IN THE SHADOWS

MICHAEL ASHCROFT

IN THE

SHADOWS

THE EXTRAORDINARY MEN AND WOMEN OF THE INTELLIGENCE CORPS

Biteback Publishing

First published in Great Britain in 2022 by
Biteback Publishing Ltd, London
Copyright © Michael Ashcroft 2022

ISBN 978-1-78590-668-8

10 9 8 7 6 5 4 3 2

A CIP catalogue record for this book is available from the British Library.

Set in Minion Pro

Printed and bound in Great Britain by
CPI Group (UK) Ltd, Croydon CR0 4YY

FSC
www.fsc.org
MIX
Paper | Supporting
responsible forestry
FSC® C171272

CONTENTS

ACKNOWLEDGEMENTS

Various people from different walks of life were crucial to this project, including many former Intelligence Corps operators who shared with me an astonishing array of experiences and recollections from when they served. While it was not possible to include the story of every individual who volunteered such information, I am extremely grateful to each of them for taking the time and trouble to make a contribution. Every briefing received was beneficial.

For security reasons, the names of some key contributors to this book have been withheld. Of those who can be mentioned, I would like to thank former Intelligence Corps officers Brigadier Brian Parritt CBE, Colonel Nick Fox OBE, Lieutenant Colonel 'Alfie' Knought MBE BEM and Warrant Officer II Alan 'Fred' Judge. Each of them advised and assisted in distinct and important ways. The guidance and wise counsel of three other former members of the Intelligence Corps – Mick Laurie, Mark Hallas and John Condon – were also invaluable. The expertise of David Erskine-Hill, the curator of my medal collection, was much appreciated as well.

Further thanks are due to the staff of the Military Intelligence Museum at Chicksands, in particular its curator, Major Bill Steadman, and its archivist, Joyce Hutton. I am equally indebted to staff at the National Archives in Kew, the Imperial War Museum in London and the Historical Disclosures Section of the Army Personnel Centre in Glasgow.

Finally, I would like to thank the formidable Angela Entwistle and her team, those at Biteback Publishing who were involved in the production of this book and my chief researcher, Miles Goslett.

FOREWORD
BY LORD HAGUE OF RICHMOND

During the four years in which I served as Foreign Secretary, I was privileged to have responsibility for two of Britain's intelligence agencies, SIS and GCHQ. I also received regular briefings from the Joint Intelligence Committee, the top-level group that fuses together the work of all four branches of the UK's intelligence network. This body includes the Defence Intelligence Staff and, by extension, the Intelligence Corps.

Collecting intelligence can be a dangerous business. No country – not least a rogue state which is unafraid of using the most brutal tactics to achieve its aims – wants to reveal its capabilities and plans to an opponent. In the interests of keeping the citizens of this country safe, however, it is always necessary for Britain to evaluate every piece of relevant information about a potential threat that can be gleaned in case it requires operational, planning or policy action. Some intelligence operators carry out their work behind the protective shield of a UK base. Others, including members of the Intelligence Corps, often have to conduct assignments in closer proximity to the enemy. For this alone, they deserve everybody's respect.

My time in government taught me that Britain sits at the top of the tree when it comes to practising the many arts of collecting, processing and analysing information. Although resources are finite and complications often present themselves, the UK can hold its own among global superpowers. Indeed, our men and women are held in great regard for their skills, inventiveness and integrity.

It is for these reasons that, as Foreign Secretary, I always felt confident in the intelligence assessments I received. When you read this book, you will understand why. Britain's intelligence capacity is not the result of high levels of funding or of clever organisational processes. Instead, it is a product of our people – their training, courage, bravado and commitment. It is also the consequence of a culture which sets great store by acknowledging the experiences of those who have gone before.

The invasion of Ukraine has been a sharp reminder that good intelligence is vital in the conflicts of the twenty-first century. Russia proved to have a poor understanding of the armed forces of the country it chose to attack. By contrast, western intelligence, with the British contribution at the forefront, alerted the world to what was about to happen and has been important in detecting and attempting to deter Moscow's next moves at each stage.

Every story in this book is a gripping individual drama, reminding us that many Intelligence Corps operators have risked, and in some cases lost, their lives in pursuit of a mission. Taken together, these accounts combine to portray a remarkable organisation which has not always had the recognition it deserves. While I suspect that most of its members are not overly concerned about that, it is only right that, a little more than eighty years after it was formally re-established, the Intelligence Corps and its many achievements should be celebrated. This book does a fine job of honouring the thousands of men and women who have served in the Corps and, by association, of saluting those who continue to do so. Every one of them should be proud.

AUTHOR'S ROYALTIES

Lord Ashcroft is donating all author's royalties from
In the Shadows to military charities.

INTRODUCTION

This book is not a conventional work of military history. Rather, it is intended as a literary salute to the thousands of men and women who have served in one of the most shadowy elements of the British Army, the Intelligence Corps. Over the past century or so, scores of them have done exceptional things all over the world in the name of their country. Some have paid the ultimate price. It seems only right, therefore, that the collective courage, judgement, skill and resourcefulness shown by Corps operators should be acknowledged.

It is understandable in some senses that the Corps is not better known because much of its work is secret. I have long been fascinated by it. Just as armies reflect the history, geography and culture of a nation, so the growing relevance of military intelligence mirrors the way Britain's armed forces have evolved. The Corps only formally came into being in July 1940, though it had existed unofficially during the First World War. Until 1940, and in the following five years, intelligence had its place in military matters, but attitudes of the day meant that arguably it was also expected to *know* its place. Its importance was understood but somehow underestimated.

Before and during the Second World War, spies and analysts were often mainstream officers, soldiers and officials who were co-opted into intelligence duties to carry out specific tasks. Alongside them worked those who have been described as 'gifted amateurs', unusual but talented people who were able to track down and utilise information which was also of use to the armed forces. All this was effective enough – and it played a part in the creation of MI5, MI6 and GCHQ – but the Second World War was the true catalyst for change. It confirmed the need for the Army to have at its disposal the full-time unit of dedicated intelligence professionals on whom Britain has so often relied in the years since: linguists, experts in human intelligence and those able to undertake surveillance, agent handling, signals intelligence, counter-intelligence and imagery analysis.

These specialists proved their worth time and again during the Cold War, in Northern Ireland and in the conflicts in the Falklands, Iraq and Afghanistan. And they continue to do vital work today. In fact, no Commander will deploy on operations without the Intelligence Corps providing knowledge and understanding. This helps to explain why, whereas other parts of the British Army have shrunk over the past few decades, the Intelligence Corps has grown. The rose and laurel cap badge, and those who wear it, have become synonymous with proficiency and dedication of the utmost kind. Frequently, ordinary people who joined the Corps have ended up achieving extraordinary things.

As the twenty-first century progresses, and international relations become increasingly complex, the significance of the Intelligence Corps has only become greater. Whether in tackling matters of security, terrorism or war, exploiting information and turning it into good and timely intelligence has never had a higher value. Successive British governments this century have questioned the need to maintain traditionally equipped armed forces, yet Russia's invasion of Ukraine in February 2022 proved that conventional threats remain. The Corps is able to provide the necessary intelligence to inform the British military and its allies of them. Indeed, the warning transmitted around the world in early 2022 of Russia's intended actions was a British initiative. Specifically, it was the idea of Intelligence Corps officers, who ran the project. This warning did not stop Russia, but it did allow nations and organisations to prepare. This book frequently alludes to the strategic impact of the Corps' enterprising approach and Ukraine is certainly the best recent example of this.

It would not be possible in a single volume to write about every operator who has represented the Intelligence Corps over the past 100 or so years. To that end, it is worth emphasising that this is not an exhaustive account of the Corps. Instead, it aims to provide insights into the Corps' many different activities and achievements through various individual members, something no previous published history has done.

A total of 282 members of the Corps have died since 1940 while involved in operations around the world, three of whom were women. Many died alone and in distressing circumstances, including several who were tortured and executed in Nazi death camps. This book is written in their honour especially. In some cases, it has been necessary for security reasons to obscure operational details and the identities of Corps personnel. Nonetheless, I hope others agree that this book offers a fair account of every campaign that it covers.

PART ONE

EMERGENCE

During the afternoon of 17 June 2008, in the searing heat of Lashkar Gah, Helmand province's capital city in southern Afghanistan, five soldiers from the British Army climbed into a Snatch Land Rover and headed east for the neighbouring province of Kandahar. They were on a mission that would take them deep into Taliban territory. The unit consisted of four SAS reservists: Corporal Sean Reeve, Lance Corporal Richard Larkin, Private Paul Stout and an individual who has only ever been identified as Soldier E. The fifth figure among them was Corporal Sarah Bryant, a 26-year-old member of the Intelligence Corps.

The aim of this hastily scrambled operation was to recapture Taliban fighters who had escaped from prison earlier that day. The quintet had been mentoring local police when they were tasked to assist in the search for the inmates and also to disrupt the enemy's lines of communication. They began by conducting vehicle checks and were then ordered to reinforce members of the Royal Scots Regiment, one of whom had killed an enemy soldier.

Tragically, as the Land Rover passed over a drainage ditch near the village of Miralzi, a huge mine detonated. The blast is believed to have been triggered by the vehicle's back wheels rolling over an incendiary device which contained up to 100kg of high explosives. The devastation was so great that it killed the three SAS men whose names have been made public. The fourth, Soldier E, survived. According to the coroner's inquest into Corporal Bryant's death, she was sitting at the back of the vehicle and died instantly.

As the first British servicewoman to be killed during the war in Afghanistan, media interest in Corporal Bryant's death was intense. So, too, was the public's sympathy for her parents, Des and Maureen, and for her husband, Carl Bryant, who also served in the Intelligence Corps as a Corporal. Although much of the Corps' work is unavoidably secret, its existence is not, and the press did offer some insights into Corporal Bryant's professional status, almost certainly because her passing drew attention to the increasing use of women on the front line in the wars of Iraq and Afghanistan. As it happens, women have, historically, played a strong role in the context of military intelligence, particularly during the Second World War. In the case of the Intelligence Corps in the twenty-first century, its soldiers have routinely been selected for operations regardless of their sex.

In the week of her death, *The Times* reported that Corporal Bryant was a member of 15 (United Kingdom) Psychological Operations Group based at the Intelligence Corps' headquarters at Chicksands in Bedfordshire. Initially, she had wanted to be a veterinary surgeon, but when an Army careers officer visited her school in the north of England she became interested in the military. Having completed her A levels, she joined the Intelligence Corps aged eighteen. She was marked out for a potential commission but insisted on rising through the ranks. With this in mind it is particularly poignant to reflect on the fact that on the morning of her death she was told she had been recommended for promotion to Sergeant. She had completed two six-month tours to Iraq and, in March 2008, was posted to Afghanistan with the 152 Delta Psychological Operations Effects Team. It was chiefly concerned with 'influencing' operations, as Carl Bryant, who is still in the Intelligence Corps, puts it. 'A lot of the work Sarah was involved in was proper, old-fashioned hearts-and-minds stuff, really,' he says.

> Sarah tried to have a positive influence on operations. What Sarah was doing was not common and she did it incredibly well. One of the reasons the team took Sarah out as much as they did was because she was a really fantastic soldier. She prided herself on that. She was a good intelligence operator, but fundamentally she could hold her own with anybody in the field. One of her greatest joys on an earlier tour was going on patrol and engaging with local people; she was particularly interested in female engagement. Sarah believed really keenly in what she was doing. She knew of an Afghan woman who was pregnant and was subsequently murdered by the Taliban and I think that affected Sarah. She knew what she was out there to do and she believed in that quite strongly.

At the time of her death, it was reported by many newspapers that Corporal Bryant spoke the local Pashto language, monitored Taliban communications by telephone and over the airwaves, and interrogated female prisoners. It is certainly true that some of her colleagues would have undertaken such knowledge-gathering duties because they are the cornerstone of the Intelligence Corps' work, but Carl Bryant says that his late wife communicated with Afghan women through a translator if they had to be spoken to at any time.

Undoubtedly, however, gleaning information and securing support from the local population formed a significant part of her work.

Without in any way diminishing the ultimate sacrifice made by Corporal Bryant or the others who died alongside her, the details of her career path and duties which emerged following her loss provide a good sense of the Intelligence Corps' *raison d'être*. The modern Intelligence Corps was formally constituted with the consent of King George VI on 15 July 1940 and formally established on 19 July 1940 under the authorisation of Army Order 112. Since the Second World War, the Corps has deployed with the British Army on every major campaign and conflict in which British troops have been involved and has developed according to the demands placed upon it in each context, starting with the continuation of the Palestinian conflict from 1945.

As well as engaging in the Cold War, the Corps has also operated in Malaya, Korea, Cyprus, Suez, Brunei, Indonesia, Dhofar (Oman), Northern Ireland, Belize, the Falkland Islands, the Gulf, the former Yugoslavia, Sierra Leone, Iraq and Afghanistan. In recognition of this service, the Corps was declared an 'Arm', defined as an entity whose role is to be close in combat with the enemy, on 1 February 1985. Corps personnel wear a cypress green beret with a cap badge showing a union rose surmounted by a crown and flanked by laurel leaves. The Corps' motto, *Manui Dat Cognitio Vires*, meaning 'Knowledge Gives Strength to the Arm', was added later. The regimental quick march is 'Rose & Laurel' and the slow march is Henry Purcell's 'Trumpet Tune and Air'.

As reflected in its name, its principal responsibilities relate to garnering intelligence. Its other main responsibility is to provide security, and security intelligence, for the purposes of force protection. Over the past eighty years or so, it has employed a hugely diverse range of people who have often supplemented their individual professional skills with extraordinary ingenuity and courage in the name of the Crown. Although it has only 1,850 serving officers and soldiers, and is therefore one of the smallest elements of the Army, the Intelligence Corps' many achievements cannot be overstated – even if, as Brigadier Brian Parritt, who served as Director of the Intelligence Corps from 1981 to 1986, says, it has often been viewed with 'great suspicion' by some in the British military. The Corps is unique in that its officers and soldiers have access to highly classified material during their daily duties. For this reason, they are required to undergo Developed Vetting, the most comprehensive form of security clearance in Britain, as part of their selection. Those who graduate to the Corps' most sensitive work must pass the Enhanced Developed Vetting process.

It is worth stating at the outset that, despite being entirely separate organisations, the ties between the Intelligence Corps and the civilian security and intelligence services have been strong since the 1940s, with some of the Corps' serving officers and soldiers being selected to work temporarily alongside the Security Service, MI5; and the Secret Intelligence Service, MI6. During the Second World War, Intelligence Corps members were also attached to the Political Warfare Executive, responsible for propaganda; and the Special Operations Executive, which carried out sabotage operations in Europe. At the same time, the Corps' signals intelligence experts worked closely with Bletchley Park and then, post-war, with Government Communications Headquarters (GCHQ). Furthermore, some Corps members have been recruited by the security services after they have left the Army. Famously, John le Carré, the author whose real name was David Cornwell, worked for both MI5 and MI6 during the 1950s and 1960s. Yet his adventures in the spy trade only came about after he had served with the Intelligence Corps in Austria during his National Service in the early 1950s. Indeed, it was during his time in the Corps, when he was stationed in the city of Graz in the British occupied zone, that he undertook secret missions with MI6 at the border with communist Czechoslovakia. Almost seventy years on from le Carré's experiences, the working relationship between the Corps and the peacetime agencies remains just as close.

Members of the Intelligence Corps are trained soldiers who are able to enter into physical confrontation with the enemy anywhere in the world. Their main role, however, has always been to advise the Army's Commanders of an opponent's capabilities and intentions while also protecting their own forces – and 'friendly' forces – from enemy espionage, sabotage and subversion. This is achieved by collecting, collating, analysing and distributing military intelligence to those who need it in time for it to be of use.

Most simply, 'intelligence' is classed by the British Army as 'information that helps senior commanders to make important decisions'. It is gathered for strategic and tactical reasons and could originate from a simple conversation with a member of a native community; from a technical asset; from a well-placed source; or perhaps even from a state secret. Once processed and analysed, individual pieces of information become intelligence. This intelligence is then passed up the chain to inform the Commander's decision-making.

By way of example, operational intelligence is the term which covers the interpretation of an enemy's capacity for action. A hostile power might want to launch an attack on Britain, but if it can be ascertained through fresh intelligence that it lacks the means to do so, it is reasonable to conclude that no immediate threat to the UK exists. Equally, if an enemy *does* have the ability to attack but it can be confirmed via the relevant intelligence channels that it has no plan to do so, it might also be concluded that no likely threat exists. Of course, events can change quickly, making the work of the Intelligence Corps so relevant and justifying its continual assessment of the intelligence picture. This recurrent process of collection, collation, analysis and dissemination is called the intelligence cycle and is one of the basic doctrines of Intelligence Corps operators.

When the Intelligence Corps advertises for new recruits, it explains to successful candidates that they may be called to serve in all kinds of conditions during the course of their career, ranging from the hostile environment of an operational deployment overseas to the secure surroundings of a headquarters or government department at home. Those in the Intelligence Corps must be able to adapt to different circumstances and cultures and the threats they pose, whether physical or cyber-based, and they are expected to have the knowledge and confidence to brief very senior officers and politicians in both tactical and strategic situations. There are many occasions when NCOs are required to brief Generals and government ministers. They must also have the ability to operate as part of a team or work alone and unsupported.

Among those who have overseen the recruitment of officers and soldiers to the Intelligence Corps in the past generation, it is generally agreed that the most crucial characteristics in prospective members are intellect, moral courage, fitness, judgement, confidence, compassion and leadership potential. Mark Hallas, a former Director of the Corps, says:

An Intelligence Corps officer needs to have the same range of talents as an officer in any other part of the Army. That being said, I'd add intellectual curiosity and a passion for intelligence as being the standout qualities that further impress. In many respects, similar qualities [are required] for Intelligence Corps soldiers, given the independent roles they often have to fill from an early stage in their career.

Another former Director of the Corps, Major General Peter Everson, says that when it came to selecting soldiers, he looked for 'interpersonal skills [coupled] with the confidence and ability to interact effectively with everyone from Corporal to General; intelligent [people] with intellectual rigour, the ability to understand complex issues and the broader context; physical and mental toughness; leadership potential.'

Not everybody who has joined the Corps since the 1980s has fitted a particular mould, however. David Burrill, a former Deputy Colonel Commandant of the Corps, recalls that above and beyond the kinds of attributes and abilities that might be expected for the military, he also looked for men and women who were irreverent and maverick in their thinking. He says:

I remember well, when as Deputy Director and Chief of Staff, that, with one exception, the young men and women candidates would appear [at interview] formally dressed. The one exception was a young man with shoulder-length, slightly unkempt hair, wearing a T-shirt and rather rough-looking jeans. He managed all the regular questioning extremely well. In fact, he was joint best with one young woman. When I asked him if he was satisfied that he had prepared sufficiently well for the occasion, he answered along the lines of 'If you are referring to my general appearance and dress, you are seeing me as I am now. If I am accepted, I will, of course, become what you would expect of me and will be damned good at it.' There and then, I decided that he was a must for the Corps. There was resistance from the other two selection panel members, and I make no apologies for being very heavy with them and talking them into dropping their rather rigid and routine thinking.

The watchword of the Intelligence Corps is to 'exploit all sources and agencies'. In order to fulfil their mission and leave no stone unturned, the Corps' officers and soldiers must be prepared to engage in a wide variety of activities, from surveillance work on the street to monitoring incoming electronic threats. This means that members of the Intelligence Corps might find themselves on an overseas stakeout or briefing a Commanding Officer in Britain about an attempt by hackers to destroy a computer network. Material could come from an infantry foot patrol or a high-level source. Before looking at the origins and development of the Corps, it is worth outlining the main methods it uses today to obtain the information and data it needs to produce actionable intelligence.

Human intelligence (HUMINT) is an umbrella term used for any activity from which knowledge can be obtained via interpersonal contact. Interrogation can provide valuable information if properly planned and directed and both officers and senior non-commissioned officers of the Corps are trained in this specialist discipline. Prisoner handling and tactical questioning represent a lower level of interrogation to exploit the shock of capture in a recently secured prisoner. Subjects who might be questioned include prisoners of war, refugees, enemy intelligence agents, insurgents, defectors and anybody else who might reasonably be considered to hold information that might be of potential value. There are varying levels of interrogation, depending on the status of the subject. For instance, somebody thought to be in possession of particularly high-value intelligence can undergo deep interrogation for protracted periods of time in special facilities.

Covert surveillance is another specialised skill used by the Intelligence Corps to collect information. It can be static – that is to say, carried out from a covert hide or stationery vehicle; or mobile, which would involve following a subject by vehicle or on foot; or a combination of both. Intelligence is also gained through technical surveillance such as telephone tapping or 'bugging'. Such methods are employed in counter-intelligence, counter-terrorist or counter-insurgency operations. Corps personnel involved in these activities historically received their surveillance training through the Security Service, MI5, but later developed their own expertise.

Agent handling, also known as source handling, is another method by which the Corps collects information. Enemy agents; disaffected members of terrorist organisations or hostile intelligence services; foreign government officials; or individuals with access to useful information who are sympathetic to an Allied mission can all be 'turned'. Agent handling, which involves 'talent-spotting', 'recruitment' and 'handling', is a specialised activity in which the natural social skills of the handler are reinforced by formal training. It is one of the more dangerous activities in which the Corps is involved, which explains why twenty-seven awards of the Queen's Gallantry Medal were made to Intelligence Corps agent handlers operating in Northern Ireland between 1969 and 2007.

Signals intelligence, or SIGINT, is collected by monitoring enemy communications with high-grade technological equipment and intercepting anything considered to be of use, from radio broadcasts to satellite communications. These transmissions are rarely conducted in 'plain language', meaning that SIGINT often involves cryptanalysis and translation. In a British military context, specialists from the Royal Corps of Signals usually intercept the material. The cryptanalysis, translation and later intelligence analysis and interpretation of the 'product' is then carried out by Intelligence Corps personnel. Both officers and soldiers in the Intelligence Corps can spend eighteen months or longer on language courses, with a particular focus on Farsi, Russian, French, Arabic and Serbo-Croat, as well as Cantonese and Mandarin Chinese.

Exploitation intelligence is a relatively new addition to definitions of the Corps' skills and activities. At a basic level, it is the intelligence gained from material or personnel via scientific, technical and specialist collection methods including forensics. This might include captured terrorist weapons or the remains of improvised explosive devices (IEDs) which have been recovered following a bombing incident. These can shed light on an enemy's technical capability and link equipment to an individual or group.

A further form of intelligence relates to imagery obtained from the study and analysis of aerial photographs. Imagery intelligence (IMINT) is the analysis of images taken from air, satellite or ground sensors including photography, electro-optical images, infrared or RADAR. During the Second World War, aerial images allowed accurate maps to be made of the beaches at Normandy for the D-Day landings, for example, and were key to identifying German weapons development sites. In the modern era, these are recorded principally by satellites and drones.

It is worth emphasising from the start that the role of women in the Intelligence Corps from 1917 to the present day has been vital. Initially, women were employed exclusively in SIGINT-related duties. As shall become clear, the 'Hush WAACs' of the First World

War, and those members of the Auxiliary Territorial Service attached to Bletchley Park in the 1940s, were prime examples of this sort of work. Their role expanded greatly from the late 1960s, when members of the Women's Royal Army Corps (WRAC) were admitted for full SIGINT analyst training. Then, in 1975, the trade of Operator Intelligence and Security was also opened to them. And with the dissolution of the WRAC in 1992, women were admitted to the Corps on exactly the same basis as men. From the beginning, whether they were attached to the Corps or were full members of it, women proved their value in all aspects of intelligence collection, both overt and covert. This is reflected in the fact that women have served in all the senior positions of the Corps, from Regimental Sergeant Major to Corps Colonel, and have fought on the front line in both counter-terrorism and counter-insurgency, three of them making the ultimate sacrifice.

● ● ●

Having demonstrated what the Intelligence Corps does in the twenty-first century, it is vital to examine its origins and development prior to its re-establishment in July 1940 in order to appreciate how it has become so pivotal to the modern British Army.

In the fourth century BC, the Chinese General Sun Tzu wrote in his fabled text *The Art of War*: 'Nothing should be as favourably regarded as intelligence; nothing should be as generously rewarded as intelligence; nothing should be as confidential as the work of intelligence.' Similarly, both the Greek and Roman Empires are known to have made extensive use of spies and intelligence gathering in their conquests. And in feudal Japan, between the twelfth and sixteenth centuries, covert agents known as '*shinobi*' were used to spy on their enemies. All of these examples help to explain why espionage is sometimes referred to as 'the second oldest profession'. In acknowledging that intelligence has been seen as the key to military success for thousands of years, however, it will come as a surprise to many to learn just how recently Britain's military intelligence operation was formalised.

It is true that the need to know about an opponent's activities and situation has been a feature of British military history for centuries, but it was probably not until the Wars of the Roses between 1455 and 1485 that intelligence was exploited to its full potential. At that time, networks of agents were run by both the House of York, represented by a white rose, and the House of Lancaster, represented by a red rose. These symbols were covert signs of affiliation and it is no accident that they are depicted on the cap badge of the modern-day Intelligence Corps. Following these civil wars, John Morton, a lawyer and priest, emerged as a member of the King's Council. King Henry VII then appointed him as head of his own secret service.

In the sixteenth century, when Henry VIII was on the throne, the post of a chief army 'reconnoitier', known as the Scoutmaster-General, was created. The holder had responsibility for intelligence matters. Subsequently, during the reign of Queen Elizabeth I, the Cambridge University-educated lawyer and fervent Protestant Sir Francis Walsingham rose to become her principal secretary and spymaster. Catholic plots to overthrow or even to kill the monarch were thwarted during his tenure. Walsingham also oversaw the development of organised intelligence gathering, both at home and abroad, as well as codebreaking.

During the Wars of the Spanish Succession, between 1701 and 1714, the Duke of Marlborough is said to have proclaimed: 'No war can be conducted successfully without early and good intelligence.' The duke's victories against the French at Blenheim, Ramillies, Oudenarde and Malplaquet, which cemented his place as one of the greatest Generals in European history, were attributed, among other things, to his 'keen knowledge of the enemy', again showing the power of military intelligence.

In the course of the Peninsular War, between 1807 and 1814, the Duke of Wellington enjoyed the advantage of having two separate intelligence organisations. Firstly, tactical intelligence was provided by the 'Exploring Officers' of his Corps of Guides, featuring men such as Colquhoun Grant and Edward Charles Cocks. Indeed, Grant was eventually appointed as Head of Intelligence of the Peninsular Army. Second, for strategic intelligence Wellington was reliant upon a network of civilian agents recruited by British diplomats in the Portuguese city of Lisbon and the Spanish city of Cádiz. Wellington's use of intelligence continued during the Hundred Days, culminating in the Battle of Waterloo. For most of the nineteenth century, however, the British Army collected military intelligence only when it was necessary to do so. No permanent intelligence unit existed.

The Boer War, fought between 1899 and 1902, inspired the founding of the Field Intelligence Department (FID). Whereas previously no formation below divisional level had had an Intelligence Officer, Colonel Hume, the Director of Military Intelligence (South Africa) from 1900, wrote a paper identifying the requirement for FIDs to have Intelligence Officers at all levels of military commands, pressing for a greater emphasis on counter-intelligence. Hume further called for the coordination of 'detective work' with 'press censorship and the reading of private mail' and the recruitment of scouts and interpreters. David Henderson, who rose to become Director of Military Intelligence during the Boer War, also tried to persuade the British Army of the need for a permanent Intelligence Corps to exist in the early years of the twentieth century. By the end of the Boer War, the intelligence element of the British forces had increased from two officers to 132 officers, plus 2,321 white soldiers and a group of native scouts. Henderson subsequently wrote two books, *Field Intelligence: Its Principles and Practice* (1904) and *The Art of Reconnaissance* (1907), both of which underlined his belief that there should be no scaling back.

Despite Henderson's warning, the FID was disbanded after the hostilities ended in May 1902 and the Directorate of Military Intelligence Section 5 (MI5) and the Secret Service Bureau (MI6) were created in 1909. Thereafter, an Intelligence Corps unit designed exclusively to deal with field intelligence did not exist until the outbreak of the First World War in August 1914, when it was founded under the stewardship of Major T. G. J. Torrie. As noted by Anthony Clayton in his book *Forearmed*, initially, the Intelligence Corps comprised about fifty men made up of existing members of the Army, the Metropolitan Police and some civilians including 'academics, businessman, journalists, writers, artists and others selected for expertise, linguistic (French or German) or other, useful for operations in France'. Nigel West, in his book *The A to Z of British Intelligence*, highlighted that the Corps comprised a 'Headquarters Wing, a Dismounted Section, a Mounted Section equipped with horses borrowed from the Grafton Hunt, a Motor-Cycle Section, and a Security Duties Section manned by detectives seconded from Special Branch'. Then, as now, the Corps collected and analysed intelligence through mapping, interrogation, aerial photography, running agents in the German-occupied territories, and wireless and telephone tapping. It also launched counter-intelligence initiatives against suspected enemy agents. By the end of the war, the model that had been developed was for regular Staff Officers to be supported by non-regulars with specialist skills.

One famous officer who served in the Intelligence Corps during the Great War was John Buchan, the author of the spy adventure novel *The Thirty-Nine Steps*, which was published in 1915. In 1916, Buchan was sent to the Western Front and attached to the British Army's General Headquarters Intelligence Section. There, he received a field commission as a Second Lieutenant in the Intelligence Corps and his duties included drafting official communiqués for the press. Later in the war, he was appointed Director of Information by Lord Beaverbrook, the Minister of Information.

Another person from this era who is of special interest, despite his name being less well known than Buchan's, is Roger West. He was one of the Corps' initial fifty or so officers in 1914 and has been dubbed 'the man who saved Paris' thanks to his stunningly audacious actions shortly after hostilities began. West's story is the first of the many extraordinary tales charting the men and women of the Intelligence Corps upon which this book will focus.

Roger Rolleston Fick West was born in London on 12 January 1891, the son of Samuel West, an eminent physician, and Margaret West (née Frankland). Through his mother, he inherited German ancestry and was a fluent speaker of that language and of French. After attending Rugby School between 1904 and 1909, he went up to King's College, Cambridge, to study mechanical sciences, graduating in 1912. He continued his studies at the Universities of Bonn, Heidelberg and Würzburg before returning to England in 1913 to begin his first engineering job with Tangyes of Birmingham, a firm which made hydraulic cylinders and rams.

As soon as Britain declared war on Germany on 4 August 1914,

West, who was unmarried and twenty-three years old, quit his job in order to join up. So desperate was this adventurer to serve his country with the British Expeditionary Force (BEF), despite having very little military training, that over the ensuing five days he travelled 1,000 miles around England by train and on his trusty Triumph motorcycle in search of a post as an Army despatch rider. Having been turned down by several recruiting depots, he was eventually directed to the War Office in London where he pleaded with a Captain E. W. Cox to be given a chance. Once his qualifications and linguistic ability were confirmed, he was appointed on 10 August as a temporary Second Lieutenant in the newly formed Intelligence Corps. Writing in his diary that day, West noted: '[Cox] took me on as one of the last of five spare men for the Intelligence Corps for six months or the duration of the war.' In view of the valour shown by West in France just three weeks later, Cox's decision to accept him would prove serendipitous.

After his recruitment, West immediately bought a second-hand uniform for 30 shillings from the military department of Moss Bros in Covent Garden and on 11 August caught a train to Southampton. There, he was issued with a Premier motorcycle and kit including field dressings and field glasses and, like many of his colleagues, detailed as a 'Scout Officer'. In this role, he would be deployed to the flanks to collect intelligence on the enemy which, using his motorcycle, he would then transport to divisional headquarters. Other new recruits to the Corps alongside West were engaged as interpreters, document examiners and interrogators, or tasked with vetting or 'contra-espionage' duties; all were told that they should not consider themselves officers, despite having received commissions.

On 12 August, West boarded the SS *Olympia* with the Corps' other new Second Lieutenants. After disembarking at Le Havre on 13 August, he and his colleagues spent six days in a squalid camp at Harfleur attending numerous briefings before eventually advancing by motorcycle along hot, dusty roads to the town of Le Cateau, which was reached on 20 August. The following morning, they were given their assignments. Along with two others – one of whom, Alfred Sang, was a French-speaking travelling salesman – West was seconded as a despatch rider to the 19th Infantry Brigade, an independent brigade and part of II Corps. It had been formed hurriedly on the battlefield and its role was to protect the left flank of the BEF and to respond to any enemy activity. As a result, it was always either on the move or in action. West and his colleagues were to courier messages between the brigade headquarters, its four infantry battalions and other formation headquarters as necessary.

For the next three days, armed only with what West described as a second-hand revolver 'of doubtful safety', he criss-crossed ramshackle countryside roads as the brigade headed north into Belgium, one night sleeping on a bed of straw at a billet so infested with fleas that one of his feet was badly bitten and became inflamed, causing him to hobble. On 23 August, the BEF was dug in at Mons, along the line of the Mons-Condé Canal, facing the numerically superior German First Army. By the end of that day, despite suffering severe losses to the determined British defence, the Germans had managed to outflank the British and were sending troops across the canal, making retreat the only option for the BEF. In an attempt to slow the German advance, the bridges across the canal were blown up by the Royal Engineers and the British battalions made an orderly withdrawal, pursued all the while by the enemy. The retreat from Mons continued, with the BEF pausing at Le Cateau to make a stand but then being forced again to withdraw south.

By 30 August, West and the 19th Brigade headquarters had reached Pontoise on the River Oise, barely 17 miles from Paris. By now, the rearguard of the BEF was formed by the 1st Battalion Middlesex Regiment, with the German advanced units not far behind. When it was discovered before dawn that morning that the rearguard had taken a wrong road, a sleep-deprived West, still limping, was sent out on his motorcycle to catch up with them and set them on the right route. Having found them, and while attempting to show them the correct road, he discovered that he had left his maps at his Pontoise billet, so he decided to retrieve them.

When he reached Pontoise, he was greeted by silence. The brigade had moved on and its inhabitants were still asleep. He searched his billet but could not find the maps. Then, just before returning to the rearguard position, he noticed that the suspension bridge across the River Oise was still standing. Although charges had been laid to its suspension straps, the resulting explosion had had little effect, while a fire that had been lit to burn the bridge down had gone out without causing any damage. Knowing that it was the only remaining bridge in the area, and that the British withdrawal had left the French Fifth Army exposed, it was clear to West that the advancing German troops could cross it easily and perhaps threaten Paris. He decided that this strategically important structure must be obliterated.

He shot back to the headquarters' new location to report the situation. Having done so, he volunteered to return to the bridge with some explosives and complete this demolition job personally. So crazy did the acting Brigade Commander, Colonel Ward, consider this plan that he told West: 'Don't be a fool and commit suicide.' A short argument ensued, after which a persuasive West was given permission to try to see out his scheme. Having secured a 14lb tin of gun cotton plus primers, fuses and detonators, West then admitted to another senior officer, a Major Walker, that his knowledge of demolitions was 'rusty' and he would benefit from having an expert engineer with him. Lieutenant J. A. C. Pennycuick, an officer of the Royal Engineers, immediately stepped forward and volunteered to accompany West on this urgent mission, hitching a ride on his motorcycle.

Weaving through troops and past horses, the pair – who were unknown to each other – travelled north as fast as they could into what they knew might already be enemy territory, arriving at Pontoise at about 7 a.m. They were relieved to find no signs of the Germans there, but they knew the clock was ticking. After unloading the demolition kit and turning the motorcycle in the direction of 'home' for a quick getaway, they stepped onto the bridge. West climbed one of the suspension towers and fixed the slabs of gun cotton, followed by Pennycuick who attached the fuses and detonators. West lit the fuse and they ran towards a nearby house, whereupon they heard only a 'feeble bang', according to West's diary. This first attempt had failed to ignite the charge and so, after West had once again scaled the same pillar, they were forced to try again with a new detonator and a new fuse. As they were completing this delicate operation, there was a sudden burst of rifle fire from across the river, heralding the advance of the German units. Having done their best, the Britons sprinted into a nearby building for cover, hearing a tremendous explosion as they sheltered. This time, the tower collapsed, and with it fell the suspension straps supporting the roadway, which plummeted 40 feet into the river below. The bridge had been blown. As it turned out, the building in which West and Pennycuick had found sanctuary was an 'estaminet' – a small café selling alcoholic drinks – so they had a couple of ciders to celebrate their success and then returned to brigade headquarters. Later that day, West noted modestly that he was 'quite pleased with our morning's work'.

It is impossible to know the precise repercussions of Second Lieutenant West's derring-do. That he was branded 'the man who saved Paris' so soon after completing his feat certainly reflects the contemporary feeling that his courage generated, even if this credit may have been amplified somewhat. With that said, his quick thinking, which unarguably did protect scores of soldiers in the French Fifth Army, was certainly deemed by his senior officers to have played a significant part in frustrating the Schlieffen Plan, the blueprint for Germany's invasion of France and Belgium: on 9 December 1914, West was Mentioned in Despatches and created a Companion of the Distinguished Service Order (DSO). The brief citation which appeared in the *London Gazette* read: 'For assisting Lieut J. A. C. Pennycuick in the demolition of the bridge at Pontoise'. It must be said that awarding a DSO to a junior officer was unusual; the order was traditionally reserved for officers of the rank of Major and above. Moreover, West's was the first decoration earned by the Intelligence Corps during the First World War. This was not the end of the campaign for West, of course. He continued to serve his country as the war raged on.

In late 1914, during the First Battle of Ypres, his engineering background meant that he was transferred to the 8th Railway Company, overseeing the construction of light railways to enable the rapid transport of casualties, reinforcements and supplies to and from the front line. In early 1915, he was with the 42nd Fortress Company, Royal Engineers, engaged in designing trench fortifications, for which, in June that year, he received his second Mention in Despatches. In September 1915, he returned to intelligence duties and was attached to the General Headquarters staff as an Intelligence Officer in the Ypres sector. In December 1915, however, he was admitted to the Queen Alexandra's Military Hospital at Millbank in London suffering from shell shock. The following year, he was released from front-line duty by the War Office and attached to the Ministry of Munitions in Edinburgh. There, he resumed his work designing trench fortifications before being sent in 1917 to the Aircraft Manufacturing Company at Hendon, where he became chief design assistant to the aviation pioneer Geoffrey de Havilland, working on wind-tunnel design and aerodynamics.

After the war, West continued working for de Havilland and was accepted as an associate member of the Institute of Civil Engineers. Between 1920 and 1930, he worked in the field of petroleum geology and seismology with the Asiatic Petroleum Company in China and the Anglo-Persian Oil Company. In July 1930, he married Barbara Morley-Horder, a stage actress who had trained with Laurence Olivier and John Gielgud and toured as an understudy to Sybil Thorndike. Initially, the Wests moved to British Columbia, where Roger lectured in seismology at the university while Barbara focused on her acting career. In 1939, they relocated to San Francisco. Roger became an advisor to Paramount Pictures in Hollywood and also used his engineering skills and expertise in seismology to make additional income by designing and building earthquake-resistant houses; Barbara continued to act. In the mid-1950s, they retired to the Californian town of Carmel, where they lived until Roger died on 18 November 1975 at the Monterey Health Centre, aged eighty-four. His widow returned to England, where she died in 1986. Roger West is remembered as a quick-witted and cheerful man, who was always self-effacing about his daring actions in

Pontoise on that late summer morning of 30 August 1914. He never forgot the war, though he was sufficiently haunted by it to be reluctant to return to England until late on in his life.

• • •

If Second Lieutenant West showed great bravery during the First World War through a single spontaneous act, another Intelligence Corps officer, George Bruce, had a comparatively nuanced, though no less momentous, experience during the same conflict which further substantiates the illustrious history of the unit and the fearlessness of its operators.

He was born George John Gordon Bruce in Edinburgh on 18 October 1883, the son of the 6th Lord Balfour of Burleigh and Lady Balfour, née Katherine Hamilton-Gordon, daughter of the Earl of Aberdeen. His father was a leading Scottish Unionist politician who served in a number of posts including as Secretary of State for Scotland. The Bruce family lineage can be traced back to Robert the Bruce, the fourteenth-century King of Scotland.

George was the second youngest of five siblings, having three sisters and one elder brother, Robert, who was the heir to the family title. He was educated at Eton College, but a bout of tuberculosis prevented him from going up to university and instead he was sent to Switzerland to convalesce. On his return, he went into insurance and banking. His brother, Robert, was a career officer in the Argyll and Sutherland Highlanders who had seen active service in the Boer War and in Sudan, but he was killed in action on 26 August 1914 at the Battle of Le Cateau during the retreat from Mons. On 8 September, less than two weeks after his brother's death, George, then aged thirty, was commissioned as a temporary

Second Lieutenant on the General List for service with the Intelligence Corps. He landed in France to join the BEF on 27 September, but in May 1915, he received a shrapnel wound to the head at Neuve Chapelle, prompting his evacuation to England for treatment. This injury would, in its way, prove pivotal.

After his convalescence, the War Office refused to let Bruce return to front-line duty and instead found a post for him behind the lines with the branch of the Intelligence Corps concerned with counter-espionage and security. By May 1916, he was posing as an Assistant Provost Marshal (an assistant head of the Military Police) and was based in the city of Amiens, 75 miles north of Paris, from where he ran a secret service which monitored suspected enemy agents. At that time, Amiens was a large British garrison area with thousands of Allied troops, communications and transport networks, all of which were prime targets for German espionage and sabotage.

From the outbreak of the Great War, hundreds of thousands of European civilians were uprooted as a result of enemy occupation or state deportation, causing a refugee crisis. Many of the displaced retreated to France. This emergency was exploited by the Germans, who considered the circumstances ideal for infiltrating their secret agents into enemy territory. In order to counter this risk, British intelligence established from late 1915 a series of what were called Inter-Ally Permit Offices. Officially, these bureaux issued documents to people travelling outside France. Unofficially, they provided a brilliant opportunity to insert Allied agents into Belgium, the Netherlands, Switzerland and Germany. They were staffed by trained Intelligence Officers who could potentially identify an enemy agent among the mass of innocent refugees, or 'talent-spot' would-be agents among the civilian population who might be willing to work for the Allies. Bearing in mind that anybody who was caught spying in France would most likely be shot, Bruce not only had to contend with risking his own life for his country, he had to persuade others to place themselves in mortal danger for the greater good as well.

One crucial activity undertaken by these Allied secret agents was train watching. By identifying the movement of German troops and supplies, it was possible to estimate with some confidence the position and timing of the next German offensive. According to one account, quoted in Michael Smith's book *New Cloak, Old Dagger*, train watchers even included housewives living near railway lines who knitted reports of German movements: a plain stitch for a carriage containing men, purl for those carrying horses. Other agents' reports, written in Indian ink on tissue paper, would be passed to a local chief agent who would then attempt to send the information back across the front line using other inventive methods. Messages were hidden in vegetables and thrown across fences; or attached to homing pigeons; or fixed to model aeroplanes. Bows and arrows were even used to pass sensitive communications on occasion.

The Paris Inter-Ally Permit Office was located at 41 Rue Saint-Roch, an anonymous building in an unremarkable street in the 1st arrondissement, close to the Jardin des Tuileries and the Louvre Museum. Initially, it was run by a Lieutenant S. H. C. Woolrych of the Intelligence Corps, but in January 1917, George Bruce was appointed in his place. The system which Bruce inherited was complicated. Following an agent's initial selection at Rue Saint-Roch, they were sent to an equally non-descript building in the Rue Soufflot on the Left Bank to learn how to identify German uniforms, insignia, weapons and equipment and how to recognise and record the movement of trains carrying German soldiers and provisions.

Once instructed, they were sent back behind enemy lines in France and Belgium, risking capture and certain death as they travelled on foot, by rail or – with the assistance of the Royal Flying Corps – by parachute. Although many agents did die trying to get information back into Allied hands, those reports that passed across the lines successfully were sent to Bruce at 41 Rue Saint-Roch. From there, they were couriered to a central bureau at Folkestone in Kent. This office, located at 8 The Parade, handled and coordinated all intelligence from the Allied secret service agencies – that is to say British, French, Belgian and Russian.

By early 1918, Bruce had simplified and accelerated this process by cutting out the Kent office so that he and his colleagues dealt directly with the General Headquarters in France. Bruce also established a new network of agents operating in Luxembourg, which had been occupied by Germany since the start of the war and through which ran much of the German rail network supplying their armies in France and Belgium. Furthermore, he addressed the difficulties of inserting agents behind the lines. By the final months of the war, the Royal Flying Corps' losses were increasing, and it was made clear that dropping agents by parachute from valuable aircraft had become too expensive. Under Bruce, the idea of using balloons to secrete agents into enemy territory was refined and utilised.

Two of the agents whom Bruce recruited and who had a significant impact on the war at a critical stage stand out. The first was the 49-year-old Madame Camille Rischard. Having visited Paris early in 1917 to see her student son, Marcel, she was keen to return home to Luxembourg and went to 41 Rue Saint-Roch to get the necessary travel papers. Bruce believed immediately that this unassuming doctor's wife would make an ideal potential agent. Unfortunately, Madame Rischard saw things differently, having no desire to get mixed up in an international spy ring. Indeed, she positively recoiled when it was suggested to her that she might smuggle out of France a message written on thin tissue paper which would be hidden in her ear. Repeated attempts to persuade this respectable lady to do her duty failed, and it was not until she attended confession in a Paris church in April 1917 that she agreed to act, spurred on by a priest. Training her and getting her back into Luxembourg via Switzerland took almost a year, but finally, in February 1918, she reached home and started sending her first messages to Bruce by planting code words in a local newspaper. She continued to do this, with growing confidence, for months.

Bruce also recruited a Belgian Army officer called Albert-Ernest Baschwitz Meau. He had worked in Africa and South America, and by the time he and Bruce met, he had already been captured by and escaped from the Germans five times. He was considered a natural agent and, incredibly, having offered himself up for duty, he travelled to Luxembourg by hydrogen balloon in order to take up his train-watching duties. Meau's devil-may-care attitude was perfectly suited to his epic voyage, as he drifted over the lines by night, risking ground fire and anti-aircraft defences. Having evaded the enemy by air, he, like Madame Rischard, was able to pick up intelligence about German troop movements on the ground right up to the end of the war, making a huge contribution to victory. After the war, both Madame Rischard and Meau were made Chevaliers of the Légion d'Honneur. Perhaps the greatest accolade paid to them and, indirectly, to Bruce for having identified them as agents, came more than a decade later, in 1940, however. That year, the Nazis reoccupied Luxembourg and they are said to have gone looking for these two notable graduates of Bruce's spy school. They failed to find them.

Following the Armistice in November 1918, Bruce was transferred to the GHQ Intelligence Staff, where he took the place of Major Stewart Menzies, who had been transferred to the Secret Service Bureau. In June 1919, Bruce married Dorothy Done, his secretary and assistant at 41 Rue Saint-Roch and someone who had herself been recruited by the British for counter-intelligence work. After the war, Bruce returned to banking, but it seems that he did not sever his links with the intelligence services entirely. There are strong indications that he was involved in the 'Z-Network' with Claude Dansey of the Secret Intelligence Service, using his connections with foreign government officials to provide economic, commercial and, sometimes, military intelligence for the British. Evidence also exists suggesting that shortly before the outbreak of the Second World War, in 1938, Bruce was involved with 'Section D' of SIS, tapping his old network to carry out undercover missions in Europe. Bruce succeeded his father as the 7th Lord Balfour of Burleigh in July 1921 and died in June 1967, aged eighty-three. He never talked about the war. It was only in 1995, when Bruce's son Robert and his wife Janet opened a chest of drawers at their house in Clackmannanshire which had been locked for almost thirty years, that the truth of his activities came to light. The chest contained files of War Office documents, notebooks, letters, maps and diagrams which showed the extent of George Bruce's spy network.

● ● ●

British women were also involved in intelligence work during the First World War, even if attitudes of the day meant they were seen by some in the military as being useful primarily in replacing men who were needed for front-line duty as opposed to being considered valuable in their own right.

Mabel Peel was one such person whose skills were called upon at the height of the conflict. She was born on 25 July 1879 at Barton upon Irwell in Lancashire, the daughter of Robert Peel, a bank official, and Alice Peel (née Dymond). Although details of her early schooling are sketchy, it is known that she developed an aptitude for languages at an early age. In 1898, not yet twenty, she was granted a permit by the British Consulate in Bordeaux to travel freely in south-west France and she set herself up there as a freelance teacher of French and of the violin. After returning to Britain, she gained a second-class Bachelor of Arts (BA) degree in modern languages (French and German) from the University of Manchester in 1906 and a Master of Arts (MA) the following year. She became an assistant mistress at Howell's School in Denbigh, North Wales, and later worked as a modern languages teacher at Bridlington High School in Yorkshire.

By the end of 1916, the British Army was experiencing a severe manpower shortage caused in part by the horrendous losses suffered during the Somme offensive, and replacement troops were needed urgently in the front-line trenches. One obvious solution to filling the shortfall was to deploy the thousands of men who had until that point been providing myriad subsidiary services behind the lines and at home. They could, in turn, be replaced by a trained corps of volunteer uniformed women. The War Office eventually accepted this idea.

Recruitment began in March 1917, though the Women's Army Auxiliary Corps (WAAC) was not established formally until July 1917. Dr Mona Chalmers Watson served as its first Chief Controller.

Initially, WAAC members were restricted to traditionally 'feminine' duties such as administration, catering and stores-related work, but the potential for some of them to undertake more specialist responsibilities was soon heralded by a letter written to the War Office by Field Marshal Douglas Haig, the Commander of the BEF. Haig stated the urgent need for female clerks at Boulogne to censor letters written by German prisoners of war.

Mabel Peel joined the WAAC in June 1917, following in the footsteps of two of her siblings who had already donned uniform. Her younger sister, Alice, had joined the British Red Cross Voluntary Aid Detachment (VAD) in 1914, an organisation that provided nursing support for military casualties in hospitals at home and abroad. And her only surviving brother, Harold, who had read theology at Cambridge and became a cleric in Australia, joined the Australian Imperial Force as a chaplain in 1916 and served throughout the Great War, including with the 1st Australian Division in France.

Peel's linguistic abilities meant that she was posted to the War Office Intelligence Branch in London as a German interpreter and censor in the rank of Assistant Administrator. She was the first woman to be admitted to this post. By the time of her arrival, the German Army was making increasing use of wireless to transmit coded battlefield messages. Intercepting these messages was relatively easy, but decoding them was more complicated. Teams of Army officers in the department known as I(e)C at the British Expeditionary Force (BEF) headquarters at Saint-Omer were already busy in this deciphering effort, but they were becoming overwhelmed by the volume of work. Rather than take more officers away from front-line duty, it was decided that German-speaking WAAC members should be sent to France.

In September 1917, Peel and five other WAACs made the journey from Folkestone to Boulogne. Initially, they were kept in the dark about what they would be doing there. They arrived at Saint-Omer on 29 September and reported for duty the following morning, entering an office strewn with papers which they later discovered was part of the GHQ Intelligence Branch. It was then they were informed they were to work as codebreakers.

In 1924, Peel wrote an account of her time in France. In it, she recalled:

> I think none of us will ever forget that first morning at the office, when we sat there, with sheets of paper in front of us on which were arranged in the form of sentences, meaningless groups of letters. We were told that they were codes, wireless messages (coming from the Germans and tapped by our operators). We were to try and solve them. Never having seen a code message in our lives before, you can imagine the despair that filled our hearts … On discussing the work at lunch time, which we had to do in very guarded terms because of the presence of the orderlies, we found a certain amount of consolation in the fact that everyone was as depressed about it all as everyone else and each felt as dull witted and stupid as the others.

She and the other WAACs took some time to adapt to the rigours of their work. They were split up, so that one woman worked alongside a team of men. As Peel also wrote in her memoir:

> We began to find our work intensely interesting, and as we began to see more and more daylight in it, found it monopolising all our thoughts both waking and sleeping … I knew that at the

end of three months, a colleague and myself decoded our daily messages quite by ourselves, handing up our suggestions each evening to be signed by the head of the room.

By early 1918, the WAAC element assisting with the codebreaking effort had been increased from six to twelve, all of whom were affiliated to the Intelligence Corps. Each woman came from an educated middle- or upper-class background and ranged in age from early twenties to mid-fifties. They lived in wooden huts and were largely separated from the other WAACs who were tasked with routine administration and catering duties. Their discomfort was compounded by their having to get used to night-time bombing raids. Having been ordered never to discuss their secret work outside of their office, the codebreakers became known as the 'Hush WAACs'. Their assignment was demanding and the hours were long, working every day of the week from 9.30 a.m. to midnight. Whereas the men in the office were allowed to take two weeks' leave every six months, the women were only granted leave every twelve months.

The WAACs did not work in isolation and there were varying levels of liaison with their American and French counterparts. They also became more actively involved in what they were doing. For example, Mabel Peel is known to have independently contributed to the catalogue of well-known phrases that could be used, through analysing context, to break codes. And her colleague Gwendoline Watkins emphasised the importance of code books of captured German soldiers to assist in the decoding process – a technique of using a 'crib', which would be instrumental in the success of the Bletchley Park codebreakers during the Second World War.

In March 1918, when the German Army commenced its last-ditch effort to defeat the Allied armies in France, known as the

Spring Offensive, it changed all of its military codes. This meant that Peel and her colleagues had to work even harder to break them, though their task became more manageable when the Americans intercepted a German message that had been sent in both the old and the new codes. This error enabled the message to be unscrambled using the old code while providing an opportunity to crack the new one.

As the German advance continued, the British and French armies pulled back. By April 1918, Saint-Omer was no longer considered safe and the I(e)C office was moved to Le Touquet, less than 2 miles from the major British base area at Étaples. Although the intensity of the work didn't change, the WAACs' accommodation did improve, with the women moving into a house. It was also in 1918 that Queen Mary, being so impressed by their work, became their patron and their group's name changed to Queen Mary's Army Auxiliary Corps.

When the war ended abruptly in November 1918, the I(e)C was dissolved and the WAACs returned to civilian life. On 11 December 1918, exactly a month to the day after the Armistice came into effect, Mabel Peel was recalled home, her service abroad qualifying her for the British War Medal and Victory Medal. She was demobilised on 11 January 1919 and then returned to teaching. In 1925, she moved to Rouen in Normandy and lived at the Rue Malpalu, only yards from Notre-Dame Cathedral. She soon became aware of the large number of veterans who had gravitated there after the war, many of whom were injured or shell-shocked and in need of help. She felt moved to join the British Legion, the organisation set up in 1921 as a single unified charity to help ex-servicemen, and later formed a British Legion branch in Rouen. It grew to a membership of more than ninety and she remained deeply involved in its running until she returned to England in 1936.

The cryptographic work undertaken by Mabel Peel was not as challenging or as strategically significant as that done by later British female codebreakers, but she was part of the first contingent to perform these duties in uniform and behind a battle front, and her input is considered to have been notable. Later, she settled in Welwyn Garden City in Hertfordshire and resumed teaching until her death on 25 January 1938, aged fifty-eight.

• • •

As can be extrapolated from the small selection of accounts above, members of the Intelligence Corps made many and varied contributions during the First World War. Once the bloodshed ended in November 1918, however, the Army decided that it should be broken up. By then, the Corps consisted of 3,000 men and had units in every area of conflict outside of France: Egypt, East and West Africa, Italy, Greece, Turkey and Russia. Some Corps members were retained to take part in covert operations against the Republicans during the Irish War of Independence between 1919 and 1921. Notoriously, on the morning of 21 November 1920, twelve Britons – including those operatives working for British intelligence known as the Cairo Gang – were assassinated in early morning raids on their lodgings in Dublin. This strike marked the first killings of Bloody Sunday and was engineered by the political revolutionary Michael Collins.

Such an intelligence failure did nothing to encourage senior military figures to maintain a permanent intelligence unit within the British Army although, following the Armistice, the Counter Espionage Section was retained in Germany until December 1929.

When the last two officers left the country that month, the Intelligence Corps was formally disbanded and ceased to exist. It would take another global conflict before a military intelligence organisation became an integral part of Britain's armed forces once again.

PART TWO

THE SECOND WORLD WAR

The Second World War was the deadliest conflict in human history. It is estimated that between 62 million and 72 million fatalities occurred after every major global power was drawn into it. Of these, approximately 25 million were military casualties. The war began on two different fronts which merged in 1941. The first was the Sino-Japanese War, starting in July 1937; the second was the war in Europe triggered by Adolf Hitler's invasion of Poland in September 1939 which resulted in Britain and France declaring war on Germany. In 1945, the Allied powers led by the British Empire, America and the Soviet Union defeated the Axis powers of Germany and Japan.

In September 1939, no full-time designated British military intelligence organisation had existed for a decade. When war broke out, it was thanks only to the work of Major (later Field Marshal) Sir Gerald Templer, aided by Captain F. C. Davies, that thirty-one field security sections were formed under the Corps of Military Police. The job of these sections was to accompany the British Expeditionary Force (BEF) – the name of the British Army operating in France and the Low Countries from September 1939 to May 1940 – in an intelligence role.

Intelligence Staff Officers were attached to the nerve centres of all the major formations: the BEF's General Headquarters; the Army, Navy and Air Force; and to each divisional headquarters. The basic Intelligence Corps field unit was the field security section (FSS). Normally, these units consisted of a Field Security Officer, a Warrant Officer, two Sergeants and a varying number of junior NCOs and Privates. Sections were attached to infantry and armoured divisions, ports, 'line of communication' areas, or raised for a particular task such as providing security to restricted areas. They were often among the first to land during amphibious operations and usually the last to leave. Their role was to collect battlefield intelligence, to conduct tactical questioning of enemy prisoners, to seek out and arrest enemy collaborators in liberated areas, and to advise on security for the formation to which they were attached. Intelligence Corps officers and soldiers involved in port security duties also worked closely with the Security Service, MI5 and, in effect, took their directions from that organisation. During the Second World War, MI5's primary concern was the detection and arrest of German agents in Britain and the monitoring of any individual suspected of being an enemy sympathiser.

Having been established hurriedly, field security sections inevitably faced difficulties, including over the recruitment and retention of people of sufficient calibre for intelligence work. Adding to these obstacles was resistance among some Field Commanders within the British Army. Some would not take these extempore units and their results seriously, almost certainly because they were populated by what might be termed 'gifted amateurs' rather than professional soldiers. The upshot was that history repeated itself.

As had been the case a quarter of a century before, in 1914, Britain began fighting the Germans on the back foot.

The writer Malcolm Muggeridge is one noteworthy individual who joined the British military intelligence endeavour during the first months of the Second World War. His recollections of that time reflect perfectly the lukewarm reception from some officers that could be expected by the motley crew of intelligencers who volunteered alongside him. After arriving at the Royal Military Police training centre at Mytchett in Surrey in 1940, Muggeridge remembered, as quoted in Jock Haswell's *British Military Intelligence*: 'The Red Caps looked with ill-concealed distaste and disdain at we Field Security men, mostly schoolmasters, journalists, encyclopaedia salesmen, unfrocked clergymen and other displaced *New Statesman* readers.' Muggeridge's words should perhaps be taken with a pinch of salt, but those with an innate respect for and understanding of military intelligence clearly felt the same way. They believed that this palpable sense of haughtiness must not be allowed to stand; a change in attitude was rapidly required.

Major W. F. Jeffries, who was in charge of military intelligence personnel at the War Office, certainly held this view. He lobbied intensively for the Intelligence Corps to be revived as a full unit. In July 1940, just weeks after the humiliating Dunkirk evacuation in which almost 340,000 troops had to be rescued, Jeffries's exertions paid off. It was decided that the field security wing of the Royal Military Police should be turned into an independent formation. All the duties of the original Intelligence Corps were restored, along with signals traffic analysis and an airborne section. The Corps was created on 15 July 1940 with the permission of King George VI and was formally established four days later under the authorisation of Army Order 112. Over the next five years, it would grow to comprise 3,040 officers, 5,930 soldiers and 1,553 attached officers. As highlighted in a Ministry of Defence pamphlet, Intelligence Corps members would be associated with many of the key aspects of Britain's military undertaking which led to victory in 1945: by working within the Special Operations Executive; by helping to break the Enigma code at Bletchley Park; and by setting up other irregular groups including the Long Range Desert Group.

Selection procedures for the new Intelligence Corps were similar to those used in 1914, but in 1940, the additional idea of advertising for recruits in the national press and via the BBC took hold. Notices would be left in the personal columns of newspapers such as the *Daily Telegraph*, specifically seeking those in possession of the twin qualities of wanting to serve their country and the ability to speak at least one foreign language. Some who applied were invited to an anonymous-sounding address in Northumberland Avenue, near Trafalgar Square in central London, where they had to take French dictation and discuss their political sympathies before they were considered for training. Alongside regular and reserve officers and soldiers, some of whom had served with the Intelligence Corps during the First World War, about 500 recruits were secured through this innovation.

A crucial challenge facing the burgeoning new Intelligence Corps concerned its location for training purposes. As it transpired, it and its predecessor, the Field Security Police, would be linked with several areas around the country during the war. As well as the depot at Mytchett in Surrey, at which Malcolm Muggeridge felt he was given such a half-hearted welcome, a field security and training depot was established at Sheerness, in Kent, in 1940. That year, two Oxford University colleges, Pembroke and Oriel, also became officer training centres, with other ranks being trained at King Alfred's College in Winchester (now the University of Winchester). From 1942, Wentworth Woodhouse, near Rotherham in South Yorkshire, was requisitioned by the Army and became the Corps' headquarters. It would remain so until 1946. This vast house, situated on an 80,000-acre estate, was owned by the Earls of Fitzwilliam, one of the wealthiest families in Britain through its extensive coal mining interests. At the time, Wentworth Woodhouse was considered the largest private residence in the United Kingdom, having a 606-foot-long façade and consisting of more than 300 rooms. To put this in context, Buckingham Palace's façade is 354 feet. Needless to say, it added some glamour to the Corps to be based at such an impressive seat, even if its personnel were housed in the stable block.

Reflecting the growth of the Corps, additional training facilities for officers and soldiers were established during the war at Minley Manor near Camberley in Surrey; at Swanage in Dorset; at Smedley's Hydro at Matlock in Derbyshire; and in Cambridge. Training consisted of a short basic military instruction course and a two-week Field Security Course covering interrogation, morale and propaganda, together with tuition in motorcycle proficiency because it was envisaged that field security personnel should be highly mobile.

As shall become clear, Intelligence Corps personnel were associated with several different groups throughout the Second World War. These included the Political Warfare Executive (PWE), which was responsible for propaganda and came into being in August 1941. The PWE's overall direction came from the Foreign Office. Many influential journalists and broadcasters were recruited to it, along with psychologists and other experts in human behaviour. Innumerable ploys were designed to influence the minds of the target civil and military population using politics, deception, sex, humour and character assassination. Several officers of the Intelligence Corps served with the PWE, two of whom died on active service.

Having established when, where and how the Intelligence Corps was brought back following its decade-long slumber, attention can now turn to the various theatres in which its operators served and the astonishing stories of individual Corps operators, beginning with Hitler's swift advance through Europe in 1939 and 1940.

FRANCE, NORTH-WEST AND CENTRAL EUROPE

On 1 September 1939, German forces crossed the East Prussian border into Poland. By 11.15 a.m. on 3 September, Germany had failed to respond to the Anglo-French ultimatum to withdraw, resulting in the Prime Minister, Neville Chamberlain, broadcasting to the nation that Britain was at war with Germany. Over the following weeks, the ill-equipped British Expeditionary Force (BEF) mobilised and shipped over to France, where, still hidebound by the trench warfare traditions of the First World War, it dug in and waited. There followed eight months of limited military operations on the Western Front known as the 'Phoney War', during which French troops invaded Saarland, a state in western Germany. This period of relative inactivity ended abruptly on 9 April 1940, when Hitler invaded Denmark and Norway. The following month, Luxembourg, Belgium and the Netherlands surrendered. And in June 1940, France fell.

It was during the frenetic springtime of 1940 that one remarkable Intelligence Corps operator, Antony Coulthard, was captured. Despite becoming a prisoner of the Nazis, his heroic story is so affecting that no account of the Corps would be complete without it.

John Antony Ronald Coulthard (always known as Antony) was born on 9 April 1918 at Windsor, Berkshire, the son of retired Captain John Coulthard and his wife, Dorothy. His father was a teacher whose career was interrupted by the First World War, during which he served initially with the London Regiment, seeing active service at Gallipoli and on the Western Front before rising to become Company Sergeant Major and eventually being commissioned into the Royal Flying Corps as an administrative officer.

Antony attended Exeter School and King Edward VI School in Southampton, his father having been appointed a schools inspector in the city. His linguistic talents then won him a double scholarship to Queen's College, Oxford in 1936 to read modern languages. While there, he joined the Addison debating society and the Student Christian Movement. In 1938, he was awarded a Heath Harrison Travelling Scholarship in both French and German, which provided funds for academic travel to those countries during vacations. In the summer of 1939, he graduated with a first-class honours degree and, representing his deep love of Germany, special mention was made of his ability in colloquial German. He also became a Laming Fellow, a bursary designed for language students wishing to enter the diplomatic service. The declaration of war put paid to the glittering career that might have been his.

On 22 September 1939, Coulthard enlisted in the Oxfordshire and Buckinghamshire Light Infantry. Having inherited left-wing inclinations from his parents, he refused a commission, opting to serve among the rank and file. Six months later, he was transferred to the Corps of Military Police (Field Security Wing), and, on 4 April 1940, after just three weeks of training, he was promoted to Lance Corporal and was soon sent to France to join 11 Field Security Police Section. It had been attached to the British Expeditionary

Force at Brest since October 1939 on line of communication duties. In mid-May 1940, he was posted to 32 Field Security Police Section at Rennes, which was attached to the 45th Division of the BEF.

A few days after arriving, Lance Corporal Coulthard was sent out on a motorcycle reconnaissance mission across northern France to find a divisional headquarters whose whereabouts had become unclear. On 20 May, as he and another Intelligence Corps operator neared Amiens, he was exposed to the horrors of war for the first time. After two days of sustained Nazi bombing, the city and its surroundings had been torn apart. Infrastructure lay in ruins, corpses and injured horses littered the streets and the area was rampant with refugees fleeing the Germans. Having scrounged some petrol from a French lorry driver at Montdidier, the young Briton, only twenty-two years old, pressed on into Amiens itself. Believing that enemy troops were nowhere near the badly damaged centre, he decided to have a look at the extent of the chaos but drove immediately into the path of a group of German troops. Being unarmed, and not having enough experience of motorcycle riding to stage a fast getaway, he surrendered without a fight and spent the night in a large temporary prison just outside the city with about 200 other British soldiers.

A gruelling nine days followed, during which Coulthard and his captured countrymen made their way across Belgium on foot. Anybody who disobeyed orders was beaten, whipped or shot by their captors. Then, most humiliatingly, the nightmare journey continued east by rail as the men were crammed onto overcrowded cattle trucks and transported through Germany and into Nazi-occupied Poland. With no proper food or water on offer, and almost no ventilation, conditions on these trains were inhumane to say the least.

Boiling hot during the day and freezing cold at night, there were no facilities of any kind, meaning the men had to urinate and defecate in their helmets or boots. Some died en route.

At the end of May, they reached their final destination, Stalag XXA, a prisoner-of-war camp near the medieval city of Toruń on the Vistula River about 100 miles north of Warsaw. At its peak, it held about 10,000 men. Coulthard would be forced to live there as Prisoner No. 5202. On 19 July 1940, two months after his capture, he was transferred to the newly formed Intelligence Corps, as were all other members of the Field Security Police sections. At that time, it was not uncommon for the War Office to administratively reassign soldiers from one regiment to another, even if they were incarcerated. Coulthard's impeccable German made him the obvious candidate for the post of camp interpreter, earning him the nickname 'The Professor'.

Coulthard was much more than just an earnest academic with a facility in languages, however. His nerve was sufficiently strong for him to make a well-planned, rousing bid for freedom on 23 August 1942. In this, he was accompanied by Sergeant Frederick Foster of the 8th Battalion the Sherwood Foresters Regiment, who had been captured in Norway in April 1940. Foster, a bricklayer's son turned solicitor's clerk who had left school aged fourteen, was a few years older than Coulthard, but the pair had struck up a steady friendship. Foster's riveting account of their daring 900-mile endeavour for neutral Switzerland, recorded by him in an official report after the war for MI9, the branch of the Military Intelligence Directorate dealing with escape and evasion, detailed the meticulous preparation that preceded it and charted the journey itself.

First, for a year before they broke out of Stalag XXA, Coulthard taught Foster to speak German. After receiving this tuition, he had a decent grasp of vocabulary and idiom, but his Nottinghamshire accent was so strong, and German therefore so obviously *not* his native tongue, it was decided that he should pose as a Hungarian advertising executive named Dr Benecz. Coulthard played the part of a German advertising man, Dr Neumann. They concealed their skeletal bodies underneath suits obtained from Polish connections in Toruń in exchange for Red Cross food and clothing. Trilby hats and civilian shoes were another key part of their disguise as two young businessmen. They carried forged identity cards copied from an authentic example which had been stolen from a German workman and also had 'letters of authority' made up with the aid of a child's printing set. These letters claimed they worked for the engineering and electronics firm Siemens. A fellow prisoner, Sergeant Wilfred Gordon, the camp medicinal dispenser, arranged their supply of traveller's ration tickets. Before making their break, they posed for final photographs to send home. Foster's would be sent to his wife, Peggy; Coulthard's to his parents in Hampshire. Finally, they agreed a cardinal rule: if either of them encountered trouble during the journey, the other must go on alone.

They fled at 2 p.m. after cutting through one of the camp's wire fences and walked to Toruń railway station, from where they caught a train to Frankfurt an der Oder, speaking German to each other at all times in case they should be overheard communicating in English. Showing how tight security was, they were soon asked to show their identity cards to a railway policeman. The forgeries worked. On arrival at Frankfurt an der Oder, they spent the night in a waiting room, and then at dawn caught a train, along with scores of Nazi troops, another 50 miles to Berlin. As they scrutinised a timetable there, an old woman approached them asking if they were together. Foster confirmed they were and thought no more of it. Then, as they left the station a few minutes later, a plain-clothes member of the Nazi Kriminalpolizei stopped them and said that a 'lady detective' had reported them as having been acting suspiciously. Again, their identity cards were put to the test, and they passed muster.

While waiting for their next train, they took a tour around the capital. Driven by the instinct to carry on serving their country, despite the potentially fatal position in which they had put themselves, they used their time to visit key sites including the Chancellery and Reichstag. Their aim was to log all anti-aircraft positions and the whereabouts of netting and other camouflage in the city streets. After this scoping exercise, they lunched in a hotel full of German officers before finding a quiet park bench from which they made shorthand notes on scraps of paper of every piece of intelligence they could remember from their earlier reconnaissance that might be of use to the British Army. In the late afternoon, they caught a train to Magdeburg and then went on to Leipzig, again looking around the city carefully for any useful information which they could pass on before travelling to Munich. 'My method in [the] train was to bury my head in the *Illustrated* I carried, and part of the time pretend to be dozing,' Foster's report to MI9 recalled. Then, showing what risks Coulthard was prepared to take in order to protect their true identities, Foster added: 'Coulthard was able to speak to fellow passengers and even take part in arguments.' Arriving at Munich, they had a quiet drink at the Bürgerbräukeller, from which Hitler launched the 1923 Beer Hall Putsch, and then ate lunch in the Atlas Hotel. By this point, they knew that they were just twenty-four hours from being able to return to Britain.

On the final leg of their nerve-racking journey, they caught a train to the border town of Lindau, a few miles inside Germany on the shores of Lake Constance. There, they had to endure a two-hour wait before the train would take them to the safety of Switzerland, and they were told they could either have their papers checked inside the train or leave their carriage and undergo a security check outside. They opted to stretch their legs and enjoy the beauty of their surroundings.

Having disembarked, Coulthard led the way. His papers were examined, he was cleared for the onward journey, and he was a free man. He walked off. Foster approached the barrier next. For some reason which was never established, the border guard hesitated over his papers and began questioning him. At this point, Coulthard broke the rule agreed between them and walked back to find out what was going on. 'May I ask if something is wrong?' he asked the guard in his faultless German. The guard's suspicion was heightened. Having established the men were travelling together, he asked to see Coulthard's papers again. Not accepting that the men were who they claimed to be, he quietly drew his pistol and told them to accompany him to the local police station. Heartbreakingly, just a couple of miles from repatriation, the game was up. When asked by Foster why he turned back, Coulthard apparently replied: 'I just thought I should, that's all.'

They had to endure two days of interrogation by the Gestapo before their true identities were ascertained. Luckily, they had managed to dispose of the pieces of paper on which they had written their intelligence notes before this cross-examination began. Then, they were returned at gunpoint to Stalag XXA and were soon separated, Foster being sent to Stalag 383 in Bavaria. They never saw each other again. Coulthard made a further eight unsuccessful escape attempts, the second of which, in January 1944, was as much a near miss as the first. Dissidents arranged for him to board a Swedish ship in Gdynia harbour on the Baltic coast. Having reached the harbour, he found that the ship had not arrived. He went into hiding for a week before desperation forced him to try to board the first Swedish ship that docked. His luck ran out again, however, when his cover was blown by an Italian dockworker and he was again sent back to Stalag XXA. A third attempt was planned with a Polish officer, but this fell through when Coulthard was unexpectedly removed to a working party two weeks beforehand. The Polish officer did manage to escape and eventually reached England.

By January 1945, the Russians were advancing into Poland, prompting the Germans to move their prisoners of war back into Germany. As they had no transport resources to waste, the men were put on forced marches in freezing conditions. Little food was supplied, and they survived by foraging in fields. Those who were sick at the start of the march, or who became sick en route, were of no concern to the Nazis. Many died where they fell, beaten by exhaustion, pneumonia, exposure or starvation.

On 20 January 1945, with the Russian Army closing in, it was the turn of Coulthard and the inmates of Stalag XXA to begin their forced march, an 800-mile trek to the Hanover region. By early March, they had reached the German town of Schwerin, in Mecklenburg-Vorpommern. Coulthard was in a poor state, suffering from dysentery and foot problems, yet he was observed at least twice giving away his bread ration to other men whom he thought were worse off than him. He had continued to act as an interpreter for the prisoners, several of whom testified after the war that he tried pleading with the guards for better conditions. Although men with dysentery were treated at a hospital in Schwerin, only the sickest were left behind. Those considered fit enough, including Coulthard, were placed into wagons. Eventually, they crossed the River Elbe and approached the town of Dömitz. On 23 March, the sick column had reached the small hamlet of Kaltenhof, near Dömitz, where it was halted for the night near a barn close to the river bank. The prisoners were to sleep in the barn. By this point, Coulthard's condition had worsened. He was barely able to walk. On the instructions of the escort Commander, Hauptmann Mackensen, a German medical orderly ordered the prisoners to wash in the icy cold River Elbe. The shock of doing this was too much for Coulthard. He collapsed and was carried into the barn where he died during the night. The following morning, four friends buried him in a small civilian cemetery in a nearby village, the name of which was never properly recorded. After the war, as he had no known grave, his name was inscribed on the Dunkirk Memorial to the Missing. On 23 November 1945, an announcement honouring him appeared in the *London Gazette*. It read: 'The King has been graciously pleased to approve the posthumous award of a Mention-In-Despatches in recognition of gallant and distinguished service in the field to Lance Corporal J. A. R. Coulthard, Intelligence Corps.'

In late 1945, the cruel and sadistic Hauptmann Mackensen was put on trial for his part in the deaths of the thirty prisoners who succumbed during the march, one of whom was Coulthard. He was convicted and executed by hanging on 8 March 1946.

Coulthard's friend and fellow escapee, Frederick Foster, survived the war and returned home to the wife he had married only months before his capture in 1940. They went on to have two children. In May 1945, Coulthard's mother, Dorothy, wrote to Foster telling him the devastating news of her son's death. Foster passed away in 1990, having had a successful career in his family building company. He became Mayor of Grantham in 1957, was made an alderman after leaving the council and was friendly with the future Prime Minister Margaret Thatcher and her father, Alf Roberts.

Coulthard's story did not die with Foster, however. In July 1947, a British Graves Concentration Team had been informed that two unknown, non-combat British soldiers were buried in a small cemetery in the village of Quickborn, near Kaltenhof. Once it had been confirmed that the remains were of British men, both were moved to the Becklingen War Cemetery near Soltau. Although one was identified as an unknown British soldier of the Duke of Wellington's Regiment, the other was entirely unknown, and their new Commonwealth War Graves Commission headstones reflected this status. In 2010, Frederick Foster's son, Steve, discovered among his father's personal papers detailed records of his time as a prisoner of war, his escape attempts and of Antony Coulthard. This inspired a five-year search to find Coulthard's grave, during which he linked up with Coulthard's niece, Barbara, to solve the mystery.

After a rigorous investigation, they gathered conclusive evidence that John Antony Ronald Coulthard was the unknown British soldier originally buried at Quickborn and then reburied at Becklingen. On 24 March 2015, exactly seventy years after his death in the barn at Kaltenhof, the Ministry of Defence officially confirmed that the Becklingen grave would be recognised as the final resting place of Lance Corporal Coulthard. In July 2015, Lance Corporal Coulthard's grave at Becklingen War Cemetery was rededicated with a new headstone in a ceremony attended by members of the Foster and Coulthard families, and by officers and soldiers of the Intelligence Corps who wanted to pay tribute to one of their own who died for his country. Antony Coulthard's bravery and selflessness can never be questioned, even if his downfall in August 1942, just a few miles from the safety of Switzerland, was, to a degree, agonisingly self-inflicted.

• • •

Another Second World War Intelligence Corps operator who did not shirk from risking his life for other people's liberty in France and north-west Europe in 1940 was Captain Norman Hope. The account of his service to his country provides sure proof that some missions carried out by Corps operators were considered so sensitive and dangerous that even those who participated in them were shielded from their ultimate objective until they were under way.

Norman Edward Hope was born on 13 March 1903 at Carlisle, the son of John and Henrietta Hope. His father was a businessman who hit hard times, but this did not appear to affect Norman's education prospects. In September 1913, he started at Dean Close School, a private establishment in Cheltenham, where he was a member of the Officer Training Corps. In 1921, he moved to France to continue his education at the École des Roches in Normandy, founded by the sociologist Edmond Demolins, and in 1923 he enrolled at the School of Arts and Crafts at Southampton Row in London. By 1929, following a year working in Canada as a harvester, he was employed by the Asiatic Petroleum Company, a joint venture between the Shell and Royal Dutch oil companies operating in the Far East and headquartered in Shanghai. He spent seven years with this firm in French Indo-China, during which time he mastered the local Annamite language and, in 1933 in Saigon, married Marjorie Martin Phillips, the daughter of a Welsh solicitor.

In 1937, Hope was posted to Colombia and then Venezuela before returning to England in July 1939. Illustrating how the British establishment worked at that time, he was approached in October 1939 through what might bluntly be called the old boy network to join Section D of the Secret Intelligence Service, MI6. Recruitment to Section D was often based on a person having been to the right school, coming from a family with a certain social standing, or through a business connection. In 1938, when the odds of Britain going to war with Germany began to shorten markedly, Section D was established under the direction of Laurence Grand. ('D' is commonly believed to have stood for 'destruction', although this has never been confirmed officially.) It was a secret outfit which operated for a spell from offices in the basement of 54 Broadway Buildings in Westminster, under the cover of the Minimax Fire Extinguisher Company, and later from the nearby St Ermin's Hotel. Its aim was simple: 'To plan, prepare and when necessary carry out sabotage and other clandestine operations, as opposed to the gathering of intelligence.' According to MI6's own official account of Section D, '[Laurence] Grand laid plans for targeting Germany's electricity industry, phone communications, railways, food supplies and agriculture. He also wrote a report on how to defend Britain against sabotage – including the protection of power stations and communications.' By December 1939, Norman Hope was one of at least forty individuals, many of them civilians with no previous military or intelligence experience, who had agreed to join this undercover organisation. The qualities which united its members were a detailed knowledge of Europe and the ability to speak foreign languages, in particular French and German.

Section D operated under a variety of nicknames during its brief existence, including 'Section IX' and the 'Sabotage Service', but the most common official guise it adopted was that of the 'Statistical

Research Department of the War Office'. It was split into departments for operational purposes, each of which focused on a country or territory under a section head who oversaw their respective administration, training, documents, equipment, plus research and development. For some reason which was not recorded, Norman Hope, a fluent French speaker, was appointed as the head of the Belgium and Netherlands section and given the code 'D/I'.

Following the outbreak of war, Section D officers were granted Army commissions, partly as cover but also to provide some measure of legal protection in the event of capture. As the Intelligence Corps did not come into being officially until July 1940, commissions were mainly to the General List, otherwise known as the General Service Corps. On 17 April 1940, Hope was commissioned as a Second Lieutenant on the General List and was made acting Lieutenant five days later. His War Office service file describes his appointment as a 'Junior Research Officer with the Statistical Research Department', in keeping with the main Section D cover identity. Along with a Belgian Army Liaison Officer, Hendrik Van Riel, he recruited evacuated Belgian soldiers in order to send them back into Belgium to carry out work for the Special Operations Executive, Churchill's underground army which undertook spying and sabotage operations in occupied Europe. Hope also set up explosives stores in all the major towns and cities – Brussels, Antwerp, Bruges and Ghent.

After the fall of Dunkirk on 5 June 1940, and the evacuation of the British Expeditionary Force, the Nazis moved to complete their 'Blitzkrieg' occupation of northern France. On 16 June, the French Prime Minister, Paul Reynaud, resigned and was replaced by Philippe Pétain. One of Pétain's first acts was to request armistice terms with the Germans. With the fall of France imminent,

Pétain was appointed President of the Ministerial Council by President Lebrun. At the same time, Brigadier-General Charles de Gaulle, who had been leading a tank brigade against the advancing Germans, had been appointed Under-Secretary for War. He bitterly opposed any thoughts of an armistice. On 17 June, de Gaulle flew to London to lead the French government-in-exile. One consequence of his taking this stand was that he was parted from his wife, Yvonne, and their three young children, all of whom remained in France.

The previous month, the de Gaulle family had left their home near Rheims and moved in with a relative at Carantec in Brittany. Yet with the German forces advancing in that direction, de Gaulle was desperate to get them to the comparatively safer shores of Britain. Upon landing in England, his first act was to visit Winston Churchill in the hope that the Prime Minister could arrange for the de Gaulles' immediate rescue. Within the hour, Churchill had made a call to Major General Stewart Menzies, the head of the Secret Intelligence Service. Menzies then contacted the Director of Naval Intelligence, Admiral John Godfrey. After this, the situation developed quickly. Menzies contacted the head of Section D, Laurence Grand, and ordered him to organise a rescue expedition using one of his fluent French speakers who had knowledge of Brittany. The first candidate on the list, Colonel Louis Franck, was unavailable, so Grand asked Norman Hope to lead the assignment. Meanwhile, Godfrey's office telephoned Admiral Martin Dunbar-Nasmith, the Commander-in-Chief, Western Approaches, at 6 p.m. requesting that an aircraft be made available for a secret mission to France. The order went down the chain of command. Dunbar-Nasmith signalled a special request to 15 (General Reconnaissance) Group of Coastal Command at Plymouth, which in turn signalled the following order to No. 10 Squadron Royal Australian Air Force (RAAF) at RAF Mount Batten, a flying boat base at the Mount Batten Peninsula in Plymouth Sound, Devon:

> One Walrus to proceed with Admiralty passenger from Plymouth Sound to north coast of Brittany at earliest 18/6. Passenger will give details of destination on arrival at about 2359/17. Aircraft to be fully armed and to keep defensive watch at all times especially when waterborne. Return to base on completion.

No. 10 Squadron usually flew Short Sunderland flying boat patrols on either anti-submarine, convoy escort or air-sea rescue duties. For this covert undertaking, the squadron 'borrowed' a Mark 1 Supermarine Walrus from the communications flight of 15 Group. The Walrus, an amphibious biplane, was considered ideal, being relatively nimble, able to put down and take-off on water or land, and having the capacity for several passengers and crew.

When Hope received his orders during the afternoon of 17 June, he was heavily engaged in organising his Belgian network. With no time to plan or prepare this assignment, he made his way to the Coastal Command base at Mount Batten and arrived just after 1 a.m. on the morning of 18 June. First, he met the officer who would pilot the Walrus, Flight Lieutenant John Napier Bell of the RAAF. The other two members of the crew were Sergeant Charles Harris, an RAAF observer who would act as gunner on the flight, and Corporal Bernard Nowell, an RAF wireless electrical mechanic. Hope did not tell his three colleagues the nature of their task. That information would only be revealed once they were airborne. The ground crew hurriedly mounted a Vickers .303 machine gun to the aircraft and at 2.55 a.m. the Walrus took off from Mount Batten and headed for Carantec on the Brittany coast.

At about 4 a.m. on that fateful day, a Frenchwoman in the small village of Kerbiquet, near Ploudaniel, heard loud noises overhead and saw an aircraft flying low with flames shooting out of its tail. A thick fog covered the countryside, but through it, the plane was observed circling as if the pilot were looking for somewhere to land. It finally came down in a field where it is thought to have hit a small embankment and broken up. Villagers ran towards the wreck and attempted to save the crew, but it was too late. All four men on board were dead. The villagers removed the bodies and searched for identification. Although they found details for the three crew members, the fourth man, Hope, carried nothing. With the Germans expected to arrive at any moment, the corpses were buried in the churchyard in Ploudaniel. The cemetery register logged Hope as 'Aviateur X'.

Although the cause of the crash was never properly established, two stories emerged afterwards. One report stated that a radio transmission had been received from the Walrus as it flew over the French coast, indicating it was being attacked by enemy aircraft. The other report, from France, stated that it came under fire from a German battery at Valeury as it crossed the coast. Whichever explanation was correct, the aircraft had strayed far to the west of its planned route when it crashed.

With no news from the Walrus by midday on 18 June, it and its occupants were posted as missing. On 19 June, with the rescue of the de Gaulle family still a high priority, another officer of Section D's Belgian section was despatched to Carantec on a motor torpedo boat to complete the job and also to try and ascertain what had happened to the Walrus. Having landed safely, the Section D officer made his way into Carantec but learned that the de Gaulles were no longer there. It transpired that Hope's rescue had been so secret that Madame de Gaulle had not been informed of it and, on 18 June, in the face of the advancing Germans, she had left for the port of Brest. En route, the car in which she and her children were travelling broke down and they missed their boat. Luck was on their side, however. The ferry they missed was sunk by the Germans on its way to England with all lives lost. Later that day, they found passage to Falmouth on one of the last ships to leave before the port was overrun by the Nazis, and eventually made it to London safely.

Captain Norman Hope and the three crew members of the Walrus were officially 'missing' until late 1941, when two French refugees who fled to Britain made a report to the British Red Cross in which they recounted the story of the crashed Walrus and the burial of the occupants at Ploudaniel. Before his fate became known, Norman Hope had been transferred to the Intelligence Corps on its formation in July 1940.

• • •

Irregular warfare played a large role in Britain's war effort after the Intelligence Corps was re-formed in July 1940. The Special Operations Executive (SOE), the secret organisation told by Winston Churchill to 'set Europe ablaze' through sabotage, espionage and reconnaissance, was the body through which much of this work was done, and several Intelligence Corps operators were linked to it.

As well as being nicknamed Churchill's Secret Army, the SOE was also dubbed the Ministry of Ungentlemanly Warfare. It operated behind enemy lines with the aim of causing as much disruption as possible to the Nazis. Indeed, Churchill's active encouragement of using guerrilla warfare in order to defeat Hitler was taken exceptionally seriously. Its formation was beset with problems, however. SOE operators were viewed with scepticism by the three 'conventional' armed services; they were starved of resources; and they were treated with disdain by the Secret Intelligence Service (MI6), which has been responsible for foreign intelligence gathering since its formation in 1909. During the Second World War, SIS continued to collect strategic intelligence abroad in all the conflict areas and mounted many behind-the-lines covert missions in the occupied countries, occasionally on joint missions with the SOE. There was, however, some justifiable unease among the SIS that SOE operations would endanger their own more subtle methods of going about things.

Before being accepted into the perilous but undeniably fascinating world of the SOE, agents were required to learn a range of skills, including how to kill with their bare hands; how to burgle a house; how to derail a train; how to operate wireless equipment; how to cut power supplies; and how to break out of a pair of handcuffs. When on a mission, they would routinely carry two suicide pills in case they should be caught. Their training also required them to undertake a parachuting course, which tested their physical courage as much as their mettle. At its peak, the SOE employed 13,000 people. About a quarter of them were women. SOE operated across the entire field of conflicts and losses were heavy. Many SOE members were captured, tortured and executed in Nazi death camps. Clément Jumeau was an Intelligence Corps officer who was attached to the SOE. His story demonstrates the essential spirit of determination that was required by those who undertook its hazardous missions in the name of liberty.

He was born on 14 September 1914 at Anse La Mouche, Mahé Island, in the British colony of the Seychelles, the son of François and Agnes Jumeau. His father was a landowner and copra planter. He was educated at the Saint Louis-de-Gonzague College in Mahé before studying first at the University of Cambridge and then at the University of Glasgow, where he completed a master's degree. He studied law in Glasgow for a further two years and was registered as a solicitor in 1939. That year, he married his first cousin, Gladys. The details of their parentage entered on their marriage certificate show that Clément's mother and Gladys's mother were sisters, both with the maiden name of Lefevre, and their respective fathers were brothers. By September 1939, Jumeau, a fluent French speaker, had moved to London, where he worked as a private tutor. According to official records, he enlisted with the Corps of Military Police on 15 December 1939, undergoing field security training at the Military Police depot at Mytchett, near Aldershot.

Jumeau was first posted to 23 Field Security Police Section, which was attached to the 42nd (East Lancashire) Division. In March 1940, during the 'Phoney War', the section moved to northern France and was employed on frontier control duties in the region of Armentières. On 10 May, it moved to the French town of Comines, on the Belgian border, with a view to establishing some form of control system for the anticipated flood of refugees. Once the German offensive started, more than 300,000 displaced people headed for France, most of whom were marshalled by Belgian officials working under the instructions of the field security section to which Jumeau belonged. Before long, the 42nd Division was ordered to withdraw towards Dunkirk and Jumeau's section followed them. It was among the last to leave, having ensured that no sensitive documents had been left behind once premises had been vacated.

Jumeau and his fellow operators were evacuated on the night of 31 May and moved straight to the field security depot, which by then had relocated to Sheerness in Kent. During his time in France, Jumeau was promoted to Sergeant and was Mentioned in Despatches for his work there, the award being gazetted on 20 December 1940. By this time, his FSS post had been absorbed into the Intelligence Corps and his war was about to take a dramatic turn.

On 4 May 1941, Jumeau was selected for agent training with F-Section (French Section) of the Special Operations Executive. He joined formally on 19 May 1941 and underwent initial paramilitary training at one of its schools in Inverness-shire, named Special Training School 25. Official reports from this period of his training state that he received a mixture of 'Very Good' and 'Good' grading in field craft, close combat and weapons use. He also excelled in explosives training, achieving a score of 93 per cent. He then moved to another training school, STS 5, at Wanborough Manor, an Elizabethan house near Guildford in Surrey. Again, his official report was glowing, describing him as 'intelligent, very keen and, with further training, a good leader'. On 16 July 1941, F-Section requested to the War Office that Jumeau be commissioned, commenting that his progress had 'justified him for work of a very responsible nature abroad'. His promotion to Second Lieutenant was backdated to 10 July 1941.

Jumeau's first assignment, in which he led a unit of four F-Section agents, was codenamed Operation Deposit. There was another Briton in the group, Jack Hayes; two Frenchmen, Jean Le Harivel and Daniel Turberville, made up the rest of the quartet. Their mission, for which

Jumeau adopted the alias 'Robert', was to establish an area of operations near Marseilles in the then unoccupied Vichy zone of France. On 10 October 1941, they parachuted from a Whitley bomber into the Dordogne region, close to the town of Bergerac. Having established their circuit, their plan was to organise '*actions insaisissables*' (literally 'elusive actions'), targeting barges, oil and rubber supplies, rolling-stock and power stations.

Regrettably, the mission got off to a poor start and only went downhill. The first problem was that Turberville landed apart from the main group and had with him the wireless and a large quantity of equipment and explosives. He was soon captured. The others lay low in a barn until 15 October, when they set off for Marseilles. They travelled separately, but their destination was the same safe house, the Villa des Bois. Their contact there was a man called Georges Turck, codenamed 'Christophe'. By the time they arrived, however, the house had been compromised and agents of the Vichy regime had set a trap. As each member of Jumeau's group arrived, the door was opened by an attractive young woman with a small child, who told them that her husband was not there but that they should meet him the following day at a nearby café at a particular time. The trio followed this instruction, but on arrival they were arrested by plain-clothes members of the Vichy police.

Having been interrogated without force or ill-treatment, Jumeau and his colleagues were incarcerated at the Beleyme in Périgueux in south-western France. Jumeau later described conditions there as 'degrading and humiliating to the last degree, hygiene and sanitation were non-existent. Food was unspeakably bad and in addition we were plagued with vermin and disease.' From Beleyme, they were sent on to a Vichy internment camp at Mauzac, east of Bergerac. Also held prisoner there was Georges Bégué, a French engineer turned SOE operator who was codenamed 'Bombproof'. He was the first SOE agent to have been infiltrated into France, landing 'blind' (meaning without anybody to meet him) on 5 May 1941, and had been captured on 3 October 1941.

Bégué and Jumeau took the lead in plotting and organising an escape. Unusually, the wife of one prisoner was allowed into the camp by the relatively relaxed Vichy guards, meaning that she was not only able to bring food parcels and other comforts to inmates but also able to take messages from them to the Resistance. Setting up this convenient postal service was not their only piece of luck. Bégué and Jumeau also made friends with a sympathetic guard, eventually bribing him into supplying them with a key which they managed to copy. On 16 July 1942, Jumeau, Bégué and about ten others bolted. After finding sanctuary with members of the local Resistance, they crossed the Pyrenees into Spain and returned home.

Despite having endured such hardship, duty came calling again for Jumeau soon afterwards. Like so many of his generation, Jumeau responded with little thought for himself, placing his life in danger again by volunteering to return to France – this time under a heightened risk because his identity was known to the Germans. On the night of 12 April 1943, he set out as the leader of the Reporter network, using the alias of André Chambon and the field name Philibert. 'Reporter' was to operate in the Lyon area with the main objective of subverting French labour in the German-controlled war munitions factories. For this mission, Jumeau was accompanied by Lieutenant Louis Lee-Graham, also of the Intelligence Corps, who was codenamed 'Surgeon'.

The aircraft which was to deliver them into France was a Halifax bomber of 138 Special Duties Squadron, piloted by a Polish Air

Force crew. They took off from RAF Tempsford in Bedfordshire and crossed the French coast near Cabourg. At this point they were flying low, at 500 feet, and the navigator requested the pilot to climb another 200 feet to enable him to get an accurate 'fix'. Having done so, they were picked up by an anti-aircraft battery and came under a flak barrage. The Halifax was hit several times, setting fire to one engine and killing the wireless operator. Despite the pilot's attempt to control the plane, it crashed at Douvres-la-Délivrande, just 7 miles north of Caen, and burst into flames. Two crew members received bad burns and were apprehended the following morning; two others evaded capture for six months before being caught; and the pilot managed to return to England without detection.

Miraculously, Jumeau and Lee-Graham also escaped from the crashed plane before it blew up, with Jumeau sustaining only minor injuries. Having survived, they buried their papers in a copse and headed south, but within an hour they were arrested by a German patrol. After being held at Caen, they were handed over to the Gestapo at Frankfurt-am-Main.

Lee-Graham, who survived the war, later recalled that they were kept in solitary confinement until March 1944. When he saw Jumeau again, ten months later, he was almost skeletal and unable to walk unaided. The pair were moved to a nearby barracks and held together in a freezing cold cell with little food. Jumeau's condition quickly deteriorated and he developed a persistent cough, chest pains and a high temperature. The next day, they were taken by train to the town of Torgau in Saxony. On arrival, they were forced to walk to Fort Zinna, the Wehrmacht's largest prison facility, by which time Jumeau was in a state of collapse and had to be carried by Lee-Graham. They were again separated, with Jumeau being transferred to a military hospital at Buch, a northern suburb of Berlin. Lee-Graham was also transferred there after a month at Torgau, soon learning from a German parson that Jumeau had died a week after his arrival. In a subsequent military report which he wrote, Lee-Graham stated that the conditions at Buch were even worse than at Torgau. It transpires that the end of Jumeau's life was unforgivably grim.

The Buch hospital was established in 1905 as a sanatorium for tuberculous patients, but from 1940, it became a truly dark place. As is well known, the Nazis pursued a policy of euthanasia that was intended to rid the world of those who were disabled, sick or mentally ill. In keeping with this programme of organised murder, patients at the Buch hospital, many of whom were children, were removed from the premises and sent to centres at Bernberg and Brandenberg, where they were gassed with carbon dioxide. The hospital was later turned into a military sanatorium for the Luftwaffe. Chronically unwell Allied prisoners of war were also sent there and housed in its older, run-down areas.

After the war, the SOE conducted investigations into the fates of those agents who failed to return. In Jumeau's case, it was established that he received no medical treatment while at the Buch military hospital. When he became so weak that he could not leave his bed or eat, he simply perished having been left to starve to death. Officially, he died from pulmonary tuberculosis on 26 March 1944. He was twenty-nine years old. His body was taken for burial to the old First World War prisoner-of-war cemetery at Döberitz, just outside Berlin. In December 1946, the Commonwealth War Graves Commission exhumed the bodies of the British burials at Döberitz, which was by then in the Soviet-controlled zone, although many of these graves were unmarked and unidentified. They were re-interred at the Berlin 1939–45 War Cemetery. It has been suggested that Jumeau was one of those reinterred, but this has not yet been confirmed. His name therefore remains inscribed on the Brook-wood Memorial to the Missing at Woking in Surrey. His name is also commemorated on the Special Operations Executive 'F-Section' Memorial at Valençay in central France.

● ● ●

Although Intelligence Corps men like Coulthard, Hope and Jumeau met tragic ends, fate looked more kindly on others. Among the noteworthy operators who survived the war was Harry Rée, an Intelligence Corps officer who was, like Jumeau, attached to the SOE and was responsible for some of its most effective work in oc-cupied France. Indeed, the military historian M. R. D. Foot, who was the SOE's official historian and who was himself a member of the Intelligence Corps, believed that of the 400 or so SOE agents active in France during the Second World War, Rée was among its very best practitioners of the black arts of sabotage.

Harry Alfred Rée was born on 15 October 1914 at Withington, Manchester, the youngest of eight children of Dr Alfred Rée and Lavinia (née Dimmick). His father was an industrial chemist and his mother was a scion of the du Pont family, one of the richest dynasties in America whose fortune came from the chemical and automotive industries. His paternal grandparents, Isidor Rée and Thekla Mathilde Beck, were European Jews who settled in Britain in the nineteenth century, his grandfather becoming a wool mer-chant in Bradford.

Rée was educated at the Craig Preparatory School in Windermere and Shrewsbury School in Shropshire. In 1933, he went up to St John's College, Cambridge, to read modern languages, graduating in 1936. While at Cambridge, he signed the Peace Pledge and declared himself to be an idealistic socialist, but when visiting cousins in Hamburg subsequently he became disturbed by the rise of Hitler. After graduating, he spent a year training to be a teacher at the University of London and in 1937 took his first job at a grammar school. With war on the horizon, he registered as a conscientious objector in 1939 and volunteered to work part-time with the National Fire Service. When war was declared, he volunteered with the London Civil Defence. As a teacher he was in a reserved occupation, but the knowledge that so many other young men were going into uniform when he was not made him ill at ease. After the fall of France in June 1940, he decided to join up, and did so within a few months, having first married Hetty Vine of Beaconsfield in Buckinghamshire. They would go on to have three children.

On 14 November 1940, Rée enlisted as a gunner in the Royal Artillery. His elder brother, Eric, was serving with the Intelligence Corps at the time and persuaded him to transfer. He did so on 14 June 1941, having calculated that he would rather die as a result of making his own mistake as opposed to following orders 'from some stupid colonel or general back at base', as his memoir put it. His first postings were with 116 Home Port Security Section at Port Talbot and then with 34 Field Security Section at Doncaster.

In October 1941, he was posted to one of the several field security sections attached to the SOE. These sections provided the military security for the various SOE training schools and establishments. They also conducted surveillance on the SOE 'students' themselves who were preparing for their missions abroad, meaning that would-be spies were effectively being spied on. Every facet of their lives, on and off duty, was monitored, including their drinking habits; behaviour with the opposite sex; and any foibles likely to make them stand out when they became operational in the field.

In September 1942, Rée volunteered to train as a field agent and, having been accepted for F-Section to undertake missions in France, he began his tuition at Wanborough Manor, near Guildford. He was commissioned into the Intelligence Corps on 27 October 1942 and six weeks later had completed his paramilitary training at Arisaig in Inverness-shire, his parachute course at Ringway in Cheshire and the sabotage course at Brickendonbury in Hertfordshire. He had completed his last course, at the SOE 'finishing school' at Beaulieu in Hampshire, by the end of December.

On 15 April 1943, Rée and another agent were dropped from a Halifax of No. 138 Special Duties Squadron close to the town of Tarbes, in the unoccupied Vichy zone in the Pyrenees. Under the field name 'Caesar', his mission was to act as the assistant to the leader of the 'Stockbroker' circuit in the Clermont-Ferrand region, developing this network in the Dijon, Doubs and Montbéliard areas. For the next three months, he toured around the Maquis camps in the area, organising supply drops and distributing arms and explosives. Despite placing his life in danger, Rée, whose spoken French is said not to have been particularly good, displayed a certain amusing nonchalance while carrying out these duties. For example, on one occasion he arrived at the railway station in Tarbes to catch a train to Clermont-Ferrand but he later recalled: 'I reached the station an hour early, so I went and got my hair cut. I could hardly understand a word but said "*Oui*" to everything and came out with a reasonable haircut.' It was around this time that he was struck by the kind of counter-intuitive thought that was second nature to those working in intelligence.

In July 1943, the RAF carried out a bombing raid on the Peugeot factory at Sochaux, near Montbéliard, because it was producing turrets for German tanks. The raid was a failure, causing heavy damage to the town but little to the factory. Realising that any future raid might produce the same result, Rée arranged with London for all bombing activity in this specific area to be suspended. He then used his charm to mastermind a cunning scheme, setting up a meeting with the factory director, Rodolphe Peugeot. During this meeting, he 'persuaded' Peugeot to assist in an internal act of sabotage on the factory's vital components, thereby leaving the Germans hamstrung. Rée personally planned and organised the attack on the night of 5 November, assisted by one of the factory foremen, overseeing the placing of explosive charges on transformers and turbo-compressors. The factory was put out of action for six months. With that mission having been a success, Rée then organised the bombing of several other Peugeot sites. (Incidentally, that same month, Eric Rée, Harry's brother, by then a Warrant Officer II in the Intelligence Corps, was killed in a motorcycle accident while serving with a field security section of SOE at their 'Massingham' base in Algiers.)

On 28 November, Rée called at the house of Jean Hauger, one of his Resistance contacts who had been setting up a sabotage group. The house, in the Rue de Belfort in the village of Vieux-Charmont, appeared quiet as he approached on his bicycle. Unbeknown to him, the Germans had carried out a search of the property earlier, finding Hauger's entire arsenal of sub-machine guns, revolvers and hand grenades. Hauger and his family had been arrested and taken into custody. Rée knocked at the front door and was surprised when it was opened by a stranger in civilian clothes pointing a pistol. Keeping the gun trained on Rée, the stranger produced the identity card of a member of the German Feldgendarmerie and ordered Rée to enter. As he went into the kitchen, Rée saw Hauger's cache of weapons on the table and realised that he wasn't easily going to be able to bluff his way out. But under questioning, Rée provided such a convincing explanation for visiting the house that the German began to relax. Rée then took his chance. He picked up a wine bottle and smashed it over the German's head. A fierce fight ensued.

In his memoir he recalled:

> I lunged at him and brought him down. I remembered *King Lear* and tried to get one of his eyeballs out by pressing with my thumb. It didn't work, so I tried biting his nose, and then put a finger in his mouth and tried to rip his cheek. That must have hurt a lot but he managed to push me off and stand up. I lunged and we started boxing again … I landed two more punches full in the face, smashing his head against the wall. He turned away and said, '*Sortez, sortez* … get out.'

During the tussle, the German fired his pistol six times. All six bullets hit Rée, but in the heat of the moment he didn't realise this and broke free, running from the house, crossing a water-filled ditch and disappearing into the countryside. It was only then that he saw blood was seeping from his arm and chest. Although weak and in great pain, he swam across the River Allan and made his way to the safe house of another contact in the village of Étupes. A friendly doctor was called who found that one bullet had entered Rée's chest, another had penetrated his shoulder and the other four had grazed him.

After his wounds were dressed, Rée was moved to a house at

Méziré and the following day he was driven in a post office van to Delle, less than a mile from the Swiss border. From there, he was smuggled into Switzerland and admitted to a hospital at Porrentruy to receive proper treatment. After ten days, he went to the Alpine resort of Wengen, above Interlaken. Although his recovery was good, SOE ordered him not to return to France but to continue controlling the 'Stockbroker' network from Switzerland. Rée remained in Switzerland until the first week of May 1944 and then crossed back into France and over the Pyrenees into Spain. He intended to return to England via Gibraltar, but on 10 May he was interned by the Spanish at Pamplona and transferred to a camp at Miranda de Ebro. Finally, on 17 June, he was released and completed his journey to Gibraltar, from where he flew back to England. He returned to SOE headquarters in London and served with the General Staff of the French Forces of the Interior (HQ EMFFI).

On 15 June 1944, Rée was appointed an Officer of the Order of the British Empire (OBE) in recognition of his 'gallant and distinguished services in the field'. Five months later, on 15 November 1944, he was also created a Companion of the Distinguished Service Order (DSO). The recommendation provides a fuller account of his brilliance in sabotaging the Peugeot factories. It reads:

This officer was appointed an Officer in the Order of the British Empire (Military Division) on 16 June 1944 for his work on a secret mission to France. A great deal of further evidence has now come to light particularly in connection with the damage done to the Peugeot factories at Montbelliard and Sochaux. Capt Rée organised, directed and personally led the sabotage attacks on these factories between 5 November 1943 and 3 March 1944. The attack on the centrifugal compressor in the compressor room necessitated his crawling up the ducts under conditions of the greatest danger and physical strain. The compressor was completely destroyed. In the same operation Capt Rée and his men destroyed a large lathe in the heavy machine shop. Later, he and his men attacked and destroyed a new compressor while it was standing on a lorry in the works yard. He also put out of action a jig borer, another compressor, a two-drill borer, the washing tower of the gas producer plant, the foundry and dryers and the bodywork transformers and destroyed six thousand tyres in the tyre depot. These activities were planned and coordinated with the Peugeot management by Capt Rée who personally led the attacks and, on one occasion, only escaped under heavy small arms fire by swimming a canal. He was twice wounded but escaped. The result of these attacks was that these Peugeot factories, which produced tank parts and aircraft engine components for the enemy, were made completely unproductive for five months and only started producing, on a small scale, in March 1944. After a short time spent in recovering from his wounds, Capt Rée again started to direct sabotage activities in this area. His prestige and authority were enormous, and his activities have become legendary. He did not cease from this work until the liberation of France. For his outstanding gallantry, his diplomacy in getting the Peugeot management to cooperate in his sabotage activities and for his devotion to duty over a long period it is strongly recommended that Capt Rée be appointed a Companion in the Distinguished Service Order.

Rée was further honoured by the French government with the Croix de Guerre in 1945, and in 1949 he was made a Chevalier of the Légion d'Honneur.

Rée's dedication to his work was also committed to celluloid. In 1944, he starred in a documentary film called *Now It Can Be Told* (also known as *School for Danger*) about the work of the SOE, which was made for the Central Office of Information. In it, he played the fictional Captain Brown. His co-star was a fellow SOE agent, Jacqueline Nearne, who played the role of the fictional Miss Williams. The film was not released officially until 1946, but it can still be seen today via YouTube and it shows brilliantly the levels of bravery required of SOE agents when doing their duty. Rée was seconded to the Services Educational Unit of the BBC until June 1946.

Back in civilian life, he returned to teaching, becoming headmaster of Watford Grammar School, where he remained until 1962. He then took up the post of professor of education at the University of York, but in 1974 he grew tired of being an academic and returned to grass-roots teaching at a comprehensive school in London. He retired in 1980 and died aged seventy-six from a heart attack on 17 May 1991 at Ingleton in the Yorkshire Dales. His wife had died on Christmas Eve 1961.

• • •

The work of women in the Intelligence Corps during the Second World War was decisive and some of it was carried out at Bletchley Park, the Allied codebreaking centre in Buckinghamshire. It was not unusual for them to take on duties there from the age of eighteen. One such teenager was Betty Webb, whose story neatly summarises the levels of responsibility they took on in a way that is perhaps unimaginable today.

Charlotte Webb (née Vine-Stevens, known as Betty) was born on 13 May 1923 at Aston-on-Clun in Shropshire. Her father, Leslie

Vine-Stevens, was a bank official who had served during the Great War as an officer in the Royal West Kent Regiment in Mesopotamia and India. Her mother, Charlotte (née Harris), had been a music teacher and school mistress at a Moravian Ladies School in Bedford.

Webb grew up in the village of Richard's Castle, near Ludlow, and was educated at home. Additional private tuition with a Miss Faraday, the niece of Michael Faraday, who pioneered research into electricity and electromagnetism, followed. The family employed German and Swiss au pairs in the 1920s and 1930s and, as a result, Webb excelled at German, which her mother spoke as well. She also taught herself Spanish. In 1937, she embarked on an exchange visit to Germany with a family who lived near Dresden. While there, she became aware of the rise of the Nazi regime.

After the outbreak of war, she started a domestic science course at Radbrook College, near Shrewsbury, but she wanted to help the war effort. Although the National Service Act had not yet been introduced, Webb decided to join up. As there were then no vacancies in her first choice, the Women's Royal Naval Service (WRNS), she applied for the Auxiliary Territorial Service (ATS) and was accepted. The ATS was formed in September 1938 as the women's branch of the Army. It had its roots in the Women's Army Auxiliary Corps (WAAC), which was formed during the First World War to release men from the support services of the Army for front-line service.

In September 1941, following her six-week basic training at Wrexham, she was ordered to report to an address in London. With no idea what to expect, she went to Devonshire House in Piccadilly where she was interviewed in German by a Major from the Intelligence Corps. She was not given any reason for the interview. Next, she was told to take a train from Euston to Bletchley, where she would be met. She was given a kit bag, a railway warrant and sent on her way. After a night in a billet in Bletchley, she went the following morning to a large house surrounded by a closely guarded perimeter, Bletchley Park. With still no idea as to what the future held, she was given a copy of the Official Secrets Act to read and sign and lectured on the need for absolute discretion. It was only then that she was made aware she would be working for the Government Code and Cypher School as one of thousands of service personnel and civilians engaged in breaking the enemy's codes.

Webb's first assignment was to the department run by Major Ralph Tester, a fluent German speaker, whose small team was working on breaking the German 'Playfair Cypher' used by the German Military Police. As the hundreds of intercepted messages were delivered from the 'Y-Stations', it was Webb's duty to register them all individually by date and call-sign on index cards. This enabled the team to make quick cross-references during the decoding and translating process. The resulting product was then sent off for intelligence analysis. In July 1942, Ralph Tester took on the challenge of breaking the German High Command's top-level code, 'Tunny'. This was a cypher system used for the transmission of messages from German Army Headquarters in Berlin to their top Commanders on all fronts. It was considered by the Germans to be unbreakable and used the twelve-wheel Lorenz coding machine, which was far more complex than the standard three- or four-wheel Enigma. Eventually, this section – known as the 'Testery' – moved into a newly constructed 'Block F' in Bletchley's grounds.

Webb remained part of the 'Testery' until mid-1943, when increasing levels of Japanese traffic made it necessary to expand the Japanese section. She stayed put in Block F but moved over to the

Japanese Military Air section. Her duties were to paraphrase the content of decoded messages so that the information extracted from them would not appear to have come from the original message, thereby concealing the fact that Japanese codes were being broken. The Japanese section was large and consisted of both civilian and military staff, the latter being made up almost exclusively of Intelligence Corps personnel and the ATS attached to them.

On 8 May 1945, the war in Europe came to an end. The war against the Japanese continued, however, and many who worked in Bletchley's Japanese section were being warned of a move to New Delhi, which was at the centre of the British SIGINT effort in the India–Burma–Far East theatre. By this point, Webb had been promoted from Private to Staff Sergeant. She was among those selected to travel to India but was then unexpectedly asked to go to Washington DC on attachment to the Pentagon instead. At Poole in Dorset, she boarded a Shorts Sunderland 'flying boat' aircraft bound for Baltimore via Newfoundland. Arriving on 1 June at Baltimore, she was taken on the final leg of her journey to the American capital.

For the next five months, Webb worked in the Pentagon as part of a small British team assisting American decoders. In effect, she reprised her Bletchley Park role by paraphrasing intelligence reports resulting from intercepted Japanese communications from Burma. Towards the end of her time in Washington, she was working in a British Joint Services Mission. On 6 August 1945, the first atomic bomb was dropped over Hiroshima. This was followed three days later by a second bomb dropped over Nagasaki. On 14 August 1945, Japan surrendered and the Second Word War was over.

On 5 October, Webb and a group of other ATS girls set sail on the liner *Aquitania* for the return voyage to England. After a one-night stay at Bletchley Park, she was posted to East Grinstead in Sussex to await her final discharge, which became effective in February 1946.

Now a civilian, Webb enrolled on a six-month secretarial course in London and then took an administrative job at Ludlow Grammar School, where the headmaster had also been at Bletchley Park during the war. From there, she moved on to a manufacturing firm in Chester, which led to her being commissioned in 321 (Cheshire) Battalion, Women's Royal Army Corps (TA). The Women's Royal Army Corps (WRAC) was the de facto replacement of the ATS, which had been disbanded in 1949. In the autumn of 1959, Webb was offered the position of the Permanent Staff Officer and Adjutant to the battalion in the rank of Captain. She remained a full-time member of the WRAC (TA) and later moved to Bristol with 71 (Bristol) Company. From 1966, she was the WRAC Recruiting Officer for the West Midlands and held that position until she retired from the Army in 1969 to take up the post of area secretary for the YWCA.

In July 1970, she married Alfred Webb, a wartime veteran of the Guard's Armoured Division, and they settled in Redditch, Worcestershire, until his death in 1978. The Official Secrets Act was lifted in 1975, allowing many who had signed it to write about their wartime work at Bletchley. Webb was among them, publishing *Secret Postings: Bletchley Park to the Pentagon* under her full name, Charlotte Webb, in 2014. She also gave more than 150 talks about her time at Bletchley. In 2015, Webb was appointed a Member of the Order of the British Empire (MBE). The following year, she learned that some of the decoded messages she had been ordered to catalogue at Bletchley were communications between members of the SS and the Gestapo in which details of the Holocaust were discussed. By any standards, however, she and many other women played a key part in an intelligence triumph which is widely considered to have shortened the Second World War by between two and four years. Webb said in 2018: 'I was rather pleased to know I had been working on an important part of the exercise. I do hope I made a contribution.' In July 2021, Betty Webb was further honoured by the French government when they made her a Chevalier of the Légion d'Honneur.

• • •

The duties of the Intelligence Corps throughout the Second World War were many and varied. It was concerned with the collection of strategic and tactical information through the interception of signals, through the retrieval of documents and via aerial photography. Counter-intelligence was also pivotal. Another crucial area was prisoner-of-war intelligence. Shortly before war was declared in September 1939, several prescient officers working in military intelligence realised there would be a need for an organisation concerned with escape and evasion. Their idea culminated in the creation of 'MI9', which was established expressly for this purpose as a section of the Military Intelligence Directorate. It came under the leadership of Major (later Brigadier) Norman Crockatt DSO MC and used as its cover address in London 'Room 900 of the War Office'.

The role of MI9 was twofold. Firstly, it was concerned with devising, manufacturing and smuggling escape aids to British prisoners of war held in occupied Europe and Germany. Inventions developed under this initiative included miniature compasses which could be hidden in uniform buttons; silk maps that could be sown into the linings of uniforms; and replacement uniforms that could be converted easily into civilian clothing. Its second preoccupation was to find and maintain escape routes from the occupied countries to neutral territories, chiefly Spain and Switzerland. To carry out this work, MI9 agents were infiltrated into the occupied countries – notably France, Belgium, the Netherlands and Denmark – usually by parachute. Generally, they cooperated and coordinated with the various Allied resistance organisations while remaining subordinate to the Secret Intelligence Service, MI6.

One Intelligence Corps operator who excelled himself while attached to MI9 was Dignus 'Dick' Kragt. He was born at Datchet in Berkshire on 18 July 1917, the son of Hendrik Gijsbertus Kragt and Edith Matilda Eberl. His father, who was originally from Rotterdam, was a merchant and company director, while his mother was the British-born daughter of a naturalised Austrian innkeeper from Windsor. During his childhood and early youth, and before his father died in 1934, Kragt and his family made frequent trips to Holland to visit relatives, as a result of which he spoke Dutch flawlessly. Following his education in England, he trained as a radio engineer and worked for the Dutch electronics firm Philips at its factory in Mitcham, south London.

In early 1943, Kragt was commissioned into the Intelligence Corps and attached to MI9 for a mission in Holland. His proficiency as a radio operator and his knowledge of the country and its culture made him a natural recruit for the assignment which, incidentally, was overseen by Airey Neave, the future Conservative MP who had escaped from Colditz in 1942 and who was assassinated by the republican communist paramilitary Irish National Liberation Army in 1979. In his book *Saturday at MI9*, Neave described Kragt as a 'brave and persistent agent'.

By this point of the war, many Allied resistance agents operating in Holland had been compromised by the *Englandspiel* (literally 'England game') counter-intelligence operation run between 1942 and 1944 by Lieutenant Colonel Hermann Giskes of the German military intelligence unit, Abwehr Section IIIF. Having captured them, the Nazis commandeered their radios and codes and sent bogus messages back to England. Although most of the agents omitted security codes from the messages – an exclusion which should therefore have warned London that an agent had been apprehended and was operating under duress – this fact was ignored by the recipients, meaning that agents and supplies continued to be sent into the Netherlands. In total, fifty-four agents – nine of whom were from MI6 and one of whom, a woman, was from MI9 – fell into German hands before *Englandspiel* was itself blown. Of these, all but four were tortured and eventually shot or died in concentration camps.

Kragt volunteered to be the first agent to be infiltrated into the Netherlands after the deception was discovered. Putting his own safety firmly to one side, he agreed to parachute in 'blind' – that is to say without a reception committee – in total secrecy. His objective was to set up a link to the existing Comet escape line so that any aircrew shot down in the Netherlands had an organised route out of the country. Comet had been set up in 1941. It consisted of a series of connections across Europe from Belgium, through occupied France, into neutral Spain and then on to Gibraltar. Although comparatively few airmen had been shot down in the Netherlands, a Dutch extension of Comet was needed to complete the network. The War Office was initially reluctant to allow Kragt to take a wireless set with him, convinced that detection was inevitable. Eventually, however, his mission was approved on condition that he dropped alone, without a wireless operator, and would therefore work his own set. His mission was codenamed Lemontree and his personal alias was 'Frans Hals'.

Four attempts were required to get Kragt into the Netherlands. The first came on the night of 10 June 1943. He boarded a Halifax bomber from 161 Special Duties Squadron at RAF Tempsford in Bedfordshire, piloted by a Pilot Officer Higgins. While trying to pinpoint the drop zone, 7.5 miles north-north-east of Apeldoorn and east of Epe, the aircraft came under heavy fire from several 20mm anti-aircraft guns. A few minutes later, the Halifax was attacked from astern by a German night-fighter, sustaining damage to the tail and the port engine. As if that wasn't enough, it then came under fire from another anti-aircraft battery. Having made three passes of the area, the drop was aborted and Kragt returned to base.

The second attempt came nine nights later, on 19 June, again in a Halifax of 161 Special Duties Squadron flown by P/O Higgins. Although on this occasion the drop zone was reached without incident, high surface winds forced the plane back to England. The third attempt, on the night of 22 June, was flown by a P/O Wilkinson, also of 161 Squadron, after P/O Higgins was on another mission. Nearing the Dutch coast at 150 feet, the aircraft was engaged by a flak ship firing a mixture of machine guns and Bofors AA guns. Although the aircraft made it through the blizzard of bullets safely, fate once again intervened while approaching the drop zone, as wind conditions made jumping too dangerous. Wilkinson aborted the drop. On their return to Bedfordshire, they learned that P/O Higgins had been shot down that night while flying a combined MI6/SOE mission to the Netherlands, with the loss of eight lives. That mission had not been a 'blind' drop and it was suspected that the Abwehr intelligence service had informed the Luftwaffe they were coming.

The fourth – successful – attempt came the following night, on 23 June, this time by a Halifax of 138 Squadron piloted by a Squadron Leader Griffiths. Things got off to a bad start for Kragt. First, he was dropped in the wrong place, narrowly missing a large tree and a building. Instead of arriving in the countryside between Apeldoorn and Epe, as planned, he landed in a suburban area between Epe and Vaassen, 8 miles from the target. To make matters worse, he became separated from his transmitter and equipment containers during the drop. It transpired they had become lodged in a tree in the garden of an enemy collaborator a few houses away who handed them over to the Germans. Not only did the enemy know, therefore, that an agent had arrived in the area, but Kragt would have to operate without a transmitter for several months.

Making careful notes of the scene around him in order to work out his position, Kragt removed his camouflaged suit and boots and hid them, along with his neatly rolled parachute, among some weeds. Armed with an automatic pistol, he decided his best bet was to leave the area, find a quiet spot and lie low. After walking for a couple of hours, dawn was approaching. He saw some tall grass near a brook and hid there for almost eighteen hours until the dead of night. Using his compass, he then made his way to a house owned by a couple who were members of the Dutch resistance. They took him to an underground dugout in some woods nearby where he linked up with Jacobus van den Boogert, known as Koos, and Joop Piller, a Jewish resistance worker in Emst. Over the ensuing months, Kragt established a highly effective link to the Comet line in Brussels. In November 1943, MI9 parachuted in a Dutchman, Jean Temmerman, to act as Kragt's wireless operator with a replacement transmitter and a spare set. Indeed, so effective did Kragt's organisation turn out to be that, up to September 1944, he sent a total of more than 100 aircrew 'down the line' to Brussels for onward passage to safety.

Fifteen months after Kragt's arrival in the Netherlands, on 17 September 1944, Operation Market Garden was launched. Its ultimate objective was to secure nine bridges, including one in the Dutch town of Arnhem, close to the German border. Although it was unsuccessful, some Allied forces did manage to evacuate across the Rhine while others avoided capture and were sheltered by the local Dutch population. These men were eventually passed to Kragt and their escape back to Allied lines was organised.

On the night of 22 October 1944, Kragt was also involved in the highly successful Operation Pegasus, organising the first extraction of more than 100 men who had been in hiding in German-occupied territory since the Battle of Arnhem. Its outcome prompted London to organise 'Pegasus II' on the night of 17 November. In fact, Kragt advised against this mission, believing that details of the first operation had been leaked to the British press, allowing the Germans to become aware of it and encouraging them to step up patrols. His instincts were right. Although *Pegasus II* went ahead, only seven men managed to cross the Rhine. Of the remainder, some were captured, and the rest were forced to disperse back into the countryside.

Like the Dutch resistance, Kragt risked his own life in order to secrete Allies out of the country, organising safe houses to feed and hide them before their escape. The area was patrolled constantly by German search parties and on one occasion Kragt was almost caught while cycling between two safe houses with some military maps rolled up in his saddle bag. Having been stopped by a German soldier and asked what the rolls were, Kragt said they were wallpaper and then engaged the soldier in a long story about how difficult it was to obtain in wartime. His story worked, because the German appeared so bored he simply waved him on.

Kragt stayed in the Netherlands until 17 April 1945, by which time it had been liberated. In total, he operated behind the lines for twenty-two months. In 1947, the British government awarded him the King's Medal for Courage in the Cause of Freedom. The following year, he was awarded the Medal of Freedom with Gold Palms by the American government. The citation read:

First Lieutenant Dignus Kragt, British Army, for exceptional hero-ism in connection with military operations against an enemy of the United States, from 23 June 1943 to 17 April 1945. Displaying extraordinary courage, superior organising ability and outstand-ing perseverance in the face of continuous danger of capture and torture, for twenty-two months Lieutenant Kragt built up and di-rected an underground chain in enemy-occupied territory which recuperated, fed, clothed and housed hundreds of Allied airmen and led them back to friendly territory where they rejoined their fighting units. The extraordinary accomplishments of this officer in saving, at great risk to himself, hundreds of Allied fighters from the enemy, reflects the greatest credit upon himself and the Army of which he was a member and merits the highest recognition by the United Nations.

In 1951, the Dutch government awarded Kragt the Bronze Lion, ac-knowledging that he 'greatly distinguished himself as the originator and leader of an escape organisation to England for Allied pilots shot down over the Netherlands. He also used the escape-route to pass on military information regarding the enemy, up to the libera-tion in 1945, to the Resistance movement in the Netherlands.'

After the war, Kragt returned to his former occupation at Philips and then moved to KLM Royal Dutch Airlines. While holidaying in Norway, he met Karin Rosted and they married in London in 1947. They had one son, Eric. In the mid-1970s, they settled near Oslo. His wife died in 1995. Dignus Kragt died at Bærum, Norway, on 8 July 2008, aged ninety-one. His neighbours remembered him as a quiet, unassuming gentleman. It was only after his death that they learned of his heroism behind enemy lines during the Second World War.

• • •

While many Intelligence Corps men were limited to operating in one country or even just one region of a country during the Second World War, others took on obligations which were far more expansive and diverse, to say nothing of life-threatening. One such example is Captain Godfrey Marchant, whose bravery and commitment to duty in Africa, Europe and Asia have earned him a place in the Corps' history. Considering that Marchant was not, to begin with, a professional soldier but instead fitted perfectly into the mould of the 'gifted amateur', some might see his war as having been even more extraordinary.

He was born on 24 September 1910 at Bolorum, near Madras in India, the son of Captain Godfrey Marchant and Frances Elizabeth Marchant (née Fry). His father was an officer in the 29th Lancers (Deccan Horse), Indian Army, and his mother was the daughter of Surgeon-Major Walter Fry of the Indian Army Medical Corps. Marchant senior served with his regiment during the Great War, seeing action in France and later in the Sinai during the Palestine campaign in 1918. He died in India in 1919.

Godfrey Marchant the younger was educated at Haileybury, the Hertfordshire public school which was founded by the East India Company in 1806. From there, he went up to the University of London, graduating with a Bachelor of Science degree in agriculture. In January 1931, he left Britain for Argentina and spent the next eight years there fruit farming and ranching. Through this experience, he became fluent in Spanish. He could already speak some French.

He returned to England on 30 October 1939, eight weeks after the outbreak of war, and on 14 December enlisted as a gunner in the Royal Artillery, training with 4th Field Training Regiment at Bulford in Wiltshire. The following month, when it appeared that Britain might have to send an expeditionary force to fight with the Finns in the Winter War against Soviet Russia, Marchant showed his sense of adventure by volunteering to join a specialist ski battalion which was being formed as the 5th Battalion Scots Guards, spending weeks training in the Alps. The unit was short-lived, however. When the Finnish operation was abandoned in March 1940, it was broken up.

Having returned to the Royal Artillery, Marchant was selected for officer training and on 7 July 1940 he attended 162 Officer Cadet Training Unit based on Salisbury Plain. Having passed the course, he was commissioned as a Second Lieutenant in the Intelligence Corps on 2 November 1940 and then attached to a new department called MO9, which recruited soldiers for what would become the British Commandos. It had been created six months earlier in response to Churchill's instruction to form a 'butcher and bolt' raiding force to continue the war against Germany following the disaster of Dunkirk.

On 4 March 1941, Marchant was taken on by the Special Operations Executive, being promoted to temporary Captain on 4 June 1941. After training, he moved to W (West Africa) Section in January 1942, where his focus was neutral colonies. In March 1942, he went to Lagos as a 'courier', routinely travelling between there and Douala in Cameroon; Fernando Po on the island of Bioko; and the port of Bata in Spanish (now Equatorial) Guinea. These trips were a cover for intelligence gathering. He remained in the region until late 1943, when he was evacuated to England after becoming seriously ill. By April 1944, he had recovered sufficiently to be posted to ME71, the Jedburgh Training Section at the Commando Training School in Scotland and at Milton Hall in Cambridgeshire. Like the Intelligence Corps' headquarters in Yorkshire, this estate was owned by the Fitzwilliam family.

Operation Jedburgh was a secret joint venture between the SOE, the American Office of Strategic Services and the Free French. In time, volunteers from the Dutch, Belgian and Norwegian Special Forces would also be included. Jedburgh teams consisted of three men: a British or American Commander; an officer from the country into which they were to be inserted; and an NCO radio operator. Initially, their role concerned the Normandy landings in June 1944, where their objective was to link up with existing Resistance networks and coordinate 'sabotage and disruption' attacks on enemy communications, transport columns and supply routes. They operated in uniform, were trained in guerrilla tactics and could arrange rapid resupply of arms and explosives for Resistance groups. They also acted as the link between the Resistance groups and the conventional ground forces as they advanced.

In August 1944, Marchant, codenamed 'Rutland', was placed

in command of Jedburgh team 'Aubrey'. The other two members of the team were a French officer, Captain Chaigneau, codename 'Kildare', and their British wireless operator, Sergeant Ivor Hooker, codename 'Thaler'. At 0155 on 12 August 1944, they parachuted from a B-24 Liberator bomber and landed without incident at the dropping zone near Le Plessis-Belleville, 20 miles north-east of Paris. They were quickly followed by two other Liberators carrying supplies. Their mission was to operate with the F-Section Spiritualist network in the Seine-et-Marne region. They were met by a group from this network, including the organiser, Major René Dumont-Guillemet, and cycled to a safe house in the adjacent village of Forfry. After two days, Marchant and Chaigneau accompanied the organiser to the northern suburbs of Paris, where at least 1,500 volunteers had been organised but required training. The resistance managed to obtain Spanish identity papers for Marchant and for the next week he travelled around the area by bicycle, instructing small groups of volunteers – including some Paris gendarmes – on weapons and sabotage.

On 21 August, following signs that the Germans were starting to retreat from the area, Marchant moved close to the village of Meaux, managing to avoid an SS and German Army unit en route. On 25 August, Allied forces liberated Paris. On hearing this, the Spiritualist organiser, Major Dumont-Guillemet, took it upon himself to begin an open revolt against the Nazis. He ordered the Free French volunteers in northern Paris to move to the Rougemont area, where he planned to set up an ambush on a section of sunken road between the villages of Forfry and Oissery. Despite an order from Special Forces HQ to wait until they gave him authorisation, Dumont-Guillemet carried on regardless.

Resistance volunteers arrived on the morning of 27 August in twenty different vehicles. As the men were unloaded, however, they were surprised by the appearance of a German light tank and a large force of infantry. The resulting battle lasted more than an hour, until Dumont-Guillemet ordered a covering party to hold the Germans at bay while the rest dispersed. With characteristic fearlessness, Marchant volunteered to remain in situ. Then another enemy tank appeared and began firing at close range. The cover party immediately fled, leaving Marchant to face the enemy alone. He crawled to the nearby Rougemont lake, where he hid, semi-submerged, for more than eight hours while the Germans machine-gunned it from two sides. When they eventually withdrew, Marchant was able to make his way back to the safe house in Forfry. The whole area was free of Germans. On 29 June, the forward units of the American VII Corps arrived. Marchant was able to meet Sergeant Hooker, but their French colleague, Captain Chaigneau, had been killed in the fighting. They both returned to Paris and on 6 September they went back to England.

In the nineteen days it was in the field, 'Aubrey' provided London with valuable information about Luftwaffe airfields north of Paris and the withdrawal preparations of the German garrison. The Jedburgh report of the mission concluded it had been a 'dangerous mission carried out with courage ... Had it not been for the training given by the Jedburgh officers, and their skill in handling weapons, the action at Forfry would have been a complete disaster.' Allied casualties numbered eighty-six. About fifty Germans were killed. Marchant's bravery was reckoned to have saved the lives of 200 people. For this, he was awarded the Military Cross (MC) and recommended for the French Croix de Guerre. His MC citation read:

This officer was dropped in the Paris area by parachute in August 1944 to assist in directing the final phases of the liberation. Capt Marchant, who spoke French indifferently, traversed this area on a bicycle, organising recruits collected in garages and warehouses. He later joined the FFI East of Paris where he and his W/T operator carried on their work at times within 200 yards of enemy forces who had been searching the neighbourhood for a transmitting set.

That was not the end of Marchant's war, however. On 20 October 1944, he flew to Italy to join Force 139, which dealt with SOE operations in Poland. He was selected to take part in Operation Flamstead, which had been planned as a support to Operation Freston, an attempt to insert a British Military Mission to the Polish Home Army which was ultimately abandoned.

Marchant returned to England on 21 February 1945 and was transferred to the SOE pool to await a further assignment. On 12 March 1945, as the war neared its end, he flew to India to join B/B(I) Section, (E-Group) Force 136, which was conducting missions into Japanese-occupied Burma from bases in India. On 1 April 1945, he led a six-man team, codenamed Hart, preparing to parachute into the Burmese jungle on a mission connected to the ongoing Operation Nation. This operation, mounted in support of General Slim's 14th Army, centred on arming, training and leading the local guerrillas of the Anti-Fascist Organisation and the Burmese National Army in the Pegu Yomas area against the retreating Japanese 15th Division. Three Britons, including Captain Marchant, and three Burmese guerrillas – Maung Ba Aung, Saw U and Maung Pyu – had with them military supplies and equipment, plus large amounts of Indian, Burmese and Japanese currency and gold leaf.

They took off in a Special Duties B-24 Liberator of 357 Squadron from RAF Jessore, in Bengal, that night. The take-off appeared normal, but as the aircraft climbed it suddenly stalled, swerved to the right, crashed and burst into flames. Tragically, Captain Marchant MC and his team and the crew of the aircraft were all killed instantly. Marchant was thirty-four years old. He was buried at Chittagong War Cemetery, in modern-day Bangladesh. His grave is inscribed with the words: 'I have fought a good fight. I have finished my course. I have kept the faith.'

• • •

If sending Allied agents to operate behind enemy lines in occupied countries was considered difficult, mounting any form of successful covert activity within the enemy's own territory was even harder. Most people who lived in Germany and Austria under Hitler's rule were either not willing or not able to involve themselves in anti-Nazi activities, meaning there was no effective resistance movement in those countries. Furthermore, Germans and Austrians everywhere had to be considered by Britain and her allies to be adversaries. As a result, very few missions to Germany were attempted by MI6 or the SOE until after the Normandy landings in June 1944 when the Allied forces were advancing towards its borders. There were some exceptions. One involved Frank Chamier, a half-German Intelligence Corps officer who was the first MI6 agent to be dropped into Germany. Putting his life on the line in the Allied cause, he worked closely with a German national called Friedrich Reschke.

Philip Chamier, always known as Frank, was born in Frankfurt on 3 January 1909 to Dr Fred Chamier, an Australian-born engineer and inventor who moved to Germany in 1906, and Elena

Stallforth, who was German. In or around 1911, his parents separated and within a year his father's business interests in Germany had collapsed. Chamier senior then left for England and began a relationship with a divorcee, Georgina Read. They never married.

Young Frank was educated in Germany, where he learned to speak several languages. In late 1932, he travelled to England to find his father. Their reunion was brief because Chamier senior died the following year, but Frank remained in England and, in September 1934, he married his father's girlfriend, Georgina Read. Initially, they moved to Bradford Peverell in Dorset and had two children, Anthony and Frederica. By the time war was declared in September 1939, the family lived in Hove, Sussex. The 1939 Register, which took the place of a census, records Chamier's occupation only vaguely as being 'on Government Service'. In fact, he was an MI6 agent whose duties included making trips to Germany to photograph airfields and gather military information.

In April 1940, the Directorate of Military Intelligence petitioned the War Office for Chamier to be called up as he was urgently required for services overseas. Chamier was commissioned as a Second Lieutenant on the General List on 24 April 1940 in the role of an Intelligence Officer 'for special duties without pay and allowances from Army funds', an administrative phrase indicating that an individual was working in the shadows. His activities for the ensuing year or so are not recorded, but on 17 March 1941 his special duties came to an end and he embarked for the Middle East with a posting to the Combined Services Detailed Interrogation Centre (CSDIC) at GHQ Cairo, where it was believed that his fluent German would be useful.

On 11 February 1942, he was transferred to the Intelligence Corps and in December 1942 he was posted to 102 Military Mission with the Libyan Arab Force (LAF) to assist with sabotage and intelligence gathering behind the lines. On 9 February 1943, he was posted back to CSDIC at Cairo under the status of being 'Specially Employed – not entitled to Army funds'. All correspondence to him was to be forwarded to Major S. J. Fulton, c/o Room 024 at the War Office, which was a cover address for MI6. The following month, the direction of Chamier's war changed distinctly after he began working with Friedrich Reschke.

A year earlier, in 1942, Reschke had walked into the British lines near El Alamein claiming to be a deserter from the 155th Panzer Grenadier Regiment. Under interrogation, he told the British that he had been a Sergeant in the French Foreign Legion in North Africa between 1936 and 1940 before joining the German military and being posted to the Afrika Korps. He had apparently deserted after refusing to fight against other legionnaires.

Initially, Reschke was sent to POW Camp 308 at Alexandria, but he was moved later to Camp 309 at Ismailia. At some point during this process, he was talent-spotted by MI6 which, under the guise of the Inter-Services Liaison Department (ISLD), combed such camps for recruits. In March 1943, he was taken to Cairo, where he first met Lieutenant Chamier, who was by then using the alias 'Robinson'. The pair shared a flat just opposite the GHQ building in the Egyptian capital. There, Reschke received instruction on codes, cyphers, Morse and various wireless transmitters. He was apparently free to move around unescorted and used the alias 'Ross'. Eventually, in July 1943, he was issued an AB 64 British Army soldier's pay book in the name of James Allan and sent on a parachute course at Haifa. Then, in February 1944, he accompanied Chamier (who had been elevated to the rank of Captain) to England, where he received further instruction on the Mark XV wireless set. On 5

April, they moved to a farmhouse near Cambridge prior to starting their mission to Germany, Operation Elm. It was concerned with gathering intelligence on German troop locations and movements prior to the invasion.

On the night of 11 April 1944, Chamier took off in a Halifax of 161 (Special Duties) Squadron from RAF Tempsford bound for Germany. Reschke, his wireless operator, was with him. Flying at 4,000 feet, the plane was picked up by a searchlight and subjected to several bursts of anti-aircraft fire, but it sustained no damage. The two men jumped out near the village of Gündringen, just west of Stuttgart. Chamier led, Reschke followed and a third parachute carried their radio and other equipment. Chamier was, therefore, the first MI6 agent to be dropped into Germany.

This was an incredibly dangerous mission. Despite being the country of their birth, the men were entering enemy home territory as British spies and there would be no friendly or sympathetic local population to help them. Although they landed safely, the aircraft was detected by an air observation post at Altensteig and the rural police were told to be on the lookout for parachutists. The following morning, Chamier and Reschke buried their wireless and equipment, made their way to the railway station at Gündringen and bought tickets for the town of Pforzheim. Following the police alert, a local constable went to the station and, seeing Chamier and Reschke, checked their German papers. He found them to be in order. Chamier carried the identification of a Major Geske of the Oberkommando der Wehrmacht, the German High Command; Reschke passed himself off as Oberfeldwebel Rudolf Berger of the artillery. They also carried a letter from a firm in Pforzheim confirming they had official business there. Satisfied, the police constable went home.

At some stage before the train arrived, Chamier and Reschke

decided to split up for the journey. When the train pulled out of the station, only Chamier was on board; Reschke was hiding in the station lavatory. As soon as the train had departed, Reschke told a railway official that Chamier was an English spy. The official immediately alerted the stationmaster, who telephoned the next station down the line at Nagold. In the meantime, Reschke went into the stationmaster's office, placed his revolver on his table and said, 'Here are my arms, so that there shouldn't be any suspicion.' A few minutes later, an official from Nagold station rang asking for a description of the 'English spy'. Reschke took the receiver and gave a detailed account of Chamier, adding, 'He's a dangerous person, armed with two revolvers, one in his pocket and one under his arm.' As soon as the train arrived at Nagold, Chamier was arrested.

Back at Gündringen, Reschke took the police to the drop zone and retrieved the buried wireless set, cyphers and other equipment. After questioning, Chamier and Reschke were taken to Berlin separately and subjected to a lengthy interrogation by the Gestapo. Chamier was then handed over to the Reich Security Head Office concerned with 'turning' captured agents and 'playing' their wireless transmitters back to their controllers with false intelligence – a process known as *Funkspiel* (literally 'radio game'). This section fell under the control of SS Sturmbannführer Horst Kopkow of the Gestapo. He was keen to use Chamier in a *Funkspiel* using Chamier's own wireless and codes, knowing he could rely automatically on the cooperation of Chamier's double-crossing wireless operator, Friedrich Reschke. All Kopkow needed to run a watertight operation was Chamier's cooperation with regard to his security codes. These were usually letter groups either inserted or omitted in each message to let his controllers in London know if he had been captured and was transmitting under enemy dictation.

After the war, Kopkow was captured by the Allies and interrogated about his knowledge of the treatment and fate of missing Allied agents, including Chamier. He recalled him and said that he had been held at the Sicherheitspolizeischule at Fürstenberg while the *Funkspiel* was being run. He added that Reschke operated the set but maintained the operation had only lasted a few weeks, after which the British became suspicious due to some error made in the transmissions. His memory was that Chamier had agreed to co-operate and was held under the pseudonym 'Mr Boston'. He denied having any knowledge of how Chamier was treated and alleged that he had been killed, along with other British agents, during an Allied bombing raid on the Berlin Polizeipräsidium.

Reschke's version of events regarding the *Funkspiel* during his post-war interrogation differed from Kopkow's. He stated that the operation failed because they could not continue without certain information from Chamier. The implication was that Chamier had refused to divulge his security codes and may even have been tortured. To this day, the true details of Chamier's death are not known or have not been placed on available record, but there is a possibility that a cover-up has taken place.

Intriguingly, while a war crimes investigation into Horst Kopkow was ongoing, MI6 requested he be sent to London and debriefed so that his knowledge of Soviet espionage methods could be exploited. Then, a deception masterstroke was pulled. In 1948, MI6 officially informed the War Crimes Group that Kopkow had died in hospital from bronco-pneumonia and had been buried in Britain. They even sent a death certificate as proof. Kopkow was not dead, however. It later transpired that MI6 was so impressed by his knowledge of Soviet espionage matters that he was offered immunity from war crimes prosecution if he worked for them. He agreed and was given the alias of Peter Cordes, returning to Germany with his new identity and pretending to work in textile manufacturing while in fact being a British agent. The SS officer who during his career had tried to 'turn' enemy agents was himself, therefore, 'turned'. In a further irony, he did die of pneumonia in October 1996. Bearing in mind MI6's vested interest in Kopkow, and his desire to protect himself from a possible war crimes prosecution, there will always be some doubt as to whether the officially authorised version of Chamier's death is true.

Reschke, who betrayed Chamier so callously, surfaced in Hamburg after the war and was investigated and interviewed by HQ 30 Corps District after claiming to have been a British agent who parachuted to Germany. Although he described his connection to Chamier in North Africa, he excluded from his account that Chamier was in any way connected to his own mission. As the Chamier case had not become an issue at the time of his interrogation, the matter was not taken any further, and in November 1945 Reschke was 'employed with a motorcycle' by 1019 Field Security Reserve Detachment, Intelligence Corps, at Delmenhorst in northern Germany. When his part in Chamier's capture *was* discovered following Kopkow's interrogation, Reschke was arrested and interrogated. Appallingly, however, it was concluded that as an enemy soldier who had succeeded in penetrating British intelligence services and then regained his own country, Article 31 of the Hague Convention prevented him from being tried for war crimes. Furthermore, there was no evidence to link him directly to the torture or eventual demise of Chamier.

Major Philip Frank Chamier has no known grave and is therefore commemorated on the Brookwood Memorial to the Missing at Woking in Surrey. His wife, Georgina, lived to the age of 102. She died in Essex in 2005.

●　　●　　●

From the 1930s onwards, thousands of Jewish German and Jewish Austrian refugees fled Hitler's tyrannical regime and found sanctuary in Britain. By 1940, when the threat of Germany invading Britain was at its height, most of these 'Enemy Aliens' were interned. Yet a considerable number of them were eager to get into uniform and join the war. By late 1941, when the prospect of the Nazis reaching British shores had passed, their loyalty was accepted and they were allowed to enlist. Throughout the conflict, about 10,000 German and Austrian refugees would serve with British forces.

Initially, these men were only accepted in non-combatant units such as the Pioneer Corps, which specialised in labour and light engineering tasks. Special 'Alien Companies' of the Pioneer Corps were formed, and foreign national recruits were sent for training to camps at Richborough in Kent and Ilfracombe in Devon. Later, these 'Loyal Aliens' were allowed to join combat units and to bear arms. Many served in the Commandos and other special service units. By this time, those working in military intelligence had realised the recruiting potential in these camps. After all, these 'Enemy Aliens' could speak fluent German, they knew the geography and culture of the enemy better than any Briton and they had more reason to hate the Nazi regime than most of the Allies. It was for all of these reasons that anonymous figures would sometimes turn up at the camps unexpectedly, accompanied by the camp security officer, and summon certain inmates for interviews. These anonymous figures were, of course, recruiters for the SOE, MI6 and MI9.

After an exhaustive selection and vetting process, those recruits who were considered suitable were subjected to the routine training schedule of a British agent operating behind the lines, undergoing testing in physical fitness, tactics, fieldcraft, weapons handling, explosives, wireless operation and codes. Some also Anglicised their surname or were provided with a suitable alias. Many were transferred from the Pioneer Corps to the Intelligence Corps and then attached for special duty to 'other organisations' – primarily the Secret Intelligence Service, MI6, for intelligence-gathering missions in Germany, Austria or on the borders of Slovakia and Hungary. Two examples of exceptional individuals who escaped to Britain to save their lives, and who later risked them again while serving with the Intelligence Corps, are particularly noteworthy.

August Jacques Wärndorfer was born in Vienna on 3 October 1900 to a Jewish family. His father, also called August, was an industrialist in Austria's automotive industry, an art consultant and collector and a textile designer. His mother, Adrienne Marguerite Hakim, was of Egyptian heritage. His parents divorced in 1910 and the following year his father married Constance Evelyn Byatt, from Midhurst in Sussex. On the outbreak of the First World War, Wärndorfer served, aged fourteen, as an officer cadet in the Austro-Hungarian Navy, but it appears that he did not pursue a military career, instead qualifying as a chemist and later becoming a self-employed explosives salesman. In 1927, he married Emilie Vlasinova in Vienna. They had no children.

In March 1938, after Austria was annexed by Hitler, the Wärndorfers fled as a result of increasing anti-Jewish persecution and settled in Scotland. Through personal connections, they lived in a property called The College, at Elgin in Morayshire. On 28 November 1939, two months after the war began, each member of the family was granted immunity from internment.

On 31 January 1940, Wärndorfer, then aged thirty-nine, enlisted in the Auxiliary Military Pioneer Corps and was posted to the training camp at Richborough on the Kent coast. For the next four years, he served with 79 Company and then with 220 Company. On 15 October 1943, he left the Pioneer Corps. His posting record shows that he was then attached to the Directorate of Military Intelligence. On 17 January 1944, he was transferred to the Intelligence Corps for special duties 'without pay and allowances from Army funds' on the authority of the Secret Intelligence Service, MI6. He was promoted to the rank of Sergeant six months later and after standard agent training was posted to No. 1 Intelligence Unit at Bari on the southern Adriatic coast of Italy. This unit was the cover name for MI6's behind-the-lines activity in central Europe and the Balkans and was controlled by P6 Division, which ran clandestine operations in the German sphere.

Wärndorfer volunteered for a mission which would require him to land by parachute near the Austro-Slovak border and then contact pro-Allied Slovak partisans, who were planning a mass revolt against their pro-Nazi government, which would become known as the Slovak National Uprising. In order to support the revolt, MI6 hoped to recruit agents and set up an underground network. The initial stage of the idea was to drop two-man MI6 teams along the Austro-Slovak border to establish advance bases through which the network could report.

On 18 July 1944, Wärndorfer took off on a special duties flight from Bari. His cover name was Major Jack Wilson and his radio operator, Frank Hensque, adopted the name Keith Hanson. Things got off to a poor start. They were dropped some 40 miles east of their intended destination near Vienna, landing near Bratislava instead. Details of their activities on landing are scarce, but it is known that they were eventually 'captured' by a group of Slovak partisans and some escaped American airmen. As Wärndorfer and

Hensque were carrying forged German identification papers, the Slovaks mistook them for German spies and they were severely beaten. Convinced that he was going to be killed, Wärndorfer tried to use his L-pill – a rubber-coated cyanide capsule – but instead of biting it, in which case death should occur within thirty seconds, he swallowed it whole and survived. After some time, the pair convinced the Slovaks of their true identities. An official post-war report confirms that they later took part in a number of skirmishes with the Germans along the Austro-Slovak border before last being heard of on 14 October.

The Slovak National Uprising began well for the rebels. By early September, they controlled significant areas of central and eastern Slovakia and were secure in their base at Banská Bystrica. Then the Germans intervened and on 17 October more than 35,000 troops were sent in from neighbouring Hungary. With superior weapons, better equipment and greater air capability, they quickly drove the Slovaks back. Furthermore, Stalin halted the Russian advance towards Slovakia, on which the rebels had been relying, and diverted his efforts against Budapest. On 27 October, the rebels and partisan groups were forced to abandon their bases in Banská Bystrica and retreat north into the mountains. Along with the insurgents, Wärndorfer and Hensque went into survival mode as winter approached. Not having heard from Wärndorfer since 14 October, MI6 initially reported him and Hensque as 'missing' and eventually as 'missing presumed killed in action'. It was not until after the war that the details of their fate came to light.

By early November 1944, Wärndorfer and Hensque had managed to join members of the SOE's Windproof team. It had been infiltrated to undertake a mission into Hungary but had become involved in the uprising. Subsequently, they all fell in with some

American intelligence agents from the Office of Strategic Services (OSS) mission and fled to the mountains. Suffering extreme cold, with few clothes or supplies, casualties mounted. On 11 November, Hensque was captured by a German patrol along with a group of the airmen from the Dawes mission. On Christmas Day 1944, the remaining survivors were hiding in a mountain shack north of Polomka when they were surrounded by the enemy. They held out for as long as they could, but the next day, 26 December, the Germans moved in, overran the shack and captured the occupants, including Wärndorfer . Also captured was the American Associated Press correspondent Joseph Morton, who had accompanied the Dawes mission to report on the Slovak Uprising.

The men were taken to the Gestapo prison at Banská Bystrica, then moved to Bratislava and eventually transferred to Mauthausen concentration camp. On 17 January 1945, they were taken to an isolated building in the camp known as The Bunker, which housed cells, interrogation rooms, a gas chamber and a crematorium in the basement. Five specialist interrogators were sent from Berlin on the direct orders of Heinrich Himmler, best known as the chief architect of the Holocaust. Wärndorfer was one of the first to be questioned. He was subjected to a torture known as the Tibetan Prayer Wheel, during which wooden rods were interlaced between his fingers and then his hands squeezed tight, causing unimaginable pain. Still unable to make him talk, his interrogators tied his hands behind his back and then suspended his arms from a gallows with his feet clear of the ground, causing his arms to be forced upwards and dislocated. The other prisoners were subjected to the same treatment.

On 12 January 1945, Sergeant Wärndorfer and the other seventeen captives from the Windproof and Dawes missions were executed on the direct order of Ernst Kaltenbrunner, an Austrian who was a high-ranking member of the SS and another leading architect of the Holocaust. A post-war report taken from a Polish prisoner who was charged with removing the bodies afterwards described how, one by one, the prisoners were ushered into a room marked 'Bath' and ordered to undress for a full-body photograph. Then they were quickly shot by SS Commander Georg Bachmayer. Their corpses are believed to have been cremated. On 18 April 1946, Sergeant Wärndorfer was posthumously awarded the King's Commendation for Brave Conduct. As he has no known grave, he is commemorated on the Groesbeek Memorial in the Netherlands. He was forty-four years old when he died.

●　●　●

Another notably brave 'Enemy Alien' who became an Intelligence Corps operator was Frederick Benson. His real name was Fritz Becker. He was a German national, born on 30 March 1923 in the city of Iserlohn. His parents, Sally and Bertha Becker, were Jewish and in the late 1930s they were arrested and transported to Poland where they were murdered in the gas chambers of Auschwitz. Their names are recorded on the Yad Vashem Holocaust Memorial database.

Becker arrived in Britain as a refugee on 5 January 1939 with the assistance of the Refugee Children's Movement and was placed in a hostel at Sutton in Surrey. He found employment as a carpenter in Croydon. In June 1940, aged seventeen, he was interned as an 'Enemy Alien' at Onchan on the Isle of Man. One story recalls that while in the camp he became popular for his comical imitations of Prussian military manners.

On 16 April 1941, he was attested for the Auxiliary Military Pioneer Corps and then sent for training at No. 3 Company at Ilfracombe. Thereafter, he was posted to 251 Company. On 14 June 1943, he applied to change his name to Frederick Benson and on 4 October 1943, he was transferred to the Intelligence Corps in the rank of local Corporal 'for special duties without pay and allowances from Army funds'. Like so many others, including August Wärndorfer, he was posted under the authority of the Directorate of Military Intelligence. On 8 November 1943, he signed a declaration acknowledging his transfer to the Intelligence Corps for special duties.

In September 1944, Benson was selected for Operation Birch, an intelligence-gathering mission in Berlin, working as the radio operator to another MI6 agent identified only by his cover name, 'Josef Bauer', a Yugoslav-born anti-Nazi who had been recruited by MI6 in Uruguay. Benson's codename for the mission was 'Brian'. The plan was for the pair to pose as cement workers employed by the firm Siemens, which was based in Berlin, and the objectives of the mission were to report 'on military and air identifications, production figures of industrial concerns, air-raid damage, morale of the population and tendency of the Nazi movement to go underground.' Even though the war was stuttering to a conclusion, entering Germany was incredibly risky, particularly for a young and inexperienced operator who was not only Jewish but also a German defector.

On the night of 2 October 1944, Benson and Bauer were dropped blind to a location near Heilbronn, in south-west Germany, from where they were to make their way to Magdeburg about 250 miles away and approximately 70 miles to the west of Berlin. It would be their base of operations. The men completed this journey uneventfully by train, arriving on 11 October. Having found some accommodation, they met an MI6 contact from the Stockholm station. During this meeting, Bauer passed the agent a secret-ink letter asking for additional German identification papers. For almost three weeks, Benson maintained his radio contact schedules while Bauer went about his assignments.

On 28 October, disaster struck. Bauer was arrested by the Gestapo, having been exposed by an informer. A post-war report described how Bauer had taken two suicide pills, but they didn't work and, under severe interrogation, he disclosed the location of Benson's lodgings. The following day, the Gestapo raided the house and Benson was shot dead while trying to escape. He was twenty-one years old and the last member of his family to die at the hands of the Nazis.

On 18 April 1946, Sergeant Frederick Benson was posthumously awarded the King's Commendation for Brave Conduct, the award being personally recommended by 'C', the Chief of MI6. As he has no known grave, his name is commemorated on the Groesbeek Memorial in the Netherlands.

●　●　●

Not every Intelligence Corps operator saw active service, of course, but that did not in any way lessen the contribution they were able to make to the war. One figure whose sterling work stands out despite never leaving his desk is John Masterman. In September 1939, Masterman, an Oxford don, was already forty-eight years old, disqualifying him from front-line duties. This spymaster was able to make a difference in another way, however, through what he called the 'high-stakes game' of using double agents. As the details of Masterman's work are themselves so fascinating, it is easy to forget that they had very significant consequences, not least that tens of thousands of Allied lives were saved through decisions made by him and his colleagues. Deceiving Hitler himself to such great effect through these 'games' would surely have been immensely satisfying as well.

John Cecil Masterman was born on 12 January 1891 at Kingston upon Thames in Surrey, the son of John Masterman, a naval officer, and Edith (née Hughes). He had one sibling, Christopher, who worked in the Indian Civil Service and became Deputy High Commissioner for India. Although the family lived at Kingston Hill, he, his mother and brother would spend long periods with his grandfather, who was a clergyman, and his grandmother while his father was at sea. As a boy, young John intended to follow in his father's footsteps, but after attending the Royal Naval College at Dartmouth, he decided that Navy life was not for him. In 1908, he won a scholarship to read modern history at Worcester College, Oxford.

After graduating, he travelled on a student exchange scheme to the University of Freiburg, where he also lectured. He was there when the First World War was declared in August 1914 and was interned as an 'enemy alien' at the Ruhleben camp near Berlin. After his release, he returned to Oxford, becoming a senior tutor at Christ Church College in 1920. There, he developed links with MI5, acting as one of their 'talent-spotters'. One student he 'spotted' was Dick White, who, uniquely, would become the head of MI5 in 1953 and then, from 1956, the head of MI6.

As well as becoming involved in the spy trade in his twenties and continuing with academic life, Masterman was an outstanding sportsman. He had already won an athletics blue as an Oxford undergraduate, but in the 1920s he also represented England at tennis, hockey and cricket; and he played singles and doubles tennis at Wimbledon. His talents did not end there. In 1933, he published an acclaimed murder mystery novel, *An Oxford Tragedy*.

In June 1940, having volunteered for war service, he was commissioned on the General List. The following month, upon its formation, he transferred to the Intelligence Corps. Initially, he was appointed as secretary to a War Office committee investigating the Dunkirk operation, until his former student, Dick White, recruited him to work for MI5. On 2 January 1941, Masterman became the chairman of the Double-Cross Committee, also known as the XX Committee and the 'Twenty Committee'. It oversaw a counter-espionage initiative that 'turned' enemy spies into double agents working for the British. The committee's members comprised officials from the Army, Navy and Air Force plus MI5 and MI6. They met every Thursday in MI5's offices at 58 St James's Street in central London.

The background to the Double-Cross Committee's formation lay in the period immediately after war broke out in September 1939. At that time, it was widely believed by the British public that scores of Nazi spies had infiltrated the country. This 'spy-mania', as Churchill called it, was stoked to some degree by the government, which used radio broadcasts and posters bearing propaganda messages such as 'Careless Talk Costs Lives' to warn people to be on their guard. In fact, the Abwehr, Germany's intelligence service, did not launch any active espionage mission in Britain until the second half of 1940. Its aim was to gather information about Britain's military capability and intentions, but it was not a success.

Between September and November 1940, just twenty-five German agents were sent to Britain by parachute, by submarine or by posing as refugees. They were poorly trained compared with

Britain's spies and, thanks to the codebreakers at Bletchley Park, they were quickly apprehended: the Abwehr's hand cypher messages, which were used to communicate among themselves and with their agents in the field, were cracked. This meant the British were expecting these imposters. Records show that all except one of them were rounded up between September and November 1940. Later on, incidentally, Bletchley Park's personnel were able to break the Enigma codes, giving MI5 an even greater ability to monitor German espionage plans and capture more agents, showing how significant signals intelligence (SIGINT) was to the Allies.

All captured enemy agents were sent to Camp 020 at Latchmere House in Ham, Surrey. During the First World War, this property had been used as a military psychiatric hospital, but it then became MI5's secret detention and interrogation centre. It was run by its chief interrogator, Lieutenant Colonel Robin 'Tin Eye' Stephens, his nickname referring to the monocle he wore. Once deposited into Stephens's care, a foreign agent was kept in a bugged cell and subjected to intensive cross-examination but never violence, which Stephens believed to be counter-productive. Neither did he favour using drugs to extract information. He preferred to exert psychological pressure by questioning a prisoner in the middle of the night, when tiredness made them easier to wear down; or by warning them that a lack of cooperation might mean they were sent to Cell 14. In reality, it was nothing but a padded cell, but it gained legendary status as the most sinister place on the site. Another method favoured by Stephens for making prisoners talk was to remind them that they could ultimately face trial and execution. Some forty enemy agents did indeed meet this fate.

As well as bolstering Bletchley Park's work in monitoring the Abwehr's communications, Camp 020's primary purpose was to assist the Double-Cross System. Having 'turned' a foreign agent, the British could not only expect to secure accurate information about the enemy but also use that agent to feed the enemy false information. In total, eleven notable Double-Cross agents came out of Camp 020, having been worked on by Stephens and his team.

In order to appear credible, double agents were required to pretend that they were developing networks and collecting military information for the Fatherland. This meant that occasionally some real, verifiable intelligence, known as 'chickenfeed', had to be produced. This mix of accurate 'chickenfeed' information and completely bogus disinformation had to be choreographed very carefully. If the Germans were to discover the deception, the entire house of cards would collapse. This is where Masterman and his committee came in. By early January 1941, the problem of blending information and disinformation had led to the creation of the Wireless Board, whose members included the heads of the intelligence services and the War Office. These high-powered individuals would only deal with broad policy, however. A subordinate layer of oversight was needed to take responsibility for the day-to-day running of the Double-Cross System in far more specific terms. The Double-Cross Committee was established for this purpose.

Masterman ran the committee expertly, steering different opinions towards a unanimous decision so that Britain's counter-espionage unit was second to none. The most famous double agent controlled by Masterman's committee was Juan Pujol García, a Spanish spy codenamed GARBO. Along with his MI5 handlers, García invented a stable of twenty-seven agents for the benefit of his German masters, enabling him to report fictitious military intelligence on a wide variety of subjects and preventing the Abwehr from discovering what was really going on. In one celebrated example of his double-dealing, GARBO told the Germans that Allied forces were going to invade French North Africa in November 1942 in what was known as Operation Torch. This was true, but it was arranged that this information would only reach Germany shortly before the Allied troops landed on the beach, rendering it useless to German High Command but giving the impression that it had been sent in good faith. It worked brilliantly. Masterman himself later summed up the success of the Double-Cross System when he said that through it 'we actively ran and controlled the German espionage system in this country'.

In the summer of 1942, the system expanded its remit from counter-espionage to include acts of tactical deception against the German High Command, again with Masterman's committee running the operations. After Operation Torch, which was the first major plot overseen by Masterman, the Allies turned their attention to the next strategic objective, the invasion of Sicily, known as Operation Husky – itself the precursor to the invasion of mainland Italy. Two of MI5's most inventive employees, Charles Cholmondeley and Ewen Montagu, planned a deception based on the use of a corpse. This idea was taken on by the Double-Cross Committee and developed into Operation Mincemeat, which was the basis for the 1956 film *The Man Who Never Was* and the 2021 film *Operation Mincemeat*. The body of a Welsh homeless man, Glyndwr Michael, dressed in the uniform of a fictional Royal Marine Major and given the pseudonym 'Bill Martin', was left to float off the coast of south-western Spain near the port city of Huelva, where it was known that an Abwehr agent was operating. An attaché case secured to the corpse's belt contained Allied Invasion plans indicating that the next objective was the assault on Sardinia and Greece rather than Sicily. The cadaver drifted towards shore and the ruse worked. Although Hitler was not totally convinced, he was worried enough to move infantry divisions and air assets from Sicily to Greece, thereby changing the course of the war and almost certainly saving the lives of thousands of Allied soldiers.

Undoubtedly, the most significant success of Masterman's committee, however, was Operation Fortitude South. This deception convinced Hitler that the Allied invasion of Europe in June 1944 would be directed against the Pas-de-Calais rather than Normandy. While the real invasion army gathered and prepared along the south coast of England, a 'dummy' army – the First United States Army Group (FUSAG) under the command of the American General Patton – was 'manufactured' along the eastern coast, the natural staging area for an invasion at Calais. Tented camps, plywood and rubber planes, inflatable decoy tanks and fake landing craft were created while false signals were sent in what ranks as one of the most elaborate military charades in history. At the same time, the double agents, acting under the control of Masterman's committee, provided a stream of carefully crafted disinformation, seemingly corroborating Calais as the main target. The operation was so successful that even when the Allied forces were streaming ashore at Normandy, Hitler refused to release the divisions of infantry and armour he had placed to counter a Calais invasion, believing that Normandy was a diversion. Operation Fortitude South was, unquestionably, the triumph of the Normandy landings. By the time it became obvious to Hitler that he had been tricked, the Allies had secured their beachhead and were already streaming inland. Who can say how many thousands of Allied lives were saved as a result of this highly innovative scheme?

The last major deception operation involving Masterman's committee came after the Normandy landings and concerned the *Vergeltungswaffen* (literally 'revenge weapons'), more commonly known as V-1 flying bombs or 'doodlebugs'. On 13 June 1944, exactly a week after D-Day, the first of these early cruise missiles hit London. Thereafter, on average, 100 of the weapons were directed at Greater London every week. Although some were shot down by anti-aircraft fire or by British fighters, more than 2,500 landed in London culminating in more than 6,000 deaths and nearly 18,000 injuries. In September 1944, the first V-2 rocket, a guided missile, hit London. The V-2 was almost impossible to defend against. It made no sound on approach and flew too high and too fast to be seen. The first warning was the explosion.

Within days of the start of the V-weapon campaign, German intelligence instructed its agents in London, all of whom had been 'turned', to report back with details of the impact sites and damage caused. This information was requested to ensure that their calculations for the targeting coordinates had been correct. This gave the Double-Cross Committee an opportunity to mislead the Germans to try to minimise the effects of the weapons by persuading the Germans to unknowingly set the missile coordinates so that they landed in rural areas rather than in built-up areas of London. The double agents reported back that the mean point of impact of the missiles was somewhat north of the intended target – central London. Accordingly, the Germans altered the coordinates so that they would land further south, which they believed would be central London. The result was that many of the missiles intended for London impacted in rural Kent. Although lives were still lost, the numbers killed and wounded were greatly reduced.

The Double-Cross Committee disbanded on 10 May 1945. Soon

afterwards, Masterman returned to academic life at Oxford as provost of Worcester College. In 1957, he was appointed vice-chancellor of the University of Oxford and in 1959 he was knighted for his services to education. He had been created an OBE in 1944. When German intelligence records were studied after the war, it was found that almost every one of the 115 Axis agents in circulation during the conflict had been identified and caught by the British. Masterman's *Times* obituary noted that he 'continued to play a behind the scenes role in MI5 in the post-war era, assisting in recruitment and acting as a peacemaker as the organisation came under scrutiny in the 1960s'. In 1972, after considerable government opposition, Masterman published *The Double-Cross System*, which is still considered one of the pre-eminent military intelligence histories to appear in print. He never married and died in an Oxford nursing home on 6 June 1977. He was eighty-six years old.

•   •   •

As John Masterman's Double-Cross Committee proved so effectively, interrogation played an essential part in defeating the Nazis and in saving Allied lives. Yet while Masterman himself may have been a brilliant puppet master, ultimately directing foreign agents who had been 'turned', he was not personally involved in the complicated business of questioning the enemy, which is regarded as having been a key element of the Intelligence Corps' duties during the war. That task fell to others.

One of Britain's most notable Second World War Intelligence Corps interrogators, who questioned prisoners of war rather than enemy spies, was Alexander Scotland. He was brought out of retirement to run the Prisoner of War Interrogation Section (PWIS),

which carried out highly secretive work at Britain's principal interrogation centre, the London Cage. Believing that 'interrogation is
an art', Scotland extracted key information from captured Germans
on a range of topics including munitions production, military
strategy and the horrors of the Holocaust. This work continued
long after hostilities had ended, when it was the turn of potential
war criminals to be grilled. Given the importance of the PWIS, as
well as Scotland's unusual background and personality, he easily
warrants inclusion in the roll call of remarkable Intelligence Corps
operators.

Alexander Paterson Scotland was born on 15 July 1882 at Mid-
dlesborough, Yorkshire, one of William and Elizabeth Scotland's
nine children. His father was a railway engine fitter. He left school
aged fourteen and found work in London, first as an office boy
at a tea merchants and then as a cheesemaker's assistant. In 1902,
he travelled to South Africa, where his brother was serving in the
Army. He had planned to join up himself but arrived after the Boer
War had finished and instead took a job with an insurance company and then a grocery business for a small trading company operating in German South West Africa. In his memoir *The London
Cage*, it was explained that many of his customers were German
colonial troops and settlers. Some became his friends, and it was
through these relationships that he learned to speak German.

Scotland also claimed in his book that a German officer he had
befriended invited him to join the *Schutztruppe*, an 'irregular' force
of volunteers within the German colonial army, which was then
engaged in a campaign against the Khoikhoi tribe in what became
known as the Herero Uprising. Using the Germanised version of his
name, 'Schottland', Scotland allegedly served with the Germans for
four years until March 1907. He is reported to have been involved

in the peace talks with the Khoikhoi leader Johannes Christian, which resulted in his being awarded the Prussian Order of the Red Eagle. Later that year, he met Major T. H. Wade, the British military attaché to the German forces in South West Africa, who encouraged him to maintain his contact with the Germans and act as an intelligence agent for the British, providing details of German military capability and equipment. In 1908, Scotland moved to the town of Keetmanshoop, 150 miles inland from the South African border, and the location of the headquarters of the Southern District Command of the German forces in South West Africa. Under the guise of a trader employed by a company called South African Territories Ltd, which dealt almost exclusively with the German military, he was in a prime position to report on military matters and used regular business trips to Cape Town to submit his reports.

Following the outbreak of war in 1914, the British government asked South Africa for assistance in destroying German long-range wireless installations in South West Africa. Accordingly, on 13 September 1914, a numerically superior South African force crossed the border to engage German forces. One upshot of this was that the German authorities interned Scotland, suspecting him of being a British spy. On 9 July 1915, however, German South West Africa surrendered to the South African forces and Scotland was released. He returned to England immediately, arriving at the Port of London on the *Llandovery Castle* on 8 October. He was accepted for enlistment in the Inns of Court Officer Training Corps and was commissioned on the General List on 11 July 1916 for special duties with the Intelligence Corps.

Scotland was first posted to General Headquarters at Le Havre with Field Marshal Haig's intelligence staff, where he worked under Captain James Marshall-Cornwall of the Intelligence Corps.

Marshall-Cornwall concentrated on intelligence relating to the German order of battle – the location and strengths of the enemy units on the front line and in the reserve areas deeper in France and Belgium. This intelligence was gleaned via prisoner interrogation, the examination of documents and from the networks of agents working deep behind the lines. Scotland's main job was as an analyst involved in determining the level of German casualties, but as he was fluent in German, he was also required to interrogate German prisoners of war and in 1918 he was tasked with the organisation and classification of the thousands of prisoners of war held in France. He became acknowledged as the 'German expert in France', providing intelligence to the British High Command. After the armistice of 1918, he received glowing references from GHQ for his work, with one senior officer noting that he had 'compiled most valuable information regarding German manpower. His experience while working with the Germans in their South West Africa campaign has given this officer an insight into the German character which he has used successfully in the present war.' Marshall-Cornwall also rated Scotland highly, describing him as a man of ability and high energy whose

> knowledge of the German character enabled him to render the greatest assistance to the British General Staff in conducting the interrogation and classification of thousands of German prisoners which fell into our hands during the battles of 1916, 1917 and 1918. Because of his competence, discretion and energy, Scotland was placed in charge of this entire duty.

On 4 January 1919, Scotland relinquished his commission and returned to civilian life. He was made an OBE for 'valuable services rendered in connection with military operations in France and Flanders'.

In 1924, he married Roma Cecile Rae and returned to South West Africa to resurrect his business career. The couple remained there until 1928, when a new business opportunity took them to Argentina. They settled in England in 1934 and when war was declared in September 1939, they were living at Clarence Gate Gardens, a mansion block in Marylebone, London. Scotland's entry in the 1939 Register listed him as being a member of the Army Officer's Emergency Reserve.

In early 1940, Scotland was fifty-seven years old, but he was happy to answer the call to resume his military service, being given his old rank of acting Captain and gazetted to the General Service Corps. Initially, he was charged by military intelligence with finding a site to house German prisoners of war for interrogation, but while choosing a suitable location at Dieppe, he discovered that there were pitifully few trained interrogators in the British Army, prompting him to recruit and train his own team. After the fall of France in June 1940, Scotland went back to Britain and was asked to set up a series of prisoner-of-war centres, known as 'cages', around Britain. His detailed knowledge of German espionage, the German military and German interrogation methods made him the obvious choice for this delicate duty. He recruited even more German-speaking interrogators, including academics, lawyers, journalists and businessmen. By July 1940, the PWIS had been established formally. Just days later, Scotland was transferred from the General Service Corps to the newly re-established Intelligence Corps, as were many of his interrogators.

To begin with, the PWIS was spread across Britain, but eventually it was centralised at nine distribution centres, one for each military district command area. Enemy prisoners of war were landed at ports throughout the United Kingdom and taken to the nearest 'cage', where they were subjected to initial interrogation. Some were SS men who had slaughtered British prisoners of war and Jewish civilians. Others were lowly soldiers who refused to reveal any more than their name, rank and serial number. Those thought to be of special interest were selected for further investigation by the Combined Services Detailed Interrogation Centre (UK). Effectively, the cages acted as transit camps and sorting centres where incoming enemy prisoners of war were identified, processed, graded, interrogated and then, if found to be of no specific value, sent off to a prisoner-of-war camp. Initially, the cages came under the control of MI9, but they were later transferred to the auspices of a specially formed branch known as MI19.

The most famous centre was the London District Cage, known simply as the 'London Cage'. It was based in three vast properties, numbers 6, 7 and 8 Kensington Palace Gardens, situated just beside Kensington Palace in what remains one of London's most exclusive streets. (Nowadays, several diplomatic missions are located there and private houses change hands for tens of millions of pounds.) Officially, the London Cage did not exist. It did not appear on any list of prisoner-of-war camps during the war and, until 1946, it was unknown to the International Red Cross. Yet this was where Scotland, who was in charge of the cage from its opening in 1940 until it closed in 1948, spent a good deal of the war, and the place through which thousands of German prisoners passed. Just like his counterpart, the previously mentioned Lieutenant Colonel Robin 'Tin Eye' Stephens, the chief interrogator at Camp 020, Alexander Scotland is on record as having said he did not believe in the use of violence to squeeze information from the enemy. Instead, just as at Camp 020, psychological techniques were used in the name of saving British and Allied lives and defeating Hitler.

With the end of the war in Europe in May 1945, the PWIS became the headquarters of the War Crimes Investigation Unit (WCIU) and was used for the interrogation of known and suspected war criminals from the European theatre. Indeed, it was only once the war had ended that some of its most valuable work was carried out. Between 1945 and 1948, Scotland and his men tracked down and interrogated many of Germany's most brutal war criminals including Fritz Knöchlein of the Waffen-SS, the fighting arm of the SS, who was responsible for the murder of about 100 men of the Royal Norfolk Regiment after their capture near Calais in May 1940 during the retreat to Dunkirk. Knöchlein had them lined up outside a barn at Le Paradis and machine-gunned to death. Two of them managed to escape and after the war testified to Knöchlein's involvement. During his trial, he was found guilty and hanged. Another notorious criminal held at the London Cage was SS-Gruppenführer Jakob Sporrenberg, who was responsible for the deaths of more than 40,000 Jews in Poland. And a third was SS-Feldwebel Erich Zacharias, one of eighteen SS and Gestapo men involved in the murder of the fifty RAF men who escaped in a mass breakout from Stalag Luft III in Poland, an incident later portrayed in the 1963 film *The Great Escape*.

The London Cage closed in 1948. Although there were allegations of brutal and inhuman treatment of some of its prisoners, MI5 conducted two investigations and nothing was ever proven. Its role in the war, and that of Alexander Scotland, is hard to exaggerate. In total, 3,573 men were interrogated there, and more than 1,000 were persuaded to give statements about war crimes.

When it closed, Scotland returned to civilian life. In 1955, he tried to publish his memoir but was prevented from doing so by the intelligence services and Special Branch. During this period, his home was raided and the original manuscript was confiscated. Two years later, he was given permission to publish a heavily censored version of the book, *The London Cage*. It inspired the 1958 film *The Two-Headed Spy*, starring Jack Hawkins as 'General Alex Schottland'.

Although he never received any honours from the British government after his OBE in 1919, Scotland was awarded the Bronze Star by the US Government in 1946. The citation noted his

> meritorious achievements while serving as Commanding Officer of the Prisoner of War Interrogation Service, M.I.(19) of the British War Office; for outstanding cooperation in enabling field interrogation detachments of G-2, European Theatre of Operations, US Army to be quickly established; for generous sharing with United States Field Interrogation Detachments of the British experience for the speedy and complete reporting of the results of PWIS interrogation; and for exceptional contribution to Anglo-American cooperation and outstanding devotion to duty.

Lieutenant Colonel Alexander Paterson Scotland OBE died at the Alexian Brothers Nursing Home in London on 3 July 1965. He was eighty-two years old.

THE BALKANS, NORTH AFRICA, GREECE AND THE GREEK ISLANDS

While many Intelligence Corps operators were engaged in duties in France, north-west and central Europe from 1939, others were required to ply their trades in southern Europe and North Africa. All Balkan countries, apart from Greece, were allies of Nazi Germany, entering into bilateral military agreements with Hitler or becoming part of the 1940 Berlin Pact, which created a military alliance between the Axis powers of Germany, Italy and Japan. Greece was invaded by Italy in October 1940, was lent British support in March 1941 but surrendered in April 1941. At the same time, the North African campaign, which lasted from 1940 until 1943, threatened the Allies' colonial interests in Egypt, Morocco, Tunisia and Algeria, including the strategically vital Suez Canal.

As previously noted, Section D was established as part of the Secret Intelligence Service, MI6. Another noteworthy Section D man, and one who fully embraced its ethos of 'irregular' warfare before eventually carrying out indispensable work for the Intelligence Corps against the Nazis in both the Balkans and then Africa, was Julius Hanau. If Winston Churchill was an admirer of those rebellious enough to adopt unorthodox methods to defeat the enemy, Hanau, whose exploits earned him a place on a Gestapo hit list, can be said to have more than justified his status among the gallery of the Corps' finest operators who risked their lives for others with Churchill's encouragement.

Julius Hanau was born in Cape Colony, a British colony in South Africa, on 25 April 1885, the son of Karl and Sophie Hanau. His origins were German-Jewish, though he later converted to Christianity. His family was prosperous and influential through its farming and diamond-mining interests. After his father turned to gold mining, however, the fortune was lost and the Hanau family settled in Britain.

Hanau had a varied education, first attending South African College in Cape Town and then the Institut Thudichum, an elite international school in Geneva. Later, he studied for short periods at the universities of Freiburg, Munich and Berlin before enrolling at the specialist Camborne School of Mines in Cornwall. After five years working in Argentina, he returned to England on the outbreak of the First World War in 1914.

His War Office service file shows that he enlisted in the Army Service Corps as a Private in January 1915, shortly before turning thirty. By May 1915, he had been promoted to acting Company Quartermaster Sergeant and the following year he was posted to a motor transport company during the Salonika campaign, fighting the Bulgarians and their allies in the Balkans, where his ability to speak German, French, Spanish, Dutch and Italian was put to use. A year later, he was commissioned as a Second Lieutenant in the Army Service Corps. As the war neared its end, Hanau came to the attention of the Secret Intelligence Service, MI6. The Foreign Office then requested his retention in the Army and he was recorded officially as being 'Specially Employed'. In fact, the intelligence service had recruited him for a semi-diplomatic mission to Belgrade, attached to the Supreme Economic Council (SEC). The SEC had been established during the Paris Peace Conference in February 1919 to advise on economic measures to be taken pending peace negotiations, which resulted in the Treaty of Versailles. Hanau's precise role is not on public record, but as the wheeling and dealing of the Allied countries commenced, so did their spying – on each other.

Hanau remained in uniform in the Balkans area until July 1921, providing military and economic intelligence in a deep cover role while officially holding the post of Deputy Assistant Director of Supplies and Training. After being demobilised, he was awarded the Order of the White Eagle (with Swords) by the King of Serbia.

Colleagues in the espionage profession considered him courageous, loyal and charming, characteristics which made it easy for him to remain in business in Belgrade during the 1920s, where he lived permanently from 1930 as a representative of the engineering firm Vickers. Through his SIS activities, he developed a brilliant network of contacts in the Yugoslav government and army. In order to protect his cover, communications to him from London were sent via the British Legation and addressed to 'Major Hanau', his honorary rank, with an inner envelope marked for 'MZ/4', his code number. As a further precaution, a separate letter would accompany each envelope, asking Hanau to pass the letter on to 'MZ/4'. In this way, if ever questioned by the legation, he could state that he was merely acting as a conduit. In July 1937, he was made a Knight Commander of St Sava of Yugoslavia, 2nd Class.

In March 1938, Hanau was absorbed into the newly formed Section D of SIS, becoming the head of its Balkan Desk, still based in Yugoslavia and still using his commercial activities as cover. No doubt spurred on by the Nazi persecution of Jews, he quickly carved out a reputation as disrupter-in-chief where German interests were concerned in the Balkans, particularly in Yugoslavia and Romania. His actions ranged from what could almost be thought of as amusing pranks – for example he once forced the cancellation of a Berlin Philharmonic Orchestra concert in Belgrade by threatening an anti-Nazi demonstration and a stink bomb attack – to serious attempts at destabilisation.

The latter included his involvement in Section D's idea to sabotage the flow of German war commodities down the Danube, such as mineral ore from the Trepča Mine in Serbia and oil from the Romanian oilfields. These plans comprised a number of methods of blocking the route such as sinking barges of cement near the

Orsova Gorge on the Yugoslav–Romanian border and causing a landslide at the Kazan Pass by detonating explosives in the cliff face. Hanau arranged for a sympathetic contractor, known as 'Bruslja', to be awarded a contract to quarry stone for local building around the cliff face during which large quantities of explosives were placed and made ready, though ultimately this scheme was never activated. A similar ploy, at a place called the Greben Narrows, where the water levels were controlled by retaining walls, almost ended catastrophically. Hanau arranged with Bruslja for explosives to be buried into one of the walls which, when detonated, would drastically lower the water level and prevent deep-water transit along the river. Two of his men were sent to guard the spot, but as they observed German barges heading along the river, they set off the charge accidentally and blew a breach in the wall. Showing his skills at handling a crisis, Hanau not only managed to have the incident written off as an innocent quarrying accident but, when Bruslja was then awarded the contract to make the repairs, arranged for another large charge to be buried in the wall.

By late 1939, the Germans were well aware of Hanau and were pressing the Yugoslavian government to expel him. Hanau countered with a raft of anti-German propaganda, including embarrassing the German Consul-General by making public his criminal record. He also arranged for three truckloads of ammunition bound for Bulgaria to 'disappear'. He even had a tunnel dug under a building in which the local Nazis held meetings, filling it with explosives and planning to blow them up. All of this made Hanau a target for the Germans, so much so that he required his own bodyguard. Ironically, some within the British Legation in Belgrade looked upon him unfavourably as well, believing his unrelenting campaign against the Nazis to be harmful to their peaceful diplomatic relations with the Yugoslavs. Their discovery that he used the cellars in their building to store explosives did not help.

In July 1940, Section D discovered German plans to assassinate Hanau. His service file shows he was withdrawn from Belgrade and placed temporarily in charge of Balkan affairs in Istanbul. From there, he was called back to London to head the West African Section, having acquired the amusingly obvious codename 'Caesar'. It was around this time that Section D was absorbed into the new Special Operations Executive (SOE), the underground army which was set up with Churchill's backing to wage a secret war. Its agents were mainly tasked with sabotage and subversion behind enemy lines. Hanau, who had been happy operating as a lone wolf, slotted in perfectly. It has even been said that he was the first agent to be employed by the SOE.

In August 1941, to facilitate his obtaining military status, he enrolled in the Army Officer's Emergency Reserve. On his application form, he described his occupation as 'Inter Services Research Bureau', the cover name for the SOE. In September 1941, he was commissioned into the Intelligence Corps in the rank of Second Lieutenant, with the normal *London Gazette* entry being suppressed.

During his tour with the West African Section, Hanau was heavily involved in the planning for Operation Postmaster, carried out in January 1942. Its objective was to hijack two Italian merchant ships off the neutral Spanish island of Fernando Po and then acquire the ship *Gascon* and its cargo. It came about following reports that German submarines were refuelling in Vichy French-controlled ports in West Africa. While investigating these reports, SOE agents became aware that the two Italian ships were anchored in the port of Santa Isabel and that one of them had a working radio. It was suspected that it was being used by the Italians to relay details of British naval movements to the Nazis. The operation, which entailed elements of deception, stealth and pure bravado, was a memorable coup for the SOE and the Small Scale Raiding Force, proving that unconventional fighting forces were capable of planning and executing a complex manoeuvre against the enemy.

It was also Hanau who recognised the strategic importance of the island of Madagascar, and a few months after Postmaster, he pushed for the formation of the SOE's South African Mission, leading to the capture of the island during Operation Ironclad. Although by this point he was aged fifty-seven, he personally conducted much of the planning for this mission and accompanied the Assault Commander during the landings, even suffering a concussion from an explosion along the way. It was also during Ironclad that Hanau contracted malignant malaria and was forced to take sick leave. He was later recommended for the Distinguished Service Order (DSO) for his part in the operation, but instead he received the OBE.

On his return from sick leave, and now in the rank of Lieutenant Colonel, he was appointed Director of the West and South African, North African and Iberian Missions in London, where he remained until October 1942. With the increase in covert operations in the Balkan theatre, his years of experience in this region led to his being appointed head of the Balkan Desk, to be based in Cairo. On 1 May 1943, he was promoted to acting Colonel. Ten days later, following a brief trip to Istanbul, Colonel Hanau was found dead in his room at the Carlton Hotel in Cairo. Initially, foul play was suspected, and his wife was convinced that Gestapo agents had poisoned him. A post-mortem examination was conducted which revealed that he died from a coronary thrombosis. He was fifty-eight years old and was buried in the Heliopolis Cemetery in Cairo.

• • •

Among the Intelligence Corps' most significant contributions to the Second World War was the reconnaissance work some of its operators carried out during the Western Desert campaign in Egypt and Libya between 1940 and 1943. Fought in intense heat in strange terrain, this battle heralded the birth of the Long Range Desert Group (LRDG). One of the Corps' foremost figures to be involved in it was Patrick Clayton, a British surveyor and former soldier whose extraordinary military career began as a young man in the First World War. The expertise which he developed subsequently while mapping the vast desert areas of North Africa in the 1920s and 1930s ensured he became invaluable to the eventual Allied victory in North Africa in May 1943.

Patrick 'Pat' Andrew Clayton was born at Croydon in Surrey on 16 April 1896, the son of Charles Clayton, a chartered accountant, and his wife Katherine (née Black). He had one sibling, Douglas, who took up typing as a profession and who typed manuscripts for the writer D. H. Lawrence. Patrick was educated at University College School in London and then went up to University College London, where he was a member of the University Officers Cadet Unit (OCU).

His studies were interrupted by the Great War. In April 1915, he was commissioned from the OCU as a Second Lieutenant into the Army Service Corps. Initially, he was posted to the 13th Divisional Train (the Army Service Corps' supply and logistics mechanism attached to the 13th Infantry Division) and then to the 28th Divisional Train. In November 1915, he moved with the unit to Salonika in Greece, where the British Army opposed Bulgarian attempts to invade Macedonia. On 5 December 1917, Clayton transferred to the Royal Field Artillery and continued to serve in Greece and then Turkey for the remainder of the war, achieving the rank of acting Captain.

In 1920, Clayton was in Cairo awaiting demobilisation when he found work as a topographer with the Egyptian Geological Survey. For the next three years, he spent extended periods in the Sinai region until, in 1923, he transferred to the Egyptian Desert Survey Department as an inspector. He continued in this role for the following fifteen years, mapping and exploring the vast desert wastes of Egypt and Libya. This included, between 1927 and 1929, a survey of the Qattara Depression, a low-lying area of soft sand and salt marshes. It was hoped that it might be a possible location for a hydroelectricity project in which the area would be flooded with seawater from the Mediterranean via a canal dug through the desert. Although the scheme was abandoned, the maps Clayton produced during this period would be immensely useful to the British during the Second World War. (Incidentally, during this phase of his career, he also devised the use of rope ladders with wooden rungs and flexible mats to extract vehicles stuck in the soft sand and salt marsh.) Just before embarking on the hydroelectricity project, he married Ethel Williamson Wyatt, a teacher employed by the Egyptian government. She was originally from Lancaster and had studied at the Manchester School of Art before taking up her post in Egypt, which had been under British occupation since 1882.

While working with the Desert Survey Department, Clayton forged partnerships with other noted desert explorers from Britain such as Ralph Bagnold and Bill Kennedy-Shaw. He also worked with Count László Almásy, the Hungarian desert explorer who later became the Nazi desert advisor to Field Marshal Erwin Rommel and, later still, the basis for the protagonist in the 1992 book *The English Patient* by Michael Ondaatje. Clayton was himself the inspiration in the same book, which was turned into an Oscar-winning film, for the character Peter Madox. In 1932, Clayton and Almásy tried to find the mythical lost city of Zerzura, supposedly located deep in the western desert of Libya. It had been the subject of legend and speculation since the thirteenth century and several explorers had searched for it in vain. During this undertaking, he encountered refugees retreating from the Italian occupation of the Kufra oasis in south-eastern Cyrenaica. Clayton ferried those he was able to help to Wadi Halfa. He then drove hundreds of miles over several days, through previously uncharted desert, searching for other groups and helped them to safety as well. For these selfless acts, he was awarded a meritorious gold medal by King Fuad I of Egypt. In 1938, he left the Desert Survey Department and took up a position with the government of Tanganyika (present-day Tanzania) in the Survey Department of Lands and Mines.

After the outbreak of war in 1939, it became clear that the enemy's sights were trained firmly on the Middle East, specifically Egypt and the Suez Canal. The biggest threat to the region came from Libya, which had been an Italian colony since 1911. By 10 June 1940, when Italy declared war on Britain and joined Germany in the Axis forces, the Italians had fourteen divisions in Libya, consisting of 230,000 troops, 1,800 guns, 340 light tanks and more than 150 aircraft. Facing them were 100,000 British soldiers, 36,000 of whom were in Egypt, plus the Free French Forces. This marked the beginning of the Desert War, which was to last until February 1943.

On the day the Italians declared war, Ralph Bagnold, then a serving officer in the Royal Engineers, was in Cairo awaiting passage
on a troopship to Kenya. Realising that a desert war was inevitable,
however, he sought an interview with General Wavell, Commander-
in-Chief Middle East, to suggest forming a small, mobile scouting
force for desert operations against the Italians. Wavell eventually
agreed but gave Bagnold only a few weeks to establish the unit and
make it operational. The Long Range Patrol, later renamed the
Long Range Desert Group, was born.

One of the first people Bagnold contacted when assembling his
team was Pat Clayton, who, although forty-four years old, was
asked to help form the new unit. Clayton returned to Cairo and
on 25 July 1940 was commissioned as a Captain in the Intelligence
Corps, which had been formally re-established six days previously.
Having overseen the organisation of vehicles and equipment, Clayton was placed in command of T-Patrol. It was one of two combat
patrols in operation at that time, the other being G-Patrol. Clayton
went on the first LRDG mission, ranging hundreds of miles behind
enemy lines with a small party of men in order to gather information about the treacherous terrain, all the time drawing on his
knowledge of reading tracks so that he could estimate how many
enemy vehicles or troops had been in the area, in the process fulfill-
ing brilliantly the core principles of intelligence gathering.

Clayton's Distinguished Service Order (DSO) citation, summa-
rising his courageous activities and achievements while commanding T-Patrol, read:

During the six months which have elapsed since he was commissioned direct from civil life, Captain Clayton has most successfully carried out four daring exploits far behind enemy lines.

Each demanded enterprise and powers of military leadership and organisation of a very high order.

Immediately on joining this newly formed unit, Clayton suggested and then organised the first long reconnaissance expedition across the Sand Sea into Italian Libya. He set out ten days after his arrival with a party of five picked men in two light cars and returned twelve days later having crossed 1,500 miles of desert. On this expedition he (i) accomplished the first crossing ever attempted by a military force of the 140 miles of immense sand dunes separating Egypt and Libya, (ii) discovered and crossed a second dune field of almost equal width, (iii) penetrated 200 miles into enemy territory and remained there for four days watching the Jalo-Kufra road in an August temperature of 125 degrees. By this pioneering feat he paved the way for the subsequent activities of the Long Range Desert Group.

On the second expedition during September 1940 he led his patrol of thirty men successfully from Siwa across 700 miles of enemy territory to French Equatoria and back, a total distance of 3,200 miles, returning with much valuable information, both military and geographical.

On a third raid across the great sands he penetrated north westward from Jalo for a considerable distance along the enemy's main road to Ajedabia, and on the way back attacked and captured the fort of Augila, 220 miles behind the Italian lines. He was pursued by enemy aircraft but successfully evaded them.

During January 1941 he commanded the British force of two patrols which travelled direct from Cairo to northern Tibesti, and thence, having picked up a small party of four Free French officers and NCOs, raided Murzuk, Traghen, Umm El Arenab and Gatrun in Fezzan before putting in at Zouar for supplies. On this outward journey the force traversed enemy territory for 1,400 miles, by a new route containing difficult passage through dune fields which the enemy had previously attempted to force without success. He reached Zouar without the loss of a single vehicle out of a total column of thirty-five. To have made these tremendous journeys over unmapped desert and across the most formidable sand dune areas in the world in peace time, at leisure and with a picked party of experts would have been an outstanding feat. Clayton made them under war conditions, in command of troops who perforce had no previous experience of the desert, in constant danger of attack by enemy aircraft and with the knowledge that the evacuation of seriously wounded would be impossible. At the far end of the journey he had, on two occasions, engaged the enemy in successful actions.

Clayton's final mission was undertaken from the Free French base at Faya in support of a French attack against the Italian garrison at Kufra, commanding an LRDG force consisting of 'T' and 'G'-Patrols. The force started out from Faya on 27 January 1941, with Clayton's men providing the advance screen. On reaching Uweinat, they found that the Italian post had been abandoned. Clayton pushed on towards Jebel Sherif leaving G-Patrol in reserve. As Clayton's patrol was approaching the jebel, an Italian spotter plane appeared. Clayton ordered his party to scatter and conceal themselves among rocks in a wadi (a dry watercourse). Shortly after, however, the plane returned and directed vehicles of the Italian 'Auto-Saharan Company' – the Italian equivalent of the LRDG – towards Clayton's position.

The resulting action was brief but decisive. The Italian force was larger, with more vehicles and heavier weapons. It attacked

Clayton's unit, supported by sustained and heavy machine-gun fire, immediately disabling three trucks and killing one of Clayton's men. He marshalled his remaining vehicles and was able to remove them from the wadi in order to circle around the Italian positions and hit them from the rear. But the sudden appearance of three Italian aircraft settled the matter. The planes made a series of low-level bombing and strafing attacks. Clayton's vehicle was hit several times and its tyres, radiator and petrol tank were taken out. Even while under attack, Clayton's crew tried to change tyres, but the aircraft continued their strafing runs and Clayton was wounded in the arm. He and two New Zealander companions were captured. The remaining vehicles of T-Patrol returned to join G-Patrol.

Clayton was first incarcerated in two Italian Camps, No. 78 at Sulmona, Abruzzo, in central Italy; and then No. 29 at Veano, in Piacenza. It was recorded that while at Sulmona he was visited by Count Almásy, who was by then Rommel's desert advisor. When Italy capitulated in September 1943, Clayton and several other prisoners walked out of the camp before the Germans could secure it, managing to remain free for four months. He was eventually recaptured by German troops in January 1944 and sent to a camp in Germany, Oflag 79 LXXIX near Hanover. While a prisoner of war there, he put his cartography skills to good use for escape activities, producing maps and forging German documents, passes and rubber stamps. He was released when the camp was liberated by the Americans in April 1945.

In October 1945, Major Clayton was appointed an MBE for his activities while a prisoner of war. His citation read:

Following his capture in the Western Desert on 1 Feb 41, Major Clayton was imprisoned at Sulmona and Veano (Italy). After his release from the latter camp on 9 September 43, he travelled South in an effort to reach Allied lines but was caught by the Germans on 22 December 43. Although he succeeded in eluding his captors, he was again apprehended on 8 Jan 44 and entrained for Germany. En route he took part in an escape attempt, but only two officers got away. Throughout the four years of his captivity, Major Clayton did valuable work forging passes, identity cards and ration cards and copying maps. He was also in secret communication with the War Office. Two senior officers have commended Major Clayton for his Intelligence activities.

Clayton remained in the Army after the war and between September 1945 and August 1946 served in a staff appointment in Palestine in the rank of Lieutenant Colonel. He retired on 1 July 1953 with the rank of Honorary Colonel and lived at Hove in Sussex. Colonel Patrick Andrew Clayton DSO MBE FGS FRGS FRICS died of an aneurism on 17 March 1962. He was sixty-five years old.

• • •

One of the most daring military operations of the Second World War was the planned assassination of Hitler's close friend General Erwin Rommel, the Afrika Korps Commander whose reputation earned him the nickname the Desert Fox. One man who was instrumental in this raid, and in other high-profile missions of the Western Desert campaign, was John 'Jock' Haselden, a successful businessman with no military background to speak of when war began. Although he was in his late thirties in 1939, he was soon drafted in to assist with the war effort and joined the Intelligence Corps, yet again proving that so-called gifted amateurs, and not just professional soldiers, were able to make significant contributions to the Allied cause through bravery and original thinking.

John Edward Haselden was born on 10 October 1903 at Ramleh, a suburb of Alexandria in Egypt. His Liverpool-born grandfather, Joseph Haselden, had moved to Egypt in 1863 to work as a cotton merchant and married Emma Saunders, the daughter of the British Consul in Alexandria, Sir Sidney Smith Saunders. Their eldest son, Henry, also worked in the cotton trade in Egypt. He married Maria Ester Angela Cazzani, from Lombardy. Jock was the eldest of Henry's four children. He was educated at The King's School, Canterbury, before he, too, returned to Egypt to follow his father into the cotton business.

In 1931, he married Nadia Ida Marie Szymonski-Lubicz at Alexandria. His wife, who was of Polish and Italian descent, was the daughter of Leon Szymonski-Lubicz, the sub-manager of the Ottoman Bank in Alexandria. They had one son, Gerald, who was born in 1932. Tragically, Nadia was killed in a road accident in March 1936. Following her death, their son was sent to England to be cared for by an aunt.

By 1939, Haselden was the managing partner in the Upper Egypt agency of the American cotton firm Anderson and Clayton. He owned a large villa overlooking the River Nile just south of Cairo, was a member of the Gezira Sporting Club and was well known among Cairo society. On 13 July 1940, he volunteered for military service and was initially commissioned as a Second Lieutenant on the General List and posted to the 1st Libyan Refugee Battalion. His fluency in Arabic, French and Italian immediately came to the attention of military intelligence in Cairo, however, and he was transferred to the Intelligence Corps upon its formation on 15 July 1940. By October of that year, he had been promoted to the rank of acting Captain. In April 1941, he was appointed as General Staff Officer Grade 3 to HQ 102 Military Mission, which had been set up to assist the Senussi Force, later known as the Libyan Arab Force, in carrying out sabotage and intelligence-gathering missions behind the Italian lines. During this period, operating under the name 'Hasel', he was able to use his knowledge of the Arab tribes to build up an extensive intelligence network.

Haselden's dark eyes and complexion allowed him to pass for an Arab, and he would often spend days in the desert disguised as a nomad in order to secretly monitor Axis troop movements. On many of these forays, he was taken to and from his missions by the so-called Libyan Taxi Service, otherwise known as the Long Range Desert Group. The previously mentioned Bill Kennedy-Shaw, who worked with Haselden, described him as

> the outstanding personality of the dozen-odd men working with the tribes in Cyrenaica behind the Axis lines. Untiring, strong, courageous, never without some new scheme for outwitting the enemy, yet with a slow and easy-going way of setting about a job which was far more successful with the Arabs than the usual European insistence on precision and punctuality which they neither like nor understand.

Haselden's valour more than warranted this tribute.

In September 1941, he was recruited by G(R) Branch, the local cover name for the Special Operations Executive, and appointed its Desert Liaison Officer at Eighth Army headquarters. The following month, he became involved in Operation Flipper, the planned raid on General Rommel's headquarters at Sidi Rafa in Cyrenaica, mounted by men from No. 11 (Scottish) Commando and led by

Lieutenant Colonel Geoffrey Keyes, the 24-year-old son of Admiral of the Fleet Sir Roger Keyes; and 'L' Detachment, led by Colonel Bob Laycock. The plan was for the commandos to capture Rommel; 'L' Detachment was to target communications sites nearby. Operation Flipper was to take place on the night of 17 November. It was timed to coincide with Operation Crusader, the Western Desert offensive overseen by the Commander-in-Chief of the Middle East Theatre, Claude Auchinleck. Haselden's role in the Rommel raid was to find suitable approach routes to the target.

The month before the audacious raid, Haselden carried out a lengthy period of reconnaissance which earned him high praise and recognition. On 10 October 1941, dressed as an Arab, he swam ashore in the dead of night from a submarine. He stayed behind enemy lines for the next nine days until being picked up by an Allied patrol. For these deeds, he was awarded the Military Cross. The citation noted that during the time he was in enemy territory he 'was in constant danger of being arrested and shot [and] he collected valuable information both regarding the local Arabs and the movement of enemy troops'. It also noted that 'the success of the recce was largely due to the high degree of courage, determination and clear thinking possessed by this officer'.

When it came to the raid itself, Haselden's job was to carry out a final reconnaissance of the target, check it was all clear and then signal the raiding force waiting offshore in two submarines. Having been dropped off by T-2 patrol of the Long Range Desert Group, Haselden and an Arab colleague walked across the desert for almost 100 miles, found the target to be clear and moved to the landing location. Regrettably, however, the mission went wrong from very early on. Once Haselden's signal had been received by the commandos, they attempted to land using small dinghies. By that point, the sea conditions had deteriorated badly and only thirty-three men – fewer than half the force – made it to shore. Keyes and those who remained carried out the attack on Rommel's headquarters, inflicting significant damage on the building with grenades and gunfire, but Keyes was killed in the process. Worse still, it transpired that Rommel was not even there. Unbeknown to the raiders, three weeks earlier he had moved his base closer to Tobruk in order to be nearer the front line. Bletchley Park's codebreakers only became aware of this from their Ultra decrypts on the day of the raid, leaving them insufficient time to relay the information to Cairo before the hazardous plan could be called off. What is more, Rommel was out of the country attending a meeting in Rome. Unable to withdraw to their submarines, the raiders were forced to fight a running battle with Italian troops and tried to scatter into the desert. Of the thirty-three raiders, two were killed, twenty-eight were captured and only three managed to make it through the desert to safety. Lieutenant Colonel Keyes was awarded a posthumous Victoria Cross.

Having moved on to the second part of his mission, Haselden was unaware of this debacle. He and his Arab colleague successfully destroyed telegraph communications on the El Fridia to Slonta road, then made their rendezvous with the Long Range Desert Group patrol and returned to Allied lines. For his part in the raid and the successful sabotage of the enemy communications afterwards, Haselden was awarded a bar to add to his Military Cross. Its recommendation read:

Captain Haselden was dropped by the Long Range Desert Group in the area of Slonta prior to the raid carried out by a detachment of Middle East Commandos on General Rommel's HQ at Sidi Rafa. Captain Haselden, dressed in British Battle-dress but wearing a djard and Arab headdress, walked a distance of nearly 100 miles through the heart of the enemy territory in order to make certain reconnaissances prior to the landing of the detachment. After ascertaining the situation regarding enemy and friendly Arab forces in the area he made his way to the selected beach and there awaited our landing, which he guided in by pre-arranged signals. Having passed on vital information about the enemy, which was immediately transmitted by the Royal Navy to Cairo, and having explained the situation ashore to our raiding party and guided us towards our objective, Capt Haselden again made his way through miles of enemy territory to his appointed rendezvous with the Long Range Desert Group. On his journey back he succeeded in disrupting vital enemy communications. I consider that Capt Haselden's fearless action is worthy of the highest praise. Such success as was achieved in the operation was largely due to information which Capt Haselden had gained during his reconnaissance. I cannot recommend too highly Captain Haselden's outstanding endurance, his cool and calculated bravery, and his unswerving devotion to duty.

After the disastrous Operation Flipper, Haselden was posted to HQ XIII Corps and remained there until March 1942, when he was promoted to acting Major and posted to HQ Eighth Army as a General Staff Officer Grade 2 in the Directorate of Special Operations. In June 1942, he was promoted again, to acting Lieutenant Colonel. It was during this period that he conceived and developed the idea for a major push against the Axis campaign in North Africa.

The previous month, following an eight-month siege, the Libyan port of Tobruk had fallen to Axis forces. This gave Rommel a point through which the Afrika Korps could be supplied – not least with fuel. As the Axis pushed further eastwards towards Egypt, however,

Tobruk fell further back behind his front line. By the time Rommel was facing the British positions at El Alamein, Tobruk was 300 miles behind him. Given the nature of the terrain, this presented a major logistical problem. If both Tobruk and Benghazi could be denied to Rommel, then his only alternative would be the port installations at Tripoli, almost 1,000 miles away. This would be a huge blow to his strategy and would likely cripple his attempt to occupy Egypt and the Suez Canal. As a result of this, Haselden conceived and developed Operation Agreement, the overall codename for a series of smaller, interlinked operations: Daffodil, Tulip, Hyacinth and Snowdrop.

The plan was for a carefully coordinated raid against both Tobruk and Benghazi from land and sea, with the main targets being the harbour installations, oil dumps, shore batteries, repair facilities and communications. For the operation, the land force, command-ed by Haselden, consisted of a squadron of 1st Special Service Reg-iment together with engineer, signals and gunner specialists. The commandos were to infiltrate Tobruk by posing as prisoners of war, concealing their weapons. Their 'guards' were members of the Special Detachment G(R) Branch, otherwise known as the Special Identification Group (SIG) – German and German-speaking Pal-estinian Jews dressed in German uniforms. Their mission was to infiltrate into the town under cover of an air raid, neutralise the guns and coastal defences and establish a bridgehead.

Offshore, a mixed force of Royal Marines, Army and engineers would be waiting on board the destroyers *Sikh* and *Zulu* along with eighteen motor torpedo boats for the signal that the beachhead had been secured before commencing their landing. Their role was to destroy the major port facilities. Supporting the seaward group were other Royal Navy destroyers and the anti-aircraft cruiser HMS *Coventry*.

Haselden's Force B left the LRDG base at Kufra on 6 September 1942 and, guided to the assembly area by LRDG patrol 'Y-1', successfully breached the perimeter surrounding Tobruk on 13 September. The six German-speaking Jews of the SIG, dressed in Afrika Korps uniforms, used their disguises to good effect and were able to collect valuable intelligence regarding the locations of the coastal guns. One member of this small group even managed to infiltrate a German officer's mess and spent the evening with them playing cards while all the time listening to their loose talk. By dusk, Haselden's group had managed to establish their temporary headquarters and they then split into two parties as planned, each with its own objectives. By midnight, both groups of Force B had signalled the success of their respective missions, and then started to await the arrival of the seaborne force.

Devastatingly, the rest of the mission went awry. Force C were to land from the motor torpedo boats at 0200hrs, but in the darkness the boats lost contact with each other and became scattered; only two managed to land inside the bay and the others eventually withdrew. The Royal Marines of Force A were supposed to land from the destroyers via small collapsible boats to the north of the port area, but by then a heavy swell had set in and many of the boats capsized. Those which did make land came ashore nearly 3 miles away. Both seaborne forces were also coming under increasing enemy artillery fire and the enemy were illuminating the harbour with searchlights. Only about seventy men actually reached the shore, and they were almost all killed or captured after a firefight. HMS *Sikh* was so badly damaged by the coastal gunfire that she was scuttled. *Zulu* and *Coventry* withdrew from the area and were later sunk by enemy bombing as they headed back to Alexandria.

By dawn on 14 September, Colonel Haselden's Force B was

coming under increasing enemy fire and had taken several casualties. In an attempt to get the wounded away from the battle area before attempting to complete his second objective – the capture of the guns on the southern side of the harbour and the destruction of the oil storage facility – Haselden loaded the wounded onto a lorry and, with covering fire from other members of his group, broke through the Italian positions. One eye witness said that he charged a machine-gun post while attempting to break out and was killed in the attempt. Haselden was reported missing and presumed killed in action at Tobruk during Operation Agreement on or around 14 September 1942. He was thirty-eight years old.

On 26 June 1946, Haselden was awarded a posthumous Mention in Despatches in respect of the ill-fated Tobruk raid. As he has no known grave, he is commemorated on the Alamein Memorial to the Missing in Egypt. Only six of his original raiding party of ninety made it back to British lines. Long after Haselden's death, his Long Range Desert Group friend David Lloyd Owen wrote of him:

> He was a man many years older than myself and I admired him intensely. He had become a kind of legend to me for he had spent months with the Arabs in the Gebel (Jebel) Akhdar where he lived as one of them. They, too, trusted him and loved him for he was sincere in all he did.

• • •

If the Desert War was a protracted campaign, Britain's involvement in the fighting which led to the Axis powers' successful invasion of Greece and Crete was brief and brutal. The occupation began in April 1941, after the Nazis decided to assist their struggling ally,

Italy, which had been at war with Greece since October 1940. Although Churchill was keen to support Greece, the country was overwhelmed in the space of three weeks, along with Yugoslavia. The British then tried to hold Crete as a naval base, but after 16,000 German soldiers were parachuted onto the island, Nazi forces gained a foothold there and it, too, was lost rapidly, ushering in one of the lowest points of the Second World War as far as Churchill was concerned. After this, it was left to Greek resistance groups and others to tackle the Nazis. In this, some men of the Intelligence Corps played a supreme role. One of them was Nicholas Hammond, who showed immense bravery and not a little guile in serving his country for the greater good.

Nicholas Geoffrey Lemprière Hammond was born on 15 November 1907 at Ayr in Scotland, the son of the Rev. James Vavasour Hammond, the Rector of Ayr's Holy Trinity Church, and Dorothy May Hammond. He was educated at Fettes College in Edinburgh and then went up to Gonville and Caius College, Cambridge, where he achieved a first-class degree in Classics and was a Montagu Butler Prizeman in 1928. He was also a noted tennis and hockey player.

After graduating, he eventually took up a post as a Classics lecturer at Clare College, Cambridge. Through this, he was able to join academic expeditions and extended vacation periods in northern Greece and Albania, instilling in him a deep knowledge of and love for this region. As a young man, therefore, he became well acquainted with both countries' language, culture and geography. He married, in 1938, Margaret Campbell Townley. They would go on to have two sons and three daughters.

In late 1938, when the prospect of a conflict with Germany drew closer, the War Office began making discreet approaches to some of

Britain's major universities in search of individuals who had what were called 'special qualifications' that might prove useful in future, with a particular focus on those with notable technical, scientific and linguistic proficiencies and knowledge of foreign countries. Lists of suitable candidates were compiled and stored for possible future use. Nicholas Hammond, who was considered unusual for his ability to speak both Greek and Albanian fluently, and to have a good understanding of this politically rocky area, was among them.

Following the outbreak of war in September 1939, the War Office circulated its 'special qualifications' lists to departments and service branches which were on the lookout for recruits. On 25 May 1940, Military Intelligence (Research), which was also known as 'MI(R)' – a War Office division concerned with covert operations until it was subsumed into the Special Operations Executive in July 1940 – informed the Directorate of Military Intelligence that Hammond was required for a secret mission to Greece. On 3 June, he was commissioned on the General List and sent on an explosives course.

Initially, his intended assignment for MI(R) was to infiltrate into Albania via Greece, contact members of the local resistance movement and then instigate an uprising against the occupying Italians. In late June 1940, he flew to Athens. At that time, however, the Greek government was suspicious of the British having any involvement in its affairs and he was refused entry. It was only once Greece had entered the war following the Italian invasion of Albania in October 1940 that the situation changed. Hammond returned to Athens successfully in March 1941. By then, he had been transferred to the Intelligence Corps and he became a member of Special Operations Executive (SOE) Force 133, using the identification code D/H-52. His pseudonym was 'Eggs' – as in 'Ham(mond) and Eggs', which had been a schoolboy nickname. By this point, his mission had changed, with his main role being to instruct the Greek irregular forces, including the communist partisans, in sabotage and demolition in preparation for an expected German invasion and possible occupation.

On 6 April 1941, a dozen German divisions crossed the Greek borders at Thrace and Macedonia, sparking the German invasion. Bitter fighting lasted throughout the month until on 23 April the Greek Army was forced to surrender, leaving only a British armoured brigade and an Australian infantry division to fight a withdrawal action prior to evacuation to the island of Crete. During this period, Hammond was able to distribute some radios and supplies to groups of men he had trained and who would form the basis of the resistance organisation. He was one of the last to leave Greece and personally travelled around destroying material which might be of use to the enemy. In doing so, he nearly missed his rendezvous with the schooner that had been sent to evacuate him.

The following month, this episode was repeated almost identically. On 20 May, the Germans launched what ranks as the first airborne invasion in military history, in which it suffered heavy losses. Although things looked favourable for the Allies, telecommunications failures allowed the Nazis to capture Maleme airfield, giving them the ability to land reinforcements. On 28 May, the British Commander gave the order to withdraw and evacuate. Once again, Hammond was kept busy demolishing equipment and stores. His last act was to blow up an SOE munitions dump at Souda Bay. He then boarded a schooner bound for Egypt and reached Alexandria unscathed, although his vessel was attacked by a German aircraft en route and two crew members were killed.

From Egypt, Hammond moved to the SOE training school at

Haifa in Palestine. There, he was involved in training Greeks in the arts of sabotage and wireless operation. His expertise in explosives led to him being nicknamed 'Captain Vamvakopvrites', meaning Captain Guncotton. His co-instructors included the future Conservative MP Montague Woodhouse and the author Paddy Leigh Fermor, both of whom were Intelligence Corps officers of SOE Force 133. As well as instructing Greek units, Hammond was also involved in training Jewish youths selected by the Zionist Agency for infiltration into Syria, prior to the British occupation. This group included Moshe Dayan, who went on to become a post-war Commander of the Israeli Army and then defence minister during the Arab–Israeli Six-Day War. Hammond further trained the first group of students from the Dodecanese islands in the use of limpet mines with a view to staging sabotage missions against German and Italian ships.

In 1942, SOE Cairo decided to send an independent mission into north-west Greece in order to establish contact with the communist-backed group ELAS (People's Liberation Army). Hammond and Rufus Sheppard, another Intelligence Corps operator, were selected for the task. With Greece having descended into a state of near chaos, Hammond's brief was to look after the military situation while Sheppard concentrated on political issues. On 20 February 1943, Hammond was parachuted into Thessaly and made his base in the Pindos mountain range, becoming the Area Commander for Macedonia with the British Military Mission. Although he had been asked to try to strike up a military resistance organisation, much of his time was spent trying to defuse tensions between ELAS and the right-wing, monarchist faction EDES. These two bitterly opposed groups spent valuable time and resources fighting each other rather than the common enemy, requiring Hammond to play a diplomatic role on top of his expected duties.

Once the Desert War had been won by the Allies in February 1943, it was decided to take the fight back to Europe, starting in Sicily and then moving on to mainland Italy. As previously described in Operation Mincemeat, in which a corpse with fake invasion documents was planted for the Germans to find, British ingenuity in conceiving deception operations came to the fore. The Husky deception plan was reinforced by Operation Animals, a series of sabotage attacks on military targets and infrastructure in Greece designed to trick the Germans into believing that they were disruption attacks prior to an invasion of Greece rather than of Sicily. On 30 May 1943, Brigadier Eddie Myers, the overall Commander of the British Military Mission in occupied Greece, received orders that all main north–south communications in Greece were to be cut between the end of June and the first week of July (the Sicily invasion was planned for 10 July). Plans had already been laid for this eventuality and Myers instructed his four Area Commanders that all targets, including roads, railways and telephone lines, were to be cut on the night of 21 June and to be kept cut by further demolitions up to 7 July, with a view to making them unusable for a further seven days.

As Hammond's citation for his DSO award later stated:

Lt Col Hammond was personally responsible to Brig Myers for ANIMALS operations in the area for the main road and railway between Kozani in the North and Larissa in the South. On 21 June until 1 July he took an active part in operations with the Andartis (Greek resistance) against the enemy. The outstanding operation was the holding up of a column of seventy German lorries in the Sarendoperon Pass. The road having previously been blocked, the enemy was ambushed in the rear and practically all the Germans in the column were either killed or taken prisoner. Having supervised the demolition of three road bridges to the South of Kozani and ensured that the Andartis were acting in accordance with Brig Myers' instructions, Lt Col Hammond returned to his HQ in order to carry out a journey to Salonika to obtain special information required by Brig Myers. Dressed up as a shepherd, he went to Salonika by bus, stayed there a week achieving the necessary contacts and returned with the most valuable information. This officer's work has been consistently of the highest order and he has displayed the greatest courage and willingness to take any risks to carry out his work.

In September 1944, Hammond was promoted to Lieutenant Colonel and took over temporary command of the British Military Mission when Brigadier Myers was removed for being considered too friendly towards the ELAS partisans. Hammond remained in command until January 1945, being replaced by Colonel Montague Woodhouse of the Intelligence Corps, and his time in Greece then came to an end. In March 1945, he was posted to a staff job with 21 Army Group, in the Allied advance into Germany, and was released from military service in October 1945. As well as being created a Companion of the Distinguished Service Order (DSO) for his outstanding service in Greece, he was twice Mentioned in Despatches. In 1946, the Greek government awarded him the Order of the Phoenix.

After the war, Hammond returned to his academic life at Clare College, Cambridge, remaining there until 1954 when he became headmaster of the Bristol public school Clifton College. In 1962, he was appointed professor of Greek at the University of Bristol. He continued in that post as a visiting professor until 1992.

He also served as pro-vice chancellor of the university between 1964 and 1966. Having retired in 1973, he was made an honorary fellow of Clare College. He was a renowned Hellenist and wrote several well-regarded books on Greek classical subjects as well as a three-volume history of Macedonia. He published the story of his exploits with the SOE, *Venture into Greece*, in 1983. Professor Nicholas Hammond died in Cambridge on 24 March 2001, aged ninety-three.

•   •   •

The aforementioned Paddy Leigh Fermor remains one of the best-known operators ever to have been part of the Intelligence Corps, thanks largely to his exploits forming the basis for W. Stanley Moss's 1950 book *Ill Met by Moonlight*. In 1957, it was turned into a feature film starring Dirk Bogarde as Leigh Fermor. His actions in staging the kidnap of a German General behind the lines during the Cretan resistance is still considered one of the most dramatic incidents of the Second World War, earning him widespread praise and enormous recognition. Leigh Fermor later called the mission 'a symbolic gesture, involving no bloodshed, not even a plane sabotaged or a petrol dump blown up; something that would hit the enemy hard'. Nonetheless, it relied on the sort of enterprise which made the Corps stand out during the Second World War.

Patrick Michael Leigh Fermor (always known as Paddy) was born in London on 11 February 1915, the son of Sir Lewis Leigh Fermor and Muriel Æileen (Eileen) Ambler. His father was a renowned geologist and chemist and a superintendent with the Geological Survey of India. His mother was the daughter of Charles Ambler, the director of a stone and slate quarry in India. After his birth, the infant Patrick was entrusted to the care of the Martin family in the village of Weedon Bec in Northamptonshire while his parents and sister returned to India. They remained apart until 1919, when his now-divorced mother returned to England and they moved to London.

He attended various schools, including St Piran's preparatory school near Maidenhead, but he was considered truculent, leading to his expulsion. He then attended Walsham Hall, a school in Suffolk for 'difficult' children, and from there moved to Downs Lodge in Surrey. Throughout this time, he developed a love of reading and excelled at French, German and Latin. Finally, he was sent to The King's School, Canterbury, but he was again expelled, this time for being found holding hands with the daughter of a local greengrocer. By then, one of his teachers had described him memorably as 'a dangerous mixture of sophistication and recklessness'.

It was considered best for him join the Army, but before he turned eighteen, the age at which he would be allowed to enter Sandhurst, he became more free-spirited and his plans changed. He decided to walk across Europe, from the Hook of Holland to Constantinople, the name by which he always called Istanbul, and left England in December 1933 carrying a rucksack containing some spare clothes, a few letters of introduction, a copy of the *Oxford Book of English Verse* and Loeb's volume of Horace's *Odes*. For the next six years, he was a gentleman of the road, making his way through Germany, Austria, Czechoslovakia, Hungary, Romania, Bulgaria, Turkey and Greece. He slept in farmyards, inns, monasteries and grand houses, mixing with vagabonds, gypsies and aristocrats. He arrived in Istanbul in January 1935, and then moved to Greece and, finally, Romania, where he was living in September 1939. On hearing that Britain was at war, he returned to England.

He joined the Irish Guards as a cadet officer but in December 1939 was taken seriously ill with influenza and pneumonia. Although he made a full recovery, any immediate chance of a commission in the Guards was dashed. The War Office, however, became aware of him. His European travel experience and knowledge of the Balkans was considered useful and he was asked to undertake intelligence work. After training at Aldershot, he was commissioned as a Second Lieutenant to the Intelligence Corps in August 1940 and then sent to the Corps training school at Smedley's Hydro at Matlock, Derbyshire, for the War Intelligence and Interrogation Course. One of the instructors was Stanley Casson, a noted Greek scholar and archaeologist. When Casson later formed the British Military Mission to Greece, he asked for Leigh Fermor to be posted to it.

The British Military Mission was short-lived. Having arrived in Athens, Leigh Fermor was sent to the headquarters of the Greek III Army Corps to monitor and report on the progress of the Greek offensive against the Italians. After several adventures during the Battle of Greece and the resulting evacuation, he sailed to Crete and was posted to Heraklion as an Intelligence Officer with 14th Infantry Brigade. Two weeks later, on 20 May, German paratroopers and glider troops captured Maleme airfield. Leigh Fermor left aboard a British destroyer. In September 1941, after a short spell in Cairo, he was posted to the SOE training school at Haifa in Palestine as a Weapons Training Officer until April 1942.

On returning to Cairo, he was told he was to be posted to the SOE for a mission to Crete. His job was to be part of a small team under another Greek classicist and Intelligence Corps officer, Monty Woodhouse, working alongside the Cretan resistance. The main objectives of the team were to organise the collection and evacuation of the hundreds of Allied troops who had been hiding on Crete since its fall and to explore the possibility of an organised resistance in the event of an Allied attempt to recapture the island.

He arrived on the island via the schooner *Porcupine* on 22 June 1942 and soon afterwards took charge of the team's activities in the western zone. For the next year, using the field name of 'Filedem' and known to the locals as 'Michaelis', he lived perilously with the local Cretan resistance. Most of the time, he was disguised as a shepherd and he hid out in mountain caves gathering intelligence on German positions and troop movements, training and organising, and arranging parachute drops of munitions and supplies. He also took advantage of the experience to indulge himself in exploring the customs, songs and culture of the Cretan people.

In late July 1943, news arrived of the overthrow of Mussolini in Italy. At that time, the Commander of the Italian garrison on the island was General Angelo Carta. Sensing change in the air, Carta soon made it known that he wished to be evacuated from the island along with his staff. Leigh Fermor was the man who oversaw an operation in which Carta was smuggled from his headquarters at Neapoli across the island to the coast at Tsoutsouros, dodging German search parties and aerial reconnaissance. Leigh Fermor accompanied Carta back to Cairo. On 14 October 1943, he was appointed OBE although he was not invested with the award until March 1950. The original recommendation for the award had been made in April 1943, when he was still active on Crete and before he arranged General Carta's evacuation. The recommendation read:

Capt Leigh Fermor was infiltrated into Crete on 22 June 1942 and has thus been there over nine months already. Infiltrated at the time of the El Alamein period, he has never been other than cheerful throughout his stay there and has been a most valuable officer in maintaining morale among the civil population in very difficult circumstances. At the same time, he has been in charge at different periods of our revolutionary and espionage services in the prefectures of Canae, Rethymno and Herakleion and has thus been responsible for the production of much valuable information on enemy activity. He has made a reconnaissance of the ports of Suda and Herakleion, the latter within the past month. Once, on his own initiative, and more recently with material supplied to him he has organised defeatist campaigns in the ranks of the German troops. He is still in Crete where his services in helping the population to retain their faith in the Allies has been invaluable.

By then, Allied plans were to invade Sicily and Italy. As a result, the SOE planned to scale down its operations in that theatre and Leigh Fermor was therefore looking for another assignment. His successful evacuation of General Carta had given him the idea of staging another highly original operation: to kidnap a German General on Crete and bring him to Egypt. The man he had in mind was General Friedrich-Wilhelm Müller, the Commander of 22nd Air Landing Division, also known as the 'Butcher of Crete', who had been responsible for the massacre of hundreds of Cretan villagers.

Having finessed the plan in his own mind, Leigh Fermor submitted it for approval and, surprisingly, was given the green light by the SOE in January 1944. He was also promoted to temporary Major. On 9 January, his team, which included his 22-year-old co-conspirator Captain Bill Stanley Moss – with whom he and several others shared a riotous house called 'Tara' when in Cairo – departed. Moss was his second in command and two leaders of the Cretan resistance joined them as they took off from Brindisi en route to their chosen dropping zone on the Omalos Plateau, south of Neapoli.

The area was surrounded by mountains, which prevented the team being dropped together, forcing the pilot to circle the area and drop each man individually. As the aircraft approached, the reception committee on the ground lit the signal fires. Leigh Fermor jumped first. Thickening cloud cover prevented the pilot from being able to see the fires on his next circuit and he was forced to return to base with the remainder of the team. Bad weather prevented any further drops and it was not until April that Moss and the two Cretans arrived by sea.

Yet even before their arrival, the plan was thrown into doubt. General Müller had been moved from his command in Heraklion to Chania, some 60 miles west, as the new Commander of Fortress Crete. He had been replaced at Heraklion by General Heinrich Kreipe. Eventually, with official approval, it was decided to carry on with Kreipe as the new target. Kreipe's residence was the Villa Ariadne, near the ancient ruins of Knossos about 3 miles south of Heraklion and the former home of Sir Arthur Evans, the British archaeologist. Through surveillance, it was established that Kreipe made two daily visits to his divisional headquarters at Archanes, 5 miles south of Knossos. He would spend the morning at work, eat lunch at home and return to his headquarters until late evening when he went back to the villa. A suitable ambush point on the road from Archanes was identified, where a downward slope and a sharp bend would cause Kreipe's vehicle to slow down.

During the early evening of 26 April, Leigh Fermor and Moss dressed as German police Corporals and waited in preparation to wave down Kreipe's vehicle. Once it was confirmed that Kreipe was inside, the rest of the team would rush out of hiding, disable the driver and capture Kreipe, then take him across the mountains of central Crete to the southern coast where he would be picked up by a British vessel and taken as a prisoner of war to Egypt.

The team took up their positions overlooking the ambush point. At precisely 9.30 p.m., a signal came through from an observation post warning that Kreipe's vehicle was approaching. Leigh Fermor and Moss walked to the centre of the road and waved the car down with a red torch. As it stopped, Leigh Fermor approached the front passenger side where Kreipe was seated while Moss covered the driver's door. As Kreipe opened his window, Leigh Fermor saluted and said, '*Papiere, bitte schön.*' Then, as Kreipe reached to his breast pocket, Leigh Fermor wrenched open the door shouting, '*Hände hoch!*' ('Hands up!'). He pressed a gun against Kreipe's chest and pulled him from the vehicle. At the same time, Moss dealt with the driver, knocking him out with a cosh and depositing his body at the side of the road. The three Cretans sprang from their hiding places, restrained Kreipe with handcuffs and pushed him into the back of the car.

Moss took the wheel and Leigh Fermor sat beside him wearing Kreipe's hat. Having shaved off his moustache, it was hoped that he could pass for the General who was in the back being held at knifepoint by the three Cretan guards. Leigh Fermor and Moss bluffed their way through Heraklion and then passed through a further twenty-two German checkpoints unchallenged. Taking the coast road towards Rethymno, they drove for 30 miles and then, at a spot above the small island of Peristeri, abandoned the car to head south on foot towards the village of Anoyeia. Leigh Fermor left a letter inside the vehicle, which he had penned earlier. It read:

Gentlemen,

Your Divisional Commander, General Kreipe, was captured a short time ago by a BRITISH Raiding Force under our command. By the time you read this both he and we will be on our way to Cairo. We would like to point out most emphatically that this operation has been carried out without the help of CRETANs or CRETAN partisans and the only guides used were serving soldiers of HIS HELLENIC MAJESTY'S FORCES in the Middle East, who came with us. Your General is an honourable prisoner of war and will be treated with all the consideration owing his rank. Any reprisals against the local population will thus be wholly unwarranted and unjust.

Auf baldiges Wiedersehen!

PM Leigh Fermor, Maj., O.C. Commando

CW Stanley Moss, Capt 2i/c

P.S. We are very sorry to have to leave this beautiful motor car behind.

The kidnappers and their captive trekked for three weeks, sleeping in caves, sheepfolds and cattle pens in the cold and wet, constantly on the lookout for German land and air patrols. They were fed and supplied along the way by the inhabitants of the many villages they walked through, even though their benefactors knew they would be killed should the Germans ever discover they had aided the abductors of their General. On the night of 14 May 1944, after journeying across Crete and finally marching over the top of Mount Ida and through the Amari valley, they made it to the isolated beach at Rodakino. Kreipe was taken off Crete by motorboat to Cairo. He was held as a prisoner before being released in 1947.

For his planning and execution of the high-stakes mission, Leigh Fermor was immediately awarded the Distinguished Service Order and Moss received the Military Cross. Leigh Fermor received the decoration while a patient in hospital after he had been admitted with severe pains in his joints and a high temperature, the first symptoms of which had started during their journey across Crete.

He was eventually diagnosed with polyarthritis and spent three months in hospital. The recommendation for the DSO read:

> This officer showed exceptional gallantry in executing the task of kidnapping Major General Heinrich Kreipe, GOC 22 Panzer Grenadier Division, at Archanes, Crete, on 26.4.44. He led a party close to the German Commander's HQ, attacked his car and overpowered both him and the driver of the car. Then, impersonating the General in his car he was driven through Heraklion through 22 German-controlled roadblocks. Subsequently, for 17 days he was hunted by considerable enemy forces, but he succeeded in moving the General over a distance of 100 miles through enemy-held territory. After several attempts he was finally successful in placing his captive on board a ship which evacuated him to the Middle East. For his outstanding display of courage and audacity Major Leigh Fermor is recommended for the immediate award of the DSO.

After convalescing in Lebanon, he was sent back to Crete on 8 October 1944, by which time the Germans had withdrawn to the western end of the island, at Chania, Maleme and Souda. He was based near the village of Vafes, 25 miles south-west of Chania, and in December moved to Heraklion. He left the island just before Christmas, which he spent in Cairo, and was posted back to England at the end of March 1945 to join the Special Allied Airborne Reconnaissance Force (SAARF). He spent some weeks in Hamburg – by then in the Allied zone – hunting war criminals and returned to England for VE Day.

After the war, Leigh Fermor, who was still only thirty years old, was taken on as deputy director of the British Council of Higher

English Studies in Athens, where he remained for just over a year. Thereafter, he embarked on a career of travel and writing, becoming acknowledged as one of the greatest British travel writers of his generation. Among his works was *A Time of Gifts*, published in 1977, about his first trek across Europe. Incidentally, Bill Stanley Moss also became a writer and adventurer, producing the aforementioned *Ill Met by Moonlight*. He died in Jamaica in 1965, aged forty-four.

In 1968, Leigh Fermor married Joan Elizabeth Rayner, the daughter of Viscount Monsell of Dumbleton in Gloucestershire. They lived in a villa at Kardamyli on the Mani Peninsula in the southern Peloponnese and also had a house at Dumbleton. Joan died in Kardamyli in 2003, at the age of ninety-one, and was buried in Dumbleton. Leigh Fermor was knighted in 2004 for bridging the cultural divide between the UK and the Hellenic world following the Cypriot insurgency. In 2007, the Greek government made him a Commander of the Order of the Phoenix. He died at his Dumbleton home on 10 June 2011, having returned from Kardamyli the previous day. He was ninety-six years old. He is buried beside his wife at St Peter's Church, Dumbleton. His guard of honour was provided by veterans of the Intelligence Corps and a bugler of the Irish Guards sounded the Last Post.

• • •

As previously alluded to, many people believe that the greatest factor in the triumph of Allied intelligence during the Second World War was the progress made in signals intelligence (SIGINT) – that is to say, the interception, decryption and analysis of enemy wireless traffic. One Intelligence Corps operator who deployed these specialist skills in the most testing conditions was John

Makower, a London businessman whose bravery on the front line during the Western Desert campaign was of tremendous value in laying the foundations for intercept units in the field.

John Moritz Makower was born in London on 6 December 1902, the son of Ernest Samuel Makower and Rachel (née Caro). The family was of Polish-Jewish heritage and was prosperous, their forebears having moved to Britain in the 1860s and founded the silk merchant M. Makower, which is still in business today. He attended Cheltenham College and then went straight into the family firm. In July 1925, he married Adelaide Franklin, the daughter of the prominent Liberal politician Sir Leonard Franklin. Between 1926 and 1946, they had five children, the eldest of whom, Rachel, worked at Bletchley Park from 1944 to 1945, where she was involved in breaking Japanese naval codes.

By the time war was declared in September 1939, Makower was the managing director of the family business and lived near Henley in Oxfordshire. He soon enrolled in the Army Officer's Emergency Reserve and on 1 February 1940 he was commissioned as a Second Lieutenant on the General List. He was transferred to the Intelligence Corps on its formation in July 1940.

Having been posted to Y-Service, which was concerned with signals intelligence, he completed his SIGINT training with No. 6 Intelligence School, located with the War Office's own Y-Group at Beaumanor Hall near Loughborough in Leicestershire. This estate was requisitioned by the War Office in 1940 and turned into a Y-station – a secret listening post used to intercept encrypted enemy signals. The traffic collected by Y-stations was recorded by hand and sent for processing to the Government Code and Cypher School at Bletchley Park, usually by despatch rider or, later, by teleprinter over post office land lines. From Beaumanor Hall, Makower was posted to his first operational unit, 40 Wireless Intelligence Section (WIS), which was attached to 101 Special Wireless Section (SWS). At that time, the unit was part of No. 1 Special Wireless Group, GHQ Home Forces.

Y-Service operated under the auspices of MI8 of the Directorate of Military Intelligence, which had evolved partially from the Radio Security Service, the body that detected radio transmissions from German intelligence to enemy agents in Britain. Every special wireless group consisted of several numbered special wireless sections, manned by Royal Signals operators. Each of these had an attendant wireless intelligence section which was managed by Intelligence Corps personnel and was responsible for translation, collation and analysis.

Both static and mobile intercept detachments were established along the eastern and southern coasts of Britain. Mobile sections operated from large trucks known as 'gin palaces'. These contained all the receivers and associated equipment. Where possible, each mobile section was connected to its reporting headquarters via a landline, but in a combat scenario this was difficult, especially when a unit was operating in the field, meaning intelligence had to be carried by hand, usually by motorcycle or jeep.

In January 1941, Makower's section, 40 WIS, together with 101 SWS, arrived at Port Said in Egypt. Fearing a German invasion, however, they were moved to Athens on 11 March and assigned to the Greek Expeditionary Force. In Athens, they were immediately tasked with monitoring both Italian and German radio traffic. With the country under siege, they were ordered to evacuate for Crete on 23 April. All equipment, records and personal kit were destroyed. On 29 April, they embarked at Crete for Alexandria.

On 7 June, both 101 SWS and 40 WIS moved forward into the

Western Desert and deployed at Maaten Bagush, a small town on the Egyptian coastal strip approximately 200 miles east of Tobruk. They had been placed under the direct command of HQ Western Desert Force for Operation Battleaxe, a British Army offensive whose objective was to recapture eastern Cyrenaica from German and Italian forces after General Rommel's dramatic advance eastwards across the Western Desert. Having secured the port of Benghazi, and then pushed onwards to take Derna and the Gulf of Bomba, he was circling Tobruk. It was the only other major port facility and was of paramount importance to British supplies. Rommel wanted it for the same reason.

Operation Battleaxe was mounted by XIII Corps, consisting of the 7th Armoured Division and the 4th Indian Division. It commenced on 15 June. In preparation for this, Makower's unit had been placed under the command of HQ Western Desert Force on 8 June and was detached to support the 4th Indian Division. The two-day battle was an expensive failure in which there were 969 Allied casualties. Although the British were buoyed by the arrival of tanks transported at great risk through the Mediterranean, two-thirds of them were lost, with only forty surviving the battle.

The following month, on 14 July, Makower was ordered to take a small detachment right up to the front line to support the 7th Armoured Support Group. This was considered an unusual – indeed, almost an experimental – move because special wireless sections were usually deployed in support of Army or Corps formations. His detachment consisted of some Royal Signals operators and one Intelligence Corps NCO analyst, Sergeant William Swain. As a result of Battleaxe having failed, the British advance had been completely stalled and only managed to escape a German encircling movement by a rapid retreat. During this period, timely intelligence of the enemy's units, strength, movements and intentions was fundamental. The pressure was on. Yet as if having to establish these details was not enough, Makower and Swain also had to work under the intensity of battle conditions.

In order to achieve the best possible reception, Makower placed his unprotected vehicles on the front line. He had no cover and chose to operate in the face of continual artillery and tank bombardment. Exhausted, working under heavy fire and with little thought for his own safety while doing his duty for his country, he deciphered the enemy's tactical signals traffic. It revealed information relating to the armoured deployment of the German forces within the division's area. This intelligence was then passed to Sergeant Swain, who also showed total fearlessness as he drove through open desert under enemy bombardment to deliver it to the Divisional Commander. Makower and Swain, who demonstrated such coolness of character, are rightly remembered as pioneers. The military artist Terence Cuneo later produced a painting depicting their activities in the desert. It hangs in the Officers' Mess at Chicksands.

On 18 February 1943, Captain Makower was promoted to acting Major and was also awarded the Military Cross, although the recommendation had been made some months earlier. His analyst, Sergeant Swain, was awarded the Military Medal. Makower's MC citation read:

This officer has served in the Western Desert for almost sixteen months. He has commanded the Intelligence Section attached to 101 Special Wireless Section for the whole of that period. His devotion to duty, his cheerfulness under all conditions, and his untiring efforts have been an example and inspiration to all ranks. Understaffed and working abnormally long hours, he has contributed greatly to the records and knowledge without which such a unit is valueless. Any success of this unit as a whole has been largely due to his efforts, and his outstanding work has laid the foundations for the future work of all such units in the field. The unit concerned has often had to work under conditions of considerable danger from enemy fire, but this has made no difference to the high standard of his work.

    B.L Montgomery

      GOC 8th Army

Major Makower went on to operate with Y-Service during the invasion of Sicily in July 1943. By this time, his unit had been redesignated as 101 Wireless Intelligence Section. The following month, he was promoted to temporary Lieutenant Colonel and on 16 September 1943 he was appointed an MBE. In March 1944, he was further honoured with a Mention in Despatches:

Lt Col Makower's technical skills and energy in organising a very wide network of intelligence have provided an extremely valuable contribution to our knowledge of the enemy during the Sicilian campaign. This officer is possessed of considerable originality and his remarkable capacity for long hours of difficult and exacting work produced results that were of exceptional value.

Following the fall of Sicily, Makower continued on through the Italian campaign and commanded 3 Special Wireless Group in coordination with the US Signal Intelligence Service. He remained in Italy for the duration of the war and was awarded the US Bronze Star medal. The citation stated that in his capacity as Chief of the

Signal Intelligence Branch, G-2 Section, 15th Army Group, he 'very ably controlled and coordinated the activities of both United States and British units in the production of Intelligence which contributed materially to the final Allied victory in Italy'. It went on:

> It was through his outstanding tact, tireless energy and sound professional judgement that it was possible to knit a closely integrated Allied Intelligence organisation which operated harmoniously and efficiently. By his perseverance and the zealous manner in which he discharged his responsibilities, Lieutenant Colonel Makower bent his every effort to the successful accomplishment of his mission and served as an inspiration to all with whom he came in contact.

After the war, he returned to his business interests and continued living in Henley. He was also active with the Royal British Legion and was a senior Freemason. John Makower died on 17 December 1989, aged eighty-seven, and was interred at Henley Cemetery. His headstone bears the inscription: 'Silk Merchant and Intelligence Officer'.

ITALY AND SICILY

In January 1943, Allied chiefs met at the Casablanca Conference to discuss the next phase of the war. Churchill favoured invading Sicily, believing it to be the 'soft underbelly of the Axis'. It was argued that sending troops onto the island would force Hitler to scatter his forces and could bring down Mussolini's regime. After lengthy negotiations, Franklin D. Roosevelt agreed to the plan. By the time the Allies had declared victory in North Africa in May 1943, detailed preparations were under way on the campaign that was codenamed Operation Husky. It began on 9 July with an amphibious and airborne operation and was followed by a six-week land campaign. Operation Husky ended on 17 August. Its success did indeed topple Mussolini and triggered the Italian campaign, which would last until May 1945.

As previously noted, field security sections were required to carry out a range of tasks, including gathering intelligence in the field, interrogating prisoners and exploiting captured enemy material. They also had to fight as infantry. In order to perform these duties, they were often the first to arrive and the last to leave any operation. One FSS man who made a notable contribution to the war effort while carrying out several of these duties was Captain Jack Dunbar.

Jack Dallas Dunbar was born on 19 April 1918 at Rosario de Santa Fe, Córdoba, Argentina, the son of Angus and Winifred Dunbar. His father was a bank manager in Córdoba, but there was a strong military link within his family: one of his grandfathers was Colonel William Mathew Duncan, a career soldier who had served during the Crimean War, the Indian Mutiny and later operations in South Africa as well as being a Gentleman at Arms to Queen Victoria. Other illustrious members of Dunbar's family included his uncle, Sir Loraine Geddes Dunbar, the treasurer of the Bank of Bengal in Calcutta.

Dunbar attended Repton School in Derbyshire until 1937. He then went to Germany for a short time to complete his education. Thanks to this experience, he developed a working knowledge of German. His upbringing in Argentina meant that he already spoke Spanish fluently. He could also speak French. He soon joined the soap and cleaning products firm Unilever, but as well as starting a career in business, Dunbar also pursued his interest in the Army. On 9 November 1937, he enlisted as a gunner in the Royal Artillery (Territorials). He served with the 54th Anti-Aircraft Brigade in the West Midlands until 26 September 1938, when he joined the regular Royal Artillery. On 16 May 1939, he was promoted to Bombardier, and on the outbreak of war in September 1939, he applied for officer training and was accepted, joining the 162nd Officer Training Cadet Unit at Bulford in Wiltshire on 11 July 1940. On 12 October 1940, he was commissioned as a Second Lieutenant in the Intelligence Corps and sent to the School of Military Intelligence at Smedley's Hydro at Matlock in Derbyshire to attend the War Intelligence Course. Having completed it, he was posted to the Arundel (Sussex) Sub-Area as an Intelligence Officer in the acting rank of Lieutenant. From there, he moved to Headquarters Eastern Command at Luton Hoo House in Bedfordshire and was promoted to acting Captain.

In June 1940, having been in office for barely a month, Winston Churchill let it be known that he was so impressed with the performance of the German paratroopers during the Battle of France that he wanted the War Office to explore the feasibility of raising a British airborne force of 5,000 parachute troops. By the end of the month, a development centre for airborne warfare, the Central Landing Establishment, had been established at Ringway airfield near Manchester. Its principal role was to train parachute troops, but it was also concerned with exploring the use of gliders for taking troops into battle. At the same time, under the direction of the Ministry of Aircraft Production, the British aircraft manufacturer General Aircraft Ltd was commissioned to design and produce a suitable glider which could carry troops and heavy equipment to a combat zone, towed by military transport planes.

Using gliders for this purpose had several advantages: they were usually made from cheap material such as wood; troops could land together in concentrated numbers, unlike parachutists; and their lack of engine made them difficult for the enemy to identify. On 1 November 1941, the War Office authorised the formation of the Headquarters 1st Airborne Division and the creation of subordinate parachute and air-landing (glider) units.

In late February 1942, Captain Dunbar and three NCOs provided security coverage at RAF Thruxton, near Andover in Hampshire. This was the departure point for Operation Biting, the pioneering parachute raid at Bruneval near Le Havre in February 1942. The role of Dunbar and his men in policing the air base before the raid began, ensuring that all details and plans were kept secret, was regarded as vital. Mounted by 'C' Company, 2nd Parachute Battalion, together with an RAF radar technician and some Royal Engineers, the objective of Biting was to capture the German 'Würzburg' radar system, which had been detected on the clifftop overlooking the beach near the French village. This narrow-beam tracking system was being used to great effect to vector German night fighters and its capture for study and analysis was considered critical if effective countermeasures were to be developed. Operation Biting was the first successful raid of the war conducted by parachute troops.

On 29 April 1942, Captain Dunbar was temporarily attached as an Intelligence Officer to the Headquarters 1st Airborne Division at Syrencot House, Figheldean, near Bulford in Wiltshire, while retaining his appointment with HQ Eastern Command. On 13 May 1942, his attachment was made permanent when he was appointed as Field Security Officer of 89 (Para) Field Security Section, which was then in the process of formation at Figheldean. FSS units were deployed with the Army wherever it operated. When the formation at Figheldean was complete, Dunbar's FSS consisted of a Company Sergeant Major, four Sergeants, twelve Corporals and Dunbar's Lance Corporal batman, all of whom were volunteers for parachute operations. Every member of the unit had to be trained in both parachute and glider-borne operations and they were dispersed between the divisional headquarters and its four constituent brigades, the 1st, 2nd and 3rd Parachute Brigades and the 1st Airlanding Brigade, which was the glider-borne element.

On 1 March 1943, Dunbar and his section embarked for North Africa with elements of the 1st Airborne Division in preparation for Operation Husky, the invasion of Sicily. Initially based at Oran in Algeria, the section later moved to Mascara in Algeria and then on to Sousse in Tunisia, overlooking the Gulf of Hammamet, across which lies the Strait of Sicily. The invasion consisted of three elements. The Western Task Force, under the command of Lieutenant General George Patton, comprised the US Seventh Army and was tasked with advancing west from their landing beaches, capturing the capital, Palermo, and then heading towards Messina, 4 miles from the Italian mainland. The Eastern Task Force, under the command of General Montgomery, consisted of the British Eighth Army and was to take the eastern route from their landing beaches towards Syracuse, Catania and then on to Messina, where they would link up with the Americans. The third element was a preliminary airborne assault, with the US 82nd Airborne Division covering the Western Force and the British 1st Airborne Division covering the Eastern Force.

As part of Operation Husky, the 1st Airborne's mission consisted of three separate objectives to support the Eighth Army. The first of these missions was Operation Ladbroke. It was to be carried out by the 1st Airlanding Brigade. The main aim was to secure the Ponte Grande

Bridge across the River Anapo, just south of Syracuse, and then hold Syracuse – including its port – until ground troops took over. Initially, the plan had been to use a brigade parachute drop, but this was later revised when it was thought that parachute troops would have insufficient firepower to complete the assignment. It was decided that a glider landing would allow heavier weapons to be transported.

This sudden change of plan introduced a set of new problems, however. First, the available gliders had been sent to North Africa from England in crates. They were not of the best quality and the maintenance crews used to assemble them were not adequately trained for the job. And second, the pilots of the 51st Troop Carrier Wing, which had been assigned to tow the gliders, had little training or experience either. Ominously, this meant that the 1st Airlanding Brigade was dependent on under-trained glider pilots and an inexperienced troop carrier wing.

On the evening of 9 July 1943, the airborne assault force boarded a total of 144 gliders in the airfields of Tunisia. Captain Dunbar, along with other members of 89 (Para) FSS, boarded their glider, which also carried members of the HQ Party of 1st Airlanding Brigade including the Brigade Commander, Brigadier Philip Hicks. At about 2215hrs, as this air armada approached the coast of Sicily, they encountered strong winds, poor visibility and heavy anti-aircraft fire. To avoid these obstacles, the pilots of the towing aircraft climbed higher or took evasive action. In the confusion surrounding these manoeuvres, the inexperienced tow pilots released too early and, disastrously, sixty-five gliders crashed into the sea with the loss of more than 250 men. Only twelve gliders landed in the right place. More than fifty gliders were scattered over a wide area, miles from their objective. The rest were either shot down or unable to release from their tows.

In Dunbar's glider, the pilot, Lieutenant Colonel Chatterton, who was the Commanding Officer of the 1st Glider Pilot Regiment, managed to make a controlled landing in the sea about a mile off the coast, allowing the glider to remain afloat. Everybody on board was able to exit the aircraft uninjured and make their way onto the wings. After about an hour, during which the glider was illuminated by an enemy searchlight and came under sporadic machine-gun fire, the passengers and crew decided to swim for shore. One witness stated that Captain Dunbar initially swam off alone but then returned to assist two non-swimmers who were in difficulty. An officer who followed Dunbar in order to help lost sight of him and the two men to whose aid he rushed. Several witnesses stated that Dunbar was wearing a lifejacket and a heavy assault jerkin which may have caused difficulties. All of the other members of the party eventually managed to swim ashore and landed in the same place, but as they reached the shallows, a Wellington bomber jettisoned its bombs over the coast and several exploded in the water near the group.

Captain Jack Dunbar was never seen again. In view of the information available concerning the incident, it was presumed that he had been killed in action in Sicily on the night of 9 July 1943. As he has no known grave, his name is commemorated on the Cassino Memorial to the Missing. He was twenty-five years old.

● ● ●

Intelligence Corps operators were often linguists, but sometimes they were required to combine this facility with other specialist skills. Richard Wood was one such man. His duties took him on a mission shortly before the momentous invasion of Italy that was so secret, full details of it remain unclear even today. Thanks to his official service record and RAF flight details, it has been possible to piece together the key aspects of his work.

Richard Humphrey Vellacott Wood was born on 26 June 1916 at Ealing in London, the son of Richard and Eleanor Wood (née Vellacott). His father, an Irishman from Cork, was a civilian architectural draftsman for the Royal Engineers at the War Office who went on to become the War Office Chief Architectural Assistant.

Wood attended Westminster School and in 1934 went up to Wadham College, Oxford, to read history. He graduated in 1937 with a Bachelor of Arts degree and in January 1938 he took up a post teaching English at the University of Prague. He remained there until December 1938, when he left to travel in France and learn the language. In September 1939, he relocated to Palermo in Sicily to work for the British Council. After Italy declared war on 10 June 1940, he returned to England.

Initially, he enrolled in the Royal Artillery, but his knowledge of Italian and French led to him being transferred to the Intelligence Corps as a Private on 24 October 1940. Two days later, he arrived for training at the Field Security Wing at Winchester. On 27 January 1941, he went to Matlock for the 25th NCOs Course, which he completed on 8 February, whereupon he was recommended for commissioning. He joined 164th Officer Cadet Training Unit (OCTU) on 16 March 1941 and was commissioned as a Second Lieutenant, Intelligence Corps, on 7 June. Between 2 August and 18 October 1941, he completed the 18th War Intelligence Course at Matlock and then the Italian Interrogation Course at Cambridge. On 11 April 1943, he was posted as an interpreter to No. 65 POW Camp at Setley Plain near Brockenhurst in the New Forest. This camp had been constructed in 1941 specifically to house Italian prisoners of war. He remained there until 31 March 1943, when he was ordered to report to the Corps depot at Oxford.

On 1 May 1943, Lieutenant Wood was posted to special duties 'without pay and allowances from Army funds'. He had been selected for attachment to the Inter-Services Liaison Department (ISLD), the cover name used by the SIS, and was sent to serve in Italy. By July 1943, his address was recorded as ISLD, Allied Force HQ, British North Africa Force.

In the weeks leading up to the Allied invasion of Italy, both the SIS and SOE were busy coordinating the intelligence-gathering and sabotage and disruption efforts of their agents on the ground. One of the most effective methods for communicating with agents was via the 'Ascension' radio system. Ascension was the codename used by the SIS for a method of direct radio contact between aircraft and agents on the ground. It had been developed by Brigadier Richard Gambier-Parry, the head of SIS's Communications Section (also referred to as Section VIII), and his team at Whaddon Hall, near Milton Keynes. This short-wave, high-frequency, air-to-ground wireless system mounted in a suitable aircraft such as the Havoc, Ventura or Hudson enabled a trained operator in the aircraft to voice-communicate directly with an agent without the need for Morse code. The system was effective at distances up to 100 miles away and had the added advantage of rendering the agent on the ground virtually undetectable to enemy direction-finding. It was used exclusively by the SIS and was not made available to the SOE.

Wood had been recruited by the SIS to work with the Ascension radio system in order to take advantage of his proficiency in Italian. On 7 September 1943, at 2115hrs – two days before the Allied invasion of mainland Italy – Lieutenant Wood took off from El Aouina, Tunisia, in a Lockheed Ventura aircraft of 624 (Special Duties) Squadron, serial number AE881, piloted by Flight Lieutenant Boothby DFC DFM. The aircraft was one of two Venturas specially fitted with the Ascension equipment. Although the exact destination of the flight is not openly recorded, the little information available indicates that the aircraft was to carry out a low-level flight over the proposed landing beaches at Salerno to enable Wood to communicate with Italian partisan groups in advance of the invasion.

The estimated time of the aircraft's return was 0130hrs on 8 September. Just before then, a searchlight canopy was switched on at El Aouina and a beacon was activated at Bizerta, the northernmost city in Africa. At 0345hrs, having received no communication with the aircraft since it took off, El Aouina made contact with the relevant sector operations organisation, but no assistance could be provided as routing details had not been logged by the pilot. It was established that the Filter Room at Sector Operations at Palermo (Sicily) had plotted an aircraft, believed to be AE881, to a point just north of the island of Ustica, flying without 'Identification Friend or Foe' (IFF), and it was the only aircraft plotted in that area at the appropriate time, height and direction. The plot disappeared in the vicinity of a large Allied convoy and it was therefore considered possible, although not confirmed, that AE881 had fallen victim to a 'friendly fire' incident, conceivably anti-aircraft fire from convoy escort vessels. A significant number of Allied aircraft fell victim to such incidents around Sicily during this period.

On 21 September, MI9 (Escape and Evasion), using its cover address of 'Room 900, War Office' and acting on behalf of the SIS, informed Casualty Branch of the War Office that Lieutenant Wood had been reported missing while engaged on an operational flight. For security reasons, the letter tried to play down Wood's role. It commented that as he was not engaged in special duties but simply carrying out an operational flight in the North African field of operations, the casualty report could be treated in the normal way. 'The only fact which we wish suppressed is that he was in our employ,' the letter stated.

Casualty Branch then made the usual enquiries for further details from the Air Ministry. It replied to the effect that it had no record of Lieutenant Wood being on the aircraft while acknowledging that it was a secret mission of which it had no details. When this reply was made known to Room 900, it was forced to reverse somewhat, and wrote back to say that it had definite information that Wood was on the aircraft at the time of its reported loss. It was suggested that Wood's next of kin be informed that he had been lost while taking part in a reconnaissance mission in his capacity as an Army Intelligence Officer, with the added warning: 'I do not think it would be wise to give the next of kin any further information in view of the fact that, as you know, Wood was engaged on a secret mission concerning which it is particularly undesirable that detailed information should be supplied.' The December 1944 edition of the Westminster School magazine *The Elizabethan* contained a short paragraph about its former pupil's loss. It recorded: '[Richard Wood] was reported missing, and is now believed to have lost his life, when he undertook a particularly dangerous mission for which he had been specially selected.'

Lieutenant Richard Humphrey Vellacott Wood was listed as 'missing, believed killed in action on the night of 7/8 September 1943'. He was twenty-seven years old. As he has no known grave, his name is commemorated in central Italy on the Cassino Memorial to the Missing.

● ● ●

During the Second World War, many Intelligence Corps men were expected to fight, but others were called upon to use more subtle skills such as tact, resourcefulness, charm and diplomacy when they became involved in secret service operations. One example of an individual who put these traits to brilliant use was René Kisray, who was based in North Africa and then in Italy. He relied on the force of his personality while working undercover to keep two groups with very distinct views – left-wing Italian political forces and the Allied administration of Italy – on good terms in the difficult period between Mussolini's deposition in 1943 and the end of the war in 1945. It is hard to imagine that many others could have maintained the balancing act that Kisray oversaw.

René 'Mac' Kisray was born René Macklouf Kisraoui in Tunis, Tunisia, on 14 January 1903. (He changed his name by deed poll in 1946 and for the sake of simplicity will be referred to below by this new, Anglicised name.) Although of North African birth, he was a British subject. His Jewish great-grandfather had been born near Glasgow and later moved to Gibraltar, where his grandfather was born a British citizen. From there, the family moved to Malta, where Kisray's father, Sauveir Yechoua Kisraoui, was born. Sauveir eventually moved to Tunisia and married Mathilde Sarfati, a French national from Perpignan. René was the eldest of their five children, the other four being daughters. The Kisraouis were a wealthy family, running a profitable import company and trading in property. They also owned the prestigious Hotel Majestic in Tunis. René was educated in Tunis and Paris. He is said to have lived something of a playboy lifestyle in his youth, owning an aeroplane and a yacht. In 1925, at the age of twenty-two, he married his first wife, Lise Haddad, and reputedly lost a fortune while gambling on his honeymoon in Nice. They had one child, Martine, but the marriage did not last and in 1931 he married Ester Carmona, from Malta. They had a daughter called Annie.

After war was declared in September 1939, Kisray travelled to England to enlist in the British Army, having already made several attempts to do so by letter from Tunisia. Such was his desperation to join up, he even paid 400 Francs to obtain a military visa and spent weeks negotiating Tunisia's tangled bureaucracy in order to prove his British nationality. Although he spoke Arabic, French and Italian fluently, his English was poor. Yet that fact did not dampen his sense of patriotic duty. After living in a YMCA hostel in central London, he enlisted in the Royal Army Service Corps (RASC) as a Private. It was only with the help of the Vansittart family, with whom he had business connections, that he was taken on.

Initially, he trained as a driver and motorcycle despatch rider. While based at Bulford, in Wiltshire, he was summoned for an interview at Farnborough, questioned about his proficiency in Italian and Arabic, and then offered a post in intelligence. He declined. In March 1941, his RASC unit was posted to Egypt and he spent time in Cairo, Alexandria and Tobruk. While in Tobruk, he was again interviewed by officials. This resulted in a second invitation to work in intelligence. He accepted, and in June 1941 he was attached to SIS under their cover name of Inter-Services Liaison Department (ISLD).

In November 1941, Kisray was part of a small team given an intelligence-gathering assignment behind German lines in the Libyan desert. It was commanded by a man calling himself 'Major Jackson'. The unit included a radio operator, Frank Burton, plus an Arab guide. First, they travelled to Kufra, which had been captured from the occupying Italians in March 1941 and was used as a base for Long Range Desert Group operations. There, they met the LRDG patrol which would take them into the desert. The going was hazardous from the start. During the journey, the patrol was spotted and attacked by an Italian aircraft and one of their vehicles was destroyed. Eventually, the team was dropped off in a wadi to continue the undercover journey on foot, the plan being that they would radio the LRDG for extraction once the mission was completed. The following day, 'Major Jackson' went out alone on a reconnaissance trip but did not return and was never seen again. When the remaining members of the group tried to use the radio to contact Kufra, they found the set was inoperable.

By this time, they were more than 150 miles from the nearest British lines with limited food and water and no means of summoning help. By chance, their Arab guide was from a tribe local to that area. He was familiar with the terrain and knew where his tribespeople might be found. Days later, he returned with two camels carrying food and water, reviving Kisray and the others. Following an arduous trek lasting six nights, the unit found its way back to British lines. Kisray was awarded a Mention in Despatches which was announced in the *London Gazette* on 14 October 1942 under his original surname of Kisraoui, and commissioned as a Second Lieutenant in the Intelligence Corps. It took him several months to recover from the perilous desert journey he had endured.

After the Operation Torch Allied landings in North Africa in November 1942, the Axis forces retreated to Tunisia. For the duration of the German occupation of Tunis, their headquarters was, coincidentally, the hotel belonging to Kisray's family, the Majestic. After Tunis was liberated by the Allies in May 1943, attention turned to the invasion of Sicily, otherwise known as Operation Husky. This was completed by 17 August, whereupon Allied plans concentrated on the next phase, the invasion of mainland Italy. By this time, SIS behind-the-lines operations in the area were being conducted under the cover name of No. 1 Intelligence Unit. One of its principal objectives was to establish organised resistance among Italy's anti-Nazi and anti-fascist elements. The Italian Communist Party was at the forefront of this fightback. It was in this context that Kisray became a notable figure, playing a key role at a pivotal moment in forging an improbable but crucial alliance between the British SIS and the Italian communists.

After the rise of Mussolini in the 1920s, many Communist Party members had relocated to Tunisia. The most prominent of these exiles was Velio Spano, a committed party member of longstanding. When Tunis fell, Kisray was sent to the city to recruit Italian communists, his connections and social standing making him an indispensable asset for such work. His primary task was to persuade the exiles to use their influence with anti-fascists in Italy to secure timely and accurate military intelligence and to help establish resistance groups. He was also asked to 'talent-spot' likely agents among Italian prisoners of war and deserters and arrange for their training prior to them being sent behind German lines.

Luck was on Kisray's side. He soon discovered that the daughter of one of his Italian neighbours was married to Spano. By using Spano's wife as an intermediary, he was able to arrange a meeting with him. As he was blessed with natural charm, he was able to convince Spano to help with the British request. With the approval of the future British Prime Minister Harold Macmillan, who was then head of the Allied Commission in Italy, Spano (who was code-named 'Rosso') was smuggled into Italy in October 1943. Kisray accompanied him.

Thanks to SIS funds and equipment, Spano was set up in a large flat in Naples. His brief was to establish a Communist Party structure in southern Italy and use his party connections in the north to organise intelligence-gathering activities there for the Allies. He did this with great aplomb, working constantly to encourage his contacts to deliver the best contemporary information available. It was later assessed that the networks established in the north were so successful that 80 per cent of military intelligence from northern Italy was provided by the communists. Kisray spent months living in the Naples flat with Spano, accompanying him daily to the Communist Party headquarters. And while SIS monitored all their signal traffic to their northern colleagues, Kisray was also able to report back to the British any political intelligence which he had gleaned personally.

Kisray's assignment with Spano came to an end after the General Secretary of the Communist Party for Liberated Italy, Palmiro Togliatti, arrived in Italy from Moscow in March 1944. He accused Kisray of being a spy and demanded that all British influence at Communist Party headquarters be extinguished. Despite this, the northern networks continued to provide intelligence to the British. On 21 March 1944, Kisray was awarded the Medaglia Commemorativa Della Quattro Giornate (the Commemorative Medal of the Four Days) for his services with the Italian resistance after the four-day uprising against the Nazis in Naples between 27 September and 1 October 1943. The following day, he was awarded the Medaglia d'Argento al Valor Militare (Silver Medal of Military Valour) for his service with the resistance in the city and province of Rome in 1943–44. The citation stated:

This Officer of the British Army had duties in connection with the partisan formations operating in Lazio. He repeatedly crossed the enemy lines, his courageous activity benefiting the formations themselves and facilitating the achievements of the leaders. This useful information helped towards the South's national achievements in the War for Liberation. He gave constant proof of his sensitivity in the interpretation of his work for the Italian people and was indefatigable in the risky work pursued in this difficult task, until the total liberation of the Fatherland, from the Nazi-fascists. During the period September 1943 to June 1944 he was a shining example of courage and dedication to the Cause of the liberation of oppressed peoples.

Kisray's role as peacemaker between the Italian communists and the Allies was also considerable. In March 1944, Churchill made a speech reminding all Italians that following Mussolini's arrest and detention, the king and Marshal Badoglio were the authorities recognised by the Allies in Italy. This angered left-wing dockers in Naples, who called for an immediate strike, thereby presenting a major threat to the Allies' authority. Kisray therefore assumed the role of mediator and, using his contacts and intelligence gained through them, a compromise was reached. The strike ended on the condition that Spano could address the dockers. He did so, reminding them that the main aim of their political movement was to see off the Germans and then to establish a socialist democracy in Italy.

Kisray's expertise was called upon again in November 1944. That month, Marshal Badoglio arrived at the British Embassy seeking British protection against communist plots to assassinate him. The ambassador informed Churchill, who replied that he was responsible for Badoglio's safety. The ambassador simply passed the buck to SIS, which once again engaged Kisray to handle the matter. Badoglio was smuggled from the embassy disguised as a British officer and installed in one of the SIS apartments, with Kisray acting as his 'babysitter'. He stayed there for a week, during which time a handful of senior Communist Party officials called in for a drink, as was their habit, unaware that the man they were searching for was sleeping behind the door. Eventually, an agreement with the communists was reached and the threat against Badoglio was lifted.

After Mussolini's execution in Milan on 28 April 1945, Kisray discovered that the communists were searching for his personal papers to use as political leverage. He was despatched to Milan and used his contacts to start his own search. Three of his friends eventually found the papers and the RAF sent a plane to fly him and the papers back to Rome, where they were placed out of harm's way.

Kisray remained in Italy until April 1945 and then returned to his home in Tunis. On 25 September 1947, he was appointed an MBE, but no citation was published with the announcement in the *London Gazette*. Back in civilian life, he was involved with setting up the Italian airline Alitalia. He also lived and worked in Korea for several years. He married his third wife, Kathryn Chou, in Seoul in 1958. In retirement, they lived in Nice for twenty years and then moved to Worthing, West Sussex. René 'Mac' Kisray MBE died on 25 January 2001, aged ninety-eight.

•　•　•

Another Intelligence Corps man who showed exceptional bravery while serving in Italy during the Second World War was John Amoore. Although he was initially employed as an interpreter, circumstances dictated that he had to lead a mission at a crucial juncture of the Italian campaign, requiring him to oversee arms drops and use his intelligence-gathering and diplomatic skills while repeatedly putting his own life in danger for the freedom of others.

John Patrick Strode Amoore, commonly known as 'Pat', was born on 16 July 1918 in La Orotava, on Tenerife in the Canary Islands, the son of Thomas and Florence (née Eldridge). The Amoore family could trace its heritage in Sussex back to at least the sixteenth century. John's father was a fruit farmer who went to Argentina to farm in 1914 before moving to the Canaries with his family in 1917. Although details of his education are not recorded, it is known that during his time in Tenerife he learned fluent Spanish and it was his knowledge of the language that eventually led to his employment with the British Consulate General in Barcelona. In 1941, having returned to England, he attended an Officer Cadet Training Unit (OCTU) and was commissioned from cadet to Second Lieutenant on 12 December 1942.

His first posting was as an Intelligence Officer to the 1st Canadian Division, which was at that time preparing for its role in Operation Husky, the invasion of Sicily. Amoore served with the Canadians right through the Sicily campaign and also during the mainland Italian landings at Salerno on 3 September 1943. By the end of that month, the Allies occupied a significant area of southern Italy and the Germans were in retreat. Once Naples was taken by the Americans, British units pushed on towards Rome and the Canadians were deployed into the central mountain range of Campagna. On 1 October, the 1st Canadian Division engaged with the enemy at Motta, the first in a series of bloody actions. It was during this period, on 6 October, that Amoore was wounded in action.

Having recovered from his wound, Amoore was posted as an Intelligence Officer to the 3rd Carpathian Rifle Division of the Polish II Corps and was with the unit between 16 and 18 May 1944 when it made its sterling contribution to the fourth and final Battle of Monte Cassino. Amoore remained with the Polish II Corps until August 1944, when he was recruited for service with the Special

Operations Executive (SOE). For his service with the Polish Corps, Amoore was awarded the Polish Cross of Valour, in 1951.

During his time in Sicily and Italy, Amoore mastered Italian and, because he was already fluent in Spanish, he could also speak the Catalan dialect. His ability to teach himself a language brought him to the attention of the Special Operations Executive (No. 1 Special Force), which was recruiting Italian speakers to act as British Liaison Officers to anti-fascist and partisan groups operating behind the German lines in northern Italy. As the group's interpreter, Amoore was assigned as the second in command of the Cherokee Mission, which was to operate in the Biella area north of Turin. This mission was led by another Intelligence Corps officer, Major Alastair Macdonald. The third member of the team was the demolitions and explosives expert Captain Jim Bell, and Sergeant Tony Birch was the wireless operator.

After parachute training, Amoore and his three colleagues were dropped to their target area on the night of 17 November 1944. Although Amoore survived his landing unharmed, it was not without some drama, as he described later in his report:

> Our drop was successful, though I landed in the middle of a pig-sty between two large pigs which climbed over the wall in their excitement; I had dropped fourth and last which accounted for my narrowly missing the roof of a farm-house situated outside ADSTONE DZ [Adstone drop zone] – this being achieved by pulling on the right-hand lift web which pushed me a yard to the right in time. DZ ADSTONE is not ideal for body-dropping being rather too small. All other members of the mission landed. The DZ was attacked two hours afterwards by the FASCIST garrison of CERRIONE but the thrust was beaten off.

The aim of the mission was to make contact with the 5th and 12th Garibaldi Divisions, which comprised about 3,000 men. They were concentrated around the Valle Mosso on the other side of Biella, which was heavily garrisoned. In order to avoid detection, Amoore and his companions had to make a long and circuitous journey at night. Having arrived safely at their destination, the mission's first responsibility was to organise the delivery of a vast cache of weapons, munitions and supplies for these ill-equipped partisans who, for the previous twelve months, had been forced to scavenge for whatever armaments were available.

A base would be required in order to receive the consignments. Although several sites were tried, they were mainly surrounded by mountains, which made approaching the area too difficult and dangerous. After chewing over the problem, the mission came up with an ingenious alternative solution. An approach was made to the sympathetic local municipal authority which agreed to announce a 'Winter Rescue' programme to provide free firewood for the local population and an appeal was put out for volunteers to cut the trees. In reality, this was a cover story. The 'volunteers' cleared the planned drop area and the German garrison was completely taken in by the ruse. On Boxing Day 1944, a daylight parachute drop from approximately twenty aircraft delivered the much-needed supplies. Indeed, it was the biggest such drop ever attempted during the Italian campaign. Explosives, fuses, detonators, light machine guns, anti-tank weapons, mortars, grenade-launchers, small arms and ammunition were all secured and were ultimately used to pose a serious threat to the Germans. Ironically, the quantity of supplies dropped was so great that organising sufficient transportation became difficult. This meant that many weapons had to be buried temporarily in a cemetery while distribution to the various partisan units could be arranged.

Even while waiting for the supply drop, the mission of which Amoore was a part did not lie idle, planning and eventually executing an attack using some of the imported explosives. The group's target was the railway bridge at Ivrea, 11 miles from Biella. The bridge was used by trains to transport steel from foundries at Cogne, in the Aosta Valley, and was considered strategically important. The mission's explosives expert, Captain Bell, identified the best positions for placing the charges, but the challenge was immense: the bridge was 250 yards long, it was heavily guarded at both ends and it faced the German headquarters building in the town. Despite these obstacles, volunteers from the partisans managed to plant devices resulting in an entire section of the bridge being demolished and falling into the river below. German efforts to repair the structure were in vain and it was not used again until after the war.

On 17 January 1945, Amoore was forced to assume command of the mission after Major Macdonald was captured. This followed an unauthorised attack by one of the partisan groups on a busload of German non-commissioned officers at Cerrione, in which every German was killed, leading to reprisals. The day after this act of sabotage, Macdonald was in the village of Magnano meeting partisan radio operators when the area was suddenly surrounded and swept by a unit of the Waffen-SS. In the ensuing attempt at flight, the radio operator was shot dead and Macdonald was picked up. Although he suffered a month of interrogation in Verona, he managed to escape to neutral Switzerland when he and his group of fellow prisoners were being force-marched from Italy to Germany.

At the time of Macdonald's capture, Amoore was at Lake Orta, undertaking one of several dangerous journeys he made alone to visit the Chrysler Mission of the American intelligence agency

known as the Office of Strategic Services (OSS). He remained unaware of the setback until the end of January, by which time the
Germans' arrest of known and suspected partisans was well under
way. Over the next few weeks, more than 10,000 fascist Russian
and German troops were drafted into the Biella area in an attempt
to annihilate the partisan resistance. On one occasion during this
period, Amoore showed brilliant quick thinking when visiting
a partisan safe house in the village of Sala Biellese, where a radio
transmitter was located. When the village was attacked by a unit of
enemy troops and search dogs, the radio operator and his companions fled with the transmitter to nearby woods. Amoore's instincts
led him to gather together some key documents and hide them in
a foul-smelling open latrine before making his own escape. The
ploy was successful: the dog-handlers, nauseated by the smell, only
made a cursory search before pulling the animals away.

Amoore remained in temporary command of the Cherokee Mission, having been promoted to temporary Captain, but he and his
team were constantly on the move, evading German search parties
by hiding in church crypts, ruins and partisan houses for a few
nights at a time before moving on to the next place of safety. On
one occasion, they hid in a well for five days. The winter conditions
in that area of northern Italy were dreadful, with deep snow ham-
pering efforts to travel during the day or night.

Once the German search offensive eased off, Amoore set about
establishing a new landing base to receive reinforcements and supplies. One of the first reinforcement officers to arrive was Major
Robert Redhead, who had been sent in to take over the Cherokee
Mission. Amoore's knowledge of the area and the people, and his
background in intelligence gathering, were of considerable help to
Redhead. Also sent in were teams of Polish officers whose role was

to induce desertion of the many Polish men who had been enlisted by force by the Germans. Once again, Amoore's previous experience of dealing with the Polish Army was put to good use.

By early April 1945, the Allied advance towards northern Italy was well progressed and the Germans were showing signs of withdrawal. The Cherokee Mission, and other similar missions operating in the north, was kept busy organising a renewed offensive among the increasingly disorganised enemy. On 24 April, Biella was liberated before any other northern Italian city and the Cherokee headquarters was moved to the Principe Hotel. As Major Redhead was posted away to other duties, Captain Amoore once again took command.

On 2 May, Amoore was staying as the guest of the famous racing driver Count Carlo Trossi at Gaglianico when he received an urgent summons to return to headquarters. On arrival, he found that the Chief of Staff of the German 75th Army Corps had been taken there under a white flag by a partisan escort bearing a letter signed by his Commander, General Ernst Schlemmer, offering unconditional surrender. It was explained that although the General had been in contact with the partisans of the Aosta Valley, he was reluctant to concede only to the partisan forces and would be reassured by a British involvement. Accordingly, Amoore drew up and signed the surrender document on behalf of the British Cherokee Mission. In excess of 100,000 German and fascist troops capitulated.

In June 1945, with the war in Europe over, Amoore left the SOE and was posted to the Allied Commission in Rome. For his services in Italy, he was awarded an immediate Military Cross, the citation of which noted his 'courage and initiative' as well as his 'great powers of leadership' and the fact that he was 'indefatigable, even during enemy drives, in the collection of information on enemy forces and intentions which was of great value to the Fifth Army in its advance'.

After the war, Amoore was also awarded the Italian Croce di Guerra al Valor Militare. Captain John Amoore MC lived in Paris after the war and died there on 1 April 1993, aged seventy-four. At his request, he was cremated and his ashes were scattered in the Biella area of Italy.

• • •

While John Amoore was forced to take temporary command of the mission in Italy on which he was engaged, another Intelligence Corps operator in the country, Kym Isolani, found himself in the extraordinary position of forming the first Italian military unit to take up arms against the occupying German forces – something he did before the Italian government declared war on its former Axis partner Germany in October 1943. This highly effective group became known as F Reconnaissance Squadron and, during much of the time it was operational, it was answerable ultimately to Isolani.

Casimiro Peter Hugh Tomasi Isolani (known as 'Kym') was born on 2 September 1917 in the Anglo-American Hospital near Milan. His father, Count Umberto Tommasi-Isolani, was an Italian infantry officer. His Cheshire-born mother, Georgina Smyth, was a wartime nurse who worked in Italy in a military hospital near the front. After the First World War, the family moved to England. Kym was educated at Aldenham School near Elstree in Hertfordshire and then went up to Clare College, Cambridge, to read modern and medieval languages, graduating with a first-class honours degree. In 1938, he and his father obtained naturalised British citizenship.

When war broke out in September 1939, Isolani was living with his parents at Bexhill in Sussex, where his mother taught Italian and offered translation services. He had completed his degree but was not yet working. He enlisted in the Royal Artillery and was posted as an assistant to the Brigadier in command of the artillery defences at the Admiralty Pier at Dover in Kent. The Brigadier soon recognised Isolani's potential, however, and recommended him for intelligence work. On 31 January 1941, he was commissioned as a Second Lieutenant in the Intelligence Corps.

Having attended the War Intelligence Course at the School of Intelligence at Matlock, he was attached to the headquarters of the 11th Battalion Staffordshire Regiment at Tiverton, Devon, and shortly afterwards he was posted as an Italian interpreter to 36 Prisoner of War Camp at Hartwell near Aylesbury in Buckinghamshire. Prior to going on active service, he married, in Oxford on 15 May 1943, Karin Zetterström, who was from Finland. After this, he was attached to HQ Combined Operations, where he concentrated on Axis order of battle and Sicilian beach defences in advance of the Allied landings in Sicily, part of Operation Husky.

Just before the Husky landings, Isolani was promoted to temporary Captain and, along with several other Corps officers, attached to the 1st Canadian Division with X-Interpreter and Interrogation Section going ashore with the first units to land. The landing craft carrying him to the beach at Pachino got stuck on a sandbank and was exposed to enemy fire, but he was fortunate because the beach defences in that area were lightly manned, and there were few casualties. On landing, he immediately took up duties in interrogation and reconnaissance work. He also had to change his identity and became known as 'Captain Arnold' due to the fact he had only relinquished his Italian citizenship a few years before and risked being shot if captured under his real name.

Ten days later, luck was not on Isolani's side when a Canadian vehicle swerved to avoid an aerial attack. He received ankle injuries in the subsequent crash and was evacuated to hospital in Tripoli for treatment. He managed to return to Italy in time for the mainland invasion, when he was again one of the first men ashore at Reggio di Calabria, and continued his interrogation duties with X-Section.

When the Italians surrendered on 8 September 1943, Captain Carlo Gay of the Italian Folgore Parachute Division took the decision not to follow his Company Commander in continuing to fight alongside the Germans. Instead, he and ten members of his unit went into the mountains of Calabria to await their chance to offer their services to the advancing Allies. The men harboured great resentment not only towards the Germans but also towards the corrupt fascist Italian authorities. They were dismayed by the poor leadership in their own Army. Their chance to fight with the Allies came when they were found by Isolani during one of his reconnaissance missions. During interrogation, they explained their position to Isolani, who quickly recognised the potential value represented by such a group behind the enemy lines. Having put his idea to Captain Sir Ian McLeod, a member of the Eighth Army Combined Services Interrogation Centre, he persuaded Army headquarters of his plans, and soon this small group formed the nucleus of the 1st Autonomous Italian Detachment.

Initially, Isolani put his Italian recruits through several test patrols behind enemy lines. Wearing civilian clothes, they were trained for intelligence-gathering missions and specific sabotage assignments. Eventually, with the cooperation of the Combined Services Detailed Interrogation Centre (CSDIC), Isolani recruited another 200 men, most of whom were prisoner-of-war paratroopers from the Folgore Division, and F Recce Squadron (the 'F' stood for Folgore) took flight.

The unit operated in small groups of two or three which would infiltrate behind the German lines, sometimes in plain clothes and other times in British uniforms. They also patrolled the Sangro region in central Italy. Isolani would escort the men through the Allied lines right up to the German front line, only returning when he was sure that the group had crossed over successfully. On one occasion when returning from an operation, his Jeep was attacked in error by a Mustang fighter of the US Air Force. Isolani later recalled: 'We played hide and seek around a prickly pear bush until the pilot eventually got bored and flew away.' As the unit grew in size and the value of its activities had been substantiated, it was taken under the wing of XIII Corps. By May 1944, F Squadron had undertaken 642 patrols in which eighty-nine Germans had been killed and 118 Germans had been captured. The contribution made by the unit was officially recognised at the end of the Italian campaign by the Corps Commander, General Harding, when he wrote: 'F Recce Squadron was the first Italian unit to take up arms against our common enemy and to show by its spirit and deeds that Italy would fight alongside the Allies to regain its liberty. You have written a bright page in the liberation of your country.' He added: 'Ours was a real brotherhood of arms … The men of 13 Corps will never forget you.'

In February 1944, Isolani handed over command of the unit to Lieutenant Alewyn Birch of the Royal Ulster Rifles, and to the previously mentioned Lieutenant John Amoore, and returned to England on leave. The following month, he returned to Italy having been attached to the Political Warfare Branch (PWB) as a

Press Officer. In May 1944, he was placed in charge of PWB's radio service 'Italia Combatte' and on 6 June he entered Rome with the liberation troops. From the Rome base of PWB, he broadcast to the partisans in northern Italy. The programmes were designed to boost morale and to pass instructions to partisan groups regarding targets for sabotage and the assassination of notorious SS officers.

In 1945, as the Allies progressed north, Isolani moved to Florence and it was from there that he broadcast the news of the German surrender in Italy. At the end of the war, Isolani was appointed head of the Allied Publications Board in Veneto before taking command of Civil Liaison with the task of reintegrating partisans into civilian life. On demobilisation in 1946, he was appointed an MBE and made an 'Honorary Partisan'. His MBE recommendation reads:

> Captain Isolani has been Editor-in-Chief of the broadcasting programme 'Italia Combatte', produced by PWB and directed to the patriots and residents in North Italy prior to liberation. He has carried out this work with remarkable efficiency and success, and his programmes have been listened to by large audiences, as has been verified since the liberation of North Italy. His work has been twofold – the development of the most effective method of conveying the wishes of the Allied Commanders to the patriots, and the strengthening of the patriots' resistance to the Germans and the maintaining of their morale. Captain Isolani's responsibilities have been great, and he has worked wholeheartedly and satisfactorily during the entire period for which he was in charge of 'Italia Combatte', i.e. since May 1944. Previous to that date he was a Press Officer in Italy for PWB.

Isolani later joined the Information Section of the British Embassy in Rome, where he was considered a first-class press attaché. He returned to London in 1961, was appointed a Member 4th Class of the Royal Victorian Order (later retitled as LVO) and took up the position of deputy director of the Institute for Strategic Studies. Two years later, he rejoined the Foreign Service with a nine-year posting as regional information officer at the British Embassy in Paris and in 1972 he moved to Brussels as counsellor at the British Embassy and to the UK Delegation to NATO. He was elevated to a Commander of the Order of the British Empire (CBE) in 1975. On retiring to his home in Pont Street in central London, he spent some years working for the United Nations University and was an active member of the Anglo-Italian Society. He was described in his *Daily Telegraph* obituary as a modest, retiring man, who had a Christian faith which deepened in his later years. Kym Isolani CBE LVO died in London on 10 September 2004. He was eighty-seven years old.

• • •

Kym Isolani was not the only Intelligence Corps man to spend part of the war working underground in Italy in an effort to defeat the Germans. Major John Henderson put his life in danger on several occasions when operating in similar conditions. For his bravery, he was decorated with a Military Cross. The Henderson medal group is part of the Lord Ashcroft collection, having been bought privately in March 2013. I feel privileged to be the custodian of this brave man's gallantry and service medals.

John Henderson was born on 17 July 1905 in Edinburgh, the son of John Henderson and Elizabeth (née Gadby). His father was a cable-tram driver in the Scottish capital who served briefly in the

Army Service Corps during the First World War before being discharged with a hand disability. John the younger had a twin sister, Elizabeth.

Before the outbreak of war, Henderson worked in Turin and spoke fluent Italian and French. He also knew some Spanish and Serbo-Croat. At the time of the 1939 Register, the national census compiled by the British government, he lived in a flat in Cambridge Street in Pimlico, central London, and described his occupation as 'interpreter'.

When war was declared, he enlisted and was initially detailed for the Corps of Military Police (Field Security). He served with a field security section during the Battle of France until the Dunkirk evacuation in the early summer of 1940 and transferred to the Intelligence Corps on its formation in July 1940. In April 1941, he was posted to serve with the newly created Persia and Iraq Force (PAI Force).

PAI Force came about as the result of the pro-British Iraqi government of Nuri al-Said being overthrown in a coup d'état on 1 April 1941 by the openly pro-German opposition politician Rashid Ali, aided by German intelligence and supported by the Mufti of Jerusalem. As Iraq was a major source of Britain's oil supplies, it was essential that this territory was kept out of German control. On 17 April, an Indian brigade was sent in and by 31 May it had occupied Baghdad and reinstated the former pro-British administration. A British garrison remained in the country until the end of the war. In August 1941, Persia was similarly occupied with no resistance. Thereafter, the Allied occupation forces in Persia and Iraq were known as PAI Force. Two field security sections – 266 and 401 – were deployed from Cairo to serve with the force and were based at Basra, in Iraq. On 1 November 1941, while still serving there,

Henderson was commissioned as a Second Lieutenant, acting Lieutenant, and appointed to the Combined Intelligence Centre Iraq (CICI), located at HQ PAI Force, as Field Security Officer of 266 and 401 FS Sections.

In 1943, Henderson was recruited into MO4, the Middle East branch of the Special Operations Executive (SOE), and was based in Cairo. In November and December 1943, he completed SOE training and in May 1944, after a spell with SOE Cairo, he was transferred to the SOE's Italy organisation, No. 1 Special Force. Initially, Henderson was earmarked for Operation Crayon, whose aim was to infiltrate an SOE team into Italian Slovenia, but this mission was cancelled. He was then designated for a similar mission, Operation Slumberland, but it, too, was cancelled. It was not long before he would be deployed, however.

On 13 June 1944, Henderson was dropped by parachute behind enemy lines in the Ancona area of northern Italy. The object of his mission was to coordinate the activities of an undercover patriot organisation which had been created by plain-clothes Italian officers with the support of the Allied armies. As the first British officer to appear in uniform among the Italian loyalists, Henderson successfully conveyed the directives of the Allied HQ to the loyalist leaders and then oversaw the sabotage and guerrilla activities which followed. According to the citation for the Military Cross which he was awarded for this mission, the subsequent action was 'recognised as having considerably assisted the advance of Allied armies on Ancona'. Once this task had been accomplished and before Allied troops finally overran the area, Henderson made his way back through the lines to report. Throughout this time, the citation read, he was in constant danger owing to enemy reprisals on the patriots as a result of which his HQ was continually on the move. His presence and his cool example were a source of constant encouragement to the patriots and were largely responsible for the courage and skill with which they executed all the tasks assigned to them.

Two months later, on 22 August 1944, Henderson reported to the Tactical Headquarters of No. 1 Special Force at Florence where another Intelligence Corps officer, Major Charles Macintosh, had been working with Italian partisans during the liberation of the city. Henderson took over Macintosh's duties until late October. Then, on 6 March 1945, he led a small SOE group parachuted into 'Drop Zone Doncaster' in the Spezia region, taking over as the British Liaison Officer to the partisans in that area. He also operated with the SOE's Blundell Violet mission in the Rossano Valley and Spezia areas in conjunction with Operation Blimey, the last SAS mission in north-west Italy before the war ended. Operation Blimey saw a team of twenty-four SAS paratroopers being dropped into the mountainous area of Chiesa Di Rossano on 6 April 1945. Their objective was to carry out hit-and-run raids against retreating German units and to assist hundreds of escaped prisoners of war back to their own lines. Most of Henderson's efforts, and those of his partisans, were devoted to constructing a mountaintop airstrip. However, the mission was overtaken by events on 25 April when American forces reached the area. Four days later, all German forces in Italy surrendered. Later that year, Henderson was awarded the Italian Partisan Medal.

In June 1945, Henderson was seconded as chief of the newly

created Venezia Giulia Police Force at its training school in Trieste and tasked with reorganising it under the Allied administration. He remained in this post for more than two years, finally leaving Italy in January 1948. Shortly before then, he was appointed an MBE and the award was gazetted on 1 January. The citation read:

> This officer has been with the Venezia Giulia Police Force since its inception in June 1945. He was a founder of the VGF Training School and at the present time the Commandant of the establishment through which all candidates must pass before entering into service. Also at this school he is responsible for the specialised education of aspirants to such police branches as Criminal Investigation, Fiscal, Mounted etc. Today the Force is within approximately 200 of its ceiling of 6,000 all ranks and the return of law and order to Zone 'A' – Venezia Giulia – where no Civil Police existed in 1945 – is proof of its effectiveness. This highly satisfactory state is due primarily to the masterly handling of indigenous police students by this officer whose devotion to duty has been outstanding at all times. In energy, resourcefulness, leadership and organising ability he is unsurpassed and these commendable qualities have gained him respect and confidence of all sections of the general public and all police recruits, irrespective of nationality and creed, who have passed through his hands.

After leaving the Army, he was employed as the secretary of Edinburgh Airport and he continued to live in the city. He was also a founding member of the Special Forces Club in London. Major John Henderson MBE MC died on Christmas Day 1982. He was cremated on 29 December and his ashes were scattered.

THE FAR EAST

The Pacific War began on 7 December 1941 with the surprise Japanese bombing of the American naval base at Pearl Harbor in Hawaii. Further strikes at Wake Island, Guam and in the Philippines brought America into the war. That month, Japan also invaded Thailand and the British colonies of Malaya and Burma and launched aerial attacks against Guam, Hong Kong, Shanghai, Singapore and Wake Island. The Japanese Empire's success during this period exceeded its wildest expectations. Between 1942 and 1945, there were four main theatres of war in the Far East: China; the central Pacific; south-east Asia; and the south-west Pacific. The war climaxed with Allied air raids over Japan and the atomic bombings of Hiroshima and Nagasaki together with the Soviet Union's declaration of war and invasion of Manchuria and other territories on 9 August 1945, causing Japan to announce its intent to surrender on 15 August 1945. It surrendered formally on 2 September 1945.

The occupation of Malaya by Japan was gradual. It began on 8 December 1941 and concluded when the Allies surrendered at Singapore on 15 February 1942. Although the Intelligence Corps had a presence in the region during this time, the extent of the Japanese attack meant that it was badly thrown off course and Malaya became a communications black spot. One man who did evade the Japanese successfully was Louis Cauvin, a young British civil servant who was recruited by the Secret Intelligence Service (SIS) and then commissioned into the Intelligence Corps. His story is one of endurance and resilience in the face of appalling conditions.

Louis Patrick Trevelyan Cauvin was born in 1915. Unusually, his place and date of birth were not logged on his service record.

His father, Lewis Patrick Cauvin, worked for the Eastern Telegraph Company, the head office of which was based at Electra
House in London, which, coincidentally, became the base of the
Political Warfare Executive in August 1941. The Eastern Telegraph
Company's existence was the result of the amalgamation of several other telegraph firms, each of which had been responsible
for laying submarine telegraph cables between Great Britain and
India. It had outstations in India, Aden, South Africa and Malta,
and Cauvin senior spent many years as a telegraph superintendent
abroad. Louis Cauvin had French, Scottish and Irish blood in his
veins. His great-great-grandfather served in the Royal Artillery
for twenty-one years; his grandfather served in the Army Service
Corps and married an Irishwoman while serving in Cork, where
his father was born. Cauvin's record is similarly bereft of any details
regarding his education. It is known that the Cauvin family lived in
Malta until 1924 when they returned to England.

On 8 October 1937, Cauvin embarked at the Port of London on
the SS *Rajputana* bound for Singapore. His occupation was recorded as 'Crown Agent' though he was in fact on his way to Malaya to
take up an appointment as an immigration official at Padang Besar
on the Malaya–Thailand border. After the war in Europe began
two years later, the threat of Japanese aggression in Asia grew,
leading the SIS station in Singapore to consider the possibility of a
Japanese invasion of the Malay Peninsula. It was thought that any
attack would come via Indo-China (modern-day Vietnam), where
the Japanese already had influence, or from Thailand. As this sense
of an imminent onslaught gathered pace, Cauvin was recruited by
Major Ernest Kumar Rosher of the SIS, who operated from Singapore, and from October 1940 he began to establish a network of
Sino-Thai agents whose counter-espionage missions he ran from

his border location into Thailand. From September 1941, when the Japanese invasion seemed near certain, the SIS set up a network of agents along the Malay–Thai border and provided them with radios to give advance warning of any Japanese movements.

When the Japanese invasion began on 8 December 1941, their 5th Division landed at Pattani and Songkhla on the eastern coast of Thailand, and their 18th Division landed on the north-eastern coast of Malaya, at Kota Bharu. Both wings of the invasion then streamed south, forcing the scattered British and Dominion troops to retreat. Cauvin headed to Kuala Lumpur and then on to Singapore. He contacted Major Rosher, who was by then hastily organising whatever intelligence-gathering networks he could cobble together at short notice.

Six months earlier, in June 1941, the Malayan Communist Party (MCP) had offered to provide recruits for the British Army in the event of a Japanese invasion of Malaya. At the time, this proposal had been rejected, but Japan's military strike down the Malay Peninsula prompted a re-examination of this decision and the Malayan Police Special Branch was told by the British authorities to begin negotiating with the MCP. Several meetings between the MCP, Special Branch and the SIS ensued and it was agreed that selected MCP members would be formed into 'Stay-Behind Parties' and employed in the Perak area for intelligence-gathering missions. Each group would be led by a European drawn from the various planters, estate managers, civil servants, engineers and police officers in Malaya who would be recruited into the SIS. These individuals would be granted an Army commission and trained and armed by the SOE's Orient Mission special training school – STS 101. Each group would be equipped with a radio and a trained Royal Signals radio operator. Even as the Japanese were advancing down the peninsula, the SIS took over the premises of the Chunjin School near Kuala Lumpur as a training base with supplies provided by STS 101. The responsibility for organisation and deployment of this force was given to Major Rosher.

From Rosher's point of view, Cauvin was an ideal candidate to lead a stay-behind party. He had already worked for the SIS, had experience of agent running and had knowledge of the jungle. Cauvin agreed to lead one of the groups and on 24 January 1942 he was commissioned as a Second Lieutenant, acting Captain, in the Intelligence Corps 'without pay and allowances from Army funds' and attached to SIS under its cover name of the Inter-Services Liaison Department (ISLD).

A few days of frantic preparation followed in which Cauvin gathered together the other British members of the team – three soldiers from the Royal Signals – plus a Chinese radio operator and his Malay personal assistant and interpreter. Twenty-five MCP guerrillas provided security and extra firepower. Radio equipment was obtained, though it was cumbersome, requiring a transmitter/ receiver, two large batteries, a two-stroke charging engine to re-power the batteries, plus petrol for the engine. Food supplies were also secured, including enough tinned and dried European fare to last six men for three months and sufficient Asiatic food for the twenty-five MCP recruits. Weapons and ammunition, cooking pots and utensils and other items necessary to sustain the group in the jungle were also obtained.

The object of the mission was to collect intelligence on Japanese strengths, dispositions, movements and equipment, and transmit this information back to Allied headquarters in Singapore. Cauvin's team was designated as 'Station A' and Singapore was 'Station B'. In the normal course of events, 'Station A' would keep in contact with

'Station B', but if Singapore fell, then 'Station A' would contact Java, in the Dutch East Indies, designated 'Station Y'. In the event that Java fell, the last resort would be to direct transmissions to Rangoon in Burma, designated 'Station R'.

By this point, the situation had deteriorated significantly. No other behind-the-lines radio was functioning and it appeared Cauvin's group would be the only link from Japanese-occupied Malaya if the enemy advance kept up. Having studied the possibilities, Cauvin selected as an operational base the jungle area around Gunung Belumut, a 3,300-foot mountain 15 miles east of Kluang. There, a perimeter could be set up and radio communication could be established with Singapore to monitor and report the progress of the Japanese as they advanced.

On 28 January, having received the latest available intelligence reports from Allied headquarters, Cauvin and his team loaded up their stores and drove the 20-odd miles to Kota Tinggi, north-east of Johor Bahru. There, they met the MCP recruits and unloaded the stores. The sheer quantity of equipment was too great for the group to transport alone, so local villagers were drafted in to help, yet their progress towards their intended base was slow and tortuous. They were hampered by ravenous insects and twice narrowly escaped capture when pro-Japanese Malays informed enemy patrols of the presence of Europeans in the jungle. They stuck religiously to the agreed signal plan and tried, unsuccessfully, to contact Station B in Singapore, with their repeated call-sign getting no response. They could, however, receive transmissions from other stations. They had the same result with Java and Rangoon. The upshot was that Cauvin and his men were unaware of Singapore's fall until after it occurred. The same applied when Java fell on 28 February.

By the end of March, the group had established a camp on the banks of a tributary of the Sungai Pengeli River. A reconnaissance party of the MCP reported back that their intended base location at Gunung Belumut was unsuitable thanks to precipitous slopes and an inadequate water supply, so the decision was taken to stay put for the duration of the mission. Through his MCP colleagues, Cauvin learned of the fall of Rangoon (Station R). With that event vanished any link to the outside world. He and his party were now effectively cut off, and the object of the mission was pointless. A senior MCP member suggested organising passage from Malaya to Sumatra with fishermen, but Cauvin dismissed this idea on the ground that the mission was not supposed to end until late April.

Months passed with no opportunity of getting a message to any of the Allied locations showing itself. The only chink of light came via the fact that they could receive transmissions from several worldwide broadcasting services and were able to keep up to date with the progress of the war. Gradually, the supplies of European food began to dwindle, however, and soon they had to live off the land, supplementing their diet of rice with lizards, snakes and on one occasion a monkey, which had an adverse effect on their stomachs. At no point were the men able to rest easy, either: the Japanese conducted regular anti-guerrilla sweeps through the jungle, forcing them to move camp to stay one step ahead of their foes. The effort of each move caused even more fatigue and hardship.

By November 1943, the MCP leadership suggested that the group move to their 4th Guerrilla headquarters at Tengkil, and it was there that they linked up with four British soldiers from the 6th Royal Norfolk Regiment, the last survivors of a group of British and Australians left behind when the Allies retreated to Singapore. The two groups stayed together at Tengkil until March 1944, when a surprise Japanese attack once again forced them into the jungle. Three times in a week they had to flee as the Japanese swept through the area. Each time, they took with them only what they could carry, and ended up with emergency rations of potato flour and some small dried fish. They hid their radio in the hope of being able to retrieve it at some future point.

On 12 April 1944, Cauvin announced a plan that he had been considering for some weeks. He and the four British soldiers from Tengkil – Brian Smith, Jim Wright, George Douglas and Fred Gooch – would strike out as a separate group in an attempt to reach north Malaya, where he had good contacts and where he hoped to be able to arrange some form of communication with the Allies. Meanwhile, his original Royal Signals team, under the command of Sergeant John Cross, would remain where they were. Cauvin and his newly formed unit set off into the jungle during the early hours of 17 April with weapons, some cash, basic rations, a medical kit, maps and a compass. Exactly three months later, on 17 July, Sergeant Cross received news that Cauvin was dead and that two of the four soldiers who had accompanied him had succumbed to a fever. It was only when the two surviving members of the breakaway group returned to the main party that the full story was disclosed.

On leaving the camp on 17 April, Cauvin and his companions had headed east, towards the Kota Tinggi to Mersing Road, about 12 miles away. They had expected to cover this distance in two days, but it took them six days. They then headed north, managing to scrounge food from villagers as they went, and by the first week in May they had reached Lubok Pusing. Three days later, they had reached a rubber estate at Kampong Kambau and met some Chinese workers. It was here that things began to go wrong. First, Smith came down with a bad attack of malaria and shortly afterwards Wright was hit by severe stomach cramps and vomiting. He was followed by Douglas, who was also laid low with a severe bout of malaria. Cauvin and the fourth soldier, Gooch, remained in acceptable health, although both were exhausted. They were all taken to an MCP camp and treated with whatever medicines the guerrillas had to hand. After three weeks, those who were ailing showed signs of at least partial recovery, but then disaster struck. Each of them, including Cauvin, came down with a mysterious fever similar to malaria but accompanied by stomach pains and severe bladder trouble. Cauvin was the first to be affected, on 28 May, followed by Douglas, who caught the bug on 12 June. Smith and Wright went down four days later. On 23 June, Douglas became unconscious and, although he was treated by a Chinese doctor, he died on 3 July and was buried in the jungle.

While Gooch remained extremely ill, Cauvin and the other two soldiers seemed to rally for a few days. On the evening of 12 July, however, Cauvin left the hut and did not return. After a while, Smith and Wright went to look for him but could not find him. The next morning, they resumed their search and found Cauvin's body in the undergrowth at the rear of the hut. He appeared to have severed the veins in his left wrist with his razor and bled to death. He was twenty-nine years old and had spent two and a half years in the jungle. He, too, was buried. Fred Gooch lingered on until 19 July, when he was overcome by the same strange fever and was also buried.

Before he died, Cauvin wrote a short note to Sergeant Cross. It read:

Dear Cross,

I am dying of an unknown fever as I write – a matter of minutes. Doug too has it bad and Fred. 'Big Jaw' [the doctor] has been splendid but arrived too late to help with obat [medicine] by a few hours. I am doped with Benzedrine in order to write this and get a few more hours. Thank you more than I can say, also the others and Liu.

Yours,

Cauvin

The surviving members of Cauvin's group remained in the jungle with the MCP, which had become the Malayan People's Anti-Japanese Army, until 31 May 1945, when they were finally extracted by HM Submarine *Thule*. Sergeant Cross was awarded the Distinguished Conduct Medal (DCM) and the other two Royal Signals members of the team received Military Medals. As Captain Louis Cauvin has no known grave, his name is commemorated on the Singapore Memorial to the Missing, Kranji, Singapore.

●　●　●

As the war in the Far East raged, signals intelligence proved essential to the British as they challenged the Japanese. In this, the Army was fortunate to have access to the well-organised mind of one extremely bright young Intelligence Corps operator, Alan Stripp. He served at Bletchley Park as a codebreaker before relocating to India and Burma where he helped to provide valuable signals intelligence about Japanese military operations. Remarkably, his work contains an element of mystery to this day.

Alan Albert Martyn Stripp was born in Battersea, south London, on 17 October 1924, the son of Alfred and Norah (née Martyn). His father, who had a BSc in mathematics from London University, was a teacher who was employed as assistant master at the Sir Walter St John's School in Battersea. During the First World War, he had served with the Royal Naval Volunteer Reserve as a telegraphist. In his spare time, he compiled crosswords for publications including *The Listener*, specialising in devising fiendishly difficult puzzles involving triple anagrams.

In 1942, Alan Stripp applied both to Exeter College, Oxford, and to Trinity College, Cambridge. He received no reply from the former but was awarded a scholarship to the latter, where he read Classics. At university, he became a member of the College Officer Training Corps. In the spring of 1943, an Army officer visited the college in search of potential recruits. Stripp's interview concentrated on questions about his linguistic ability, and he was able to confirm that he spoke French, Greek, Latin and some German. He was also asked whether he had any interest in playing chess, solving crosswords and music. Having described his father's work with crosswords, and his own ability to read a musical score, the officer's ears pricked up and he asked Stripp whether he wanted to be considered for a Japanese language course.

Two months later, when he was still only eighteen years old, Stripp was informed that he had been selected for a course beginning in August 1943 being run by 'Y-Service' at Bedford. The course instructor was Captain Oswald Tuck, a naval officer who had been brought out of retirement. He had taught himself Japanese forty years previously and persuaded the War Office that he could produce proficient Japanese speakers in six months or less, as opposed to the two to three years it usually took to master the language. Little about this intensive tuition programme was straightforward, however. As Stripp wrote forty-six years later in his book *Codebreaker in the Far East*, 'Japanese is not just a difficult language, it is totally different in form from most European languages and it suffers from being largely written in Chinese characters despite the difference between the languages.' The students had to learn at least 1,200 of these Chinese–Japanese characters and then put their newly acquired knowledge to use by embarking on some rudimentary codebreaking exercises.

By February 1944, Stripp and twelve of his fellow students were called up by the Army and placed in the Intelligence Corps. After military training at Wentworth Woodhouse, Stripp received his posting order to the Government Code and Cypher School at Bletchley Park. By this point of the war, its staff had been vastly increased so that alongside members of the three services worked mathematicians, linguists, physicists, philosophers, plus non-academics like chess players and crossword fanatics who happened to be gifted when it came to thinking laterally.

At Bletchley, Stripp joined Block F, the Japanese Military Section. It consisted of twenty young men, most of whom were also undergraduates, working on the Japanese Air Force code known as '6633', which was used over a wide area of operations. Code 6633 had been almost entirely broken before Stripp's arrival. His job was to translate from Japanese to English the signals that had already been decoded in order to assemble the most accurate picture available of squadron movements, equipment, fuel and ammunition stocks and maintenance problems. Although most of the codes originated from Japanese units in Burma, some came from further afield, including the Dutch East Indies and the Philippines.

By September 1944, Stripp, still only nineteen years old, had been promoted from Private to Sergeant. Soon afterwards, he was commissioned to Second Lieutenant and posted to India to join the Wireless Experimental Centre (WEC), which was located on an isolated hill called Anand Parbat, just outside Delhi. The WEC was the cover name for signals intelligence in India. It was concerned with monitoring Japanese targets in Burma and the occupied areas of south-east Asia. Stripp was assigned to Section C, which broke and translated the main Japanese Army and Air Force codes being used in Burma. Again, he focused on radio traffic transmitted in code 6633. By the time of his arrival, the WEC was intercepting about 2,000 signals every day. On occasion, Stripp and his Japanese-speaking colleagues from the WEC were also called upon to assist with the interrogation of Japanese prisoners of war being held at the Combined Detailed Interrogation Centre located at the Red Fort in Delhi. Although the CDIC interrogators were themselves Japanese speakers, they often required the more specialist technical vocabulary of signals and codes.

By late 1944, the tide of war in Burma had turned against the Japanese, with General Slim's 14th Army having made advances at Imphal and Kohima. From then, the Allies mission was to maintain momentum and inflict a decisive blow on the Japanese before the monsoon made further progress impossible. Advantageously to the Allies, the Japanese were weaker aerially. Not only were their aircraft outdated compared with newer Allied machines, their numbers had also fallen markedly, having been forced to withdraw squadrons from Burma to face American forces advancing through the Pacific islands towards Japan.

Against this background, the intelligence provided by Stripp's section was increasingly important. Through decrypts, it monitored and even predicted the movement of enemy forces around Burma, providing contemporary reports of Japanese unit strengths and positions. Understanding the status of the Japanese Air Force was essential to the planning of air and ground operations. Indeed, during this period Stripp's section produced indispensable intelligence showing that the Japanese were pulling back an entire air regiment. This, in turn, helped to determine the strategy of the Japanese to fight from behind the River Irrawaddy rather than in front of it, enabling Allied planners to revise their own strategy so that they struck the nerve centre of Japanese operations at Meiktila. This plan effectively led to Japanese defeat in Burma in May 1945.

That defeat was followed three months later by the atomic bombing of Hiroshima and Nagasaki. Then came the Japanese surrender. Yet Alan Stripp's Corps career did not end at that point. After taking his leave at a hill station in the foothills of the Himalayas, he was posted to the Indian Special Wireless School at Abbottabad in the North-West Frontier Province of India, later to become part of Pakistan and later still to gain notoriety as the last refuge of Osama bin Laden, the leader of the Islamist militant group al-Qaeda. Stripp's new posting required him to take a crash course in Farsi, the main language of Persia and Afghanistan, and then to monitor communications relating to a dispute between Russia and Persia about Azerbaijan. He also decoded Afghan traffic concerning the insurgency being conducted by the Faqir of Ipi. Stripp was also tasked with monitoring Afghan signals traffic because the language and coding were similar to Persian.

In late 1946, Stripp was posted to Singapore, to 800 Special Intelligence Unit, to learn Russian. Shortly after starting this course, however, orders for his release from the Army came through. He returned to academic life at Cambridge, changing subjects to read Japanese, classical Chinese and Far Eastern history. After graduating, he worked for ten years for the British Council in Indonesia and Portugal and then as an administrator for Cambridge University's Board of Extra Mural Studies, occasionally lecturing on cryptology. He married Mary Wadsworth in Oporto, Portugal, in 1949. In retirement, the couple lived at Linton, Cambridgeshire, where they organised an annual music festival. His book *Codebreaker in the Far East* was published in 1989. Four years later, he co-edited with Sir Harry Hinsley *Codebreakers: The Inside Story of Bletchley Park*.

In what might be regarded as a coda to his military career, Alan Stripp published a dramatic novel in 2001 called *The Code Snatch*. This contained a suitably cryptic clue concerning his work in the Far East during the war and debate as to the authenticity of its plot continues to this day. The book is set in Asia in 1944 and tells how intercepted signals suggest that the Japanese planned to change a long-established code for a new one. When the Allies learn of this, an audacious plan is concocted to secure the only two volumes of the new codebook in existence by sending a fake radio signal to a Japanese Intelligence Officer in Rangoon, swearing him to secrecy and ordering him to bring the two volumes to an aeroplane at Mingaladon airbase where a 'Japanese general' will be waiting to receive them. It is almost impossible for anybody to know whether this series of events really occurred. Stripp, however, claimed the novel was steeped in fact and, tantalisingly, while writing it in retirement, he did reveal to his wife for the first time since marrying her in 1949 that he had been flown behind Japanese lines in Burma.

Alan Stripp died at Linton, Cambridgeshire, on 18 February 2009. He was eighty-four years old.

●　　●　　●

Another Intelligence Corps officer who was active in the Far East was Rupert Turrall. Having already fought with distinction in the First World War, he was in his fifties when he did some of his most important – and daring – work on the ground in Burma towards the end of the Second World War, for which he was decorated. He was only 5ft 6in. tall, yet his physical strength and tough character – hewn over years working alone in hard conditions – were pivotal to his successful activities there and, by extension, to the British war effort. That he also risked his life serving with the Corps in Africa and in Crete before undertaking his duties in Asia makes him all the more remarkable.

Rupert Guy Turrall was born on 27 October 1893 at Great Torrington, north Devon, the son of William and Agnes Turrall (née Adams). His father was the headmaster of the local bluecoat school who, upon retirement, became a printer and bookseller. Rupert had two elder brothers, Richard and George, the latter of whom became an Engineering Lieutenant Commander in the Royal Navy. Rupert was educated at the Queen Elizabeth Grammar School in Crediton, Devon, and then went up to Cambridge University to read engineering.

In 1914, his studies were interrupted by the Great War. Having been a member of the University's Officer Training Corps, he was commissioned as a Second Lieutenant in the Royal Engineers on 29 October 1914. A year later, on 17 October 1915, he joined the British troops at Gallipoli. His arrival coincided with the campaign having descended into trench warfare following the debacle at Suvla Bay that August. After Turrall arrived, conditions worsened as the winter bit hard. Hundreds of men on both sides were gripped by severe frostbite and hundreds more froze to death. By the time the Gallipoli campaign ended in January 1916, many units had been transferred to the Balkan theatre of operations in Macedonia to fight the Bulgarians, who had entered the war on Germany's side. Turrall fought with 127th Field Company, Royal Engineers of the 22nd Division. For his service in the Balkan campaign, he was twice Mentioned in Despatches, in 1917 and in 1919. He reached the rank of Captain.

After the war, he completed his degree at London University, graduating with a BSc in engineering, and then went up to Trinity College, Cambridge, to read for his master's in astronomy and geology. His professional interests allowed him to travel far and wide. In 1920, he was involved in desert exploration around Haifa and Baghdad. Between 1920 and 1924, he worked as a reconnaissance geologist exploring for mineral deposits in British Somaliland – a period interspersed with his studying exploration geophysics at Potsdam and The Hague under Dr Wilhelm Schweydar. Between 1924 and 1925, he worked in the United States carrying out subsurface exploration for the oil industry in Texas, Louisiana and Oklahoma. Thereafter, he took on professional assignments in Greece, Serbia, Hungary, Venezuela and, between 1934 and 1937, Kenya and Tanganyika (present-day Tanzania), where he became involved in gold exploration. As a result of these varied experiences, he acquired a reputation for being immune to the hardships of the desert and the wilderness and was nicknamed 'Tough Tim Turrall'. He was made a fellow of the Royal Geographical Society in 1921. On 31 March 1930, he married Eily Nadine Bolton in Kingston, Jamaica. She was the daughter of British parents, was educated in England and returned to Jamaica as a qualified music teacher. They had a son, William, in 1932, who died in 1962, and a daughter, Phoebe Ann, born in 1939.

In April 1939, with the clouds of war gathering, the War Office offered Turrall a post as an Intelligence Officer. By then, he was living in Kent and, although he accepted, he was not called forward until 24 October 1940, when he was commissioned as a Second Lieutenant in the Intelligence Corps. The following month, he was appointed as an Intelligence Officer in Middle East Command, taking up this post on 15 November. On 8 January 1941, he was attached to the 2nd Brigade, Sudan Defence Force (SDF), under the command of the brilliant but eccentric Lieutenant Colonel Orde Wingate, who had been charged with the defeat of the Italian occupation forces in Abyssinia (modern-day Ethiopia) and the restoration of Emperor Haile Selassie. There was doubtless a sound reason for Turrall's attachment to Wingate's elite Gideon Force. During Turrall's time in British Somaliland in the early 1920s, he had undertaken a 2,700-mile trek around the Abyssinian frontier and become an expert in the topography of the area. For the duration of this successful Middle East campaign, he served with the Frontier Battalion under Colonel Hugh Boustead. Using a combination of conventional forces and irregular guerrilla units, about 1,700 men of the SDF fought some 20,000 Italians to a standstill and then surrender. Turrall was involved at the sharp end of the fighting, receiving a head wound in action. He was awarded the Military Cross in July 1941. The citation read:

Lt R Turrall, Frontier Battalion, Sudan Defence Force, Sudan, July 1941. During the night 25/26.3.41, Lt Turrall carried out a mortar attack on the South flank of the strong enemy positions covering Debra Marcos, later withdrawing his force across the enemy's flank to the North of their position. These operations lasted the whole night and it was learnt that considerable casualties had been inflicted on the enemy as a result of them. On 28 March Lt Turrall took up a position on the Northern flank of the same defences and successfully bombed them with the three-inch mortar inflicting a large number of casualties. On the night of 31 March/1 April, Lt Turrall, in conjunction with El Bimbashi [Major]

MacDonald, carried out a night bombing attack with hand bombs on the rear of these same defences. El Bimbashi MacDonald was killed while only five yards from the enemy position and Lt Turrall took charge of the operations and at their conclusion, himself with two NCOs carried back El Bimbashi MacDonald's body a distance of some five miles in the dark. These operations were carried out in pouring rain and a high wind under the most trying conditions. As a result of these night and day attacks in all of which Lt Turrall displayed coolness, resolution and courage, the enemy were forced to hasten their withdrawal from the strong covering positions West of Debra Marcos and lost a large number of killed and wounded.

At the conclusion of the Abyssinian campaign, Turrall was posted to special duties and attached to G(R) Branch, one of the cover titles for the Special Operations Executive in the Middle East. In December 1941, he became part of the seven-man team run by Captain Xan Fielding of the Intelligence Corps which landed in Crete from HM Submarine *Torbay*. Turrall was the sabotage and explosives expert. The mission was to disrupt enemy ships docked in Souda Harbour and other targets in the Rethymno and Chania areas. Fielding later described Turrall thus:

His small, sinewy body was hard and knotted after a lifetime spent in the more remote parts of Central Africa and South America. So, in many respects, was his mind. Years of comparative solitude in the wilds had made him scornful of most forms of urban civilisation but had developed in him qualities essential for the mission which he was about to undertake: sabotage of enemy shipping in Souda harbour.

The team was put ashore at Soutsouro Beach, on the southern coast of the island. One member of the Cretan resistance who assisted them, George Psychoundakis, later recalled: '[Turrall] the sabotage officer carried with him many and strange explosives … there must have been six loads of various types of very high-powered explosives, magnetic ones with time fuses and delays, etc., also two rubber boats.' Psychoundakis also recalled that Turrall had a rucksack full of physio-geological books which he studied 'all day long'. The explosives were hidden in a mountain cave while the mission details were planned, but the enterprise was eventually overtaken by events when the Germans mounted a protracted counter-guerrilla operation in that area. In any case, Turrall disagreed with the sabotage policy in Crete, believing such missions to be highly risky and difficult to justify given the inevitability of German reprisals against the Cretan population. Three months later, on 15 April 1942, Turrall was recalled to Egypt and posted back to the Frontier Battalion of the Sudan Defence Force.

In January 1944, he was posted to India to rejoin Orde Wingate, who would run the behind-the-lines Chindit operations into Japanese-occupied Burma until his death in a plane crash in March 1944. Initially, Turrall was appointed as the Operations Staff Officer, but he also took part in deep-penetration patrols with XVI Brigade in the north Burma area. In September 1944, after a brief period commanding the Hong Kong Volunteers, he was selected for service with Force 136 – the SOE's cover name for Burma and Far Eastern operations. By this point, having turned fifty-one, Turrall was placed in command of the 'Hyena' area for Operation Character. With Japanese forces in Burma on the back foot, Character was the umbrella codename for the British and Allied special missions run by Force 136 to recruit, organise, support and lead groups of

Burmese guerrilla fighters in the Karenni region of central Burma in support of General Slim's 14th Army offensive.

Character was divided into three zones – north, central and south – into which a Special Group was inserted by parachute. Each group, with its own codename, consisted of a British officer, a British radio operator and about twenty specially trained Burmese guerrilla fighters. They were to provide intelligence of Japanese positions; harass retreating enemy units when instructed to do so; keep surveillance on the roads and railways running south; and be prepared to oppose Japanese reinforcements coming up from the south or their forces moving down from north and central regions.

On 20 February 1945, Turrall led the 'blind' parachute drop of the first wave of his team into the jungle in the southern zone of operations, named 'Hyena', near Pyagawpu. On the second night, he was standing by to receive the second wave led by Captain Duncan Guthrie, but Guthrie had a bad landing and broke both ankles, forcing Turrall to delay in the area while finding a suitable hiding place for him while Japanese units closed in on their location. Guthrie was eventually carried to safety by elephant. On 15 April, after two months of recruiting and training, Turrall led an attack against a Japanese Kempeitai base at Kyaukkyi in the Sittang Valley. The surprise attack on these notoriously brutal Military Police was successful, but during it, Turrall was wounded by grenade splinters. Despite this, he still led his group into the Karen Hills to continue recruiting and training. In subsequent operations east of Kyaukkyi, he and his guerrillas killed over 500 Japanese fighters and provided intelligence which led to air and artillery strikes resulting in the killing of several hundred more. Further detail is provided by the citation for his award of the Distinguished Service Order (DSO), which was gazetted on 7 November 1946:

This officer who, at the age of 54 [note: he was in fact fifty-two], commanded the original 'blind' parachute jump of Force 136 personnel to Pyagawpu (QB 63) on 25.2.45, organised the reception of Operations OTTER and FERRET a few nights later in spite of Japanese forces having arrived from in the area from Papun. He also organised and trained several hundred Levies who eventually became the hard core of Operation HYENA. On 15.4.45, he personally led the successful attack on Kyaukkyi which resulted in enemy supplies, spare arms and a W/T set being destroyed. Later, he operated in the area East of Kyaukkyi and with his Levies killed over 500 Japanese and gave intelligence for air strikes and artillery which resulted in 924 estimated enemy casualties. For his outstanding powers of leadership and great gallantry shown on numerous occasions I recommend very strongly that this officer be awarded the Distinguished Service Order.

Signed, Maj R de L King OC Tac HQ Force 136.

Despite the enormous success of Turrall's bravery, and that of those who operated with him, a further test of his physical and mental courage lay in store. On 15 August 1945, when the Japanese Emperor Hirohito announced the unconditional surrender of all Japanese forces, Turrall was still in the Burmese jungle where the isolated Japanese units were fighting, despite thousands of leaflets having been dropped to inform them that the war was over. After learning of the surrender, Force 136 broadcast an order to all guerrilla groups in the jungle forbidding any contact with the Japanese troops, but a communication failure meant that Turrall remained ignorant of the order. The following day, accompanied by one of his Karen guerrillas, he walked into the nearest Japanese headquarters to tell them that hostilities had ended. The Japanese either didn't believe or didn't *want* to believe that they had been defeated. Turrall was seized as a prisoner and beaten up and his Karen companion shot in the back. Turrall remained in captivity for a week before escaping, but he was soon recaptured and forced to march south for two days. Eventually, another airdrop of leaflets convinced the Japanese that their war was over, and Turrall was abandoned alone deep in the jungle. Showing his trademark tenacity, however, he found his way back to his own group.

Assessments made by the SOE at the end of the Burmese campaign calculated that Operation Character killed more than 10,000 Japanese troops, wounded another 600 and took eighteen prisoners. Many more were killed and wounded by the airstrikes called in by the Character agents on the ground. Turrall's contribution to this military success was immense. General Slim, who commanded the 14th Army, later explained the effect of men like Turrall:

Our own levies led by their British officers were a most valuable asset and had a real influence on operations. They were tactically controlled by wireless from Army Headquarters, told when to rise, the objectives they should attack, and given specific tasks. They could not and were not expected to stand up to the Japanese in pitched battles, but they could and did in places harry them unmercifully. Their greatest achievement was the delaying of the 15th Japanese Division on the Loikaw-Mawchi area, thus enabling IV Corps to reach Toungoo first, but they have rendered almost equally valuable services. They had an excellent jitter effect on the Japanese, who were compelled to lock up troops to guard against attacks on the lines of communication.

After the war, Turrall became involved in the ill-fated Tanganyika

Groundnut Scheme, working as a water-diviner in territory he knew well from his time there in the 1930s. The scheme was the brainchild of the post-war Labour government of Clement Attlee and was overseen for a time by the United Africa Company. The aim was to grow peanut crops on 150,000 acres of land for the production of peanut oil which, after the war, was in short supply in Britain. After much exploration and the outlay of a considerable amount of money, however, the project was found to be unworkable and was abandoned.

Rupert Guy Turrall DSO MC died on 22 January 1988 at his home in Holland Park, London. He was ninety-four years old. His wife died in June 1999, aged ninety-six.

• • •

As previously noted, when the Intelligence Corps was founded initially in 1914 under the stewardship of Major T. G. Torrie, it drew its operators from many areas of life, including the Metropolitan Police. During the Second World War, the Corps continued to recruit from some of the same sources, and it was most likely via this route that a Yorkshireman, William Lambert, came to serve in it. His poignant story, which covers the tail end of the conflict, in many ways shows the utter futility of war. Lambert's is the last account of the Intelligence Corps men connected with the Second World War. Like so many others who were called to do their duty, his courage and cheerfulness in the face of sheer horror stand out.

William Lancaster Lambert was born on 19 April 1911 at Sculcoates, near Hull, the son of Joseph Patterson Lambert, a locomotive fitter, and Annie May Lancaster. After finishing school, he found employment as a farm worker, but in February 1930, he enlisted as a gunner in the Royal Artillery on a three-year engagement and served as a signaller, initially with the Royal Horse Artillery, and then with 16th Field Brigade. On being discharged to the Army Reserve, his final report described him as 'a clean, honest, sober, hardworking man – a good signaller who could be trusted to work without supervision'.

In September 1933, he applied to join the Metropolitan Police and New Scotland Yard requested details from his Army service from the Royal Artillery Records Office. Whether his application was successful is not recorded. The following year, he married Florence Youll at York, where they lived. They had two children, Walter and Patricia.

On 5 December 1938, still being liable for Reserve Service, he requested permission from the Army to leave the United Kingdom, having been appointed as a police constable with the Palestine Police Force. Permission was granted and he embarked for Palestine on the SS *Ranchi* on 16 December 1938. The Palestine Police Force was a colonial police force established in 1920 when Britain acquired the mandate to administer Palestine from Ottoman Turkey at the end of the First World War. On its formation, it consisted of a hard core of twenty British officers, fifty Palestinian officers and just over 1,000 Palestinian policemen. The greatest challenge faced by the force lay in the Palestinian population's resentment of Jewish immigration and land purchase, and similar antipathy towards British rule. Tensions grew and in 1936 the Arab Revolt took hold. This nationalist uprising, in which thousands died, lasted for three years. More than 50,000 British troops had to be deployed in the country to support the police.

In early 1941, Lambert's service in Palestine came to an end. His return to England made him liable for his Army Reserve Service.

He was mobilised on 19 March and posted to 2nd Reserve Field Regiment in the rank of gunner. On 21 November 1941, he was transferred to the Intelligence Corps. It is likely that his years in the police marked him out as a suitable candidate for field security duties. Having completed his basic field security training, he was promoted to Lance Corporal and posted to the newly formed seven-man 78 Field Security Section at Winchester. Those records that survive suggest that the section was initially earmarked for service in North Africa, with the language specialisations among its members being German, French and Arabic.

In December 1941, 78 FSS was sent to Gourock in Scotland and dispersed on two troopships, *Empress of Australia* and *Warwick Castle*. Their destination was eventually revealed as Java, in the Dutch East Indies (DEI). The Japanese invasion of Malaya and Hong Kong on 8 December prompted the military planners to forecast that the DEI could well be next. On 4 February 1942, just eleven days before the fall of Singapore, the ships docked at Tandjong Priok, the port of the Javanese capital, Batavia (modern-day Jakarta), where they were attached to the Military Police.

At that time, British forces in Java consisted of about 5,000 troops under the command of a British Major General, who was subordinate to the Commander of the 20,000-strong Royal Netherlands East Indies Army, whose troops were generally regarded as ill-trained and poorly organised. Although the British and Dutch had some advanced warning that the Japanese invasion force were about to arrive, their assault was rapid and the result was inevitable. The enemy landed on two fronts on 1 March 1942, from the north and the west, and quickly overran the defenders. On the morning of 8 March, the Dutch Commander-in-Chief announced the surrender of all Allied troops.

Captain George Bruce ran from Paris an underground espionage ring which operated behind enemy lines in 1917–18. Among Bruce's network of agents was a middle-aged housewife, Madame Rischard, and an adventurer, Baschwitz Meau. Bruce took his secrets to the grave.

CAPTAIN BRUCE A.P.M.
AMIENS

Mabel Peel was posted to France with the Women's Army Auxiliary Corps in 1917 and later affiliated to the Intelligence Corps, becoming one of Britain's first female codebreakers. After the war, she dedicated her life to helping veterans.

David Henderson became Director of Military Intelligence in 1901, during the Boer War. As an authority on tactical intelligence, he tried to persuade the British Army of the need for an Intelligence Corps, though none would exist until August 1914.

In 1940, Antony Coulthard, a brilliant linguist, was incarcerated in Stalag XXA near Warsaw, where he was known as 'The Professor'. In 1942, he and Frederick Foster escaped and travelled 900 miles to the Swiss border, collecting intelligence on the Nazis along the way. Their bid for freedom was more than a year in the planning and is considered one of the most thrilling escapes of the Second World War.

Dignus Kragt, a fluent Dutch speaker, was commissioned into the Intelligence Corps in 1943 and attached to MI9, helping to set up and maintain escape routes from Holland to neutral territories. Kragt's own covert assignment to Holland was overseen by Airey Neave, the future Conservative MP.

In June 1940, Captain Norman Hope ran a top-secret operation to rescue from France the family of Brigadier-General Charles de Gaulle. A Mark 1 Supermarine Walrus amphibious biplane was chosen for the task. After it crashed in mysterious circumstances, four bodies were recovered. Although rescuers found identity details for the three crew members, Hope carried no papers and was initially registered by a cemetery in Ploudaniel as 'Aviateur X'.

ABOVE LEFT John Haselden, a businessman, epitomised the idea of the 'gifted amateur' non-professional soldier. He helped to organise the daring but unsuccessful assassination attempt on Hitler's close friend General Erwin Rommel, the Afrika Korps Commander, and often spent days in the desert disguised as a nomad in order to monitor Axis troop movements.

ABOVE RIGHT Julius Hanau, who worked undercover for British intelligence in Yugoslavia for many years. He ended up on a Gestapo hit list. Communications to him were sent via the British Legation and addressed to 'Major Hanau', with an inner envelope marked for 'MZ/4', his code number. As a further precaution, a separate letter would accompany each envelope, asking Hanau to pass the letter on to 'MZ/4' so he could pretend he was acting as a conduit. He was commissioned into the Corps in September 1941 and later carried out secret work in Africa.

John Makower, a businessman, was transferred to the Corps in 1940, aged thirty-seven. He served in the Western Desert for fifteen months in the most testing conditions and had command of the Intelligence Section attached to 101 Special Wireless Section. He was awarded the Military Cross in 1943. Terence Cuneo later produced this painting depicting Makower's activities in the desert. It hangs in the Officers' Mess at Chicksands.

SOURCE: HQ INTELLIGENCE CORPS

Paddy Leigh Fermor (*right*) remains one of the Corps' best-known operators thanks to his exploits in Crete in 1944, when he was involved in kidnapping General Heinrich Kreipe (*centre*). Leigh Fermor later modestly called the mission 'a symbolic gesture, involving no bloodshed, not even a plane sabotaged or a petrol dump blown up; something that would hit the enemy hard', yet it was at the least a major propaganda coup.

Philip Chamier, known as Frank, a half-German Intelligence Corps officer who in 1944 became the first MI6 agent to be dropped into Germany. To this day, the true details of his death are unknown or have not been placed on available record. There is a possibility that a cover-up has taken place.

Rupert Turrall operated in the Far East during the Second World War, when he was in his fifties, having already fought with distinction in the First World War. Some of his most daring work was done on the ground in Burma. He was only 5ft 6in. tall, yet his physical strength and tough character were pivotal to his success. Remarkably, he also risked his life serving with the Corps in Africa and in Crete.

ABOVE LEFT Theodoros Pantcheff (*left*) was commissioned as a Second Lieutenant in the Intelligence Corps in March 1942. He was trained as an interrogator and later recruited by MI19 to collect intelligence from prisoners of war. Pantcheff was also involved in the investigation of the Emsland Massacre and its perpetrator, Willi Herold (*right*), who, aged nineteen, became known as 'The Executioner of Emsland'.

SOURCE: RICHARD PANTCHEFF

ABOVE RIGHT Sergeant Norman Turgel of the Intelligence Corps, who interrogated Nazi criminals at the end of the war, and his bride Gena, whom he met and fell in love with during the liberation of Belsen, where Gena was a prisoner. Her wedding dress was made of British parachute silk.

Captain Lionel Savery (*left*) risked death working as an Intelligence Officer in Malaya and Cyprus in the 1950s. In Cyprus, he became a target of the EOKA terror campaign, led by Georgios Grivas, prompting Savery to hire as his driver and bodyguard a Turkish butcher who was 'fearsome' with a knife. Savery always carried a gun and grenades and also changed his car once a week. Among his quarry was Grigoris Afxentiou.

PRIVATE COLLECTION

The Greek military coup in Cyprus in 1974 threatened British interests. Thanks to an agent recruited and handled by Intelligence Corps operator John Condon, who was based on the island, the Army had some advance warning of the impending crisis.

LEFT AND BELOW

During the Cold War, it was not unusual for western military figures to be involved in traffic 'accidents'. In 1976, Sergeant Bob Thomas of the Intelligence Corps was in this Opel Admiral car when it was rammed by an East German URAL-375 truck. He later endured a botched operation on his injuries by East German surgeons and a disturbing sixteen-day stay in hospital before returning to the British Commanders'-in-Chief Mission to the Soviet Forces in Germany (BRIXMIS).

PRIVATE COLLECTION

ABOVE LEFT The Soviet Mission to the British was known as SOXMIS. British military and civilian personnel were required to carry sighting cards and report suspicious activity involving vehicles with a SOXMIS number plate.

© MILITARY INTELLIGENCE MUSEUM

ABOVE RIGHT Staff Sergeant Graeme Davis was sent to the former British colony of Belize in 1977, when the Army maintained a presence there to act as a deterrent against aggression from Guatemala. His experiences illustrate how unusual and varied the roles of some Intelligence Corps members have been in out-of-area operations, requiring improvisation and the ability to work in isolation.

PRIVATE COLLECTION

The ingenious 'Four Square Laundry' played a key role in intelligence-gathering in Republican West Belfast. Operators posed as the members of a fictional laundry firm. Once collected, dirty clothes and linen were subjected to forensic testing for explosives and weapons residues before being washed and given back to customers. The laundry van was fitted with surveillance equipment and there was space in a false roof compartment enabling undercover soldiers to take photographs of targets. The operation was compromised in 1972.

Interrogation in warfare is the oldest method of gaining strategic and tactical information from the enemy and has always been a key Intelligence Corps skill. During the Falklands War, Corps operator Nick van der Bijl (*left*) used his training to great effect when interrogating Argentine prisoners.

PRIVATE COLLECTION

ABOVE In the 1990s, the Intelligence Corps was involved in assisting with stability operations in Bosnia. The quick thinking of one Corps officer helped to expose an Islamist terrorist training camp in a ski chalet. Booby-trapped toys and weapons seized during the raid showed that students of this guerrilla warfare training school were prepared to inflict horrors on civilians and children.

PRIVATE COLLECTION

LEFT Corporal Sarah Bryant, who died on 17 June 2008, was the first British servicewoman to be killed during the war in Afghanistan. Her husband, Carl Bryant, says, 'Sarah was a good intelligence operator, but fundamentally she could hold her own with anybody in the field. One of her greatest joys on an earlier tour was going on patrol and engaging with local people; she was particularly interested in female engagement.'

When word of the imminent invasion reached 78 FSS, the Commanding Officer, Captain D. P. Glasgow, advised the unit that it was 'every man for himself' and said there might be a means of escape by ship from Tjilitjap, on the south coast. Yet no ship was found and all seven members of the section were captured. After they had been disarmed, they were grouped together with other British and Dutch personnel and sent by train to Tandjong Priok. There, they were held in a camp formerly occupied by native troops which was under the command of a Colonel Nagawo. On 22 September, Lambert was one of a group of prisoners shipped to Singapore and incarcerated in Changi jail for three weeks. From there, they were put on another ship and taken to the Batu Lintang prison camp at Kuching, Sarawak, on the island of Borneo. This camp was commanded by a Colonel Tatsuji Suga.

Bill Lambert, who came to be known as 'Palestine Billy', was held in great esteem by his fellow prisoners and widely admired as a man of integrity, invention and ingenuity. On one occasion, he was even asked to exercise his policing skills by investigating the disappearance of the prisoners' payroll, swiftly finding the culprit. The private memoir of one prisoner recorded that Lambert had an impressive Victorian-style moustache that he would methodically twirl between his fingers when deep in thought. Occasionally, he would disappear from the camp at night and return just as dawn was breaking, sometimes with a chicken or some eggs, but always with something that would be of use.

As he was minded to come and go at will, other members of the camp began to rely on his sheer courage and he was placed in charge of the 'Old Lady', a radio that had been painstakingly – and illicitly – built by some prisoners. The Old Lady was the most treasured possession in the camp, providing some measure of diversion as well as enabling inmates to keep track of the world outside and the progress of the war. Its discovery by the Japanese would have meant death to those who had built it and who were responsible for it. Thanks to Lambert's resourcefulness, however, the radio remained undetected.

In common with all Japanese prisoner-of-war camps, Batu Lintang was unimaginably harsh. The guards were vicious, there was little to eat, the sanitation was appalling and there were almost no medical supplies to treat the many diseases that were prevalent or the injuries caused by slave labour in the work parties. Being in such a place was nothing more than a sustained assault on a person's mind and body. Having to survive on less than a cup of rice each day meant that malnutrition soon took hold, leading to malaria, dysentery and tropical ulcers. It has been estimated that the Japanese captured almost 140,000 Allied military personnel during the war, more than 30,000 of whom died from starvation, disease and torture.

On 17 May 1945, Lambert collapsed and was taken to the camp hospital suffering from exhaustion and general prostration. He clung on for three months but eventually succumbed due to lack of proper medical attention. Tragically, he died at 8.45 a.m. on 19 August 1945 – four days after the surrender of the Japanese but shortly before the camp was liberated by Australian troops, on 11 September 1945. When the camp records were searched, two 'death orders' were found. They described in detail the Japanese plan to execute every prisoner before the Allies arrived. The first order was scheduled to be carried out in August but had not been completed. The second order was scheduled for 15 September – four days after the Australians arrived.

Agnes Newton Keith, an American author who was held as a civilian internee at Batu Lintang camp for more than two years, published an account of her experiences in 1947 called *Three Came*

Home, which was made into a film of the same name in 1950. Keith was able to identify the individual who was responsible for so much of the barbarity which Bill Lambert and thousands of others suffered. 'At Sandakan and Ranau and Brunei, North Borneo, batches of prisoners in fifties and sixties were marched out to dig their own graves, then shot or bayoneted and pushed into the graves, many before they were dead,' she wrote.

> All over Borneo hundreds and thousands of sick, weak, weary prisoners were marched on roads and paths until they fell from exhaustion, when their heads were beaten in with rifle butts and shovels, and split open with swords, and they were left to rot unburied. On one march, 2,790 PoWs started, and three survived … For these black chapters in captivity Colonel Suga, commander in Borneo, must be held responsible.

On 12 September 1945, Suga was arrested at the camp and, with his officers, flown to Labuan, Borneo Island, to await trial on charges of war crimes. On 16 September, before he was brought to trial, Suga committed suicide. His officers were later tried, convicted and executed.

Lance Corporal William 'Palestine Billy' Lambert was thirty-four years old when he died. He is buried at Labuan War Cemetery in Malaysia.

POST-WWII WAR CRIMES INVESTIGATION IN GERMANY

Reports of the Nazi persecution of Jews and rumours of labour camps trickled out of Germany and Austria from the 1930s, when refugees began fleeing for Britain and America. It was not until the final phase of the war, however, that the full extent of the barbarism became clear. Death camps were discovered at Belsen, Auschwitz, Buchenwald, Dachau and elsewhere. Often, the retreating Nazis tried to cover up their crimes, but given 6 million Jews were murdered in Europe between 1941 and 1945, killing on such a scale was too vast to hide. Some senior Nazis tried to disguise themselves by dressing as ordinary soldiers, while others went into hiding or escaped to South America. All the while, more war crimes came to light. When the prisoner-of-war camps were liberated, stories also emerged of the massacres of surrendered Allied soldiers – shot out of hand by German troops, mostly by the SS. Two such incidents involved British soldiers during the Battle of France in 1940. In both cases, a few men survived, despite having been left for dead and sent to prisoner-of-war camps. They were witnesses in the post-war hunt for those responsible. Those members of the Intelligence Corps in the front line of the Allied advance were the men of the field security sections and were among the first troops into the concentration camps as they were discovered. Following Germany's surrender in May 1945, the arrest and detention of known and suspected war criminals became the Corps' first priority and the field security sections, aided by the Intelligence Corps interrogators and collators of the newly formed War Crimes Investigation Unit, led the way. Most field security sections in Germany had access to 'CROWCASS' – the Central Registry of War Criminals and Security Suspects, set up by the Americans and British – and many arrests were made using this directory. The following stories outline just a few of their successes.

On 15 April 1945, 317 (Airborne) Field Security Section was among the leading units to arrive at the Bergen-Belsen concentration camp, about 25 miles north of Hanover. Some 60,000 inmates were discovered there, all severely malnourished, chronically ill and having been subjected to long-term physical and mental abuse. Additionally, more than 13,000 unburied corpses were scattered about. Disease ran rampant. The camp commandant, SS-Hauptsturmführer Josef Kramer, was still in place along with several of his staff, but most of the guard force had long since deserted. It is said that Kramer was quite unashamed of the camp and happily took the British officers on a tour of it to explain how it operated. Having joined the Nazi Party in 1931, and the SS the following year, Kramer had been a camp guard at Dachau, Sachsenhausen and Mauthausen but thereafter was rapidly promoted to become deputy commandant at Auschwitz and then commandant of the Natzweiler-Struthof camp. He was eventually appointed commandant at Auschwitz before being put in command at Belsen in December 1944. He was arrested by members of 317 FSS and then interrogated by Sergeant Norman Turgel of 53 FSS, which arrived soon after the camp was discovered. The details obtained by Sergeant Turgel were used in evidence at Kramer's trial. He was sentenced to death and hanged by the British executioner, Albert Pierrepoint, at Hamelin prison on 13 December 1945.

While Sergeant Turgel was in the Belsen camp, he met and fell in love with a prisoner, Gena Goldfinger, a Polish Jew then aged twenty who had already survived the Kraków ghetto and the death camps at Auschwitz and Buchenwald. She had been working in the camp hospital and had nursed the dying Anne Frank. Although separated for a time when Sergeant Turgel had to move on from Belsen, their romance blossomed and they married in a synagogue at Lübeck on 7 October 1945 – Gena's wedding dress having been made of British parachute silk. They were married for nearly fifty years before Sergeant Turgel's death in 1995. Gina died in 2018 at the age of ninety-five.

• • •

On 21 May 1945, just two weeks after the German surrender, two men wearing the uniforms of the German Secret Field Police and carrying documents identifying them as recently released from military service approached a British checkpoint on a bridge spanning the River Oste at Bremervörde, about 35 miles west of Hamburg. They were stopped and their documents examined. Unfortunately for them, the checkpoint was an intelligence screening post set up by 45 Field Security Section to apprehend known and suspected war criminals and leading members of the Nazi Party. On questioning, the men explained that they were part of a group of recently released soldiers and the rest of the group were following on behind. The duty section German speaker at the checkpoint was Sergeant Ken Baisbrown of the Intelligence Corps. He suspected that something was amiss immediately and he was right. Sergeant Baisbrown's sixth sense led directly to the arrest of one of the most notorious Nazis of all – SS Reichsführer Heinrich Himmler, the architect of the Holocaust.

Although they were using false identities, the two disguised Germans were in fact Himmler's aide and his personal physician, both of whom were senior members of the SS. They were part of a small cluster of senior Nazis – including Himmler – who were attempting to escape south to Bavaria disguised as members of the German Field Police. Himmler had shaved off his moustache, wore an eye patch and carried false identity papers in the name of Sergeant Heinrich Hitzinger. Unknown to the Nazis, the German Field Police had been placed on the automatic arrest list of the Allies War Crimes Investigation Unit. Having managed to cross the River Elbe, the group were confronted with the Bremervörde

checkpoint. While the two Germans scouted ahead, the remainder
of the group, including Himmler, took cover in a nearby deserted
farmhouse. Sergeant Baisbrown's suspicions led to a manhunt and
eventually to the capture of 'Hitzinger' and his companions. Although initially interrogated by Baisbrown, Himmler remained unidentified for another two days. But in an unguarded moment, he
removed his eye patch and was recognised by another senior Nazi
prisoner. Then, having replaced the eye patch, Himmler requested
an interview with the commandant of the detention camp and was
brought before Captain Thomas Selvester. Himmler removed the
eye patch again and put his distinctive pince-nez back. In a quiet
voice, he identified himself with the words 'Heinrich Himmler'.

A full clothing and body search was carried out during which
a brass case with a phial containing poison was discovered in a
jacket pocket. When another, empty container, was found, it was
assumed that Himmler still had a phial concealed about his person
somewhere. At this stage, his mouth was not searched although he
was given something to eat and drink in order to see if he tried
to remove anything from his mouth. Himmler was then taken to
a house in Lüneburg, which had been taken over to detain very
high-ranking prisoners. A medical officer carried out another
search and found what he described as a 'blue tit-like' object in the
sulcus (groove) between cheek and teeth – as he tried to sweep it
out with his finger, Himmler enacted his own 'Final Solution'. In
the words of the medical officer: 'Himmler clamped down on my
finger ... wrenched my hand out of his mouth, swung his head
away and then with an almost deliberate disdain faced me, crushed
the glass capsule between his teeth and took a deep inhalation'. The
officer commanding the camp security detail, Major Whittaker,
was also present. He later recorded in his diary: 'We immediately

upended the old bastard and got his mouth into the bowl of water which was there to wash the poison out. There were terrible groans and grunts coming from the swine.'

Their attempts to keep him alive were in vain. Himmler was dead within a few minutes. Soon afterwards, his body was taken to a secret location near Lüneburg and buried in an unmarked grave.

• • •

At 11 p.m. on 11 March 1946, members of 92 Field Security Section raided a farmhouse near Flensburg. There, they arrested SS-Obersturmbannführer Rudolf Franz Ferdinand Höss, the former camp commandant of Auschwitz. The information leading to his detection had come from his wife. When members of 92 FSS had initially interviewed Frau Höss, she claimed that her husband was dead. A decision was taken to jail her in the hope that this might persuade her to talk. For five days, she was visited and asked just one question: 'Where is your husband?' She refused to talk. On the sixth day, she was told that the train which had just pulled into the sidings behind her cell was there to take her to Siberia if she did not come clean about her husband's whereabouts, and she would have just five minutes to bid her children farewell. The bluff worked and she revealed where Höss was hiding. She also revealed that he was using the name 'Franz Lang' and was posing as a former Kriegsmarine Petty Officer, now working as a gardener.

Höss was born in 1901 into a staunchly Roman Catholic family. He had served in the German Army in Mesopotamia and was decorated for gallantry several times. He joined the Nazi Party in 1922. A year later, he was part of a gang who beat to death a schoolteacher, Walther Kadow, on the wishes of Martin Bormann, who later became Adolf Hitler's private secretary. Kadow was suspected of informing the French authorities of acts of sabotage by Nazi paramilitary groups. Höss served four years in prison for the crime. He joined the SS in 1934 and was assigned to Dachau concentration camp as a guard block leader. Promoted to SS-Hauptsturmführer in 1938, he was appointed adjutant of the Sachsenhausen camp and then in May 1940 appointed as commandant of the Auschwitz camp complex in Poland. After three years, he was removed while being investigated for having an affair with a female inmate. Subsequently, he returned to supervise the execution of 430,000 Hungarian Jews. They were murdered in a two-month period in 1944. Having experimented with various poison gases, it was Höss who came up with the idea of using the pesticide Zyklon-B, which produces hydrogen cyanide gas, as an extermination method.

On 15 April 1946, Höss testified at the International Military Tribunal at Nuremburg. In his evidence, he made the following statement:

I commanded Auschwitz until 1 December 1943 and estimate that at least 2,500,000 victims were executed and exterminated there by gassing and burning, and at least another half million succumbed to starvation and disease, making a total of about 3,000,000 dead. This figure represents about 70 per cent or 80 per cent of all persons sent to Auschwitz as prisoners, the remainder having been selected and used for slave labour in the concentration camp industries. Included among the executed and burnt were approximately 20,000 Russian prisoners of war (previously screened out of prisoner-of-war cages by the Gestapo) who were delivered at Auschwitz in Wehrmacht transports operated by regular Wehrmacht officers and men. The remainder of the total number of victims included about 100,000 German Jews, and great numbers of citizens (mostly Jewish) from The Netherlands, France, Belgium, Poland, Hungary, Czechoslovakia, Greece, or other countries. We executed about 400,000 Hungarian Jews alone at Auschwitz in the summer of 1944.

On 25 May, Höss was handed over to the Polish authorities for trial on charges of war crimes by the Supreme National Tribunal. Having admitted to the murders of more than 2.5 million people, he was convicted and sentenced to death. Apparently with an eye to poetic justice, the Poles carried out the execution on 16 April 1947 using a short-drop gallows erected beside the crematorium at the former Auschwitz concentration camp.

• • •

Theodore Xenophon Henry Pantcheff, known as 'Bunny', was born on 29 December 1920 at Buckhurst Hill in Essex, the son of Sophocles Xenophon Pantcheff and Elliot Jesse Ramsbotham. The paternal side of his family was from Greece by way of Bulgaria. His father, a Lieutenant in the Bulgarian Army during the First Balkan War of 1912, had been wounded and nursed back to health by his future wife, Ella, who had studied medicine at Durham University. They settled in London in 1913 and Sophocles took British citizenship. Bunny attended the Merchant Taylors' School in Northwood and then went up to Gonville and Caius College, Cambridge, to read modern languages. He graduated with a first.

In 1941, he went to an Officer Cadet Training Unit and in March 1942 he was commissioned as a Second Lieutenant in the Intelligence Corps. His fluency in German meant he was trained as an interrogator, and by early 1943 he was recruited by MI19, the branch of military intelligence concerned with collection of intelligence from prisoners of war. Pantcheff was assigned to the 'London Cage' in Kensington Palace Gardens, the facility run by Lieutenant Colonel Alexander Scotland of the Intelligence Corps, who also ran the other 'cages' located around the UK. They received German and Italian prisoners who, having already been processed by field interrogation teams, were considered to be in possession of valuable information.

In December 1944, Pantcheff was assigned by Colonel Scotland to investigate a plot by diehard Nazi prisoners at Camp 23 in Devizes, Wiltshire, in which about 7,000 men would break out and form a 'Fifth Column' by overpowering nearby British Army barracks, obtaining weapons and tanks and then joining up with escapees from other camps. There were indications, never confirmed, that this was a conspiracy dreamt up to cause maximum disruption in Britain during the German offensive in the Ardennes. The British and Americans heard about the plan and activated hidden microphones in the camp until they had its full details, at which point the ringleaders were rounded up and transferred to another camp for hard-line Nazis at Comrie in Perthshire, where the inmates were kept in line by Polish guards. But then the plotters began to suspect that they had been betrayed by a traitor. They singled out an anti-Hitler prisoner called Wolfgang Rosterg, whose equivalent rank was Sergeant Major. Rosterg was subjected to a brutal 'kangaroo court' during which he was beaten with red-hot iron bars and hanged, although a post-mortem revealed that he was by then already dead. Following investigation and interrogation by Pantcheff, eight Nazis were charged with Rosterg's murder and put on trial in London in July 1945. Five were convicted and hanged at Pentonville Prison.

With victory in May 1945, the London Cage was reassigned as a War Crimes Investigation Unit and Pantcheff and his fellow interrogators went all over Europe to investigate reports of war crimes and to arrest and interrogate known and suspected war criminals. After the Channel Islands were liberated in May 1945, Pantcheff was sent to Alderney to establish whether war crimes had been committed by the Germans. He had a personal interest in the island and had spent time there in his youth as his uncle was the only doctor there in the 1930s.

Pantcheff's main focus was Sylt, the southernmost of the four labour camps, where the inmates were mostly Ukrainian, Russian, Polish and French Jews who were brought to Alderney during the German occupation to build defences which prevented the Allies liberating the island until after VE Day. Pantcheff later calculated that he took more than 3,000 statements from former prisoners to put together the brutal story of the camp, where he found evidence that between 300 and 400 prisoners had died during the occupation, though the true figure may have been far higher. He recommended bringing charges against one German officer, but a lack of evidence meant that no charges were ever brought.

Pantcheff was also involved in the investigation of the Emsland Massacre and its perpetrator, Willi Herold, who became known as 'The Executioner of Emsland'. In April 1945, Herold, a nineteen-year-old German Army paratrooper, either deserted or became separated from his unit en route from Italy to Germany. Wandering alone near Aschendorfermoor, in the Emsland region close to the Dutch border, he came across an abandoned German staff car and found a suitcase containing the full uniform of a Luftwaffe Captain. He donned the uniform and, apparently emboldened by the sense of power it gave his sadistic character, continued to pose as a

German officer, eventually gathering around him a group of other lost or deserting soldiers over which he took command.

On 11 April, the group arrived at the Aschendorfermoor penal camp for German Army deserters and other military defaulters. Located near the Dutch frontier, it was one of fifteen such camps in the area known as the Emslandlager. Having heard from camp guards that 150 men had recently tried to escape, Herold convinced the commandant that he had been sent on the personal orders of Hitler to take command of the camp. Bizarrely, over the next week, he and his group executed an estimated 172 inmates for real or imagined transgressions. They are said to have been shot with an anti-aircraft gun or blown up by hand grenades before being buried in pits they had dug before their executions. Herold's extraordinary reign of terror was only halted when an Allied air raid enabled most of the surviving inmates to escape, following which Herold and his crew escaped. They went on to commit further murders.

In the chaos surrounding the German retreat from the advancing Allies, Herold's group arrived in the town of Aurich, where their appearance brought them under the suspicion of the local garrison Commander. During questioning, Herold confessed to the Aschendorfermoor killings and, although held for later trial, by some administrative mistake he was released. He made his way to the German port of Wilhelmshaven and, following the German surrender, he was arrested by the Royal Navy for stealing bread. While in custody for this relatively minor offence, he was identified as a wanted war criminal and held in custody pending investigation. Having been assigned to the investigation, Pantcheff travelled to the Aschendorfermoor camp to collect evidence and interview members of the original guard force. He also arranged for the transfer of Herold and his group from prison to carry out the exhumation of the mass grave of their victims – a total of 195 bodies were finally exhumed, examined for evidence and then reburied with due ceremony. Pantcheff's investigation secured the conviction of Herold and five of his group for the murders of 125 of the Aschendorfermoor inmates. They were all executed by guillotine at Wolfenbüttel prison on 14 November 1946.

By mid-February 1946, Pantcheff – still only twenty-five years old – reported that his work in Europe was almost over and he considered that he and his team had apprehended most if not all of the major war criminals. They had arrested 120 individuals against whom there was strong evidence of inhumane treatment, murder and worse, including every then living concentration camp commandant.

In 1948, Pantcheff transferred to the Intelligence Division of the British Control Commission in Germany, the body responsible for the administration of the British zone of occupied Germany and its Intelligence Division, which provided cover for the post-war activities of the Secret Intelligence Service (MI6). By 1951, he was a member of MI6 and he remained in Germany until 1958, running agents into the Soviet zone. He then moved to Africa under diplomatic cover and worked out of the British embassies in Lagos as the SIS Head of Station, later taking on the same role at Kinshasa. He returned to London in 1963 as Controller, Africa, but in 1964 moved to the Directorate of Counter-Intelligence. During that time, he was one of two SIS officers assigned to the FLUENCY committee, a joint MI5–MI6 operation which had been set up to investigate suspicions of a deep-penetration agent in MI5. He was also involved in the investigation of a retired SIS officer, Dick Ellis, who had worked in Berlin and Paris before the war. Ellis finally admitted to Pantcheff during interrogation that, pre-war, he had been passing information to the German military intelligence service, the Abwehr, for money. The case was closely guarded within MI6 and Ellis was never prosecuted.

In 1977, 'Bunny' Pantcheff retired from the intelligence world and settled on Alderney. For his services with 'the Foreign Office', he was appointed a Companion of the Order of St Michael and St George (CMG). In retirement, he wrote two books based on his wartime and war crimes investigation experiences, *Alderney – Fortress Island* (1981) and *The Executioner of the Emsland* (1987). He died of leukaemia on 28 November 1989.

• • •

The Second World War gave those members of the Intelligence Corps who took part in it the opportunity to refine the range of skills that had been developed by their predecessors during the First World War and to introduce new capabilities in both overt and covert intelligence gathering which proved crucial to its various successes. Despite the notable contribution it made to the war effort, however, some within the mainstream Army – including those in senior positions of command – still argued that the Corps was surplus to requirements. Alongside a general scepticism of its remit lay a view that perhaps too many of its personnel were drawn from the ranks of 'gifted amateurs' or that its operators were somehow lacking in aptitude. As a result, a threat hung over the very existence of the Intelligence Corps in the years immediately following the end of the war. The 1950s were well under way before that threat was removed and it found itself on a surer footing.

PART THREE

WORLDWIDE OPERATIONS
AND DEPLOYMENTS

B y necessity, members of the armed forces spend most of their
time in training. This allows individuals to hone a variety of
skills; it encourages teamwork; it refreshes familiarity with combined operations, from platoon level to large formations; and it
readies men and women to carry out their duties in conjunction
with other services and other nations. Given the nature of war,
such preparedness is crucial. The Intelligence Corps is different.
Indeed, in effect, the equation is reversed. Most of its members'
time is spent on active duty, for example providing surveillance expertise in a hostile environment or, at a strategic level, carrying out
photographic analysis.

As will be discussed in the next section of this book, if the
years the Army spent in Northern Ireland between 1969 and 2007
can be classed an anomaly (albeit a seminal one in terms of the
Intelligence Corps' development), then it is fair to say that since
the Second World War, UK forces have been involved in three
main areas of strategic conflict. The first was the Cold War, which
began in 1947 and ended soon after the Berlin Wall fell in 1989. The

Intelligence Corps was engaged throughout this time, mostly in the struggle with Russian espionage efforts, and this will be the focus of a subsequent section of this book. The Cold War overlapped with the second area of conflict, Britain's end-of-empire obligations, when for several decades the UK either helped to prevent insurgent attempts to seize power or acted in a peacekeeping capacity in some of its former possessions. The third conflict area has seen the UK assist with attempts to stabilise the world order by deploying to failed states or those whose security has been threatened for other reasons such as poor governance or militant insurgents.

The next stage of the Corps' history turns to some of the individuals who took part in these operations, providing a detailed context for their work. It is important to emphasise that in this section it has sometimes been necessary to protect the identities of certain individuals who are still alive. It has also been called for to camouflage details of some tactics, techniques and procedures on the grounds that they are still in use today. Other authors may have exposed some of this information previously, but this book has chosen not to do so, particularly because they are not central to the stories of those involved. Areas of vagueness may be apparent, and some names and dates out of focus, but the essence of what follows remains true.

THE PALESTINE EMERGENCY

Despite the Second World War ending in September 1945, the British Army was immediately forced to engage in the long-running conflict between Arabs and Jews in Palestine. Under the 1917 Balfour Declaration, Britain had promised to support the establishment of a Jewish national home in Ottoman-controlled Palestine in return for

Jewish backing in the Great War. Yet Britain had also pledged to the Arabs that a united Arab country, covering most of the Arab Middle East, would be created if the Ottoman Turks were defeated. Neither promise was met. In 1920, Britain was given responsibility for Palestine under a League of Nations mandate. Over the next twenty years, more than 100,000 Jews entered the country, angering the Arabs and leading to the Arab Revolt of 1936–39. During the Second World War, the British restricted the immigration of European Jews into Palestine, provoking strong Jewish resistance. As a result, two Jewish terrorist groups were formed – Irgun Zvai Leumi and Lohamei Herut Israel (Lehi). After the Second World War, about 250,000 Jewish refugees were stranded in displaced-persons camps in Europe seeking a new homeland. Yet Britain maintained restrictions on Jewish immigration into Palestine, prompting the terrorists to try to drive out the British with riots and bombing. Many of the terrorists had fought with the British during the war and had a grounding, or better, in weapons, explosives and fieldcraft. They also had the support of local Jews and were a ruthless, effective and elusive threat in the face of martial law and curfews. About 100,000 British troops were deployed to Palestine, where they faced attacks and kidnappings, often in retaliation for death sentences passed on members of Irgun and Lehi. The violence and murders continued into 1947, with almost daily bombings and shootings. Once the British government concluded that Palestine was an intractable problem, the mandate was surrendered, and on 15 May 1948, the British Army left Palestine. During this campaign, 338 British lives were lost, including six members of the Intelligence Corps.

It was into this cauldron of simmering tensions that two young Intelligence Corps NCOs, Clifford Martin and Mervyn Paice, stepped in 1947. It is no exaggeration to say that their fates proved a turning point in Britain's involvement in Palestine.

Clifford James Victor Martin was born on 27 September 1926 in Cairo, Egypt. His father, Arnold, was an official of the Sudan Government Railway. His mother, Fernanda Rinalda Procaccia, was an Italian from Livorno in Tuscany whose parents also lived in Egypt. Clifford had two elder sisters. He was educated initially at the English School in Cairo. In March 1939, when he was thirteen, the family returned to England and took up residence at Didcot in Berkshire. His father became a civilian ledger clerk for the Royal Air Force. Clifford attended the King Charles I School in Kidderminster. He could speak French, Italian and Arabic. On 4 February 1942, at the age of seventeen, he enlisted in the General Service Corps straight from school and was posted to the Army Technical Training School at Arborfield, near Reading, where he trained as a fitter. His reports at that time described him as being of 'above average intelligence and education ... a sound, alert youth who can think and has a wider experience of life than most lads of his age ... [who] is quite a good linguist'. In October 1942, with his training complete, he was transferred to the Royal Electrical and Mechanical Engineers (REME). Between then and November 1945, he served in REME workshops in the UK and on 29 November he embarked for the Middle East. On 14 September 1946, he was compulsorily transferred to the Intelligence Corps, almost certainly because of his linguistic skills. He was promoted to acting Corporal and posted to Palestine with 292 Field Security Section at Ashqelon. In January 1947, he was posted to 280 FSS and then eventually posted again to 252 FSS at Sarafand, a military base located between Jerusalem and Tel Aviv, in the rank of local Sergeant.

He was detached to the Palestine Police headquarters at Tulkarm, where he was concerned with Arab affairs.

Mervyn Harold Paice was born on 1 July 1927 at Stoke Bishop, Bristol, the son of Harry and Rose Paice (née Kick). His father was a customs and excise officer at Bristol Docks. He was educated at Bristol Grammar School and in his spare time played the clarinet, read poetry and was interested in football and hockey. He enlisted in the General Service Corps on 4 October 1945 but transferred to the Intelligence Corps on 14 February 1946. He completed his training in July and was promoted to acting Lance Corporal. On 7 August 1946, Paice embarked for Egypt, arriving at the Intelligence Corps Wing at Cairo Base Depot on 16 August. On 14 November, he was promoted to Corporal and posted to 260 Field Security Section at Tripoli, Libya. This section was mainly involved in port security duties. Later, Paice, like Martin, was posted to 252 FSS at Sarafand and promoted to Sergeant. He was placed with the detachment at Natanya, concerned with Jewish terrorist activities.

Between 1945 and 1948, five field security sections were employed in Palestine, three of which were original sections left over from the war. The other two – 3 FSS and 317 FSS –arrived with the reinforcement 1st Division and 6th Airborne. A Combined Services Detailed Interrogation Centre (CSDIC) was also established. The work of the field security sections was conducted in extremely difficult conditions. Intelligence from the ground was almost impossible to obtain as the majority of the population was sympathetic to the terrorists, meaning local sources were few and far between. When captured, terrorists generally refused to talk, even when facing the probability of execution. The net result was that advanced intelligence of a terrorist attack rarely emerged via the usual channels and most military operations were reactive rather than pre-emptive.

Some Corps personnel operated in plain clothes and mingled with the crowds in areas where uniformed military patrols could not go. Known or suspected terrorists and sympathisers were placed under covert surveillance, as were known meeting places. Corps personnel were also involved in searching ships that had slipped through the naval blockade. They would screen the crew and passengers, detaining anybody who aroused suspicion.

Another basic, but fundamental, role for the Corps was to provide security training of other military units. Having previously served with the British Army, many of the terrorists had kept their old uniforms and accoutrements. These garments enabled them to impersonate British officers and NCOs while planning and executing attacks, meaning British soldiers had to be on the lookout at all times. During one such incident in the Sarafand area in March 1947, nine Irgun terrorists dressed in British Airborne uniforms presented themselves at the camp of the King's Own Hussars, overpowered the guards and made off in a truck with an entire store of ammunition. Following a brief firefight and hot pursuit, the truck was recovered, together with most of the ammunition. And on 4 May 1947, members of Irgun – some dressed as British soldiers – carried out a prison break on the Central Prison in Acre by blowing a hole in a wall. Twenty-seven Irgun terrorists escaped, though five were captured by Parachute Regiment soldiers who were in the area. On 16 June 1947, three of the captured were sentenced to death by hanging for their part in this attack.

This formed the backdrop to the events of 11 July 1947. Martin and Paice – both just twenty years old – were on duty that night as usual in plain clothes meeting a Jewish contact of Paice in the

Café Pinati on the main street in Natanya. The contact was Aaron Weinberg, a civilian employee of the British Army who was also a member of the SHAI, the intelligence branch of the Haganah, the main Jewish paramilitary group. The trio remained in the café until after midnight, when they left to return to their billets. Suddenly, while walking along the street, a taxi pulled up. Several armed men in masks jumped out and held them at gunpoint. Martin and Paice were bundled into the back of the car, chloroformed and hand-cuffed; Weinberg was bound and blindfolded but not chloroformed because he claimed to suffer from asthma. After driving for twenty minutes, Weinberg was removed from the car, taken to an orange grove and told to lie on the ground and stay there. The terrorists warned him that if he was seen in the company of British spies again, he would be shot like a dog. After some time, Weinberg left the area and informed the British authorities of the incident.

Martin and Paice were driven on to the disused Feldman's diamond-polishing facility located in an industrial zone in south Natanya. There, they were placed in an underground, soundproofed and airtight bunker and supplied with bottled oxygen. Food and water were left for them and they were warned to refresh the air only occasionally with the oxygen. Shortly after the incident, the Irgun issued a statement in which they confirmed that the Britons were being held as hostages against the reprieve of the three condemned men. An exhaustive search operation was launched by the military, the Palestine Police and the Haganah. On at least two occasions, the Feldman's building was examined, but the bunker had been constructed and camouflaged so expertly that the searchers never came close to finding it. Despite appeals from the executive of the Va'ad Le'umi in Jerusalem, the Zionist Federation of Great Britain, the Chief Rabbi, the Pope and personal appeals from the two men's families, they were not released. On the morning of Tuesday 29 July, the three condemned Jewish terrorists were allowed a final visit from a rabbi and then taken out one by one to be killed. Following their deaths, the search for the two hostages intensified. Natanya, already under strict curfew, was sealed off and more than 5,000 troops and police with tanks and armoured cars scoured the entire town.

Irgun's Chief of Staff, Amichai Paglin, had planned Martin's and Paice's kidnap. When he learned that his three colleagues had been killed, he went immediately to the safe house of the Irgun's leader, Menachem Begin, the future Prime Minister of Israel, and received the final go-ahead to 'execute' the British Sergeants. Paglin then took personal control of the matter. He decided that the killings could not be carried out in the open due to the very heavy military and police presence and should instead take place amid the secrecy of the Feldman's property. The bodies could then be moved to a place where they could be ceremonially 'hanged'. Begin approved the plan and Paglin returned to Natanya to collect four of his men. That evening, they drove to the Feldman's plant and took Martin and Paice from the bunker into another room. After eighteen days of living in the darkness underground, with almost no air, they were removed. Then, in a replication of a judicial hanging, they were ordered to stand on a chair, bound hand and foot, hooded, and a noose was placed around their necks before the chair was kicked away. Also, as with a judicial hanging, the bodies were left for twenty minutes before being cut down.

The next morning, the bodies of Martin and Paice were wrapped in bags, placed in the boot of a Tel Aviv taxi and driven by a pre-reconnoitred route to a eucalyptus grove near the village of Even Yehuda. They were hung by the neck from two trees and a notice was attached to Martin's body bearing the message:

Two British spies held in underground captivity since July 12 have been tried after the completion of the investigations of their 'criminal anti-Hebrew activities' on the following charges:

1. Illegal entry into the Hebrew homeland.
2. Membership of a British criminal terrorist organisation known as the Army of Occupation, which was responsible for the torture, murder, deportation, and denying the Hebrew people the right to live.
3. Illegal possession of arms.
4. Anti-Jewish spying in civilian clothes.
5. Premeditated hostile designs against the underground.

Found guilty of these charges they have been sentenced to hang and their appeal for clemency dismissed. This is not a reprisal for the execution of three Jews but a 'routine judicial fact.'

After twenty-four hours, the bodies still had not been found, so the Irgun telephoned the mayor of Natanya and disclosed their location. In turn, the mayor contacted the headquarters of the 1st Guards Brigade. Immediately, a retrieval party of soldiers and police, including two members of the Royal Engineers with mine detectors, went to the spot and found them. The report produced by the Palestine Police details the scene:

They were hanging from two eucalyptus trees five yards apart. Their faces were heavily bandaged, so it was impossible to distinguish their features ... Their bodies were a dull black colour and blood had run down their chests which made it appear at first that they had been shot ... The press were allowed to take photographs of the spectacle. When this had been done, it was decided to cut down the bodies. The RE captain and company sergeant major lopped branches off the tree which held the right-hand body and started to cut the hang rope with a saw.

Shockingly, however, worse was to follow. A bomb had been hidden on one of the corpses. The report went on:

> As the body fell there was a large explosion ... The two trees had been completely blown up and there were large craters where the roots had been. One body was found horribly mangled about twenty yards away ... The other body had disintegrated, and small pieces were picked up as much as 200 yards away.

The Royal Engineer who had cut down the body was wounded. Both sets of remains were taken to the British Hospital at Be'er Ya'akov, where identification was confirmed. In his evidence to the subsequent court of inquiry, the Officer Commanding 252 FSS, Captain J. L. Valls-Russell, commented that although the two NCOs were from different detachments and dealt with different aspects of the Palestinian situation, the duties of both men were closely connected and could bring them together in any area, on some specific task. He also explained that all his detachment NCOs worked independently and arranged their own daily programme of work – unless otherwise detailed to carry out a specific enquiry.

The double murder was picked up in London immediately and a photograph of the two Sergeants hanging from the trees was published on the front page of the *Daily Express*, then the largest circulation newspaper in the world. This sparked a wave of violent anti-Jewish riots in some British cities. Synagogues were vandalised,

Jewish graves were desecrated, Jewish-owned businesses had their windows smashed and threats were made against prominent Jews.

In his book *The Revolt*, published in 1951, Menachem Begin claimed that the incident was one of the key events which tipped the balance in the British withdrawal from Palestine. In 1991, during what was to be the last interview he gave before his death, Begin commented that the decision to hang the Sergeants was the most difficult he made as the Irgun Commander but added that 'after the brutal act there were no more hangings of Jews in Palestine'. Arthur Creech Jones, who had been the British Colonial Secretary in Palestine in 1947, later commented that the 'deadly blow against British patience and pride caused by the hangings was one of four major factors that pushed the British cabinet to the decision to evacuate Palestine in September 1947.'

In what could be considered a glaring irony, the *Jewish Chronicle* tracked down Clifford Martin's sister, Vicky Kemp, in 1981. She produced what she said was clear proof that her brother was halachically Jewish, having come from a large family of Cairo Jews. Whether Menachem Begin knew that Martin was Jewish remains unclear.

Sergeant Clifford Martin and Sergeant Mervyn Paice were buried with full military honours at Ramleh War Cemetery, near Tel Aviv, on 1 August 1947.

THE MALAYAN EMERGENCY

Just as the British Army was preparing to pull out of Palestine, there was increasing turbulence thousands of miles away in another part of the British Empire, Malaya. Communists in this ethnically diverse area of south-east Asia had helped defeat Japan during the Second

World War, leading to the revolutionary political activist Chin Peng being awarded an OBE for his services as the Liaison Officer between the Malayans and the British military. But in the spring of 1947, Chin Peng became the secretary-general of the Malayan Communist Party (MCP) and it began an independence campaign. This led to MCP guerrillas blowing up trains, attacking British-owned rubber planta-tions and tin mines and murdering foremen who worked on colonial estates. In June 1948, a state of emergency was declared after three expatriate managers were killed in the northern state of Perak. The insurgency was only described as an 'emergency' because insurers would not have compensated plantation and mine owners if it had been called a 'war'. The communists established camps in the jungle and were backed by landless Chinese 'squatters' who lived there. As the campaign progressed, the British implemented the Briggs Plan, named after Sir Harold Briggs, a retired Lieutenant General who was appointed Director of Operations with orders to organise, coordinate and implement anti-insurgent operations of the military and police. This plan was the first example of counter-insurgency (COIN) techniques, which would be used in future operations around the world. Terrorist activity peaked in 1951 with the assas-sination of the British High Commissioner to Malaya, Sir Henry Gurney. Under his successor, General Sir Gerald Templer, efforts were focused on intelligence, with Templer famously remarking: 'The answer [to the uprising] lies not in pouring more troops into the jungle, but in the hearts and minds of the people.' Good intelligence and coordination of intelligence gathering were key to the Briggs Plan and the Intelligence Corps was at the centre of the process. By 1955, many insurgents had been killed or captured and two years later Malaya was granted independence. By 1960, the communists were driven out and the emergency had ended. About 40,000

British and Commonwealth troops were involved at the height of the conflict, against about 8,000 communist guerrillas. During hostilities, 1,345 Malayan troops and police were killed, as were 519 British troops and Commonwealth personnel from Australia, New Zealand, Fiji, Southern Rhodesia, Kenya, Northern Rhodesia and Nyasaland.

As Nick van der Bijl explains in his book *Sharing the Secret*, not as much as might be expected is known about the activities of the Intelligence Corps in Malaya between 1948 and 1960 because most field security sections were integrated into the Malay Police Special Branch (an arrangement considered to have been so successful that it was replicated in Northern Ireland in the 1970s). At the start of the emergency, four field security sections were already in theatre. Additional personnel were added as the campaign escalated, but the emergency occurred at a time of post-war reductions in the Corps, with most intelligence staff appointments held by non-Corps officers. Members of the Corps were also integrated into the Malayan Security Service, a local version of MI5. Special Branch had primacy in intelligence-collection matters.

In 1947, the military garrison in Malaya comprised six Gurkha, three British and two Malay battalions. When the communists began their campaign, a defensive strategy was pursued, with small groups protecting mines and estates, but although the guerrillas were able to be contained, they could not be stopped altogether. After August 1948, reinforcements were sent from Britain, many of whom were National Service conscripts. Military Intelligence Officers provided the link between Special Branch and the British and Gurkha infantry battalions that came and went, or reinforced a particular area because of an increase in the terrorist threat. One of the functions of a Military Intelligence Officer was to obtain intelligence from Special Branch as it was gathered and process it so that it could be used quickly by the Army. Working in collaboration with Special Branch colleagues, Military Intelligence Officers were also involved in the recruiting and running of agents and the handling of surrendered enemy personnel, who would then be used in counter-insurgency operations against the Malayan Communist Party.

It was while operating in this latter role that Lieutenant Peter Hunt died. His inclusion in this catalogue of Intelligence Corps men and women is deemed worthy because he is believed to be the only Intelligence Corps officer to have been killed in action during this protracted conflict.

Peter William Hunt was born on 18 May 1926 in Belfast, the son of Stanley Tyndale Hunt and Janie (née Carson). His father was born in Gloucestershire, educated in Worcestershire and worked as a tax inspector. During the latter stages of the Great War, he had served as a Private with the Gloucestershire Regiment and was commissioned into the Royal Air Force on its formation in 1918. In the early 1920s, Stanley Hunt moved to Northern Ireland and married his wife Janie, the daughter of a County Antrim farmer, in 1924. At the time of Peter's birth, they were living in Wellesley Avenue, Belfast. Peter was educated at the city's Methodist College and when the family moved to Portrush, on the North Antrim coast, he attended Coleraine Academical Institution, from where he matriculated in September 1944.

He enlisted in the Queen's Royal Regiment at Belfast in October 1944 and, following basic training at 13 Infantry Training Centre at Maidstone in Kent, embarked for officer cadet training at Bangalore in India in July 1945. In June 1946, he was posted to Palestine and appointed Platoon Commander with the 1st Battalion, seeing service in Jerusalem, Haifa, Natanya and Gaza. He was promoted to Lieutenant in October that year. A posting with British Troops Austria preceded a spell at the Platoon Commander's Course at the School of Infantry Tactical Wing at Warminster. Lieutenant Hunt then applied for a regular commission in the Royal Ulster Rifles, with the Royal Signals being his second choice. In order to assess his suitability, he was attached to 24 Brigade Signals, British Element Trieste Forces, between September and November 1947. Having returned to the UK, he was on the permanent staff of the Irish Brigade Training Battalion in Northern Ireland, and on 14 August 1948 he was posted to the Intelligence Corps depot at Maresfield and appointed as Platoon Commander. On 1 September 1948, he was granted a regular five-year short service commission in the Intelligence Corps. He then attended the Field Security Course and the Short Interrogation Course. On 3 August 1949, he was posted to British Troops Austria and served with 410, 68 and finally the Carinthia FS Section, returning to the Maresfield depot in June 1950.

The following month, he was posted to Malaya, arriving at Singapore on 5 August. Initially, he was assigned to the Intelligence Officers Pool for duty at the Combined Operation Room at Johor. By that point, a lack of good intelligence had been cited as a key reason for not having put down the insurgency, but the recently appointed Director of Operations in Malaya, Lieutenant General Sir Harold Briggs, was about to change the situation markedly. Realising that the aforementioned Chinese 'squatters' represented an important recruiting source for the communists, Briggs focused on resettling them in more than 400 new kampongs with access to housing, clean water, education and medical care. These villages were patrolled by police, thereby separating the inhabitants from the insurgents and instilling in them a sense of faith in the authorities that made them more willing to provide information about the MCP. This was known by some as 'political pacification', and later became known as the 'hearts and minds' policy. Briggs also isolated the guerrillas from their supplies and food sources. Furthermore, committees with representatives from the civil and military agencies involved in the campaign were established so that a coordinated response to the guerrillas could be formulated. Added to this, the Malayan Police Special Branch was reorganised and given specific intelligence-gathering objectives to assist with military planning.

Given that British troops were not always able to pick out the enemy, the main intelligence contribution was in developing evidence of communist activities and support in an area. Any means was used to achieve this, including recruiting informers, obtaining documents, interrogating prisoners and aerial photography. Photographic interpretation and the resulting 'imagery intelligence' was provided by Corps personnel of 103 Air Photo Interpretation Section at Kuala Lumpur with a detachment at RAF Butterworth. Intelligence obtained via this source was all-important in identifying insurgent movements and hides in the jungle, enabling air strikes or patrol ambushes to be launched effectively. The Field Security Wing (Malaya) was responsible for screening, vetting and issuing passes for civilian labour in the military establishments.

On 30 April 1951, Lieutenant Hunt was reassigned as the Intelligence Officer to HQ 26 Gurkha Infantry Brigade at Seremban, in the South Malaya District, and moved to HQ North Malaya Sub-District on 16 January 1952. Two weeks later, he married Frances Birkinshaw in Singapore. The couple had met during his tour in Austria, where she was working as a teacher for the post-war

British military administration. All of the available evidence suggests that by this stage Lieutenant Hunt was employed as a Special Military Intelligence Officer (SMIO) attached to the Malayan Special Branch.

British Malaya was made up of several different ethnic groups. According to the 1947 Census of Malaya, there were 2.4 million Malays, 1.83 million Chinese and 534,000 Indians. This latter group were mainly Tamils from the south of India who worked on the rubber plantations. They were among the lowest castes of India's hierarchical social structure and had been in Malaya since the second half of the nineteenth century working as cheap labourers. Having endured their lot for generations under British rule, they were some of the Malayan Communist Party's strongest supporters and many joined the ranks of the guerrillas.

On 29 April 1952, Lieutenant Hunt was travelling in a Land Rover on the road between Maxwell Hill and Taiping, accompanied by a Warrant Officer and four Tamils. Suddenly, they found the road was blocked by a felled tree and they were forced to stop. As they did so, a party of at least six terrorists opened fire on their vehicle from the surrounding treeline. Lieutenant Hunt was killed outright, as were two of the Tamils. The Warrant Officer and the other two Tamils were wounded. The official report of the incident included in Hunt's service file stated merely that he had been on an operation in support of the civil power. Although the full nature of what Hunt was doing remains unknown, it is more than likely that the mission was linked to the presence of the four Tamils, and quite probable that they were intelligence agents or surrendered enemy personnel. The details of the ambush also suggest that it was planned carefully by the gunmen and that they were acting on prior knowledge of the vehicle's movements rather than making a random 'pot-luck' attempt. If it is true that he was on a hit list, this poses the tragic possibility that Hunt was betrayed by one of his supposed assets.

Lieutenant Peter Hunt, who was twenty-five years old, was buried at Kamunting Christian Cemetery in Taiping. After his death, his widow remained in Malaya until January 1953, when she returned to England to reside in Bournemouth. She never remarried and died in December 2010.

THE KOREAN WAR

After Japan's defeat in the Second World War, Korea was partitioned into areas of Soviet and American military control along the demarcation line known as the 38th parallel. Unsuccessful attempts at reunification caused elections in 1948 which led to the creation of the Republic of Korea in the south and the Democratic People's Republic of Korea, under Soviet influence, in the north. In 1949, American troops were withdrawn from the south. Then, on 25 June 1950, North Korean troops invaded the Republic of Korea. The United Nations Security Council called for their withdrawal and UN forces, including American troops led by General Douglas MacArthur, were sent to the region, though they were soon overwhelmed by the North Koreans. In August 1950, two British infantry battalions joined the UN forces and were called into action at the Naktong River. The following month, reinforcements arrived from Canada, France and Turkey and made a surprise amphibious landing at Inchon, forcing the North Koreans back into their own territory. That month, an Australian battalion joined the British battalions, forming the 27th Commonwealth Brigade. After Seoul was liberated, UN and South Korean troops captured the North Korean capital of Pyongyang

and it appeared that the short war had been won. MacArthur's
fierce opposition to communism inspired him to keep driving north,
however, which the People's Republic of China viewed as a threat. It
sent hundreds of thousands of peasants to assist the North Koreans,
forcing the UN troops back. The Chinese retook Pyongyang and in
January 1951 launched another offensive, moving the UN forces back
further and eventually reoccupying Seoul. MacArthur was relieved
of his command, the UN regained some ground and peace negoti-
ations began in July 1951, but fighting continued until an armistice
agreement was reached in July 1953. In three years of conflict, around
1,100 British soldiers died and more than 2,000 were wounded. No
peace treaty has ever been signed between any of the forces.

The Intelligence Corps' involvement in the Korean War was limited, mainly because of the relatively small size of the British contingent in the region. On the field security side, 904 FS Section
arrived in Korea in August 1950 and to begin with was based at Seoul
before moving to Pyongyang. When Pyongyang was recaptured
by the Chinese, the Corps moved to Busan. The section's role was
initially restricted to the British 29th Brigade and Busan but was
later expanded. Its routine duties were counter-espionage; counter-
sabotage and the security of key points; civilian movement control
and vetting; and the detection and arrest of enemy agents and 'black-
list' suspects. On the photographic interpretation side, 104 Air Photograph Interpretation Section was sent to Korea in 1951 and fulfilled
the usual role of producing a daily print of the enemy areas to detect
enemy troop movements and providing intelligence to brigade and
battalion level for patrol briefings. Some NCOs of the section were
engaged in the rather more delicate task of handling Korean agents
who were prepared to 'line-cross' on both long- and short-term

intelligence-gathering missions. One senior NCO, Staff Sergeant Clifford Jackson, a decorated veteran of the Second World War, specialised in this activity.

Clifford Jackson was born at Foleshill, Warwickshire, on 15 December 1922, the son of Clifford and Selina (née Richards). His father was a maintenance labourer. After leaving school, he trained as a manual miller and toolmaker. By the outbreak of war in 1939, his mother had died and the family lived at 45 Chapel Street in Bedworth, Warwickshire.

Jackson first enlisted in the Royal Berkshire Regiment in 1939 and was successively transferred to the Army Air Corps and then the Black Watch before finally serving with the 9th Battalion Royal Fusiliers, with whom he saw action during the final stages of the Tunisian campaign in North Africa and then during the Salerno landings in Italy in September 1943. The battalion was with the 167th Infantry Brigade, 56th Division. Three months later, while the 9th Royal Fusiliers were in action during the Battle of Monte Camino, Jackson, who had by this point been promoted to Lance Sergeant, was involved in an act of bravery which led to the first of his three major gallantry awards, the United States Silver Star medal. This award was gazetted on 14 May 1948. The citation describes the action:

On 3rd December 1943, near Mt. Camino, Italy, when the advance of his platoon was delayed by a German machine gun post, Lance Sergeant Jackson ordered his section to attack the enemy position under cover of fire from the rest of the platoon. Moving forward toward the objective, he found the enemy fire so potent that he directed his men to seek cover, and with complete disregard for his own life, ran straight at the enemy gun, firing his submachine gun as he advanced. Before he could reach his objective, his gun jammed, and without hesitation he drew his machete and charged the enemy gunners, driving them from their position and single-handedly captured their gun. This outstanding act of courage coupled with a total disregard for his safety, was an inspiration to his comrades and was in keeping with the highest traditions of the military service.

By late January 1944, the battalion had advanced to the River Garigliano, which formed one of the preliminary obstacles in front of the German Gustav Line – one of three defensive lines constructed across Italy south of Rome and anchored on the heights of Monte Casino. For his gallantry during an enemy counter-attack, Jackson was awarded the Distinguished Conduct Medal (DCM), then the second highest honour below the Victoria Cross that could be given to an enlisted man. The citation, which was gazetted on 4 May 1944, reads:

On the night of 21/22 January 1944 this NCO was acting as platoon commander holding a defensive locality over the River Garigliano. On the morning of 23 January, a shell landed near his sanger and partially blinded him with the blast. A quarter of an hour later his platoon was heavily counter-attacked, and his men started withdrawing. He immediately rejoined his men and led them back under heavy automatic and mortar fire to their original positions. He kept them there, by his personal example and control, and inflicted heavy casualties on the attacking enemy. This man's personal example and fine leadership at a critical time restored a situation which might have become completely out of control: and his tenacity and courage in refusing to leave until the danger was over, when he eventually had to be led back to the regimental aid post still partially blinded, were beyond praise.

Jackson remained in Italy at the end of the war and continued to serve there until 1948. That year, he was based in the city of Trieste and transferred to the Intelligence Corps. In October 1950, he was deployed to Korea with 904 Field Security Section, which was given responsibility for military security in the 29th Brigade and Busan areas. In October 1951, he was promoted to acting Staff Sergeant and appointed as the NCO in command of the Special Detachment, a position he held for about eighteen months. This joint UK–US unit recruited, trained and managed 'turned' North Koreans, using them as agents to be infiltrated back behind enemy lines on covert intelligence-gathering missions. This was risky work yet, in keeping with the astonishing courage he had shown several years before, Jackson did far more than just find and train these men. On many occasions, the former infantry soldier put his life in danger, just as he had done during the Second World War, by accompanying them right up to and across the line into North Korean territory to ensure that they negotiated the crossing successfully. The precise nature of some of his activities remains unknown because, regrettably, much of the material relating to Far East theatres of war from the 1950s was destroyed for security and other reasons. It is widely acknowledged, however, that for long periods of time Jackson lived almost on the border in the most primitive conditions, wishing to be on hand for his agents while they were engaged on a mission.

Jackson's approach typifies the characteristics one so often finds in the Intelligence Corps. During the long journey by troopship out to Korea, he decided to learn Korean but had no books or any other way of studying the language. There was, however, a Japanese cook in the galley, so he engaged him so that he could learn Japanese instead in case it helped. None of the Koreans in his unit spoke English, but Jackson found one who did speak Japanese. He was used as an interpreter. This was not always effective, so Jackson taught his team to use hand signals when guiding him through the Allied and enemy lines and minefields. He carried a pair of white bandsman's gloves in his pocket and, when operating at night, would put them on so that he could be seen making the signals. He was in command of the unit overseeing these HUMINT operations until 30 June 1953. In recognition of a particularly hazardous spell in which he operated between 1 January and 30 June 1953, he was awarded the Military Medal. The citation reads:

> During the period 1 October 1951 – 1 June 1953 Sgt Jackson has performed the duties of NCO i/c Special Detachment, 1 Commonwealth Division. These duties involved raising, administering, training and operating this detachment. The activities of this unit are TOP SECRET and therefore cannot be disclosed at this time. In these operations, S/Sgt Jackson has shown boundless energy, efficiency and outstanding personal courage which are above the normal requirements of his specified duties. It is due to S/Sgt JACKSON's determination and high courage that the Special Detachment of this division has been successful in its task.

Jackson was recommended for this award by the Commander-in-Chief of the British Forces in Korea. This recommendation was approved by Major General M. M. A. R. West, GOC 1st Commonwealth Division, who added the handwritten comment: 'I can personally substantiate the citation.' During the period in question, the fighting was of particular intensity as the North Koreans strived to obtain as much territory as possible prior to the armistice, which had been planned to take effect on 27 July 1953.

After the war in Korea, Jackson went on to see further active service with the Intelligence Corps on Mau operations in Kenya between 1953 and 1954. He was also involved in field security work in Germany between 1956 and 1957 and counter-terrorist operations in Cyprus in 1957 and subsequently in Aden. He retired from the Army in 1963 and was employed in various management roles with Marks & Spencer and then in the hotel industry. In his retirement, he lived in York with his wife, Florence, later spending some time as a Chelsea Pensioner, where he was the most highly decorated soldier. Clifford Jackson died on 2 December 2002. He was seventy-nine years old.

● ● ●

The Intelligence Corps suffered only one casualty during the Korean War, the details of which are still shrouded in mystery, despite several official inquiries. It is only right that this book should pay tribute to the man at the centre of that riddle, Sergeant Edward Hall.

Edward Morland Hall was born on 14 January 1928 in the market town of Shipley, near Bradford in Yorkshire, the son of George Hall, a post office civil servant, and Annie (née Hirst). He had two brothers and five sisters. He enlisted in the General Service Corps as a Territorial soldier aged seventeen, on 24 April 1945, and transferred to the Intelligence Corps on 27 September. His first posting was with 316 Field Security Section (London Port Section), where he achieved the rank of Sergeant. In September 1947, he transferred to the Royal Army Education Corps and was posted to Egypt, where he remained until June 1948, when he was released to the Reserves.

In April 1951, almost a year after the Korean War had begun, Hall re-enlisted in the Intelligence Corps on a five-year regular engagement. He completed the No. 45 Other Ranks Security Course that June and was posted to the Depot Holding Wing. On 13 December 1951, he embarked for Korea, via Japan, on a posting to 904 Field Security Section, arriving on 20 January 1952. He was promoted to acting Sergeant on 1 February.

At that time, 904 FSS had responsibility for all aspects of military security in the 29th Divisional area and for Busan, with some members of the section being attached to infantry units engaged in the apprehension of North Korean guerrillas and agents. Because they infiltrated the Allied zone, members of 904 FSS spent a considerable amount of time following up leads regarding these suspects. The leads came from a variety of sources including civilians who had become suspicious of strangers among them; intelligence received from other captured agents during interrogation; and from SIGINT.

The most popular method for enemy infiltration into South Korea was via the steady streams of refugees moving from the front-line areas to the safety of the rear. However, 904 FSS had worked out an effective way of detecting hostile agents who tried to use this means. As Brigadier Brian Parritt, a former Director of the Intelligence Corps, relates in his 2011 book *Chinese Hordes and Human Waves*:

They would stop a refugee column and then, through their interpreters, ask all grandmothers and grandfathers to move aside, then all the women and children. Finally, they would ask the grandmothers to pick out their relatives and this would leave a number of single males who could be investigated in detail. This selection process provided a good filter, but given that so few United Nations soldiers spoke Korean, the interviewing or interrogation had to be done using an interpreter which slowed down the process and reduced the impact.

In 1952, the section headquarters was located near the village of Kang Pa Ri, close to the so-called stay-back line, beyond which Korean civilians were forbidden from travelling. The NCOs enjoyed a significant degree of autonomy and were expected to investigate their own leads and to develop and maintain their own contacts. One example of this autonomy concerned the case of Sergeant R. Davies of the Intelligence Corps, who received a Commander-in-Chief's Commendation for single-handedly catching a North Korean agent who had blown up a British ammunition dump.

At approximately midnight on 31 March 1952, Sergeant Hall arrived unannounced (and without any sign of transport) at a British Army laundry of 57 Company Royal Army Service Corps near the village of Hwang Bang Ni, which used locally employed Korean women as labour. He was armed with a pistol and accompanied by a Korean youth acting as his interpreter. When the officer commanding the company arrived, Hall explained to him that he was searching for a female suspect. It was later assumed that he was engaged in searching for an enemy agent. He asked to be allowed to examine the faces of the women and then did so by torchlight. Having failed to positively identify anybody, Hall allowed the women to return to their quarters and left with the youth, refusing an RASC officer's offer of a lift to his unit lines. He was last seen walking up the road with his interpreter.

To this day, questions surrounding Hall's fate are unresolved. It is strongly suspected that in the course of continuing his investigation that night, he was captured and, perhaps, killed by North Korean agents. When questioned later, Hall's interpreter claimed that, after leaving the laundry, Hall flagged down a civilian vehicle travelling in the opposite direction to the unit lines and asked for a lift, which he was given. Despite extensive searches over a wide area, no trace of him was ever discovered.

Initially, the Army authorities listed him as 'unlawfully absent', this being the decision of a court of inquiry convened shortly after his disappearance. This finding was annulled by the War Office in December 1953, however, and Hall's status was changed to 'missing in action'. In December 1954, the War Office once again changed his status to 'killed in action on or after 31 March 1952'. One theory, which has never been proved or disproved, is that he was engaged in some form of counter-espionage activity and was killed by enemy agents, of which there were many operating behind British lines.

As Sergeant Hall has no known grave, he is commemorated on the Commonwealth Memorial, United Nations Memorial Cemetery, Daeyeon-dong, Busan, in the Republic of South Korea. At the time of his disappearance, he was twenty-four years old.

THE SUEZ CANAL ZONE

The Suez Canal in Egypt was a vital strategic and economic route for Middle Eastern oil and trade with the Far East. Britain's association with the canal began in 1875, when Benjamin Disraeli's government paid £4 million for a 44 per cent share in the company which controlled it. In 1882, Britain invaded and occupied Egypt and ultimately took control of the canal's finances and operation. Yet Egypt was never a British colony. Instead, under the terms of the Anglo-Egyptian Treaty of 1936, Britain had the right to garrison troops and to maintain a base in the Suez Canal zone for twenty years, until 1956. Between 1939 and 1945, this base played a key role in Britain's war effort in North Africa, Palestine, the Mediterranean, the Aegean and the Balkans. Britain's presence in Egypt was resented by Egyptian nationalists, however, and from 1945 disturbances and rioting were commonplace. That year, a British soldier was also killed. In 1947, as demands for Britain's withdrawal from Egypt grew, British troops were moved from the cities to the area immediately beside the canal. Then, in October 1951, the Egyptian government repealed the 1936 treaty, placing still more pressure on the British. Rioting and attacks on military personnel and establishments intensified. Fifty-four British servicemen were killed between 1950 and 1956. The British garrison was strengthened so that by 1954 there were about 70,000 British troops in the Suez Canal zone. With tensions mounting, King Farouk of Egypt dismissed his militant government and ordered his Army to control the civil unrest, but this exacerbated the situation and the monarch was overthrown by senior Egyptian Army officers. In April 1954, Colonel Gamal Abdel Nasser was installed as President of a new regime and an agreement reached which gave Britain twenty months to leave Egypt. Being posted to Egypt was deeply unpopular among British troops because of poor accommodation, the heat and the risk of catching a malaria-like disease as a result of the canal being little more than an open sewer. It is said that everybody who served there suffered diarrhoea for much of the time. Yet as unappetising as these conditions were, they ranked below the real dangers presented by the hostile local population.

There were three field security sections in Egypt in 1950, detachments of which were located around the main towns and settlements of the Suez Canal zone. Members of each section were involved in the mass screening of civilians during cordon and search operations and were also involved in the arrest and disarming of the auxiliary police known as the Bulak Nizam, the force which had been used by the nationalists to mount terrorist attacks. Some members of the Intelligence Corps ran informants among the civilian population to collect intelligence on the terrorist ringleaders, while others were involved in the collation and analysis of captured documents. One Intelligence Corps officer, a Photographic Interpreter, Charles Kelsey, put his life on the line to save others during rioting in November 1951.

Charles Langhorne Kelsey was born on 28 May 1912 at Leeds, the second son of Henry and Hetty Kelsey (née Johnston). His father was an assistant reader at Leeds Grammar School, but he died, in his forties, in 1915. Charles had an older brother, Philip, who eventually became a teacher at Leeds Grammar School. Charles attended Leeds Grammar School from 1920 to 1932, where he was a member of its Officer Training Corps. Having completed his education, he became a buyer for a clothing business in Leeds. When war broke out in September 1939, he was already engaged to Norah Mander, a clerk who worked in the same firm, and he lived with her family. The couple married in 1940 and had two daughters, Susan, born in 1944, and Anne, born in 1950.

On 25 September 1939, Kelsey enlisted as a gunner in the Royal Artillery and completed his basic training with the 24th Anti-Aircraft Training Regiment. He was then selected for officer cadet training. After attending the 124th Officer Cadet Training Unit (OCTU) at

Llandrindod Wells in Radnorshire, he was granted an emergency commission as a Second Lieutenant in the Royal Artillery, the commission being gazetted on 28 February 1941. As an artillery subaltern, he served with 9th Reserve Regiment and then on the staff of 7 Heavy Anti-Aircraft Practice Camp before being attached to the Royal Artillery (HAA) Record Office in September 1944 and promoted to Captain. In May 1945, he was posted to 21st Army Group, North West Europe (British Liberation Army), in the rank of acting Major. In April 1949, his original emergency wartime commission was changed to a regular short service commission with the rank of substantive Captain, acting Major. He was then posted to No. 2 Prisoner of War Centre. At that time, there were still considerable numbers of German prisoners of war being processed prior to release.

In late May 1949, Kelsey was posted to 211 German Civilian Labour Organisation (GCLO) Artisan Group in Berlin. The GCLO was made up of former German prisoners to provide a much-needed labour and transportation pool for the post-war reconstruction of Germany. Kelsey was concerned with organising the GCLO to provide work parties in the unloading and transportation of goods brought in during the 1948–49 Berlin Airlift when supplies were carried to the people of West Berlin. It appears likely that, as a result of his contact and interaction with the Germans during this time, Kelsey became known to the intelligence community in the German capital.

As soon as the Berlin Airlift was completed on 30 September 1949, Kelsey was posted back to England to attend the No. 9 Advanced Intelligence Course at the Intelligence Centre, returning to 211 GCLO in November. On 24 January 1950, he was granted a short service commission in the Intelligence Corps, retaining his seniority as Captain. In April 1950, he returned to the Intelligence

Corps depot and was sent on the Inter-Service Photographic Interpretation Course at RAF Nuneham Park in Oxfordshire. He was then posted to the Army Photographic Interpretation Unit in the UK and in February 1951 to the Air Photo Interpretation Unit in the Middle East. This unit was headquartered at RAF Deversoir at the head of the Great Bitter Lake, just north of GHQ Middle East at Fayid, some 18 miles south of the town of Ismailia.

When nationalist discontent gripped Egypt in 1951, the Bureau Sanitaire, a former Egyptian Hospital in Ismailia, was taken over by the Egyptian Auxiliary Police as a barracks. On the night of 17 November, a civil disturbance broke out in the vicinity of the barracks during which groups of auxiliaries opened fire on British servicemen and vehicles. Although the trouble died down during the night, it flared up the next afternoon, with some incidents of shooting at both British service and civilian personnel. During this gunfire, several British soldiers were killed and wounded. At approximately 3 p.m. on 18 November, Captain Kelsey was in the company of an RAF officer in Ismailia when they heard shooting coming from the direction of the Bureau Sanitaire. They went to investigate and, having established that British servicemen were being targeted, Captain Kelsey went to their aid. As he approached the grounds of the building accompanied by the RAF officer and several other British servicemen, he was confronted by an Egyptian policeman who was armed with a rifle. Standing his ground, and in an attempt to try and assert some authority, Kelsey ordered the policeman to drop his weapon. At this, the policemen ran back inside. Kelsey then turned to warn his colleagues to take cover. As he did so, a short burst of small arms fire came from a basement window. Kelsey was hit and fell to the ground. While the other British servicemen covered the windows, a Sergeant of the Royal Electrical and Mechanical Engineers rushed over to him, dragged him out of the grounds and got him into the street. Sadly, it was too late; he was dead. His body was taken to the Medical Reception Station where death was confirmed. It was established that he had been hit by one bullet in the chest.

Immediately after this incident, the British Commander ordered all British families in married quarters in Ismailia to be evacuated. The number of terrorist incidents increased, however, most of them involving police auxiliaries. Eventually, in January 1952, the decision was taken to disarm the Egyptian police. By that time, British casualties due to terrorist acts had risen to thirty-three, with another sixty-nine wounded. On 25 January, a company of the 1st Battalion Lancashire Fusiliers, supported by a Centurion tank, assaulted the Bureau Sanitaire and the Caracol, the main police station. After a four-hour operation during which forty-one police were killed and seventy-three were wounded, the remaining 800 police surrendered.

Captain Charles Langhorne Kelsey was buried with full military honours at Moascar War Cemetery in Egypt. His wife remarried in the autumn of 1952 and died in 2010, aged eighty-nine. In 1952, Captain Kelsey was posthumously awarded a Queen's Commendation for Brave Conduct.

THE CYPRUS EMERGENCY

Britain's link with Cyprus dates back to 1878 when the Ottoman Empire leased the territory, placing its majority Greek Cypriot and minority Turkish Cypriot population under British administration for the next eighty-two years. As the twentieth century progressed, the Greek Cypriots' desire for 'enosis', or union, with Greece grew.

By 1954, independence demands had spread, yet they were rejected
by Britain, which planned to transfer its military headquarters
from Suez to Cyprus. On 1 April 1955, the National Organisation
of Cypriot Fighters (EOKA) began a bombing campaign under the
leadership of General Georgios Grivas, a Greek Cypriot former
officer with the Greek Army. Also involved with the 1,250 EOKA
guerrillas was Archbishop Makarios III, a clergyman and politician
who would eventually become the first President of an independent
Cyprus. Amid the unrest, Field Marshal Sir John Harding was
appointed Governor of Cyprus and additional British battalions
were despatched. Harding tried to replicate the counter-insurgency
(COIN) measures used during the Malayan Emergency, including
a combined Army and police command structure with an emphasis
on intelligence gathering and processing. These measures had some
success, but local informants were thin on the ground. In 1955, EOKA
killed five British servicemen and a state of emergency was declared.
The terrorists were active in many towns and villages, but their main
power base was in the Troodos Mountains. They also ran a campaign
of intimidation against Greek Cypriot police, forcing the British to
rely on Turkish Cypriot policemen. There were 17,000 British service-
men in Cyprus by mid-1956. When 2,000 of them conducted a sweep
of the Troodos using spotter planes and helicopters, seventeen ter-
rorists were captured, though Grivas escaped. Hides were found and
documents were discovered which, when analysed by the Intelligence
Corps, proved to be an intelligence goldmine, giving details of EOKA
members across the island. However, attacks against British service-
men and their families escalated. By early 1957, a more coordinated
intelligence process led to greater British operational success. In
March 1957, a ceasefire was agreed and negotiations between the
British and Archbishop Makarios began. When Grivas resumed his

bombing campaign in March 1958, the new Governor, Sir Hugh Foot, was ordered by London to find a diplomatic solution. Eventually, in 1960, negotiations led to the Zürich and London Agreements by which Cyprus became an independent republic, with Britain retaining control of two military bases at Akrotiri and Dhekelia.

Intelligence Corps personnel were involved in three main areas during the 1950s Cyprus Emergency: the provision of Intelligence Staff Officers and NCOs at formation headquarters; field security sections; and port and travel control security. Headquarters personnel included operational intelligence staff, interpreters, a headquarters security section, the Security Identification Section (whose members were attached to the Cyprus Police Special Branch) and a Corps Captain who controlled 'counter-gangs', that is to say 'turned' former EOKA terrorists who were used to spread fear among their former comrades. Their activities were covert and 'non-admitted' or recorded.

There were two field security sections, one each for the western and eastern halves of the island. The Port and Travel Control Security Unit had detachments at the major port facilities of Famagusta, Limassol and Larnaca, and also at RAF Nicosia. Their primary task was the prevention of arms and explosives smuggling, requiring them to search all vessels entering and leaving the ports and to detect the movement of insurgents. Although one former wartime member of the Intelligence Corps was assassinated by EOKA in April 1958 (at the time of his death, he was a Colonial Office security officer attached to the Cyprus Police Special Branch as an interrogator), there were no fatalities among serving Corps members during the crisis. Several Corps men, however, were targeted personally by EOKA. Notable among them was Captain Lionel Savery.

Lionel Frank Savery was born in Cardiff on 17 August 1929, the son of Ernest, a cinema manager, and Irene (née Porter). He was educated at Cathays High School in Cardiff and then the Royal Military Academy at Sandhurst. He received an emergency commission as a Second Lieutenant in the Royal Artillery on 24 September 1948. His first posting was to Hong Kong as a naval gunfire control officer aboard a cruiser on the Far East Station. He then moved to London to learn Mandarin at the School of Oriental and African Studies. In April 1950, he was promoted to Lieutenant and his commission was changed to a regular, short service commission. Having finished his studies in 1952, he was selected as a Military Intelligence Officer in Malaya, where the terrorist insurgency had peaked the previous year with the murder of the British High Commissioner, Sir Henry Gurney.

As a Military Intelligence Officer, Savery provided a link between the Malay Special Branch and the rotating British Army units on the ground, both British and Gurkha. His area of responsibility was around Bentong, a small town between the capital, Kuala Lumpur, and Kuantan, dealing with captured and 'turned' communist terrorists who were used as informers and guides for Army patrols against terrorist camps in the jungle. During this period, he saved the life of a British soldier whose knee was blown off by a dumdum bullet fired at close range. A medical orderly was unable to staunch the flow of blood, so Savery tied a tourniquet around the wounded man's thigh using a knotted towel, an apple that he happened to have and a sten gun magazine to screw the dressing tight. For the work he did in his three-year tour, he was awarded a Mention in Despatches in May 1955. The previous year, he had married Marisa Hanscomb, the daughter of Intelligence Corps officer Major 'Hank' Hanscomb. They went on to have two sons.

In August 1956, Savery was promoted to temporary Captain and posted to Cyprus. He was attached to the Intelligence Corps and appointed as the District Intelligence Officer in the Pano Platres area of the Troodos Mountains, a major stronghold for Grivas and his EOKA terrorist organisation. As a mark of how dangerous the island had become, the morning after Savery arrived in Nicosia, a British Army officer was assassinated in a street which he had walked down just twenty minutes earlier. Indeed, trouble seemed to stalk him from his arrival in Cyprus. On his first visit to police headquarters, he was briefed on the highly secretive nature of his work and then photographed for his identity card. He later discovered that the photograph was copied and leaked to EOKA by an informer in the station.

Although his cover had been blown, he carried on regardless, deciding to actively pursue his foes – often by night – rather than becoming a sitting target. He hired as his driver and bodyguard a Turkish butcher who was reputed to be 'fearsome' with a knife. He always carried a gun and a bag of grenades and also changed his car once a week and his number plate daily. His wife, who had accompanied him on his posting, was eventually recruited as a special constable with the Cyprus Police and used for searching women during operations and typing up her husband's intelligence reports.

Mirroring his Malayan experience, Savery became involved in the formation and running of 'counter-gangs' against EOKA. Captured and 'turned' terrorists were organised into patrols who would venture out on intelligence-gathering missions in the villages known to be sympathetic to the revolutionaries, often posing as EOKA fighters to win their confidence. It was highly risky work. Once actionable intelligence was obtained, a follow-up operation would be mounted by fast-moving hit and snatch teams, sometimes

– but not always – backed up by the Army. The 'counter-gangs' also recruited their own informers when circumstances allowed, widening the intelligence coverage. Very often, Savery's group, officially known as X-Platoon, operated in conjunction with the 2nd Battalion of the Parachute Regiment. Its Commanding Officer, Lieutenant Colonel Bredin, had been involved with Orde Wingate's 'Special Night Squads' in Palestine during the Arab Revolt of the 1930s. On numerous occasions, Savery personally led his group on patrols through the forests of the Troodos Mountains. He also ventured out alone disguised as a Cypriot peasant.

On 31 December 1956, Savery received intelligence from an informer that Grivas was hiding in the house of an EOKA supporter called Minas Constantinou in the village of Zoopiyi, about 8 miles east of Pano Platres. He led a patrol there using an old taxi as cover, but, in a moment of confusion, the patrol mistakenly raided the house of Constantinou's father next door. As it turned out, the terrorist in hiding wasn't Grivas but his second in command, Grigoris Afxentiou. Another EOKA man, Michael Georgallis, was with him. Both guerrillas fled with their weapons and a firefight ensued. Savery and his men fatally wounded Georgallis; Afxentiou was shot in the leg but escaped into a forest and walked over six hours to another EOKA hideout in the village of Papoutsa. Eventually, he secreted himself in the Monastery of Machairas on the slopes of Mount Kionia near the village of Lazanias. The abbot, Ireneus, was a fervent EOKA supporter and allowed Afxentiou to disguise himself as an Orthodox priest. With no clue as to the radical's whereabouts, Savery continued to hunt for him and Operation Whisky Mak was created. Its objective was to arrest or kill Afxentiou.

On 21 January 1957, Savery got his break. During an intelligence-led search operation in the village of Omodhos, an EOKA hideaway was discovered in the home of Aristos Theodorou. This hidden room, in a dugout underneath the house, had been assembled on the instructions of Afxentiou in October 1956 and was accessed via a slab beneath the fireplace. When the secret hatch was opened by British troops, two EOKA men were discovered. Savery took charge of them and eventually 'turned' them.

Under questioning, one of terrorists, who had been a member of Afxentiou's group, pointed the British towards the Machairas Monastery. He also revealed the existence of another hideaway used by EOKA in rocks close to the monastery and said that a local shepherd, identified as 'Petros', took supplies there when it was occupied. The monastery became the prime focus for Whisky Mak. On Friday 1 March, 'Petros' was arrested and interrogated. He confirmed that Afxentiou had been hiding in the monastery along with four of his men but said they had moved to the hide on the evening of 27 February. It later transpired that the details of Whisky Mak had been leaked to EOKA by a sympathiser in the Cypriot Special Branch.

'Petros' was persuaded to take the Britons to the hide in return for a reward. On 2 March, he led a patrol of the Duke of Wellington's Regiment there, also digging up two EOKA pistols buried in the ground. It soon became apparent that more manpower would be required to flush the terrorists out, so the whole of 'D' Company was tasked. At dawn the next morning, the men of 'D' Company were divided into five groups to cover all the possible escape routes and provide an assault team. Cornered, Afxentiou ordered his companions to leave the hide but decided he would sit tight and fight to the end. A gun battle ensued in which one British soldier was killed. Another soldier managed to get close enough to the hide's entrance to throw a grenade inside. An officer then ordered one of Afxentiou's men to find out if he had been killed and, if he was still alive, to persuade him to surrender. He did so and, finding that Afxentiou had been wounded, rejoined his leader.

Knowing that the hide was well supplied with ammunition and grenades, the Commanding Officer ordered that the two terrorists should be burned out or buried by a large explosive charge. An initial attempt to ignite petrol which had been poured around the hide proved fruitless as it had been raining heavily overnight, and an explosive charge detonated against the roof was also ineffective. Eventually, a supply of highly flammable aviation fuel was delivered by helicopter and poured around the hide. When it was ignited, it went up with a bright flash. Through the flames, a smouldering figure emerged and ran into nearby bushes. It was Afxentiou's companion. He was quickly killed by soldiers, but of Afxentiou there was no sign. The fire burned so intensely that the hide could not be approached until the following day. The charred remains of Grigoris Afxentiou were found inside. They were taken away for a post-mortem which revealed a bullet wound to the head. The coroner concluded that it had been the cause of death and was most likely due to a round cooking off in the fire. The possibility of suicide, or of the shot being administered by another person, seems not to have been considered. Afxentiou's body was buried in a small cemetery in the yard of Nicosia Prison used for the burial of executed EOKA men. After Cyprus gained independence, several thoroughfares in major towns were named after him.

Captain Savery continued to lead the 'counter-gangs' in the Troodos Mountains. During one patrol in June 1957, he was engaged in a firefight with a group of terrorists and received a serious gunshot wound to the thigh. He spent months in hospital before returning to duty. By then, he was on the EOKA death list. On 23 July 1957, his award of the Military Cross was announced in the *London Gazette*. The recommendation had been made in March of that year and read:

> Captain Savery has built up an intelligence organisation in Platres which has been responsible for many successes against terrorism in the Troodos area. In particular he has developed entirely on his own initiative a most valuable small unit of ex-EOKA sympathisers who now work for the security forces. He has frequently led patrols by day and by night in pursuit of information and on at least one occasion he has had to fight for it. Raids in which he took part at Zoopiyi, Kannaviou and Omodhos in particular yielded twelve badly wanted terrorists with their weapons. In all these operations it was his tirelessness, driving force resourcefulness and lack of regard for his own personal safety in most difficult country and climatic conditions which provided the inspiration leading to success. There is no doubt that during the period October 1956 onwards he was a man marked out for assassination by the EOKA leaders, so much had they learned to fear his knowledge of them and his unceasing efforts against them, though he thought nothing of it he went in daily danger of his life from ambush.

Savery's tour of Cyprus ended in 1958 and he returned to England where his long association with the Intelligence Corps was formalised when he became one of the 'First 100' regular officers transferred to the Corps in July of that year. During his remarkable service in the Army, he had become fluent in Italian and Chinese and also spoke Spanish, Greek, Turkish and French. He remained in the Corps until 1963, when he resigned his commission to take up the appointment of Deputy Head of the Royal Malaysian Police Special Branch in Sarawak. In 1968, he left Malaysia and joined the International Publishing Group (IPC) as a labour advisor in its magazine division. In 1980, he joined the Institute of Practitioners in Advertising in the same capacity.

In retirement, Lionel Savery lived in Frome, Somerset. For a time, he was chairman of the Special Forces Club historical sub-committee. His wife predeceased him. He died on 4 January 2012, aged eighty-two.

BORNEO

The Borneo campaign, also known as the Indonesian–Malaysian Confrontation, was an undeclared war fought from 1963 to 1966 between Britain and President Sukarno of Indonesia following Malayan independence in 1957. In 1962, the northern area of Borneo consisted of the British protectorate of Brunei and the colonies of Sarawak and North Borneo. The rest of the island was made up of the Indonesian provinces of Kalimantan. Britain hoped to incorporate Brunei, Sarawak and North Borneo, all of which were close to gaining independence, into the Federation of Malaysia along with Singapore and the Malayan Peninsula states. Sukarno, however, wanted to tighten Indonesia's grip by adding these areas to the rest of Kalimantan. In December 1962, pro-Sukarno rebels staged an attempted coup against the Sultan of Brunei, prompting the British to send in the Gurkhas from Singapore. They were joined by the Queen's Own Highlanders and 42 Royal Marine Commando and easily put down the rebellion. Then, in April 1963, Sukarno attacked North Borneo. This time, five battalions of British and Gurkha troops defended the territory, which consisted of almost 1,000 miles of mountainous jungle. As the

*campaign progressed, the military effort expanded to include troops
from Malaysia, Australia and New Zealand and stretched to thirteen
infantry battalions. A Special Air Service squadron was also called
upon together with supporting artillery, engineers, logistics and several helicopters. Intelligence was of particular importance. The Director
of Operations was senior Army officer Walter Walker. His experience
fighting the Japanese in Burma during the Second World War and the
communists in Malaya encouraged him to use medical and agricultural projects to help win the 'hearts and minds' of the local population, some of whom were also recruited into an irregular force known
as the Border Scouts. Eventually, Sukarno had to use his own regular
troops to help the insurgents, forcing the British to counter with more
artillery and stronger patrolling. In March 1966, Sukarno was overthrown by President Suharto, who withdrew Indonesia's forces from
the border areas and signed a treaty with Malaysia that August. The
confrontation claimed the lives of 114 Commonwealth personnel and
wounded 180.*

The success of the Borneo campaign relied heavily on the production of good intelligence and the ability of the British units to act
quickly enough to use it to its best effect. This allowed them to
dominate the jungle using a series of forward bases from where continuous patrolling could be mounted. The performance of the Intelligence Corps in providing the necessary intelligence product was
outstanding from the start. At the heart of the intelligence-gathering
process were Field Intelligence Officers who were mainly Warrant
Officers and senior NCOs. They lived in the jungle, often with or
close to the local community, and dressed in plain clothes. They had
two main jobs: extracting information from tribesmen regarding the
insurgents' movements and activities; and recruiting informers who

could be directed for specific tasks. The FIOs worked with the local police, and many learned local dialects to generate the best results. Other members of the Corps were engaged on the interrogation of captured insurgents, while some formed intelligence platoons for attachment to the various formation headquarters. The Corps also provided signals intelligence and aerial photographic interpretation specialists. Tony Shilcock was one Intelligence Corps operator who was posted to Borneo. His account represents the typical duties expected of him and his colleagues.

Anthony 'Tony' Shilcock was born in Manchester in 1944, the son of a serving Army officer. He was educated in schools in Britain and Malaya and then on the Isle of Wight, where he joined the Sea Scouts and the Army Cadet Force. He also learned to sail, a skill which came in use while serving a spell with the Special Boat Service (SBS) during the Borneo Confrontation.

In December 1961, he enlisted directly into the Intelligence Corps at Portsmouth, the sixth generation of the family to join the armed forces. After training at the then Intelligence Corps depot at Maresfield in Sussex, he qualified as an Operator Intelligence and Security and was posted to 13 Intelligence Platoon, HQ 20 Armoured Brigade at Detmold in Germany. While there, he undertook further training including surveillance and counter-surveillance together with winter warfare training in the Harz Mountains.

In early 1963, the Intelligence Corps sought volunteers to serve with Special Forces. Shilcock and another Corps NCO volunteered for the Royal Marine Commandos, enduring the arduous Commando Course at the RM Commando Training School at Lympstone in Devon. They were the first members of the Corps to attempt it. Having passed, Shilcock received the coveted commando 'Green Beret' and was posted to the Intelligence Platoon of HQ 3 Commando Brigade in Singapore. In January 1965, HQ 3 Commando Brigade RM were deployed to Borneo to cover the second and third divisions of Sarawak and take operational control and responsibility of both divisions, undertaking confrontation and intelligence-gathering duties.

Once in theatre, Corporal Shilcock and other members of the intelligence platoon were deployed as FIOs throughout the divisions. Shilcock's area covered a 25-mile stretch along the border of the Second Division south of Song and on the Rajang River near Kapit, close to the South Kalimantan border where his base camp was located. Having been given his instructions, he received his kit which consisted of a personal weapon; 200 rounds of ammunition; a 28-day mixed box of 24-hour rations; and some Australian lightweight gear. He then embarked on a five-hour river trip in a native longboat accompanied by the local Malay Liaison Officer (JCLO) to the border base camp, which was manned by the Royal Malay Regiment (RMR).

Life as a Field Intelligence Officer in Borneo was tough. For the exclusive purpose of contributing to this book, Tony Shilcock has kindly provided his recollections of his duties. He writes:

Having to deploy as a Field Intelligence Officer in Borneo was like being thrown into the deep end very quickly, with little directive from the Military Intelligence Officer other than to gather intelligence on the insurgents – the North Kalimantan National Army, or TNKU – and at the same time conduct a 'hearts and minds' operation. There were no Malay government representatives in my border region other than my Malay liaison officer (known as a JCLO) who was a bit vague on the understanding of intelligence-gathering or conducting a hearts and minds programme. The basic operational intelligence phrase that came to mind being to 'collect, collate, interpret and disseminate intelligence gathered'. As a Field Intelligence Officer, I operated alone with the JCLO: there was no radio back-up, no military assistance that could come to my aid in the event of an Indonesian incursion during my intelligence-gathering trips to the longhouses or while conducting hearts and minds activities. Such a situation sharpens your mind very quickly, makes you stay alert and constantly evaluate your options continually in the event of meeting the enemy. Prior to my arrival, a 100-strong force of TNKU had invaded the area, but swift action by UK forces had cut off the insurgents' line of retreat, most of whom had been killed or captured. The local Iban headman who had alerted the British forces on that occasion had been given a large cash sum with which he built a very modern longhouse. He also requested a car, which he was given, but with no roads in our area, or petrol station, it remained static! At base camp, I had a small room located on the perimeter of the base camp which I shared with the JCLO, while the boat crew slept in the nearby longhouse. There was no running water, so I had to use water sterilization tablets for all drinking water drawn from the river; no electricity other than to supply the radio operator; no washing facilities – but we did have a hole in the ground as a loo. All jungle greens were washed in the river and dried in the sun on the river rocks. Cooking was by hexamine burners which came with the 28-day ration pack. I will always remember that on my second 28-day jungle insertion, I was given a pack which I did not check before leaving for base camp, only to find that I had not been given a mixed pack but one containing 28 days of Irish stew. The Iban tribes in my area were very friendly and an eye-opener as to how they lived but I also found out that their rice wine is very potent. From recall, every longhouse I visited had a picture of the Queen hanging on the wall alongside the skulls of their slain enemy and some had never seen a white man before. The Ibans were always coming forward with information which allowed me to assess if it indicated a threat from the TNKU. The remoteness of my area meant that there were no medical facilities in the area. Any serious illness required a journey by longboats back up the river Kapit to Song, where there was a local doctor, or onward travel to the hospital located in Sibu. It was during one of my visits to a longhouse that the Iban headman asked if I had any medication for one of his family who had stomach ache. Considering my role in the 'hearts and minds' effort this was a problem that had to be solved, but I was not medically trained and neither did I have any medical supplies. So, I invoked 'Smartie Power'. In several of the Army-issue ration packs there were boxes or tubes of Smarties and, being partial, I had a box in my rucksack. The power of 'medical Smarties' prevailed. I had to designate different colours for different minor ailments such as headaches, stomach-aches and so on. The word soon spread and at each longhouse there was always a queue of minor ailments with Smarties being dished out according to colour and ailment. Whether this was the placebo effect or not, 'Smartie medicine' seemed to do the trick, but then maybe they just liked the taste and wanted more. After 28 days in the jungle I was airlifted out by a Naval Air Squadron helicopter to take seven days rest and relaxation at the Brigade location in Sibu. But my R&R lasted just 12hrs when I was ordered to go back into the jungle and undertake a Special Branch request to get details and, more importantly, a photograph of a Communist sympathiser who was stirring up trouble with the Ibans. The information coming through from Special Branch was that the individual was going to be attending a local cockfight. So, without too much trouble the suspect was identified, temporarily befriended by me putting my arm forcibly around his shoulders, with the JCLO covertly taking his photo – job done. I was withdrawn from the FIO post when the Brigade returned to Singapore. But because of serious threats from Indonesia, our Intelligence Platoon was tasked to conduct various test operations to establish how safe Singapore would be from any aggression from Indonesian troops stationed in the islands just offshore. I was attached to the Special Boat Service and met Paddy Ashdown, who was their section OC. I subsequently qualified in the SBS skill of swimmer canoeist – unfortunately without additional pay!

On leaving 3 Commando Brigade, Tony Shilcock's career progressed into other intelligence specialist training and organisations in various theatres of operations. He left the Army as a Captain in 1986 having served for twenty-four years. In civilian life, he worked as a recruiter for the General Mining Corporation of South Africa, an area crime investigator with Kent Police and as an educational officer for pupils with special educational needs in Kent. Latterly, he established a radio-control business manufacturing models and high-specification drone wings for a major defence company.

THE ADEN EMERGENCY

The port city of Aden, situated at the south-western tip of southern Arabia in present-day Yemen, became a British colony in 1839 and was used originally to protect the shipping route to India. It developed as a coaling and resupply station and was also important for protecting access to Middle Eastern oil supplies. The emergence of

General Nasser as President of Egypt in 1954 coincided with a rise in Arab nationalism in the region. In response, in January 1963, the British persuaded the Aden protectorates to merge with the Colony of Aden to form the Federation of South Arabia (FSA). The following year, Britain announced that independence would be granted to the FSA by 1968, though it was stated that it planned to maintain a presence in Aden. Motivated by Nasser, Arab nationalists in Yemen formed the National Liberation Front (NLF), a Marxist paramilitary organisation which itself wanted control of Aden and other areas.

The NLF insurgency against British rule began on 10 December 1963, when a grenade was thrown at the British High Commissioner, Sir Kennedy Trevaskis, at Khormaksar Airport. Among my medal collection is the George Medal and bar awarded to George Henderson, the former RAF officer who as Assistant High Commissioner of Aden saved the life of Sir Kennedy Trevaskis by pushing him away from the terrorist grenade. One member of his entourage was killed and fifty other people were injured. A state of emergency was declared and a violent campaign against the British followed. Initially, off-duty British servicemen and their families were targeted. In early 1964, attacks switched to the mountainous Radfan area near the Yemeni border, leading to British reinforcements being sent to the region. After a short but arduous campaign, the insurgency was crushed. From November 1964, the guerrilla campaign concentrated on Aden itself. British troops and their families, local security forces and government supporters were attacked, prompting the British Army to conduct patrols, sweeps, search operations and to set up roadblocks, yet supplies of arms and explosives continued. The NLF's intimidating tactics made intelligence gathering difficult, with the local population unwilling to help. In 1966, London announced that all British forces would be withdrawn immediately on independence, playing no further role in Aden. As the NLF continued its campaign, however, a second nationalist military group, the Front for the Liberation of Occupied South Yemen (FLOSY), launched a terrorist offensive against the security forces. In January 1967, supporters of both groups began weeks of rioting in Aden. This presaged further violence, which escalated following the Arab–Israeli Six-Day War. A mutiny in June 1967 by members of the Federal Army and the Aden Police ensued, resulting in the deaths of more than twenty British servicemen in Aden. By November 1967, the NLF and FLOSY began fighting each other for control of Aden. That month, the British government withdrew its remaining 3,500 troops, and by the end of the year, Britain had left Aden altogether.

As with previous insurgent campaigns, members of the Intelligence Corps were involved in the full spectrum of intelligence duties during the Aden Emergency. A few NCOs had served in Aden during the mid-1950s, providing support to the British Protectorate Levies and Aden Levies, and had been grouped together as 4 Field Security Section. When the Aden Emergency was 'recognised' in 1963, 15 Intelligence Platoon provided support to the 39th Infantry Brigade and were engaged primarily in collating and analysing information from captured weapons, documents, roadblocks, patrol reports and observation points – in other words, the basic sources of operational intelligence. Intelligence Corps officers were employed in staff appointments at formation headquarters such as Joint Staff Intelligence (Middle East); HQ Middle East Land Forces; HQ 24 Brigade in the Aden hinterland; and the Aden Brigade in the townships. What had been 4 Field Security Section morphed into the Counter-Intelligence Company Aden. It provided all physical and personnel security plus vetting and investigation of insurgents, suspects and known sympathisers. While interrogation had been the province of the Aden Police, the breakdown of the force led to that role being undertaken by the Intelligence Corps at a holding and interrogation centre at Fort Morbut, using Arabic speakers. Several recently commissioned subalterns in the Corps served their mandatory eighteen-month infantry attachment with battalions serving in Aden – three of whom went on to become Brigadiers in the Corps. Colin Parr served with the Intelligence Corps in Aden during the emergency.

Colin David Parr was born in Belfast on 22 February 1944. He was educated at the Royal Belfast Academical Institution and in 1961 he enlisted in the Royal Ulster Rifles in the ranks. In 1963, having been recommended for a commission, he was accepted at Sandhurst and in 1965 he was commissioned into the Intelligence Corps. His first posting on leaving Sandhurst was to Singapore and from there he served in Malaya and in Borneo. In 1966, he went up to Worcester College, Oxford, to read Arabic and Islamic history, but, while he enjoyed the work, he missed the Army and applied to return to regimental duty. He recollects:

In 1967, I had been in the Army for five years, during which I had served as a Rifleman and Local Lance Corporal of the Royal Ulster Rifles, a cadet at RMA Sandhurst and been commissioned into the Intelligence Corps. My introduction to the Corps was an 'under instruction' tour to Singapore, West and East Malaysia (Borneo) and briefly to Brunei, in all cases to watch, learn and gain some insight into the work of the Corps. In June 1967, I embarked on the next phase which the Corps regarded as appropriate for a regular officer, in order to develop understanding of the combat arms and of the field conditions under which operational intelligence is collected. The postings roulette wheel assigned me to the 1st Battalion The Prince of Wales Own Regiment of Yorkshire (PWO), at that time in garrison in Colchester as part of the Strategic Reserve, participating in the roster for emergency tours in case of urgent operational circumstances where HMG regarded military intervention or reinforcement as necessary, especially overseas.

I did not have much time to study the strategic reserve concept. I joined the battalion in June 1967 when it was taking its turn as 'Spearhead' i.e. first reserve, and five days later, at five hours' notice, deployed as OC 7 Platoon, Charlie Company 1 PWO to Aden. I learned my soldiers' names on the VC10 en route to Aden via Cyprus. This was the battalion's third tour to Aden in nine years and what the NCOs thought of a non-infantry squirt as their boss beggars description.

Aden at this time was violent. Britain had announced that protectorate status would end and that the garrison would be withdrawn in 1968. The two major local revolutionary organisations – the National Liberation Front (NLF) and the Front for the Liberation of Occupied South Yemen (FLOSY) – frequently attacked each other, but both conducted frequent attacks on the colonial power. 1 PWO had its rear elements in Maala and had the operational responsibility for Tawahi and Steamer Point. The forward patrol company base was in HMS *Canute*, a former RN establishment, and Battalion HQ was at Clock Tower Hill. Maala had been the married quarter area for the now evacuated British families and our rear area accommodation was in their apartments, empty when we arrived. We therefore had to clear the buildings, and during this clearance I was shot at for the first time – but by the British Army. The flats on the opposite side of the main road were occupied by another battalion and their rooftop guard had not been warned of our arrival. When their LMG gunner saw in the twilight the silhouette of a figure with a long rifle, he fired an immediate but luckily inaccurate burst. The figure (me) rapidly dropped back through the roof hatch and has been jovially rude to officers of that battalion ever since.

My first street patrol gave me my first insight into the priorities of the Yorkshire soldier. I had prepared the patrol orders with fervour, leaving – I thought – no detail uncovered. I delivered them crisply and finished with a confident 'Any questions?' There was silence and then a quiet, polite but firm Yorkshire voice said, 'Us ahn't coomin.' The only thing I could think to say was 'Why?' The answer was clear and concise – 'Us ahn't 'ad us tea.' So, we 'ad us tea' and then went on patrol.

Thus began the lifelong respect and affection for 'Yorkie' which has accompanied me undiminished. For the next five months, life alternated weekly for the battalion's rifle companies between patrols, guarding installations, manning of observation posts and specific targeted operations, normally intelligence based. My agonisingly cryptic platoon diary, updated daily, lists some twenty active incidents of which nine involved hand grenades, and the rest split between mortar attacks, small arms fire, explosive charges and arson. A number of successful searches also took place. We even searched the public sewage tanks and the Platoon Commander had of course to set the example.

Fifty-three years on, I have been asked to describe the incidents. Not easy, but typically one retains: the tension from the first steps out of the patrol base which continued throughout a three-to-four-hour patrol unless suddenly, the rhythm is broken by the ping of a grenade lever retention spring, a shot, a running figure, an explosion or unexpected movements near – a door, a window, an alleyway. Training kicks in – cover every entry or exit to the area e.g. alleyways, steps, shutters, windows, doors; on the radio, get neighbouring observation posts to link in, inform company HQ, snap-search any likely area of threat. Check own troops by voice and in case of non-response, send others to check – if we have wounded or worse, order the necessary reaction. In one incident, I did all this and turned to my driver who turned out to be bleeding profusely but waiting for me to finish my business.

As we settled into the tour, I now know I became consumed by adrenalin, urgency and above all pride and trust in the performance of my soldiers. I also know that my older NCOs were becoming concerned that I was seeking action. This culminated in a moment when my Company Commander asked me to accompany him to the battalion second in command (2IC) for an interview. The 2IC said: 'Colin, I gather you have had seven incidents on platoon patrols. No other platoon has had more than one.' I swelled with pride until he continued: 'Has it occurred to you that you may be presenting the softest target?' A less inflated subaltern returned to his platoon. On a later occasion, a very senior officer was visiting the battalion when my patrol was involved in a double grenade incident (we survived and captured the grenadier). The senior visitor asked to visit the scene. When he arrived, I was taken to meet him with the caveat from my Company Commander: 'Don't forget to salute!' I did not realise I had a blood-stained shirt. The senior officer, a very tall man, put his hands on my shoulders and spoke warmly. 'Dear boy, you might have been killed!' One of my platoon, a few feet away in the security cordon, said in a stage whisper: 'Good thing he weren't hurt worse – he'd have got fucked!'

After leaving 1 PWO, Colin Parr served in the Intelligence Corps and fulfilled a variety of other roles in the British Army all over the world for a further thirty-two years. He was made an OBE in April 1985 and was awarded the United States Legion of Merit in 1998. Brigadier Parr retired from the Army in 1999 to work in an intelligence capacity in the Cabinet Office until 2006.

OMAN

Britain has enjoyed a mutually beneficial relationship with the Sultanate of Oman since the two countries signed their first treaty in 1798. By the mid-twentieth century, the importance of Oman's strategic position at the mouth of the Persian Gulf was hard to overstate. It had controlling access to the Strait of Hormuz, through which most of the world's oil is shipped, and British influence had increased to the point where Oman had effectively become a colony. Yet trouble in this completely closed country was brewing. In 1954 and 1957, rebellions broke out in the Jebel Akhdar region among followers of the Imam Ghalib al-Hinai, posing a threat to the authority of the ultraconservative sultan, Said bin Taimur. These uprisings were triggered by the imam's opposition to the sultan's plans to permit British-influenced oil exploration. Both rebellions were put down swiftly, primarily by the Special Air Service (SAS) and Royal Air Force. A 1958 defence agreement cemented the relationship between Muscat and London, with Britain committing to help develop Oman's military in return for an airbase in Oman. In 1962, more problems came, this time in the southern Omani region of Dhofar. Marxist-influenced guerrillas of the Dhofar Liberation Front agitated against the sultan's medieval rule with support from the People's Democratic Republic of Yemen, a group which then escalated tensions under the banner of the

Popular Front for the Liberation of the Occupied Arabian Gulf. At its height, it had about 2,000 full-time fighters and 4,000 part-timers. From 1968, Russia and China trained and armed the rebels, and the insurrection became a war. On 23 July 1970, Sultan Said bin Taimur was deposed in a bloodless coup by his Sandhurst-educated son, Qaboos, who embarked on plans to modernise his country using its new-found oil wealth. By then, most of the province of Dhofar was dominated by the insurgents, with only the narrow coastal strip in the area of Salalah unaffected. Having wrestled control of the country from his father, the new sultan requested British assistance to crush the revolt and save Oman from communism, safeguarding western interests in the process. Intelligence Corps men were associated with two highly significant incidents during the Dhofar Rebellion, which ended in 1976.

Within days of Sultan Qaboos's request in 1970, an SAS squadron arrived in Oman under the guise of the British Army Training Team (BATT) to carry out Operation Storm. At that time, the SAS was almost entirely unknown to the wider British public, meaning it was in effect a shadow force engaged in a far-off and little-known war. Officers and NCOs of the Intelligence Corps were involved in Operation Storm from the beginning – indeed, the inclusion of an intelligence section had been one of the five requirements listed by the SAS for the successful conduct of the operation – and were represented in Oman in three ways. They were called upon to support the SAS's own intelligence cell; to support the sultan's Army; and they had a presence in their own right carrying out interrogation and photo imagery. Several Corps officers were also placed into staff positions at Salalah, the RAF base. Other Corps officers were already serving as loan officers or were on secondment to the sultan's Army. Later in the campaign, both officers and NCOs established a detailed interrogation centre.

The BATT intelligence cell fulfilled a number of roles including initial debriefing of captured and surrendered insurgents (known as 'Surrendered Enemy Personnel' or SEPs); talent-spotting and 'nurturing' those SEPs considered for recruitment to the small fighting squads known as 'firquats'; collation and analysis of all captured information, especially weapons analysis; compiling the order of battle; and compiling a league table of personalities and organisation of the rebel groups. Perhaps one of the most important contributions of the intelligence cell was its work with the various Dhofari tribes, especially in the 'hearts and minds' campaign and in countering the revolutionary and anti-religious ideology spread by the insurgents to shape the tactical and strategic conduct of the war against them. The campaign eventually resulted in an erosion of the guerrillas' influence and fighting capability, and though there were few examples of set-piece combat, of those that did take place, the most notable is the Battle of Mirbat. In this, one Intelligence Corps officer, David Venn, played a crucial role.

David Venn was commissioned into the Intelligence Corps from Sandhurst. He passed out third in the Order of Merit, played rugby for the 1st XV and won the Russian language prize. He was the hundredth of the 'First 100' – the first 100 regular officers either commissioned or transferred into the newly reconstituted regular cadre of the Corps. After courses at the Small Arms School at Hythe and the School of Infantry at Warminster, he served initially in the British Army of the Rhine, followed by a tour as a seconded rifle Platoon Commander with 2 Para in the Middle East and as OC 3 Commando Brigade Royal Marines Intelligence Platoon based in Singapore, where he was taught basic Malay and Thai.

He volunteered for loan service with the Sultan of Oman's armed forces and arrived in Dhofar province in January 1971, together with a fluent Arabic-speaking Intelligence Corps Major, Peter Boxhall. Venn subsequently served for twenty months in the combat zone, earning the Distinguished Service Medal from the Sultan of Oman.

At about 5 a.m. on 19 July 1972 – coincidentally the 32nd anniversary of the Intelligence Corps' formal creation – a nine-man SAS team from B Squadron, plus a small force of local Omanis, was taken by surprise by up to 400 insurgents just outside the fishing village of Mirbat. The subversives were winning the war at this point, and the garrison at Mirbat was the last frontier stopping them from opening up a route to Muscat. Defending this area was vital if the rebels' plan to bring down the sultan was to be thwarted. Against the odds, the Britons withstood a six-hour onslaught of Kalashnikov bullets, mortars and rocket-propelled grenades. Remarkably, each man had only one rifle. Their Commander, Mike Kealy, had a pistol. The only other firearms at their disposal were a Browning anti-aircraft gun which could fire just two rounds at a time; one machine gun; two mortars; and a Second World War 25-pounder artillery piece which was by a smaller fort near the BATT house – the main building used by the SAS. Equally striking is that one SAS man, Corporal Talaiasi Labalaba, managed to operate this long-range weapon alone despite rebel fire seriously wounding his jaw and badly injuring his Omani loader early on in the battle. Usually, it would require four men to handle, yet Labalaba, originally from Fiji, used it like a rifle to fire a round a minute at the approaching rebels for as long as possible, switching their attention away from his colleagues' positions. Captain Kealy and SAS soldiers Tommy Tobin and Sekonaia Takavesi ran what has been described as a suicide mission of about 500 yards through enemy fire to reach Labalaba but were ultimately too late. Tragically, Labalaba died of the injuries he sustained during the battle. Takavesi and Tobin were also hit, the latter also dying some days later from complications relating to his injuries.

Although no Intelligence Corps individuals were involved in the Battle of Mirbat, it is widely accepted that the quick thinking of David Venn was instrumental in overcoming the enemy. Venn was at that time a Captain and a loan service officer in the role of Operations Officer to the sultan's armed forces, meaning that he was ultimately in charge of coordinating everything in the field including the sultan's armed forces and the Dhofar Gendarmerie, an armed force with some police duties.

When the first shots had been fired at Mirbat at dawn, an on-duty police officer radioed SAF headquarters at Umm al Ghawarif, about 40 miles away. Venn received the call which, given the pressure of the situation, was not encrypted. He was told hurriedly: 'Send jets!' Venn knew it was not unusual for the local police to overreact to any sign of enemy contact, and that such action was not in fact always necessary, yet despite having no firm details to go on, he sensed that action was warranted. For one thing, he radioed back to the police fort but was not able to get through. As Roger Cole and Richard Belfield note in their 2011 book *SAS Operation Storm: Nine Men Against Four Hundred*: 'A very experienced intelligence officer, Venn knew that the smart thing was to carry all possibilities in your head until things became clearer ... Good military intelligence analysis is all about sifting rumour from fact and spotting the moment when the former becomes the latter.'

Although heavy rain and mist rendered flying conditions unsafe that morning, Venn quickly ordered a helicopter along the coast.

It tried to land, but under heavy fire, it was forced to leave the area, the pilot having almost been killed. Venn also ordered two Strikemaster jets of the Sultan's Air Force, flown by RAF pilots, to scramble. Their arrival, armed with 500lb bombs and machine guns, saved the day. With the enemy yards away from the BATT house, the jets provided close air support with machine guns and light rockets, ensuring the rebels were pinned back just when the battle might have turned in their favour. Reinforcements arrived by helicopter in the form of G Squadron SAS. The insurgents were forced to withdraw, having lost as many as 100 men.

As the SAF Operations Officer, David Venn – an Intelligence Corps Captain and later Brigadier – read the runes correctly and ordered the air strike that helped to win the Battle of Mirbat. Yet he is considered to be an overlooked hero. Without him, the outcome of the skirmish would almost certainly have been entirely different. He recollects:

The morning of the Battle of Mirbat commenced for me at about 0430, when I was woken by the duty signaller with a voice message from our Dhofar Gendarmerie outstation at Mirbat requesting jet-strike support in the face of a major ground attack. The weather conditions were poor, but the attack fitted a pattern; the Adoo had been jolted by SAF establishment of a battalion astride their western supply routes on Operation SIMBA, had launched a diversionary assault on the SAF Fort at Habrut on the western border between Yemen and the Sultanate, been repulsed there and were seeking to relieve the pressure. As I had done for the Habrut operation, I coordinated the jet strikes which tipped the balance. The Dhofar Gendarmerie (DG) were not 'policemen' in the conventional understanding of the word. They performed with distinction at both Habrut and Mirbat and their contact report came through long before the SAS/BATT were in a position to relay the same information. At Mirbat, a DG section was manning a piquet position above a water point known as Jebel Ali, north of the town which was attacked in overwhelming force, some members of the piquet escaped alive and raised the alarm. All air assets, recce, strike and casevac were controlled by SAF. The chopper pilot who got shot up on the first recce was Squadron Leader Neville Baker, now deceased. The first strike pilots, all SOAF, were Sqn Leader Bill Stoker and Flt Lts David Milne-Smith and Nobby Clark.

The date 19 July 1972 marked a turning point in the war in Oman. The rebels' failure to take Mirbat triggered the beginning of their decline. By securing a victory for the sultan, the interests of the west were protected from communism. The rebels remained active for a further four years, however.

With this in mind, victory at Mirbat can be linked directly to a subsequent development of essential proportions in Oman's struggle. In the months afterwards, it was reckoned that the sultan's forces had killed, captured and injured at least 1,000 enemy fighters in total. A further 570 surrendered enemy personnel had also defected, many of whom offered valuable information which was obtained by the Intelligence Corps. Late in 1972, one such captive was being driven to the Omani capital, Muscat, to be debriefed. He was escorted by an Intelligence Corps senior NCO. They stopped en route for a meal in the souk at the small town of Muttrah, where the enemy soldier noticed a man who was wearing a distinctive pair of yellow plastic shoes. 'I didn't know Muhammad Talib had surrendered as well,' he said. He then explained that Talib was the political commissar in the Popular Front for the Liberation of the Occupied Arabian Gulf. He always wore yellow shoes, whereas everybody else wore open-toe sandals. Having established that Talib had not in fact surrendered but was an active senior Commander in the war who represented a potential goldmine of information, he was immediately put under round-the-clock surveillance in an operation codenamed Jason.

For security reasons, only a handful of people were aware of this operation: the Intelligence Corps members involved; Major General Timothy Creasy, who was Commander of the sultan's armed forces; and the sultan himself, whose determination to root out the insurgents meant that Jason was a no-holds-barred operation. Yet it was, fundamentally, an exclusively Intelligence Corps operation. Talib and his network were tailed for months until it was apparent that they were hatching a plot of great magnitude. Shockingly, it involved the driver and military assistant to Colonel Malcolm Dennison, who was the head of the sultan's intelligence service. The details that the Corps was able to put together showed that Talib's plan was to assassinate on Christmas Day 1972 every figure in the British and intelligence operation in Oman and to kill the sultan as well.

Preparations were made to arrest and interrogate the forty conspirators involved in organising this coup. Three Corps operators who spoke Arabic were moved to Muscat before Omani forces swooped, picking up every rebel bar one who was linked to the plot. These interrogations, carried out by the Intelligence Corps, led to the discovery of a huge cache of weapons including ten tons of AK-47 assault rifles plus thousands of rounds of ammunition. By the end of 1972, more than 100 Omanis were under interrogation, ultimately revealing the methods being used to supply the rebels' weapons and confirming the extent of the opposition to the sultan's rule. This allowed him, over time, to put in place the structures around which he could remedy the situation and transform Oman into one of the most open and prosperous states in the Middle East. He ruled for fifty years until his death in January 2020, making him by far the longest reigning leader in the Arab world. He was also said to be close to the Queen.

The Dhofar campaign is universally regarded as one of the most successfully conducted counter-insurgency campaigns ever, and the Intelligence Corps played a highly significant part in it. Indeed, the Corps is the common denominator in both the Battle of Mirbat and in the collation, analysis and intelligence planning for Operation Jason, as well as the subsequent interrogations of its culprits. The end of the war was formalised in March 1976 with a peace agreement negotiated by several neutral Arab governments.

CYPRUS, 1974

As previously described in this section, the Intelligence Corps was active in Cyprus during its struggles of the 1950s. In August 1960, Cyprus became a republic, but under the treaty which brought about its independence, Britain retained the Sovereign Base Areas (SBAs) of Akrotiri and Dhekelia. These areas continue to form a strategically vital part of Britain's surveillance-gathering network in the Mediterranean and the Middle East today. Post-independence, the dream of enosis survived among the more extreme right-wing element of the Greek Cypriots, leading to the return of General Grivas, the rebirth of the EOKA movement and ultimately in the Greek military coup on 15 July 1974. The sitting President of Cyprus, Archbishop Makarios III, was deposed and replaced with the pro-unionist nationalist

Nikos Sampson. Sampson's regime was considered a puppet of the Greek junta, its aim being to unite Cyprus with mainland Greece. Clashes ensued, and on 20 July 1974, Turkey invaded the island, taking control of the north and dividing Cyprus along what became known as the Green Line. Sampson later resigned; the military regime that had appointed him collapsed; Makarios returned; and the Turkish Cypriots established an independent government. This divided the island between Turkish Northern Cyprus and the Greek Cypriot Republic of Cyprus. The Intelligence Corps' presence in Cyprus throughout the fraught period of the 1960s and 1970s was considered hugely valuable. Unlike most of the rest of the British military presence, the Corps operated – albeit unofficially but with the tacit acceptance of those who mattered – outside of the SBAs, picking up crucial intelligence from the local community.

One Intelligence Corps operator who undertook this work was Corporal John Condon. When the 1974 coup took place, it was one of his contacts who provided him with advance knowledge of the impending crisis.

John Patrick Condon was born at Deal in Kent in 1950 into a family with a strong military heritage. His paternal grandfather served with the 8th (Irish) Battalion of the Liverpool Regiment during the Great War and was awarded a Divisional Commendation for gallant conduct after taking part as a volunteer in the famous trench raid of that battalion at Blairville, near Arras, in April 1916. He was mortally wounded six months later on the Somme. Condon's father was a career Royal Marine who enlisted in the Royal Marine Artillery in 1923, served almost continuously at sea until 1944 and retired in 1946. And Condon's elder brother was with the RAF Police for thirty years, specialising in counter-intelligence in

Germany, Libya, Aden and Cyprus. He was later recruited to MI5. Continuing the military tradition, his son, Andrew, served with the Army Air Corps and saw active service in Afghanistan, being awarded a Commander Joint Helicopter Force commendation.

After school, John Condon studied clinical biochemistry and agricultural science before enlisting in the Intelligence Corps in 1970, joining Squad 32 at Ashford and passing out as an Operator Intelligence and Security. His first posting was to Northern Ireland with the Intelligence Support Section at the main Army HQ. In October 1972, he was posted to a security section in the Eastern Sovereign Base Area at Dhekelia in Cyprus. Coincidentally, his brother was employed on counter-intelligence duties on the island at the same time.

After six months engaged on military security, Condon was selected for security intelligence work, defined as 'the intelligence required to counter the covert threat posed by hostile intelligence services and other organisations'. The Soviets were considered the main menace when it came to Britain's SBAs, but the fear of a right-wing coup d'état loomed large as well thanks to the re-emergence of the EOKA terrorist movement and the subversive influence of the mainland Greek military junta on the Greek-officered Cypriot National Guard.

Intelligence Corps security intelligence operators, and their RAF counterparts, were the only members of the British forces in Cyprus whose main operational role was concentrated outside of the SBAs. Having qualified to a minimum of conversational Greek, operators were required to develop a network of sources and contacts in their areas of interest. Targets included the Cyprus Police and Intelligence Service; the National Guard; trades union officials; local businessmen; plus bars, nightclubs and other entertainment venues all over the island.

Condon's area covered the city of Larnaca and the surrounding villages. There, he ran two right-wing sources within the National Organisation of Cypriot Fighters (EOKA) sphere. One was particularly useful in matters pertaining to the Communist Party of Cyprus; the other was closer to the EOKA leadership in Larnaca. Condon maintained regular contact with them, building up a useful picture of the unionist cause in Larnaca and the penetration of EOKA into the public services and the National Guard. 'In those days, source development involved long hours over a couple of bottles of Cypriot brandy, leisurely mezes into the small hours of the morning and being introduced into the body of their families for weddings and christenings,' Condon recalls wryly.

Crucially, though, on more than one occasion during such sessions, one of his sources promised to warn him of any coup before it happened. Meanwhile, another source was able to produce evidence of an EOKA 'safe house' – in fact a restaurant – in an outlying village where the local cell met infrequently, thereby enabling identification of other hard-line EOKA members. The same contact also provided Condon with reports of arms shipments being smuggled in from mainland Greece. This all pointed to the possibility of an attempted coup. But when would it begin?

The answer came at about 7 a.m. on Monday 15 July 1974. Condon had just arrived in the section office in Dhekelia when the phone rang. It was his EOKA source who said in Greek without any preamble: 'John, in thirty minutes. I promised!' He rang off. Within a minute, Condon and his three colleagues deployed to their own areas – Condon plus a newly arrived Sergeant to Larnaca, and the others to Famagusta. By 7.30 a.m. in Larnaca, it was obvious that a major operation was about to take place. The National Guard had two barracks in the town and the opposing (anti-unionist) Police

Tactical Reserve Unit's headquarters was situated directly between them. A civilian police station was close by. At both National Guard locations, armed soldiers were being lined up in full kit and the perimeter defences were being augmented with sandbags and machine-gun posts. The Tactical Reserve Unit and police also appeared to be reacting to the obviously militant atmosphere, although so far not a shot had been fired.

Having witnessed this frantic activity, Condon and his colleague drove immediately to Lion House on Grigoris Afxentiou Avenue, the families centre for married British servicemen who lived in Larnaca. It had a direct telephone line to the Dhekelia switchboard which they needed to alert their boss of the deteriorating situation. Many distressed British wives and children who had become aware that something was amiss had begun to gather there. A National Guard roadblock supported by a heavy machine gun prevented Condon from escorting the convoy of women and children back to Dhekelia and it was made clear to them that they would be shot if they tried to force their way through, so Condon ran the mile or so back to Lion House to appraise Dhekelia of the situation and get help in rescuing the convoy.

On Grigoris Afxentiou Avenue, however, with some distance still to go and now positioned directly between the opposing National Guard and Tactical Reserve Unit barracks, everything erupted. The opening mortar and heavy machine-gun fire from the advancing National Guard was immediately answered by the Tactical Reserve Unit, with the main axis of fire being the avenue. Condon was now effectively in 'no-mans-land', caught between both sides. Unbeknown to him, the National Guard had just assaulted the Presidential Palace in Nicosia. Archbishop Makarios had narrowly escaped and this sudden burst of fire was the Larnaca National Guard's overture in moving against the pro-Makarios police and TRU. It was the start of a civil war and Condon was stuck in the middle of it.

Having made it to the relative safety of Lion House and alerted Dhekelia to the plight of the convoy, Condon was instructed to stay put for as long as possible and report on the progress of the fighting. Every hour or so he would carefully climb to the top of the fire escape running up the front elevation of the building which gave him a clear view in both directions along the avenue. The Tactical Reserve Unit was fighting a purely static defensive action, hunkered down in its headquarters, while the National Guard were advancing slowly along Grigoris Afxentiou Avenue towards Lion House. Eventually, during one of his afternoon telephone reports back to Dhekelia, Condon was told Cyprus Radio was reporting (inaccurately, it turned out) the death of President Makarios, the fall of the government and the installation of Nikos Sampson as the new President. He was told to make his way back to Dhekelia 'by the best way you can'.

By late afternoon, the firing from both sides had stopped, but there was no way to tell how far the National Guard had advanced. Condon knew the Army Land Rover issued to the staff of the families centre was parked in the forecourt and the key was easily located in the office, but not wanting to be mistakenly targeted by either side, he decided his best chance of getting out in one piece was to change out of his civilian clothes and into a recognisable British Army uniform. Luckily, the office showed the location of houses occupied by British families and there was one not too far away. He sneaked through several gardens and broke in, finding the combat jacket and beret of a Corporal in the Royal Electrical and Mechanical Engineers. The jacket was far too small, but Condon donned it and made his way back to the Land Rover. He recalls:

With a very cautious start, I deliberately left the engine running for a few minutes so that the protagonists on both sides would have a chance to get accustomed to the noise before I moved off. Then, slowly, I drove out of Lion House into the main avenue, now in full view of both sides. After the previous hours of intense gunfire, it was eerily quiet and the streets were totally empty although I had no doubt that the advance elements of the National Guard were close by. I was also aware that they and the TRU would be nervous and trigger-happy. My plan was to drive slowly west along Grigoris Afxentiou Avenue for about half a mile and then turn right onto the ring road which skirted around the town and eventually joined the main Larnaca-Dhekelia road. That slow half-mile took for ever and the hairs on the back of my neck were literally standing to attention. But eventually I reached the turning and was clear of the main axis of fire. Thereafter, it was pedal to the metal until I reached the boundary of the SBA, where I was brought to an abrupt halt by a young nervous-looking British cavalry subaltern from the resident armoured squadron drawn up in defensive positions along the boundary line. It was quickly apparent that RMA Sandhurst doesn't teach their young officer cadets how to deal with an individual suddenly appearing out of a war zone, wearing a combat jacket, a REME beret, tan flared trousers, a purple shirt while waving a Special Authorisation Card. And he didn't get a salute either!

On 20 July, as a result of the coup and the installation of Sampson as the new President, Turkey invaded Cyprus and within two weeks had effectively occupied everything north of the Green Line running from Kato Pyrgos in the west, through Nicosia, to Famagusta in the east. An uneasy ceasefire was finally agreed on 16 August, but with the fears that the Turkish forces could at any time resume their offensive. Barely a week later, an isolated act of stupidity by the Cypriot National Guard in Larnaca placed the already tenuous truce in great jeopardy and had the potential to provide the Turks with an excuse to expand their occupation of the island.

The Hala Sultan Tekke Mosque, otherwise known as the Mosque of Umm Haram, sits beside the Salt Lake in Larnaca. It is venerated in the Islamic faith as the fourth most important religious site in the world after Mecca, Medina and Jerusalem, and therefore the most important Islamic religious site in Cyprus.

Condon continues:

A few days after the second ceasefire, I was looking for one of my sources – a Sergeant in the National Guard – and learned that he was on duty commanding a guard detail at the Hala Sultan Tekke Mosque. I walked into the main mosque to be confronted by a scene of devastation. Several National Guardsmen were in the process of trashing the place. The wooden pulpit and staircase had been pushed over onto its side; and the glass of a locked bookcase had been smashed and the sacred tomes of Islamic scripture removed. Even as I arrived, a couple of the guardsmen were ripping them apart. My source appeared at the entrance of an ante-room containing the tomb. There, I found evidence of further desecration. The embroidered and patterned fabrics which normally shrouded the stone sarcophagus had been torn away and a failed attempt had been made to remove the heavy stone lid by sliding it aside. This was a potentially explosive situation both militarily and politically, considering the already tenuous state of the Turkish ceasefire. I remonstrated with my source and was eventually able to make him realise the ramifications.

With his assurances that he would try to put things right, I took about two-dozen undamaged books and texts for safe-keeping, returned to the section and reported what had happened to the boss. By then, he had been appointed as the British Liaison Officer to the Commander of the National Guard in Larnaca. He arranged an immediate meeting with him which I attended. When I described the vandalism to the main mosque area, the Greek Commander looked incandescent, but when I went on to describe the attempt to open the tomb, he turned white! It was agreed the books would be handed over to him until they could be returned to the Turkish authorities. He also made assurances that the situation at the mosque would be dealt with.

After Cyprus, John Condon served again in Northern Ireland, and with the Joint Services Interrogation Wing at Ashford. On returning to civilian life, he set up a surveillance and investigations business. In 1999, he established the first Intelligence Corps Association region in Northern Ireland and became a trustee of the Intelligence Corps Museum in 2005, eventually taking over as chairman of the trustees between 2009 and 2015.

BELIZE, 1977

Known until June 1973 as British Honduras, Belize is a country about the size of Wales situated on the north-eastern coast of Central America, east of Guatemala. It was part of the British Empire from 1836 until it was granted self-government in 1964. It achieved full independence in 1981. Guatemala historically laid claim to Belize, necessitating a British military presence there from 1948 to act as a deterrent against any aggression. The experiences of one Intelligence

*Corps operator in Belize at this time, Staff Sergeant Graeme Davis,
illustrate how unusual and varied the roles of some of its members
have been in out-of-area operations, requiring initiative, improvisation and the ability to work in isolation, often in difficult conditions.*

Staff Sergeant Graeme Davis, the son of a Second Word War veteran who was wounded during the D-Day landings, was born in
Kent in 1950. Originally, he enlisted in the Royal Engineers in 1967.
After a year, he left the Regular Army and became a Territorial
soldier with the Queen's Regiment Territorial and Army Volunteer
Reserve. In 1969, he re-enlisted with the Regulars, this time with
the Intelligence Corps. Before being deployed to Belize, he had
already served in the UK, Germany, Northern Ireland and Hong
Kong. Davis recounts his memories in his own words:

I was sent to Belize in May 1977 to take over as Field Intelligence
NCO (South) based in Punta Gorda in the Toledo district. I remained there until February 1978. I received no formal training
for the role but spent one day with the SAS in Hereford on a
crash course in handling snake bites and other tropical nasties.
I travelled via Gander, where the temperature was -20°C, and
arrived in Belize City a few hours later, where it was 30°C. This
was quite a shock to the system! After a day of briefing, I was
driven down to Punta Gorda in the back of a Land Rover, 200
miles over broken up dirt tracks without any hint of tarmac.

My accommodation in Punta Gorda was a small house – or
shack – on stilts, close to the centre of town. I was lucky in that I
had an internal flush toilet, indoor water supply and a cold shower,
all of which were a rarity at that time. I also had the luxury of a
two-burner kerosene stove and a kerosene-powered fridge which

was later replaced with a modern electric one. Sadly, I shared this house with rats the size of cats that lived in the ceiling and fought each other regularly; large spiders that lived behind the cupboards; and snakes in the yard. I did not appreciate the local diet of mainly rice and black beans, but initially, that was all there was, so I had to make the most of it. Later, I was able to scrounge ten-man compo ration packs from the local regular Army units in the area. After nine months of this fare, all of the menus tasted the same. As a result, I lost a lot of weight! I made good contacts with an American helicopter company based just outside Punta Gorda who serviced the oil rig further south and I was able to score an occasional free meal of lobster and steak flown in fresh from the USA. They took a liking to English cigarettes which I obtained from NAAFI supplies, so a productive trade was established.

For transport, I had an old, quarter-ton, air-portable Land Rover, which was probably the worst type of vehicle possible considering the local road conditions. Needless to say, it literally shook to pieces. FINCO (North) apparently had a long-wheelbase Land Rover better suited for my local conditions and mine would have been fine for him as there was much more tarmac in his area. I asked for a swap, but the Army, in its wisdom, said no. I was also able at times to hitch rides on the RAF Puma or AAC Scout helicopters and the locals helped with dugout canoe trips when necessary.

The equipment provided to me was rudimentary: a 9mm Browning pistol, which was pretty useless in the jungle against snakes; a couple of smoke grenades; and a SARBI rescue beacon. I asked for a shotgun, which would have been ideal for my visits into the jungle, but again the Army said no.

When I arrived, the local Army unit was a detachment of Royal Engineers engaged in building Rideau Camp a couple of miles out of town. This consisted of old-style Nissen huts and, when completed, formed a company base. This camp was initially occupied by the Left Flank Company of the Irish Guards and I got the impression they would have preferred ceremonial duties to the dirt and flies. They were replaced by 1st Bn the Staffordshire Regiment, with whom I got on extremely well. My only problem with the 'Staffs' was when the CO decided that it was wrong for a lowly Staff Sergeant to have a house in town when he had to live in a tent, and he made moves to have me relocated so that he could enjoy my 'facilities'. Luckily, the British Force Commander in Belize City thought otherwise and the CO was put firmly in his place.

I was expected to work with members of the local Special Branch, who really were quite useless. Their leader was not particularly friendly and appeared to resent my presence. He seemed to consider the FINCO his personal 'cash cow' and took advantage whenever possible, even running up accounts in local 'restaurants' in the FINCO's name. I stopped this very quickly. The other team members consisted of a Creole and a Mayan Indian, both of whom were constables. They were friendlier but almost unemployable. Only the Mayan constable would ever venture to the jungle villages with me.

Soon after I arrived, I initiated a system based on ethnicity, as I realised that there was a racial divide even in a country where several races seemed to live in apparent harmony. From then on, we each dealt with the people from our own ethnic group, which seemed to work quite well.

Initially, I spent time becoming known around town, getting to know the locals and cultivating contacts. In such a small community, one's identity was soon known by the locals and a good rapport seemed to have been established. Later, I spent time visiting the more outlying villages that could be reached by road and then regularly ventured to the jungle villages on foot. I regularly visited the observation post (OP) at Cadenas, perched on high ground on the border. This was permanently manned by the Army but was only accessible via a very hairy landing by helicopter on a pad only slightly larger than the wheelbase. This OP provided good sightings of the military traffic traversing the major road from north to south Guatemala.

I found that the locals were in the main proud of their nation and very receptive and friendly to the Army presence, which made my job easier. They were good at noticing anyone arriving from Guatemala by sea and the jungle village natives always knew if any Guatemalans had crossed over the unmarked border through the jungle. I became, by default, the local liaison between the military and local government and population and was often called upon to help solve local problems, arrange local trackers for a patrol member lost in the jungle and assist in the interpretation of the local (very broken) English language.

I established contacts with a wide range of expatriate individuals, including an American family who owned a rice farm some miles out of town who had made their money providing the earthworks for Disneyworld in Florida; a Briton who worked occasionally as a soil scientist for the UN and lived in a jungle hut; and a hard-drinking, gun-toting American Jesuit brother who built schools and toilets in the jungle villages.

There was a regular boat service to Punta Gorda from Puerto Barrios in Guatemala and I often acted as the de facto immigration officer for the Belizean government. This was, I discovered, a good way of obtaining information about any military movements in the area, where there was a Guatemalan Marine base.

During my time in Belize, the threat from Guatemala increased. The Irish Guards Company was replaced by the Staffords, plus a Royal Artillery 105mm pack Howitzer battery, and became 'Battle Group South'. This was reinforced by a Royal Navy frigate offshore from Punta Gorda to act as guard ship. SAS patrols were also in the jungle close to the Guatemalan border and I acted as liaison for their Intelligence NCO.

In the event of an invasion from Guatemala, Punta Gorda would have been directly in the firing line as it was situated across the bay from Puerto Barrios; it had an accessible mangrove-free beach for landing craft; a jetty; and a small airstrip capable of taking STOL aircraft. For a time, it began to look as if Guatemala might be gearing up for an attack, although none of the local information that I received indicated any immediate threat.

Tensions were palpably higher, though, especially amongst the expat community. Battle Group South deployed in a limited way, but when a flight of Harriers was flown from the UK and sent on a very low and noisy show of force around the Belizean border, the threat was effectively over. I think the Guatemalans eventually realised that they would suffer badly in any confrontation as their armed forces were in the main poorly trained and badly equipped.

My ten months in Belize was enjoyable. I was my own boss, I worked and operated as I wished and I had the freedom of movement and decision-making that was necessary and without which nothing could have been achieved. I was on my own, with little or no support, and had to operate 'on the run' with no guidance or direction from above. No other regiment or corps would or could have expected individual NCOs to operate alone in these circumstances. For the Intelligence Corps, this was the norm.

Graeme Davis left the Army in 1981, when he and his wife emigrated to Australia, settling in Queensland, where they have remained. He served in various roles with the Queensland Prison Service for over twenty-five years before retirement in 2011.

THE FALKLANDS WAR

The Falkland Islands have been in Britain's possession since 1833. Argentina has long disputed Britain's right to the South Atlantic territory and in 1965 the UN General Assembly approved a resolution encouraging Britain and Argentina to find a peaceful solution to the disagreement. Years of diplomatic wrangling followed. Then, in a surprise move on 2 April 1982, Argentina's military dictator, Leopoldo Galtieri, ordered an invasion. The next day, the separate British dependency of South Georgia, 800 miles away, was also seized. For the first time in decades, British sovereign territory had been captured by a foreign power. Margaret Thatcher's government quickly assembled a Task Force that started heading south on 5 April. Ultimately, about thirty members of the Intelligence Corps were despatched to participate in what turned out to be a ten-week war in which 255 British troops lost their lives and 775 were wounded.

Interrogation in warfare is the oldest method of gaining strategic and tactical information from the enemy. It has been considered a key skill of the Intelligence Corps since the First World War and can be broken down into three elements: tactical questioning of prisoners near the front line; interrogation of selected prisoners at specific centres at divisional level; and in-depth interrogation of selected prisoners such as senior officers and technicians.

Although interrogation is governed by the 1949 Fourth Geneva

Convention, the European Commission of Human Rights ruled in 1976 that the five interrogation techniques used by British security forces in Northern Ireland amounted to torture, leading to significant changes in approach. So determined was the British government to ensure that the Falklands Task Force interrogators conformed to a 'no coercion' interrogation policy that it was decided prisoners should be 'interviewed' instead. Nick van der Bijl was the only Intelligence Corps operator in the Falklands in 1982 qualified to carry out interrogation. Of the twenty or so cross-examinations which he undertook during the campaign, the following story is a good example of the effectiveness of prisoner handling, when the shock of capture is used to obtain as much intelligence as is reasonably possible.

Nick van der Bijl was born in York in 1946. His father flew for the RAF during the Second World War and, after hostilities, his family moved to East Africa. In the mid-1950s, he returned to Britain, attending Aldenham School in Hertfordshire. After leaving in 1964, he joined the Royal Armoured Corps but failed the Commissions Board. He found a job and after joining the Territorial Army in Canterbury in 1967, he re-enlisted into the 1st Royal Dragoons (amalgamated as the Blues and Royals in 1969), spending three years on tanks in West Germany. He transferred to the Intelligence Corps in 1970 and was posted to protective security and operational intelligence duties in West Germany, Northern Ireland, Hong Kong – where he was awarded the British Empire Medal for security duties – and Belize. In mid-1981, he was posted to the 3 Commando Brigade Intelligence Section of Royal Marines as the only Intelligence Corps operator. His roles were operational intelligence, including interrogation. In 1982, a week after he had completed a winter warfare course in Norway, Argentina seized the Falkland

Islands and van der Bijl was sent to the South Atlantic on board the amphibious assault ship HMS *Fearless*, analysing intelligence en route.

After six weeks at sea, and equipped with significant intelligence, 3 Commando Brigade landed on 21 May at San Carlos Water, a bay on the west coast of East Falkland, as part of the Battle of San Carlos, which was fought until 25 May. Low-flying land-based Argentine jet aircraft made repeated attacks on ships of the British Task Force. Although the British sustained losses and damage, they did manage to land troops successfully.

During the afternoon of 23 May, after the Special Boat Service reported to brigade HQ that they had captured a prisoner at Fanning Head, van der Bijl was instructed to interrogate him, in particular for information relating to the Argentine defending forces known as Task Force Mercedes, which were spread between Darwin and Goose Green. Van der Bijl was under pressure to acquire accurate operational information in preparation for a forthcoming British attack which would turn out to be the Battle of Goose Green, lasting between 28 and 29 May.

'I had carried out plenty of counter-intelligence interviews and interrogations under various conditions, and although I had been on a Spanish course for my tour of Belize, I was not certain my Spanish would survive the rigours of a combat interrogation in which accuracy was crucial,' van der Bijl says. Deciding that accuracy was paramount, he put in a request for an interpreter.

My first choice was a Spanish-speaking Royal Marine on board *Fearless*, but brigade HQ instructed Captain Rod Bell, a Royal Marine of Puerto Rican extraction, to interpret. This was the first time I had had to interrogate with an inexperienced interpreter, which is different ball game to what I was used to, and therefore I insisted I would control the mechanics of the interrogation.

Van der Bijl's training kicked in automatically. 'Interrogation is all about psychology. Provided you hit the right buttons, you're half-way there,' he says.

But attacking the brain can be difficult, particularly with a resistant prisoner. Methods to convince prisoners and suspects to share information include faked anger and faked boredom with repetitive questions. But with decency and kindness, you usually win results, as long as you're always probing, probing, probing to identify information. The 'softly, softly, catchee monkey' philosophy is usually effective because prisoners respond to normality. My view was always that prisoners of war generally don't know when they will next see family and friends. It's a lonely [situation to be in] and certainly emotion can be a lever. I didn't know much about the character of the average Argentine, but from my experiences in southern Belize on the border of Guatemala, I knew there was a perception that British fair play was highly regarded in Central and South America, especially from those used to regimes which were prepared to shoot and execute their own people. I knew I would need to deflect any mention of Northern Ireland.

Shortly before dark, van der Bijl and Captain Bell were helicop-tered to Red Beach on Port San Carlos and taken to the settlement farmyard where the prisoner was being held. After a short briefing from Captain Giles Orpen-Smellie, the 3 Para Intelligence Officer, they learned that his name was Sergeant Rene Martin Colque, that he was suffering from the expected shock of capture, and that his resistance could be weak. Before meeting him, van der Bijl examined a small bag found among Colque's equipment and noted it contained British Army webbing, Northern Ireland-issue military gloves, a sleeveless jerkin from the British outdoor equipment shop Millets, two hand grenades and two photographs of a family.

He and Captain Bell then walked into a dimly lit stable. Colque stood up. Aged twenty-eight, he was stocky with jet-black hair topped by a khaki woollen hat and he wore a grey-green Argentine Army jacket and trousers and calf-high boots. Under his jacket was a British heavy-duty sweater with Royal Marines cloth shoulder titles and a Colour Sergeant's rank insignia. 'He looked at me blankly and was clearly anxious,' recalls van der Bijl. 'I strip-searched him and asked for a medical orderly to check for any wounds or injuries.'

Colque admitted that his unit was the 25th Infantry Regiment and that it was based in central Argentina and had arrived in the Falklands very shortly after the Argentine invasion. His captors concluded that he was probably used to the cold and damp weather they were experiencing. According to notes van der Bijl made shortly afterwards, '[Colque] was therefore subject to a period of discomfort, unpleasantness and pressure, made worse by the approach of night and a cold and dripping wind.'

The Argentine maintained his silence about military matters until van der Bijl removed the two photographs from his pocket. On seeing them, Colque broke down and reached out for them. 'The photographs were of his family,' van der Bijl remembers. 'Nevertheless, I told him "You can't have them back until you tell me what I want to know about Goose Green. Then you may have them."'

At this, 'the floodgates opened', according to van der Bijl, as Colque spoke in some depth about the minefields and trenches surrounding the Darwin School House, withdrawal routes to Goose Green along the beaches and the organisation of 25th Infantry Regiment. He also drew badges of insignia and rank and indicated on a map the holding areas of reserves and deployment areas of 12th Infantry Regiment at Darwin Peninsula and explained that he had left his billet at the Darwin School House three weeks earlier and been sent to Port San Carlos. He claimed to have been in the Recce Platoon of Command and Special Company and had been recruited from the south of Argentina. His unit had apparently been the first conventional infantry unit ashore in April.

When questioned about the British equipment in his bag, he said that his Quartermaster had given it to him. Van der Bijl challenged him over this, alleging he had stolen it from the Royal Marines Barracks at Stanley in contravention of the Geneva Convention. Colque denied the allegation, yet ultimately it elicited more information, in particular that his unit had been attached to 12th Infantry Regiment to form a composite company. 'He said that 12th Regiment was held in low regard and he felt it was suffering badly,' van der Bijl goes on.

> He admitted that he had little time for his officers and voiced his belief that Argentina would be defeated. This was our first indication of a possible weakness that could be exploited, although he was obviously a tough and competent solider. In discussing his capture, he said that he had not eaten for two days.

After the first interrogation, Colque was allowed to sleep and, having eaten a good meal, he was transferred to MV *Norland*, the

P&O car ferry requisitioned by the Ministry of Defence for use as a troopship which was by then being used to hold prisoners. He was questioned on *Norland* by an RAF Flight Sergeant with interrogation experience and following a yet more detailed search of his 'belongings', a ladies' wrist watch he had secreted was used as a repeat lever to keep up the pressure of accusing him of breaching the Geneva Convention by looting private property. The interrogations lasted until midday on 24 May. Van der Bijl summarised the information gleaned and passed it to brigade HQ.

Colque was repatriated to Argentina with other prisoners shortly after the Battle of Goose Green. Other interrogations in which van der Bijl was involved over the following week included that of a Mirage pilot shot down near HMS *Fearless* and a Marine officer found within Britain's beachhead perimeter.

Van der Bijl departed from the Falklands after the war ended on 11 June, returning on the SS *Canberra* with 3,000 soldiers and arriving at Southampton on 11 July 1982. He remained in the Intelligence Corps until 1989 and on discharge was employed as a security manager in the defence industry before being appointed one of the first NHS security managers. In retirement, he re-enlisted into an infantry battalion as a Private and was commissioned. He has also been a Justice of the Peace in Somerset. He is the author of twenty books, mostly on British campaigns between 1945 and 2000.

THE GULF WAR

After the Iran–Iraq War ended in 1988, tensions between Iraq and the emirate of Kuwait spiralled. Kuwait refused to cancel a $65 billion Iraqi debt. It also increased its oil production by 40 per cent, ultimately triggering accusations from Iraq's dictator, Saddam

Hussein, that it was stealing oil from an Iraqi field on the border between the two states. On 2 August 1990, Hussein ordered the annexation of Kuwait. In the ensuing invasion, it was estimated that more than 4,000 Kuwaitis were killed in fourteen hours. The UN Security Council unanimously passed a resolution calling for Iraq to withdraw, but Iraq ignored it. As a peaceful resolution was sought during the autumn of 1990, America assembled a military coalition of which Britain was a significant member. On 17 January 1991, war commenced with a five-week aerial and naval bombardment of Iraqi positions in Kuwait. On 24 February, the ground assault started. Iraqi forces were put down easily and a ceasefire was declared on 28 February. Operation Granby was the codename given to British military operations during the war, in which 53,462 members of Britain's armed forces were deployed.

The Intelligence Corps' contribution to the Gulf War was significant. It oversaw covert surveillance before the multinational military campaign began; it provided small detachments to embed with the tactical US drone units in Saudi Arabia; and it supervised photographic interpretation services. Following the Iraqi invasion of Kuwait, a threat assessment conducted by the Ministry of Defence and British intelligence concluded that British bases in Cyprus were potential Iraqi targets for their then suspected 'Weapons of Mass Destruction' (WMD) and also for smaller scale sabotage attacks planned and organised by locally based Iraqi Intelligence Officers.

At that time, the Iraqi Intelligence Service, also known as the 'Mukhabarat', was suspected of having a base on the third floor of the Iraqi Airways offices at Makarios Avenue in the Cypriot capital, Nicosia. The airline occupied the first floor while the second floor was used by the Military Affairs Office of the Iraqi Embassy.

The building's role in covert Iraqi intelligence activities had led to it being attacked twice previously by dissident Iranian-backed Iraqi terrorists during the Iran–Iraq War, first in May 1984 and then again in November 1985. On the second occasion, the airline's manager – who was also believed to be an Iraqi Intelligence Officer – was killed by a booby-trapped car bomb.

A threat assessment was carried out which was centred to a major extent on the role that the British bases in Cyprus – especially the airbase at Akrotiri – would play as a forward staging post for British troops and equipment in the impending ground war. A perceived danger to military personnel also existed, specifically those with families who lived in the neighbouring dormitory towns and who therefore did not enjoy the relative security of the bases. To counter the latter threat, the two security sections of 11 Security Company were reinforced by members of the Intelligence and Security Group (Volunteers) who conducted critical counter-terrorist surveys of these houses.

In August and September 1990, 11 Security Company in Cyprus received a request from one of the national agencies to monitor two Iraqi Airlines officials in Nicosia who were also thought to be members of the Mukhabarat. This surveillance was required to provide warning of any activity by the airline staff which might indicate planning or an imminent attack on the British bases. The operation was handled by members of 111 Security Section, which was located in the Eastern Sovereign Base Area at Dhekelia. By that time, the workload of the seven-strong section was already burdensome as a result of their existing military security and security intelligence duties. In addition, the small section was also involved in a review of the Eastern Sovereign Base Area's counter-terrorist security and contingency plans.

The target offices were in a particularly busy part of Nicosia, in the middle of the central business district, where vehicle and pedestrian traffic was heavy. This made establishing suitable observation points extremely difficult. An added complexity was that only one or two of the available team were trained surveillance operators, increasing the likelihood of the operation being compromised. Furthermore, the section did not have access to any of the specialist surveillance or communications equipment required for such an operation. They therefore had to rely on more basic methods, for instance observing targets on foot and noting who they were meeting.

Regardless, and in the face of the high late summer Nicosia temperatures, the team began its duties with its customary dedication and professionalism. By October, however, the operators were exhausted by the long hours of surveillance interspersed with their routine duties. It was clear that they could not continue to work on the operation effectively. Authority was sought and granted to request the deployment of a team from the Specialist Intelligence Wing (SIW) at Ashford in Kent. Having received authority to proceed, the operation was codenamed Operation Swordfish.

When Operation Swordfish was activated and it was agreed that observation of the Iraqi Airlines office in Nicosia would begin, the senior officer led the deployment of the entire six-strong team of instructors to Cyprus, together with an SIW Royal Signals communications specialist. Flying from RAF Brize Norton to Cyprus on a C-130 Hercules, they took with them specialist surveillance and communications equipment such as radios, aerials and remote cameras, which could be installed in locally hired vehicles.

They stayed in Larnaca in an Army hiring, a rented civilian-owned house used to accommodate married servicemen and their families. Their administrative support was provided by 111 Security Section in Dhekelia. With accommodation, vehicles, specialist equipment and communications organised, the team were briefed on the background to the operation and commenced viewing the building and its occupants. Much of the detail of the operation is still sensitive and cannot be divulged here. What can be stated is that the surveillance was concentrated on one particular Iraqi who was believed to be an Intelligence Officer but whose office and residence were located in the town of Limassol, the dormitory town of the Western Sovereign Base Area. It contained both the Headquarters Near East Land Forces at Episkopi and the large and strategically vital Akrotiri air base – the latter being a prime potential target for sabotage. Accordingly, the team's base was switched to a secure location, away from prying eyes, at the end of the Akrotiri runway.

With the main target and his residence having been identified, he was subjected to round-the-clock monitoring. Most evenings he left his home and patronised a local Cypriot social club, but while watching him at the office location, two Soviet trade mission personnel were seen visiting him there. This sighting was considered to be particularly significant as it had long been known that such Soviet missions were used as 'legal' cover for Intelligence Officers of both the KGB and the GRU. No such connection between the target and the Soviets had previously been established, however. At the time, it was unclear to the team just what the Soviet interest or involvement was concerning Iraq. Their instinct was that this would be of note to somebody further up the intelligence food chain, perhaps providing an important piece of the overall intelligence jigsaw. Throughout the period of the operation the team made detailed daily surveillance reports which were enhanced by still and moving photography. These were disseminated 'upwards' for analysis by the staff. As is often the case, the surveillance team was not fully aware of the outcome of the analysis, which was on a 'Need-to-Know' basis.

Apart from the sighting of the Soviet trade mission individuals, the operation uncovered no evidence or indication that the Iraqis were planning any offensive action against British bases, leading to its eventual termination. The team returned to the UK, but in line with other personnel stationed in Cyprus who were involved in supporting the Gulf War, they were awarded the Gulf War Medal.

Having been able to provide reassurance that no threat existed, the staff at HQ Near East Land Forces were able to properly reassess and allocate their resources and efforts accordingly. The operation also proved the value of maintaining a highly trained, specialist surveillance capability which was able to operate worldwide at short notice.

•   •   •

Before the coalition ground assault began, Imagery Analysts of the Intelligence Corps were deployed to the Middle East to obtain aerial imagery of Iraqi positions. Given the desert conditions, this was indispensable work which made a major contribution to the overall war effort. One of the key practitioners involved was Staff Sergeant Nigel 'Sam' Southam.

Staff Sergeant (later Lieutenant Colonel) Nigel 'Sam' Southam enlisted in the Intelligence Corps in 1980 with Squad 86. After qualifying as a Photographic Interpreter, he spent the late 1980s in Rheindahlen with 6 Intelligence Company, mainly 'looking' at and analysing Soviet forces' equipment and dispositions in East

Germany. Part of 6 Intelligence Company's role included Photographic Interpreter support to 32 Regiment, Royal Artillery, for the Midge drone. After three years with 6 Company, and a six-month deployment to the Falkland Islands, Southam fulfilled his ambition to serve with The British Commanders'-in-Chief Mission to the Soviet Forces in Germany (BRIXMIS). No sooner had he arrived in Berlin in the autumn of 1990, however, he was told to prepare to deploy to the Gulf War. He was one of a team of five Photographic Interpreters working with a senior collator who joined the Royal Artillery for pre-deployment training in Dortmund before arriving in Al Jubail in Saudi Arabia on 3 January 1991. The full unit designation was Drone Troop, 57 (Bhurtpore) Locating Battery, 32 (Heavy) Regiment, Royal Artillery. Their key asset was the Canadair Midge drone.

The Midge's role was target location and battlefield surveillance. It was effectively a guided missile with a Zeiss or Vinten camera system attached which could be pre-programmed to make either two or three turns and then recover, by parachute, to a homing beacon. It had a theoretical maximum range of 140km. A typical mission might involve it flying north from launch for 50km, then turning to 80 degrees for a further 40km, then turning to 120 degrees and flying for 25km before recovery. The camera systems could be switched on for two exposures, or 'runs', during the mission, resulting in either stereoscopic, mono black and white or infrared imagery. The hundreds of feet of 9-inch 'wet film' produced would be processed in the battlefield processor on the back of a 4-tonne truck and analysed by Intelligence Corps Photographic Interpreters from the film negative. Photographs of select frames could be produced to order if required. The Midge flew at an altitude of between 200 and 1,200 metres with an operational speed of about 300 knots. Its relatively high speed and low battlefield signature gave it a guarantee of reliability. Sam Southam recalls:

> It was touch and go whether the locating battery would be used in the ground war at all. It was, after all, ancient equipment which had been brought into service to be used against potential Soviet hordes streaming westwards over the German plains, but it did fill a hole in tactical recce spectrum for Op Granby. The decision was to be made by Commander US VII Corps, General Frederick M. Franks, who visited 57 Battery to assess our worth. In his presence, we flew the Midge over our guns aligned in the desert in parade review order, causing palpitations among the Royal Artillery safety-conscious Sergeant Majors instructor gunnery, and within forty-five minutes had the best imagery the Midge was ever to produce during the conflict: pin-sharp stereo imagery of the gun line. The Commanding Officer, otherwise invisible at the drone troop, was last seen scurrying away with a cut of the film, still drying, to show to the General. And so off to war we went. The General's visit was only overshadowed by the visit the day before by the BBC War Correspondent, Katie Adie, with the joke being that we must really be in for a fight if she had turned up!

The battery deployed to the 'quarry', our designated piece of desert from where we continued to exercise (PT, nuclear biological and chemical (NBC) training – lots of NBC, first aid and law of armed conflict), and from where we carried out ten drone practice flights, which gave a return of nine lots of useable imagery, a strike rate never to be bettered. However, with no on-board GPS, it became apparent very early on that it was not possible to confirm where the drone had actually flown, and therefore impossible to accurately identify target locations. Maps provided no reference points, as one bit of empty desert looks pretty much like any other except for the proliferation of newly constructed Iraqi trench systems evident on our imagery. Therefore, while we could identify equipment and activity, we could not say exactly, or even roughly, where it was. This was an issue which would reverse General Franks's decision but was resolved by Intelligence Corps ingenuity and a stroke of fortune.

As Intelligence Corps soldiers routinely working at strategic level, we were used to accessing the highest classification of information, so it was quite a shock to discover that at battery level there was none! This information-void was very off-putting, so we decided to embark our own intelligence-collection plan. Commandeering our 4-tonner, which none of us had a licence to drive, we invited ourselves to the 1 (UK) Armoured Division's Intelligence Section. Fortunately, we knew the Corps blokes in the division and we were able to strike up a relationship very quickly. There followed a daily trek to Divisional HQ where we attended, albeit as interlopers, several of Major General Rupert Smith's (GOC 1 (UK) Division) twice-daily briefings, right until he lost patience with the amount of 'unnecessary' people in his tent each day and banned all uninvited visitors. We had at least gained some valuable situational awareness and were able to brief the locating battery accordingly.

However, and more importantly, during the time we were welcome in the Divisional HQ, we were delighted to discover literally piles of secret 'overhead' photographs, measuring about a square metre each, providing photographic coverage of our entire frontage. The imagery had a map trace with it, so we could cross-refer it to our maps. Even better, it had been imaged after the Iraqi trench system had been constructed. As no one in Divisional HQ had any idea what to do with the imagery, we pilfered the lot and used it to plot our subsequent missions and to confirm the flight paths once the Midge had returned. The much-needed 'lock-on' was provided by marrying up the trench systems on the drone imagery with the trench systems on the overhead imagery. This represented hours of intricate work, but it was vital.

We had cause to put our new-found system to use on 19 February in support of the divisional preparation for crossing the start line. A mission went at 1645hrs from which twelve targets were identified, including a very large, occupied logistic site with an adjacent ammunition dump, which I duly reported by 2100hrs. At the end of the shift, I was pleased to be able to get my head down but was woken a couple of hours later with the demand from division to provide the exact ten-figure grid references of the perimeter extremities of the site, which covered about two square kilometres, so the Multiple Launch Rocket Systems (MLRS) could strike. MLRS makes a lot of noise when launched, especially if you haven't been warned it has moved close to your position. In the middle of the night, not knowing if the fire is incoming or outgoing, the previously practised NBC drills come into sharp focus, and you find yourself able, even from deep sleep, to get your respirator on with a perfectly airtight seal in significantly less time than the 'Mask in Nine' training requirements urge. Almost as much fun was, in full NBC kit, having to immediately move location to avoid Iraqi counter-battery fire. Still, I guess I was having a better night of it than those poor souls in the Iraqi logistics location.

As we moved to further operational flying, the reliability of the system got progressively worse. But the demand for the product remained sky-high, especially for photographs. Once we crossed the start line on 24 February, we fired a further nineteen missions with diminishing returns. The speed of the UK advance put the drone at the very limits of its range and many did not return. However, prior to crossing the line, and as the air war continued miles above us, we did conduct missions in support of our own division, the Egyptian Division (conducting a 'Forward Passage of Lines' through Egyptian positions in hours of darkness is an experience all of its own), the US VII Corps, and in support of the advance into Iraq and Kuwait. During this time, we spent considerable time moving as a mile-long convoy in complete darkness, much of it in full NBC kit, especially when subject to SCUD alerts, and a lot of time drying uniform. Who would have thought it rained so much the in the desert?

We found that at battalion level, the US Army 1st Division were very generous, especially when we were able to provide them with photography of the Iraqi defensive systems to their front, and sharp bartering got us one Meal Ready to Eat (MRE) pack per photo. MREs are the US equivalent of 'compo', the dry rations issued to UK forces, but more exotic. We also perfected the art of digging in at each and every stop we made, quickly discovering that the desert is not all soft sand. Where the desert was soft sand, the 4-tonne truck carrying our processing equipment invariably got stuck and had to be pulled out by the REME recovery vehicle. The weight of the processing equipment and fluid made it too heavy for the four-wheel chassis and drive system. So, using our initiative, we visited 6 Ordnance Battalion, somewhere ten hours' drive away in the rear, and 'swapped' the 4-tonner for a 14-tonne Bedford 6 x 6 flatbed truck, which we also did not have a driving licence for, but at least we were mobile.

After we went through the breach at the start line, we found ourselves repeatedly re-subordinated, firing missions in support of several different units. As the conflict drew to a close, we continued moving, passing increasing quantities of wrecked Iraqi armour, when an alarming report over the operations radio net warned of incoming Iraqi T-55's – Soviet-manufactured main battle tanks – causing us to ponder if grenades would be more effective than SMGs. When the tanks hooved into view, it was only to surrender, which was a relief! On another occasion, the battery took a further 100 POWs, passed rearwards for processing.

Finally, we ended up in a holding position north of Kuwait City on 1 March. On 2 March, the Iraqi government agreed to talks and it was all over bar the talking. On 3 March, as we handed our operational ammunition back, we were mightily relieved to be finally issued with our body amour! We were repatriated to Germany on 26 March.

The first drone mission was fired on 22 January with the last on 27 February, six weeks during which we mounted ten training and sixty-one operational flights, with an operational success rate of just over 25 per cent. That we were able to provide tactical level intelligence in a timely manner to a variety of customers, some of whom even paid us, was down to excellent PI skills and experience; good Corps skills of liaison with the UK Division Intelligence Section and being alert to opportunities as they presented themselves, notably pilfering their photography; good fortune that the Divisional HQ had the imagery in the first place; and our trade skills which allowed us to juxtapose strategic and tactical imagery to accurate and, ultimately, deadly effect.

The Midge drone was retired from service shortly after Op Granby. Sam Southam was eventually appointed Regimental Sergeant

Major of 1 Military Intelligence Battalion and then commissioned. His career progressed through operational tours on Op Herrick 4, in Helmand province, Afghanistan, with 16 Air Assault Brigade and later on attachment to the US Marine Corps. His staff appointments included Permanent Joint Headquarters (PJHQ), Defence Intelligence, HQ Int Corps and HQ 1 Military Intelligence Brigade. His final appointment as Lieutenant Colonel was Chief of Staff HQ Int Corps. He retired from the Army in 2015 but returned as a retired officer as Corps Secretary. For his services in Northern Ireland with the Reconnaissance Intelligence Centre (NI), he was awarded the Queen's Commendation for Valuable Service (QCVS).

SIERRA LEONE

For most of the 1990s, the former British colony of Sierra Leone was ravaged by civil war. It began in 1991 when the rebel army of the Revolutionary United Front attempted to overthrow the government. Violent gangs and militias, including the notorious West Side Boys, were also active, creating further chaos and instability. By May 2000, a UN-backed peace process was coming unstuck and the rebels were advancing on the capital, Freetown, prompting the British government to deploy troops to secure the airport and evacuate international citizens. British forces stayed on to support UN peacekeepers and to train the Sierra Leonean Army. In August 2000, a vehicle patrol consisting of eleven British soldiers, plus one Sierra Leonean soldier, entered West Side Boys' territory. They were taken hostage and held in appalling conditions. Members of the Intelligence Corps played an essential part in Operation Barras, the ensuing rescue mission carried out by the SAS.

The so-called West Side Boys inflicted a regime of fear on Sierra Leone, beating and butchering at will over a period of years. Yet despite being a group of vicious thugs, they were so well trained and well armed that nobody underestimated their abilities as a fighting force. On 25 August 2000, an eleven-strong patrol of the Royal Irish Regiment, together with a Sierra Leonean Lieutenant Liaison Officer, encountered members of the gang in their base village of Magbeni. Following an unprovoked attack, the British soldiers were overpowered and held prisoner in a house deep in the jungle. After initial negotiations, six were released on 31 August. The five who remained were kept captive in a room barely 6-foot wide and were subjected to assaults and mock executions. Musa Bangura, the Sierra Leonean Lieutenant, had to endure worse treatment. He was locked in a sewage pit outside the house with only stale urine to drink in order to stay alive.

An SAS rescue mission, codenamed Operation Barras, was soon ordered, although those involved in it are said to have referred to it as Operation Certain Death such were the perceived risks of the raid. The contribution of the Intelligence Corps to the resulting mission formed a key plank of its success.

A military intelligence detachment had been attached to HQ Commander of British Forces, Sir David Richards, for several months in 2000 as part of the overall effort to train and improve the Sierra Leonean Army. The detachment consisted of a Captain, a Warrant Officer and a junior NCO. As early as June 2000, there was also a clear requirement to deploy a field human intelligence team into theatre. In order to achieve their objectives, the military intelligence detachment was expected to conduct all trade skills (less surveillance) and provide a timely intelligence product.

Additionally, the detachment OC not only acted as Sir David Richards's Staff Officer but also oversaw all the intelligence functions including direction, collection, analysis and dissemination.

Following the capture of the Royal Irish soldiers, and alongside the usual menu of intelligence products, the detachment managed a number of casual contacts who provided various degrees of low-level actionable intelligence regarding the hostage situation. Then a more significant source materialised. One morning, a 'walk-in' from Freetown approached the guard at the entrance to the Commander of British Forces' HQ asking to speak to someone about the hostages. Two detachment NCOs took the young man to a quiet area to debrief him. It quickly became clear that he had significant actionable intelligence: his brother was a West Side Boy hostage taker. The young man said he knew where the hostages were being held because he was responsible for running errands between the location and Freetown. His motivation for helping was based on his knowledge that the British Army had brought peace to his community. He also wanted support in seeking employment opportunities.

While holding him on site, a discussion ensued to determine how the military intelligence detachment could best exploit the young man's knowledge and access. In order to confirm his reliability, he was asked to draw a plan of the hostage site. By this stage, it was known that the hostages had been moved from Magbeni and it was thought they had been taken across the Rokel Creek to a remote village upstream called Gberi Bana. There was no clear evidence to support this assessment, however.

To the exasperation of everybody, it soon became apparent that the young man could neither read nor write. After some coaching, he was asked to draw a plan of the Commander of British Forces'

HQ compound where he was currently located. He was told to imagine he was a bird and to look down on the site and then draw what he could see. After a reasonable stab at providing a plan of the compound where he was standing, he then set about drawing a plan of where he believed the hostages were. On examination of the plan, and to everyone's amazement, it was a very close replica of satellite imagery of Gberi Bana.

By this time, SAS plans were already well advanced for Operation Barras, the rescue mission. Sending in troops by river was vetoed as there were too many sandbanks, while the jungle was known to be too thick for a land attack, so they decided they had to go in by Chinook helicopter. Under close direction of his detachment 'handler', the young man made several visits to the hostage location, allowing him to provide further actionable intelligence regarding the location of the West Side Boys' camp as well as information about key characters in the group. This development in the detachment's human intelligence activities resulted in experienced operators being deployed to the theatre to provide support.

In the days leading up to the hostage rescue, multiple lines of information requirements were being pursued by the military intelligence detachment through the 'walk-in', the UN Mission in Sierra Leone, the Sierra Leone Police and other contacts. All of this tactical level information was passed into the UKSF J2 Cell, fusing this together with its own operational picture and strategic intelligence assessments. By the evening of 9 September, the West Side Boys' demands, passed through trained negotiators, were becoming more unrealistic. With no sign of the hostages' release and the potential for their being moved further into the jungle, the hostage extraction operation was given authorisation for the following morning.

At 0630 on 10 September, the Special Forces assault began with a covering force securing the southern bank of Rokel Creek and Magbeni while the main force successfully assaulted the West Side Boys camp at Gberi Bana. All hostages, including the Sierra Leone Liaison Officer, were successfully rescued and by 0650 were flown by Chinook to a Royal Fleet Auxiliary vessel in Freetown. At least twenty-five members of the West Side Boys were killed in the operation and their leader, Foday Kallay, was captured having been found cowering under a bed. He was handed over to the Sierra Leone Police. Sadly, one SAS soldier was killed in action.

The head of the Sierra Leone Police Special Branch offered the British Army the chance to interview Kallay, in case he was willing to reveal where in the jungle those members of the West Side Boys who had escaped during the raid were hiding. The field HUMINT team was despatched to the prison. During the interview, Kallay was said to be 'laid back and cooperative'. He provided a detailed account of where the remnants of his group would likely head and the information was briefed to the Sierra Leone Chief of Defence Staff by a senior Intelligence Corps operator that evening. The Sierra Leonean Army's advance into the strongholds identified by Kallay was hugely successful and was supported by an information operation which included a leaflet drop into the area. The leaflets included a photograph of Kallay in his prison cell, which was taken by the field HUMINT team. More than 300 West Side Boys and their families handed themselves in. A large number of them were eventually reintegrated into to the Sierra Leonean Army.

•   •   •

Between 1946 and 1957, the Corps survived in large part simply by proving its worth in Palestine, in Malaya and during the Korean

War. Despite its obvious qualities, however, it still had no regular group of officers and the idea prevailed within the military that 'intelligence' was not a suitable career choice for professional soldiers. It was not until 1957 that, thanks to the foresight of the former Director of Military Intelligence and then Colonel Commandant of the Corps Major General F. H. N. Davidson, the 'First 100' cadre of regular officers from a variety of regiments was transferred into the Corps. This marked the point at which the Intelligence Corps began to be accepted as a necessary and permanent element of the regular Army in both peace and war, a change of attitude which, as we have seen, resulted in its important contribution to the British Army's activities for the remainder of the twentieth century.

PART FOUR

THE COLD WAR AND NORTHERN IRELAND

The Cold War describes the protracted period of deep hostility that existed between America, the USSR and their respective allies. It began at the latest in 1947 with the Truman Doctrine, in which America promised to provide political, military and economic assistance to all democratic nations under threat from external or internal authoritarian forces; it ended in 1991 with the dissolution of the Soviet Union. It was characterised by arms races, proxy wars and diplomatic emergencies such as the Cuban Missile Crisis and the building of the Berlin Wall, but it never spilled over into outright military action. The concept of it having been a 'cold' war came about because of its proximity to the Second World War which had been a 'hot' or 'shooting' war.

In 1945, President Roosevelt, Winston Churchill and Joseph Stalin met at Yalta to plan the restructuring of Germany and Europe. It was eventually agreed that, among the various implementations, Germany and Austria would be carved up into four military occupation zones – American, British, Soviet and French.

Misunderstandings about the newly reorganised territories meant these arrangements were rarely straightforward, however, and further unease came with the creation of East and West Germany in 1949 and the spread of communism and USSR domination over Eastern Europe.

The Intelligence Corps' presence in Germany post-1945 consisted mainly of field security sections which served with the 21st Army Group, plus some specialist units. Initially, the Corps provided combat intelligence and security. It also assisted with tracking down suspected war criminals. Later, Corps units adopted a Cold War stance concerned with the emerging Soviet threat to the stability of Western Europe, notably after the Warsaw Pact was signed in 1955 which established Soviet-dominated opposition to NATO.

Vienna was situated 90 miles inside the Soviet zone, but unlike Berlin, the four occupying powers were scattered around the city rather than being in single composite areas. Twelve field security sections rapidly became involved in the complete span of intelligence and counter-intelligence work in a mirror of the stand-off in Germany. In 1948, the Vienna Field Security Section penetrated Soviet communications in a coup known as Operation Conflict. An Intelligence Corps operator, Sergeant Robin 'Bob' Steers, played a key role in this classic piece of espionage.

Robin Austin Steers was born in India in 1929, where his father was serving with the Indian Army. The family returned to England in 1947 and Steers enlisted in the Royal Sussex Regiment. In 1948, he transferred to the Intelligence Corps and was posted to the City Detachment of Field Security Section (Vienna). Around the same time, a friendly official from the Austrian government informed the British that a telephone cable running under a particular street in the British Aspangstrasse District carried a lot of Soviet military telephone traffic together with international lines to Prague, Budapest and other capitals under Soviet domination. It was decided that a telephone-tapping post should be established, overseen by Steers's field security section.

Initial investigations revealed that the cable ran alongside a terrace of single-storey warehouses with deep basements. As property could be requisitioned by an occupying power without question, three of the warehouses were obtained. In the basement of the middle of the three, a tunnel was dug by six Royal Engineer sappers under the direction of an officer. The excavated soil was covertly transported by the city field security section to the premises of another section on the other side of the city and dumped in a back garden. When the tunnel was completed and the telephone cables exposed, the Royal Engineers were all posted to Singapore to limit the chances of the plan leaking.

The next stage in the operation was the arrival of a team of engineers and telecommunications specialists armed with a variety of listening and recording equipment. Unfortunately, due to a blunder, the team did not arrive as anticipated at Aspang station, opposite the warehouse, but in the Russian zone. Having got off a train, they stood on a platform with their equipment, inevitably attracting the attention of suspicious Russian Military Police. A hasty exfiltration executed by the field security section meant the team was soon brought back to the safety of the British zone. There, they set to work on breaking into the main cable and connecting up the listening and recording equipment, located in the warehouse cellar. For cover, the warehouse was disguised as a Railway Transport Officer (RTO) store.

Once established, the monitoring and recording was carried out by Bob Steers and his field security section colleagues, working round the clock in shifts. At any one time, six men would be in the cellar for a 24-hour period. Three men would monitor and record for three hours while the others slept. Security was tight, and any callers to the building were greeted by the three heavily armed off-duty men in a specially choreographed protocol. There was no ventilation in the cellar, and the endless supply of free cigarettes meant that the operation soon gained the unofficial title of 'Smokey Joe's'. During the quiet hours of the early morning when telephone traffic was light, those monitoring would be able to listen into conversations between female operators at the Vienna switchboard talking to their counterparts in other locations. Often, they discussed the graphic details of their sex lives, unwittingly broadening the horizons of the field security section men.

The recordings were made on Edisonphone wax cylinders, a type of phonograph cylinder which could record and reproduce sound. Each morning, the previous day's recordings would be collected and taken away under guard for analysis. Although those engaged in the operation rarely knew the value of the traffic they were intercepting, on one occasion they learned that information had been discovered that the Hungarian Intelligence Service was planning to arrest Cardinal Mindszenty, the anti-communist Primate of Hungary, who was suspected of working for the Americans. On 26 December 1948, Mindszenty was indeed arrested on charges of treason and sentenced to life imprisonment, eventually being released in 1956.

One Sunday morning, there was a major scare when the field security men heard activity outside. They found workmen digging up the road directly above the tunnel, having been sent to repair a depression in the road surface. The panic phone was activated and within the hour the General Officer Commanding arrived with the Austrian minister for communications. As the senior man on duty, Bob Steers acted as interpreter. The General Officer Commanding told Steers to order the Austrian to return to his office, call off the workmen and not to ask any questions or he would be in deep trouble. Steers apparently added his own variation to the translation by warning quietly in colloquial Austrian: 'Keep your gob shut, otherwise you'll be dead within the hour.'

By the summer of 1951, it became evident that the Soviets had rerouted the bulk of their telephone traffic and 'Smokey Joe's' was closed down. But the operation's idea took root with the intelligence community and another, similar, British venture codenamed Operation Silver was mounted in Vienna. Meanwhile, in Berlin, a joint British–American operation, codenamed Gold, was put in place. Both Silver and Gold were compromised when George Blake, the British MI6 officer and traitor, informed the Russians.

Following his part in the monitoring operation, Steers returned to field security duties, mostly involving the interrogation of the many people who were caught illegally trying to enter the Allied zones of Austria from Soviet-occupied Hungary and Czechoslovakia. Some were genuine refugees, in which case they would be questioned for whatever intelligence they could provide. Others were Soviet agents. Steers's section was also involved in assisting Allied penetration agents to cross into Hungary and Czechoslovakia.

In 1956, having been commissioned in the Corps, Steers took part in the Suez invasion, Operation Musketeer, and was seriously wounded in the heavy fighting following the airborne assault. Although he recovered and became an instructor at the School of Military Intelligence, he was forced to retire from the Army in January 1958 on account of his injuries. He worked in publishing until 2016. In 1996, he wrote at the request of the Intelligence Corps Association the book *FSS: Field Security Section*. He died in March 2020, aged ninety.

BRIXMIS AND SOXMIS

In 1946, Britain and the USSR set up official military liaison missions to each other's occupation zones, allegedly in the interests of maintaining good relations. In reality, they developed into a method of monitoring, particularly as the Cold War intensified. The British Mission to the Soviets was known as BRIXMIS and the Soviet Mission to the British was known as SOXMIS. Representatives from each country were allowed to travel in each other's zone of occupation under certain restrictions, providing useful opportunities for intelligence gathering, both overt and covert. These were known as 'tours'. This work was not without risk, however, and Britons who were suspected of spying were on occasion attacked or even shot at.

Those involved in BRIXMIS did take advantage of the freedom of movement available to them, generating intelligence from the Soviet zone (later East Germany). As the Cold War progressed, and especially after the Soviets completed the Berlin Wall in 1961, East Germany became heavily reinforced with advanced Soviet military equipment on account of its geographical position on the front line of the Iron Curtain. BRIXMIS reported on troop movements and garrisons, military technological advancements and major structural changes in the landscape. Although some areas were, technically, off-limits, BRIXMIS personnel very often deliberately flouted the rules by going off-piste, thereby putting themselves in danger in order to collect vital intelligence. Hazards they met included occasions when BRIXMIS vehicles were deliberately rammed by heavy East German trucks, resulting in severe injuries. The East German Secret Police, the Stasi, also tried to keep the tours under surveillance but generally failed in the face of superior British training and determination. It was not unknown for specially adapted and strengthened BRIXMIS vehicles to drive at full speed down a railway line to escape a Stasi surveillance vehicle, which was unable to follow. In his later years, one Corps officer received a substantial disability pension for mobility problems caused by wear and tear to his spine after carrying out this manoeuvre too many times.

On a tour, each vehicle was self-sufficient, containing all the supplies and equipment needed to support a three-man team consisting of Tour Officer, Tour NCO and a specialist highly trained driver. Although the 'Tourers', both officers and NCOs, were drawn from across the British Army, they included a significant number of Intelligence Corps personnel, and the support collators were also members of the Corps. The vehicles used varied over time. Initially, they were either Opel Senators, Kapitans or Admirals. Although they appeared on the outside to be standard examples of each car, some were modified with four-wheel drive, upgraded suspension and extra fuel tanks to give them a longer range. Perhaps the most effective vehicle used at this time was the Mercedes Geländewagen (G-Wagen), with its enhanced cross-country capability, winch and other refinements. Tours could revolve around routine monitoring of other vehicles including aeroplanes and trains or any activity of interest, or they could be a response to specific taskings by British military or civilian agencies. Often, this involved collecting evidence on specific Soviet vehicles or new items of equipment.

Although BRIXMIS was headquartered in the old Olympic Stadium complex in West Berlin, the tours were run from the BRIXMIS 'Mission House' in the town of Potsdam, just outside the capital. With their ability to monitor troop movements and apparatus, the BRIXMIS missions were acknowledged to be one of the most important means by which the western powers could obtain advance knowledge of a pending Soviet offensive across the inner German border.

There were some notable intelligence successes by BRIXMIS in relation to Soviet hardware, each of which illustrates the type of person who was selected to perform this type of work, which required a cerebral approach to intelligence gathering and problem solving. In April 1966, a Soviet Yak-25 fighter (NATO codename Firebar) crashed into the British-controlled part of Lake Havel in Berlin. This was the first time the aircraft had been seen outside the USSR and it was, needless to say, of great interest to the west. During a week-long operation, members of BRIXMIS were engaged on a stalling exercise with high-ranking Soviet officers who had taken up position on the opposite bank, while Royal Engineer divers covertly detached the engines and radar from the aircraft. Once removed, they were towed underwater to a secret position, sent off to London for analysis, then returned to the crash site before being very publicly 'recovered' and given back to the Soviets.

Another triumph based on spontaneous ingenuity came in 1983, when a Tour NCO spotted several newly upgraded Soviet BMP-2 armoured fighting vehicles on a stationary train. He jumped aboard to investigate the calibre of its cannon. Having only his lunchtime apple with him, he rammed it against the muzzle of the weapon to obtain an imprint and then high-tailed it back to his vehicle. The apple was later 'analysed' and the calibre confirmed as a 30mm, meaning that crucial intelligence had been captured thanks to some quick thinking.

In the 1970s and 1980s, the Soviets were known to have been experimenting with explosive reactive armour (ERA) for their main battle tanks, a technology which, when refined, could provide additional protection against opposition fire. In 1987, technical intelligence asked BRIXMIS to look out for Soviet tanks fitted with this new initiative. Within a week, during a search of a tank range at Lieberose, about 50 miles south-east of Berlin, a Tour NCO 'found' an ERA box in a vehicle pit. Days later, the box was on the desk of a boffin working in technical intelligence in London.

A further significant BRIXMIS operation that ran for many years was codenamed Tomahawk. It involved the systematic trawling of Soviet training areas, deployment sites and military installations in East Germany. Sifting through the detritus of military exercises and garrison rubbish dumps was found to be a valuable technique which often provided gems of intelligence, albeit at a relatively low level of security classification, rarely higher than 'Secret'. Work undertaken during Tomahawk was often unpleasant, even requiring operators to come into contact with human excreta, especially when exploiting Soviet military hospital rubbish tips. It was discovered that it was not unusual for Soviet conscripts on exercise to use whatever was within reach for lavatory paper, meaning that signal message pads, letters from home and technical manuals were recovered, often providing previously unknown information. One such find concerned training notes referring to a new anti-aircraft system called 2S6. This was deemed important because it was not known until then whether it was a combined gun-and-missile system. The notes confirmed that it was, and this had a direct impact in the development of counter-measures. Details of various types of new equipment, organisations and personnel were frequently found this way.

One Corps operator whose BRIXMIS experience was particularly perilous was Bob Thomas. Robert 'Bob' Thomas originally enlisted in the Junior Leader's battalion of the King's Shropshire Light

Infantry in 1964 and served as an infantryman for more than four years in Singapore, Malaya, Thailand, British Honduras, Mauritius, Thailand and France. He transferred to the Intelligence Corps in August 1968 and served in Hong Kong, Germany, Berlin, Northern Ireland and the Falkland Islands.

In February 1976, while already serving with a Corps unit in Germany, he was posted to BRIXMIS and spent an introductory fortnight with the mission in Berlin before going on to complete the BRIXMIS course at the Soviet Studies Wing at Ashford. He returned to the mission in Berlin and took over responsibility for the observation of Soviet logistics, including all military and paramilitary bases in East Germany. He also collated East German vehicle number plates and tactical markings to identify individual military units. This was painstaking but essential work.

September was the Soviet military exercise season, and in September 1976, Sergeant Thomas was the Tour NCO for a mission into East Germany, tasked with mapping a location on the edge of a Permanent Restricted Area. Such areas were marked by the Soviets to deny Allied missions access to their more sensitive bases and training areas. En route, the team passed an Early Warning Site and then went off the metalled road to scout and map the area. At one point they noted a 'Nark' – a member of the East German Stasi – on a motorbike. While returning, their Opel Admiral car was confronted by two East Germans on motorbikes, forcing the driver to take evasive measures up onto the verge on the far side of the road. At that moment, the car was deliberately rammed by an East German URAL-375 truck weighing about 9 tonnes. The truck ran over the passenger side of the car and came to rest on top of it. It had been pushed about 30 feet off the road. The front left wheel of the truck was on the roof with the other front wheel on the bonnet. As the Tour NCO, Sergeant Thomas was in the front passenger seat. He was unconscious. The other two crew members were uninjured but severely shocked and bruised.

When he eventually regained consciousness, Thomas found himself outside the wreck of the car bleeding heavily on a ground-sheet, having been pulled out of the vehicle by the Tour Officer. Although the extent of his injuries was not yet known, his right leg was positioned at an unnatural angle, and when the Tour Officer tried to straighten it, Thomas passed out again, this time as a result of the pain. He later learned that he had been in the vehicle for over an hour before the East German officer present at the scene would allow him to be taken to safety. When Thomas woke up again, he was in the back of a moving Soviet ambulance on a wooden bench seat, but the violent accelerating and braking of the driver soon made him lose consciousness a third time. Initially, he was taken to a cottage hospital where he came to again, this time lying on a canvas stretcher on a damp concrete floor as his boots and trousers were cut off. Realising that he was being attended to by medical personnel, Thomas managed to reach into his pocket for his Soviet tour pass in order to explain that he had diplomatic cover. But his injuries were so severe – a fractured skull, right leg broken in five places, three fractured ribs and facial lacerations – that he was transferred to a hospital at Lauchhammer. There, East German surgeons operated on his leg and inserted a plate and rod running from his thigh to his ankle. When he awoke after the five-hour procedure, he found his leg tied to a board with a variety of wires attached as traction.

Every morning after the operation, he was woken at 4 a.m. by nurses administering an antibiotic injection which turned his skin a jaundiced-like yellow colour. The syringes they used were made from non-disposable glass and their needles had become blunt by the frequent autoclaving, leaving him with a very sore arm. A few days after the operation, he awoke to find a lady in a white coat taping wet electrodes to his ankle with wires connected to a large trolley-mounted machine containing various humming and buzzing valves. He was much relieved to learn he was not about to undergo a Stasi interrogation session but merely an examination to check the circulation in his injured limb. Yet not everybody whom he encountered was as benign. Late one night, four uniformed East German police burst into his ward accompanied by a hospital physician who was a Communist Party member. They immediately directed a tirade of abuse at Thomas and started to knock him about until the hospital director arrived and ordered them to leave.

After sixteen days, Sergeant Thomas was released from hospital, two stone lighter. He was returned to Berlin in a British Army ambulance, escorted by BRIXMIS, where he was placed under care of the British Military Hospital. He was able to resume light office duties before going back to Britain shortly afterwards. In December 1976, while stepping off the plane at Heathrow, his injured leg gave way when the surgical plate fitted by a Soviet surgeon broke apart. It was found that all of its components – plate, screws and rod – were cheap East German copies of the Swiss-made original.

Sergeant Thomas returned to BRIXMIS in January 1978 for a further six months. Thereafter, he served in Northern Ireland, the Falkland Islands and as an instructor at the Attaché Wing, School of Service Intelligence at Ashford. He left the Corps as a Warrant Officer in 1986 and later obtained a Territorial Commission as a Captain in the Royal Army Medical Corps TA.

● ● ●

If Sergeant Thomas's BRIXMIS experience put his life and health in danger in the 1970s, the risks attached to BRIXMIS tours were little different a decade later, as Nick Rowles discovered. He joined the Army in 1974. Having qualified as an Operator Intelligence and Security, his first postings were to Germany and Northern Ireland. In the spring of 1982, while serving in Berlin, he applied for the German Interpreter Course. When he completed the Army Language Aptitude Test, he was informed that he had scored highly and been selected instead for the Russian Interpreter Course at the Army School of Languages at Beaconsfield. During the course, an Intelligence Corps BRIXMIS officer visited to brief several of the officer students who had already been selected for the mission and asked Rowles if he had considered this role himself. He was offered a slot with the mission once his language course was completed. Eighteen months later, having qualified in Russian and a subsequent French colloquial course, he was posted to BRIXMIS before completing the four-week BRIXMIS course at Ashford. In July 1984, he finally arrived back in West Berlin, by then promoted to Sergeant, for a two-year BRIXMIS tour.

For the first fifteen months, Rowles worked in the research section in the mission's West Berlin HQ and alternated as a tour NCO in East Germany. Then, in June 1985, the team were deployed near Cottbus, south-east of Berlin. They were enjoying breakfast early one morning on a country road near the deployment area of Russian Air Assault Brigade units in the hope of spotting some Soviet traffic when they saw a column of Soviet vehicles. The team swung into their routine. Sergeant Rowles was identifying and calling the equipment and vehicle numbers into his Dictaphone while the Tour Officer was photographing from the rear of their recently procured Mercedes G-Wagen. Suddenly, a medium-sized Soviet GAZ-66 truck turned away from the column and drove towards them at speed, with the clear intention of ramming them. On a previous tour, Rowles had been rammed by a BRDM-2 Soviet armoured patrol vehicle while sitting in an Opel Senator. On that occasion, the highly trained tour driver was able to avoid the collision, but a chase ensued. This time, the G-Wagen was boxed into a local training area and struck by the Soviets at 40 kilometres per hour. The force of the impact lifted the vehicle off its wheels, moving it sideways and removing two of its tyres from their wheel rims. A group of Soviet soldiers then attacked the vehicle with shovels and bricks. Rowles and his two colleagues managed to get out and limp off to the nearby village of Schorbus where a local garage owner offered to help them retrieve the G-Wagen.

They were in the process of changing the damaged wheels when the Soviet troops returned. The mission crew retreated into their vehicle as the troops loaded their weapons, signalling that anybody who got out would be shot. Eventually, the regional Soviet Commandant arrived and calmed the situation, authorising the BRIXMIS vehicle to be released so that the crew could complete the wheel change. As this was going on, one of the Soviet officers managed to reach into the G-Wagen via the passenger side window and remove one of the tour bags containing maps, notebooks, the Dictaphone, compass, torch and a list of suspected Stasi vehicle registrations to help identify surveillance. The Tour Officer protested, to no avail. The Soviets later claimed the bag had been left behind following the detention. It was subsequently returned – minus the maps, notebooks and Dictaphone.

Between 1979 and 1990, BRIXMIS crews were rammed and detained twenty-five times and there were four shooting incidents, though fortunately none was fatal. The French and US missions were not so fortunate. Each had one mission member killed, one as the result of a ramming and the other after being shot.

Nick Rowles left BRIXMIS in the spring of 1989, six months before the fall of the Berlin Wall. Less than twelve months later, the Allied and Soviet missions were stood down on the eve of German reunification on 2 October 1990. He went on to qualify as an advanced surveillance driver and as a German interpreter, being employed on HUMINT duties in Germany. He also served as the Regimental Sergeant Major at Ashford and was closely involved in the move of the Corps from Ashford to Chicksands in 1997 before being commissioned. He returned to intelligence duties in Germany and later served in Bosnia, Northern Ireland and CENTCOM in the USA, for which he was made an MBE. Further deployments and postings followed to Djibouti, Afghanistan and various staff appointments in Germany and the UK. He was promoted to Lieutenant Colonel in 2009 and retired from Regular Army service in 2013 but continued to serve on Full Time Reserve Service with one of the Corps Reserve battalions.

•   •   •

The corresponding Soviet version of BRIXMIS was SOXMIS, the Soviet Military Mission to the British Commander-in-Chief. Its mission house was in a compound in Bünde, 11 miles north of Bielefeld. In the same way that BRIXMIS personnel and vehicles operated in East Germany, so SOXMIS did in the West, albeit while subject to similar limitations of exclusion zones in sensitive areas. Despite the perceived threat posed by SOXMIS, there was no covert counter-intelligence effort against it. Until 1960, field security held the task of monitoring SOXMIS but only on a limited basis due to their other commitments.

Yet from a British perspective, SOXMIS had for too long been able to travel throughout the former British zone almost with impunity and with greater freedom of movement than Soviet diplomatic staff enjoyed. Meanwhile, members of BRIXMIS were – as we have seen – subjected to harassment. Although it had long been suspected that SOXMIS was used for clandestine purposes, the Commander-in-Chief was loath to raise the stakes against them for fear that reciprocal Soviet action against BRIXMIS in the East would mean a loss of, or reduction in, its intelligence-gathering operations. It was a delicate balance. It became abundantly clear to the British that SOXMIS must be of great importance to the Soviet authorities, and it was suspected that SOXMIS personnel were members either of the KGB or the foreign military intelligence agency, the GRU, but there was no detail as to the extent of that value, nor the ways and means of its achievement.

For this reason, the special '5-Star' committee was created by the Commander-in Chief in 1966. This put in place suitable measures – overt and covert – to ascertain the value to the Soviets of SOXMIS. One such measure was the SOXMIS sightings process. Every member of the forces, all civilian personnel and their families carried a SOXMIS Sighting Card, which asked anybody who saw a SOXMIS car, identifiable by its distinctive number plates, to call a particular number. Additionally, 19 Support Platoon of the Royal Military Police was created. Nicknamed 'The White Mice' due to the fleet of high-powered white Ford Granada saloon cars they drove, the unit was tasked with overt surveillance of SOXMIS vehicles. Its personnel were highly trained advanced police drivers and patrolled the 'Permanent' and 'Temporary Restricted Areas' during specific periods to protect sensitive units and exercise areas from SOXMIS attention. This new intelligence-collection operation against SOXMIS was the responsibility of 'S3', a small team of Intelligence Corps personnel comprising a Captain (with HUMINT experience) and five analysts within HQ Intelligence and Security Group (Germany), based in Rheindahlen.

Perhaps the most important measure directed by the 5-Star committee was tasking the Intelligence and Security Group (Germany) to create a covert surveillance capability. Detailed analysis of SOXMIS operations and touring activity could be used to identify Soviet intelligence requirements and gaps in their knowledge. This could, in turn, give an indication of Soviet war plans. Information could also be collected about individual SOXMIS officers and their personalities. At that time, however, no dedicated military covert surveillance capability existed in Germany or, indeed, anywhere in the Army. So, as part of the new measures, the Commander-in-Chief authorised the establishment, from scratch and under strict secrecy, of a dedicated unit to undertake this role. It was given the title '8 Detachment' (known as '8 Det'), under the command of HQ Intelligence and Security Group (Germany) reporting to S3, which became the all-source analysis cell for these matters.

Setting up 8 Det was a major undertaking, exacerbated by the need to employ extreme security measures given the assessed 'reach' of the Soviet and Warsaw Pact intelligence agencies. In line with a policy of maintaining secrecy, a small group of NCOs were hand-picked, taken 'off-grid' and placed under the command of an Intelligence Corps Warrant Officer, Dougie Whysall.

In the early years, the recruitment of operators for 8 Det was based on individual recommendations. Anyone deemed to have the right qualities was considered, placed under scrutiny and then discreetly approached with a 'tap on the shoulder'. If their reaction was favourable, and after an interview, the chosen few were called to attend the Det's demanding course in Germany. Later, a more formal selection and training process was established, and in 1974, with the growing need to sustain 8 Det and generate more capacity for covert operations in Northern Ireland and elsewhere, the Specialist Intelligence Wing (SIW) was opened in Repton Manor at the Intelligence Centre at Ashford in Kent.

Those who worked at 'the Manor', a fifteenth-century Grade II listed building, were responsible for selecting and training personnel for 'Special Duties', including covert surveillance and agent handling, until 1997 when the Corps moved to its present location at Chicksands in Bedfordshire. Students included men and women from the Corps for surveillance and from across all three services for agent handling.

Standards required for both 8 Det and agent handlers were, by necessity, extremely high. The instructors for both disciplines were experienced operators and a posting for them at 'the Manor' was an accolade, reflecting successful experience and the ability to teach others. The Army policy has always been that you can only teach, and be credible, if you have done it well yourself.

The qualities required for special duties operators in 8 Det were broad. They needed to work within a team and be able to think and act on personal initiative; to follow orders; and to lead regardless of rank. There were strict rules of engagement, protocols that had to be followed and limitations on action. But faced with a situation on the ground, with what were then very poor communications, sometimes relatively junior soldiers had to make decisions without being able to ask for guidance in order to avoid missing an opportunity.

Alongside these characteristics, operators needed to excel at communication, navigation, advanced driving and photography.

Fitness was also imperative. An 8 Det working day could last for eighteen hours, a work rate that sometimes had to be sustained for a period of days or even weeks. On top of all this, they needed a good understanding of hostile intelligence-collection methods and a sharp and enquiring mind. A pre-selection process sifted volunteers for those with the required aptitude and then arduous training followed. Initial training in Britain had to be augmented and adapted to suit the conditions in Germany. Operators spent long hours familiarising themselves with the ground, developing local mannerisms and environmental awareness and becoming competent in the German language. Many operators reached interpreter level. Additional specialist driver training prepared them for the different road systems in a country where few autobahns had speed limits.

There was no 'standard' operation in 8 Det. Timings and locations were dictated to a great extent by the target, guided by intelligence from S3. The deployments varied in duration. One mission required operators to be out on the ground for a total of 100 days. The teams needed to develop tactics to deal with a target that was different to those encountered by most western surveillance teams. The Robertson–Malinin Agreement of 1946, which allowed BRIXMIS to explore the Soviet zone of Germany, meant SOXMIS had to undertake their work in 'uniform' in vehicles bearing a distinctive identification plate. This meant SOXMIS were readily identifiable and could afford to employ completely overt anti-surveillance tactics to lose any followers. This was a comparative luxury for Intelligence Officers, particularly those under diplomatic or other cover who usually maintain a low profile and for whom even the suspicion of their use of anti-surveillance techniques would mark them out as being in a clandestine role.

In contrast, 8 Det's surveillance effort against SOXMIS necessitated the use of continuous covert tactics to avoid loss or compromise, with the aim of identifying the target's specific task. For example, SOXMIS could burn off down an autobahn at 140 kilometres per hour, requiring enormous skill from 8 Det operators to tail them without blowing their cover. Detection would mean the target immediately abandoning their covert mission and rendering the entire operation pointless.

One former Intelligence Corps 8 Det operator, whose request for anonymity means they can only be described here as Operator X, explains the methods used by both sides.

'We were constantly looking at tactics to reduce our exposure and therefore extend our surveillance coverage,' says Operator X.

SOXMIS would typically 'Dry Clean' for seven hours plus – Dry Cleaning being the term used by an Intelligence Officer to cover activities designed to identify the presence, or not, of surveillance. If you are a covert Intelligence Officer, your dry cleaning would need to be subtle, choosing traps that afford you a discreet look back, or a route that, while logical for you, would be illogical for anyone following you. SOXMIS were overt, they usually wore uniform and they drove around in vehicles with a big red and yellow number plate with a hammer and sickle on it. They didn't need to be subtle. Typically, one of their drills would be to U-turn for no apparent reason and without warning, and then make a point of recording the details of all following vehicles caught out by that action. The surveillance vehicle in control would then assume that their number plate had been recorded and change it. Each vehicle would deploy with up to twenty different number plates and regularly change them so that they were rarely caught out of area by such a drill. All such potential compromises were recorded, number plates often rested or replaced, cars rested, re-sprayed or replaced. Operators had to change their appearance, get a haircut, wear glasses, grow a beard or wear a wig and so on.

SOXMIS made frequent use of Germany's complex autobahn junctions, including certain exits used only by police and other emergency services, to rapidly change direction. Over time, 8 Det developed procedures to cope with this, keeping the target within a loose box. As you can imagine, the target was frequently 'un-sighted', as keeping it under control was maintained from a long distance, typically half a mile on the motorways, or just the extent of the visible horizon when on minor roads in the country or on parallel routes in urban areas. The mark of a good team was how well they could regain control following a loss. The drills were practised often and everyone knew instinctively where to check. We knew every road in our operational area, which was huge. However, when transiting from one area of interest to the next, ideally control would be best if it were minimal. [We aimed to achieve] long periods of 'unsighted', interspersed with brief peri-ods of control, thereby arriving at the next area of interest with all our cars and a target who believed they were not being followed.

Over time, S3 generated an excellent database of SOXMIS person-alities, vehicles, activity patterns, targeting and likely roles. This was based on collation and analysis of overt information, such as SOXMIS sighting and intelligence from 8 Det. While much of SOXMIS's touring appeared to be straightforward first-hand intel-ligence gathering around barracks and other military sites, there were operations which provided evidence of SOXMIS involvement in covert activity. For example, 8 Det saw and recorded SOXMIS officers servicing dead letter boxes – 'drop' locations where intelligence, money or weapons could be passed between individuals without them having to meet in person. There was little question about what some SOXMIS tasks consisted of. For example, it became known that one officer who had served in SOXMIS and later worked in Soviet embassies in the west was the author of the training manuals 'Running Agents in a Rural Environment' and 'Running Agents in an Urban Environment'. Another SOXMIS task was to identify stretches of autobahns that could be earmarked as runways. And 8 Det also collected evidence of SOXMIS personnel setting up communications antennae deep in forests and close to airports. Other intelligence confirmed by 8 Det indicated likely SOXMIS support to 'Spetsnaz' Special Forces preparation, plus likely targets in preparation for hostilities.

As 8 Det's capability grew, so did its remit, which was widened in the mid-1970s to include covert surveillance against civilian employees in contact with Soviet Intelligence Officers. By the late 1970s, other counter-intelligence cases had developed, reflecting the widespread and consistent effort by the Warsaw Pact intelligence services to recruit sources within all elements of NATO forces, including family and civilian components.

In 1979, a new Intelligence Corps unit – 2 Intelligence Company – was formed under the command of Intelligence and Security Group (Germany) to take a more aggressive approach to countering the hostile intelligence services threat. It was tasked to take over and regularise the recruitment and use of Covert Human Intelligence Sources (CHIS), to supervise the use of the surveillance effort, and to oversee all military counter-intelligence operations. It absorbed 8 Det, which doubled in size and became known as 28 Section. Over time, many of 2 Company's operators were experienced in both surveillance and agent running, giving both capabilities far greater depth, able to mount a well-coordinated multi-faceted attack on Warsaw Pact intelligence operations, and developing a concept for the future. Although the Berlin Wall fell in 1989, surveillance operations and 2 Intelligence Company's work did not stop. Soviet agents who had worked for the GRU and been compromised during the reunification hiatus continued to be arrested.

By the late 1980s, the biggest IRA terrorist target outside Northern Ireland and Britain was the British forces based in Germany and the Low Countries, where they were attacked sporadically between 1980 and 1990. The CO of Intelligence and Security Group (Germany) was able to provide 28 Section as a specialist capability with considerable capacity. British Forces Germany was the principal IRA target in Europe, and it was sensible, if not implicit in the Commanding Officer's mission, for his units to make the maximum contribution to countering this threat. As a result of various policy agreements, 28 Section maintained a surveillance team on standby ready to respond to terrorist-related intelligence. A series of successful surveillance operations against Irish terrorists took place. 28 Section's skills were also used to undertake a wide range of anti-terrorist surveys and other covert tasks for HQ British Army of the Rhine.

It was against this background that the expertise of 8 Detachment, 2 Intelligence Company and the instructional facility provided by the Specialist Intelligence Wing at Repton Manor was gradually 'exported' to counter the ever-growing terrorist threat in Northern Ireland and elsewhere. It would also meet a growing demand later on for covert intelligence-collection capability in support of 21st-century military campaigns and operations.

CYPRUS

If the phrase 'strategic envy' was ever to be used in the context of the Cold War, it might neatly summarise the Soviet attitude to British military assets in Cyprus. This former British colony has been described both as a gigantic aircraft carrier situated in the eastern Mediterranean and as a hotbed of espionage and intrigue – two ideas which are not mutually exclusive.

When Cyprus gained its independence in 1960, Britain maintained two Sovereign Base Areas (SBAs). The Western SBA incorporated the British garrison of Episkopi and the major airbase at RAF Akrotiri; the Eastern SBA incorporated the Dhekelia garrison and the highly sensitive SIGINT monitoring base at Ayios Nikolaos, roughly halfway between Dhekelia and Famagusta. Also included in the 1960 agreement were the signal and radar station at Mount Troodos, together with various signals and monitoring stations at Cape Greco and Mia Melia, which the Americans also used to monitor Soviet nuclear weapons tests.

Soviet policy towards these British and American assets was simple. In the short term, they were to be spied upon, infiltrated and considered for possible future sabotage. In the longer term, there was a desire to undermine and erode the British presence on the island and increase Soviet influence on the Cypriot government with the assistance of Soviet-friendly organisations such as the Communist Party of Cyprus and Soviet-friendly Arab nations such as Syria.

By the early 1970s, every Soviet bloc country had its representative embassy in Nicosia, each with a complement of diplomats which was totally disproportionate to the levels of trade and commerce between their country and Cyprus. In truth, most of these 'diplomats' were Intelligence Officers working under 'legal' cover. For the Russians, the KGB was concerned with more strategic and political matters while the foreign military intelligence agency, the GRU, was mostly concerned with military matters. Soviet bloc countries had their own equivalent services, albeit they generally acted directly under Soviet direction. Alongside the various embassies were Soviet commercial and trade organisations which were also used as cover for Soviet Intelligence Officers. They included TASS; the Soviet airline, Aeroflot; and the Soviet state mercantile agency, Morflot. As far as the British intelligence and security agencies were concerned, these were hostile intelligence services (HIS). Between the 1960s and 1980s, the various HIS threats were the main targets of interest for the security intelligence operators of 11 Security Company, previously known as Counter-Intelligence Company (Cyprus).

At the west end of the island, the main HIS target was RAF Akrotiri, which housed fighter, bomber and reconnaissance aircraft. In the Sovereign Base Area on the eastern side, including the towns of Larnaca and Famagusta, HIS activity was especially prevalent. Their main target was the sensitive and highly classified SIGINT intercept station at 9th Signal Regiment at Ayios Nikolaos, and especially its personnel – for talent-spotting and subversion. Other Army units in Dhekelia from which low-grade intelligence might be obtained were also subject to the interest of Soviet spooks. Apart from 'talent-spotting', the Soviets were also involved in the reconnaissance of British military key points. Their task was made easier by the fact that the SBAs were open to public traffic. It was not unusual for known vehicles of Soviet bloc embassies to park on a quiet stretch or road, or up a narrow track, in order to photograph buildings of interest to them.

In the 1970s, Larnaca also was home to a large and active Communist Party membership and the Cyprus–Syrian Friendship Society, whose organiser was an import–export merchant of Syrian extraction and long suspected of having contact with Soviet intelligence. Larnaca and Famagusta also provided the 'fleshpots' around which some of those in the military based their social life such as discos, clubs and brothels. All were 'exploitable' from an HIS talent-spotting point of view. HIS posed a real, immediate and long-term threat to the security of the sovereign bases and to the security of British interests in Cyprus. As such, their subversive activities, both within the boundaries of the SBAs and in surrounding towns and villages, became legitimate targets of interest for security intelligence personnel.

The following is an example of counter-Soviet activity which took place in the 'patch' in Larnaca of a former Intelligence Corps operator who has chosen to be known only as Corporal Y. He recalls:

In late 1973, a Hungarian mining company, Geominco, set up shop in the Troulli area, very close to the Dhekelia SBA. Their stated objective was to exploit the old copper mine site, which had previously been worked by the British Mining Corporation, and they had obtained the necessary clearances from the Greek Cypriot government. The mine had been abandoned by BMC in the 1960s, as being 'worked out' and uneconomical. Despite this, the Hungarians shipped in masses of mining and laboratory equipment and alleged specialist mining personnel, all of them Hungarian or other Eastern bloc nationals. The obvious suspicion was that the entire operation was an elaborate cover to infiltrate HIS onto the island. As a result, 111 Section was briefed to keep a watchful eye on things. At that time, I was living in an Army hiring in Larnaca. The landlord and his extended family lived on the top floor and they owned a neighbouring ground-floor flat which had been vacant for some time. One Sunday, I was invited to the engagement party of the landlord's daughter. As usual on such occasions, there were dozens of guests, both local and foreign, and during the meal I was introduced to a very distinguished looking middle-aged European gentleman and his wife. He was introduced as the new tenant of the flat adjoining my hiring and had only moved in the previous day. My astonishment can be imagined when, in idle conversation, he explained that he was the chief mining engineer of Geominco. Thus it was that a routine 'off-duty' social function had led me to one of the most senior members of the very organisation I had been briefed to monitor. The following day, I reported the contact. The report was immediately passed upward. Very soon afterwards, the word came down from above that I was to nurture the contact and find out as much as I could about him, the company and its activities, and also arrange for some covert photography of the gentleman for ID purposes. The latter was done with little trouble via the assistance of an accommodating British Army officer whose hiring directly overlooked the target's flat. Meanwhile, I was made aware that 'other inquiries' were being made in the UK to contact former members of the British Mining Corporation with personal experience of the mine. Later, I was told these inquiries had confirmed that, in the opinion of the experts, the mine was worthless for the purposes of copper exploitation. So it appeared that the only reason for their presence was for covert intelligence purposes.

Over the following months, the relationship developed and

there were several invitations to each other's homes for meals and drinks. There was little point in trying to conceal my being a British soldier and probably the fact that I was always in civilian clothes caused him to wonder about the nature of my duties, although in casual conversations I made oblique references to police work. However, he never directly asked. Eventually, a casual after-dinner conversation about religious suppression under the communist regime led indirectly to my being invited to visit the mine site. He had expressed an interest in Greek Cypriot churches of which there were several good examples in the immediate area. I offered to show him several and he readily accepted, suggesting that he could show me around the mine at the same time. One Sunday afternoon soon afterwards we visited the churches, following which he took me to the mine. I have no knowledge of mining matters although I did have some pre-Army knowledge of scientific matters. There were piles of mining, engineering and scientific analysis equipment scattered around – but strangely none of it showing signs of actually being installed or organised. I could only assume that they were seriously trying to exploit the site and were suffering delays (this was some seven or eight months after their arrival) or that they were prepared to spend copious amounts of money on maintaining good cover – although I supposed the Hungarian Intelligence Service would be unlikely to depend on a spade and a rack of test tubes for the purpose. However, I made what I hoped were signs of being suitably impressed while inwardly becoming more suspicious as the visit went on. The investigation had no end as the matter was overtaken in July 1974 by the coup and resulting Turkish invasion of the island. The Geominco staff were evacuated along with hundreds of other foreign nationals, never to return.

The Cold War lasted for forty-five years and would prove to be the Corps' longest continuous commitment. It had already been running for twenty-three years when, in 1969, the Northern Ireland Troubles erupted on the streets of Belfast and Londonderry. Thereafter, for the next twenty-two years, the Corps was heavily committed to both conflicts, and Northern Ireland would eventually become its second longest continuous operational involvement. Necessity was certainly the mother of invention when it came to the Corps' evolving expertise in covert intelligence gathering, borne out of the need to counter the Soviet threat. By trial, error, determination, flair and imagination, operators of the Intelligence Corps developed and refined the arts of surveillance and agent handling in Germany and Cyprus to such a degree that the need to formalise this expertise was recognised in the creation of the Specialist Intelligence Wing at Repton Manor. It was from there that those skills were exported to counter the threat of Republican and Loyalist terrorism in Northern Ireland.

NORTHERN IRELAND

The chequered history of British–Irish relations took a new turn in the 1960s when a new generation of Nationalists began to move away from using force and instead focused their energies on civil rights. The Northern Ireland Civil Rights Association called for an end to what it perceived as discrimination against the province's Catholic Nationalist minority. The governments at Westminster and Stormont tried to suppress the ensuing protests, but in August 1969, British troops were deployed on the streets of Belfast and Londonderry after clashes between Catholics and the Protestant Loyalist majority overwhelmed Northern Ireland's police force, the Royal

Ulster Constabulary. By 1970, the Troubles began in earnest. The IRA, which had been inactive for almost a decade, had splintered into the Dublin-based 'officials', who advocated peace, and the Belfast-based Provisionals or 'Provos', who were prepared to take up arms against the British. Non-violent Catholics came to regard the IRA as their protectors and listened to the propaganda of the hard-line Republican elements in their communities. The extremists exploited the situation, resulting in British soldiers being seen as op-pressors. Throughout the 1970s, the Troubles escalated into a blood-bath of shootings and bombings. Soldiers, RUC officers and anybody associated with the Crown forces was deemed a legitimate target, with shops, bars, restaurants and offices also being blasted by IRA bombs. The death toll of security forces and civilians mounted as the IRA campaign spread to targets in mainland Britain and British servicemen in Western Europe. In 1985, the Anglo-Irish Agreement was signed, giving the Republic of Ireland some input into Northern Ireland's affairs. The killing continued, however. Peace talks during the 1990s led, in 1998, to the Belfast Agreement, which ended most of the political conflict. By 2005, the British government stated that it considered the IRA campaign to be over. According to figures produced by Conflicts and Politics in Northern Ireland (CAIN), 3,532 people died during the Troubles between 1969 and 2001. It has been estimated that 52 per cent of the casualties were civilians, 32 per cent were members of the British security forces and 16 per cent belonged to paramilitary groups. Republican paramilitaries were said to have been responsible for 60 per cent of these deaths, Loyalists for thirty per cent and the security forces for the remaining 10 per cent.

The Troubles placed great demands on the Intelligence Corps. At times during the thirty years that the British Army was in Northern

Ireland, one quarter of the Corps' available manpower served there. Yet to begin with, the intelligence picture was almost non-existent. When the first reinforcement Intelligence Corps operators arrived in 1969, there were only a few dozen names on a card personality index at HQNI (there were no computers) bearing the details of IRA men who were almost drawing their pensions. As one former Corps operator puts it, 'the intelligence cupboard was empty.' Over the next three decades, the Corps undertook the full range of intelligence duties, from agent handling and surveillance to imagery and signals intelligence, while working in conjunction with police Special Branch and the Army. Meanwhile, other specialist members of the Corps fulfilled roles in security and counter-intelligence and provided unit security surveys, training, vetting and security investigations.

The years of the Troubles required rapid learning and development in the application and adaption of intelligence doctrine in what was then a modern counter-terrorist role, especially one conducted in the UK and in the full glare of the press at home and abroad. Prior to Northern Ireland, many in the military in general – even those at the higher levels of command – had regarded the Corps, its people and its remit with a level of distrust while others derided the need for intelligence at all. The Corps' performance during the period changed all those perceptions and incontrovertibly proved the point that no Commander should commence a mission without good, timely intelligence – information which embedded members of the Intelligence Corps could provide. It has been necessary to obscure some identities and other details in the following accounts of Intelligence Corps activities in Northern Ireland during the Troubles.

• • •

The dangers to which these early special duties operators were exposed are well illustrated by the story of Corporal Robin 'Roo' Rencher of the Intelligence Corps, whose involvement in one of the most famous undercover operations in the province at the time saw him come within a whisker of assassination.

Robin Langdon Rencher was born on 8 February 1944 in Plymouth, the son of Arthur, an Army Captain, and Muriel. In 1948, the family shipped out to Mombasa in Kenya, where his father was serving and where Rencher spent some of his formative years. In his early twenties, he decided to relocate to Australia, eventually enlisting in the Australian Army with Delta Company 6th Royal Australian Regiment, where he was nicknamed 'Pom'. In May 1966, the battalion deployed to Vietnam and was based at Nui Dat in Phuoc Tuy province. There, Rencher took part in Operation Smithfield, later known as the Battle of Long Tan, serving in his capacity as the Company Commander's signaller and orderly. He remained beside Major Harry Smith, calmly relaying radio messages as reports came in from the platoons. Seventeen men of 'D' Company were killed during the battle and others, including Rencher, were wounded. D Company was awarded the US Presidential Distinguished Unit Citation for its collective gallantry. Later in that tour, Rencher was wounded again when an artillery salvo was misdirected by an inexperienced New Zealand artillery officer, killing the Company Sergeant Major and four other soldiers. On returning to Australia, Rencher transferred to the Australian Intelligence Corps, completed a Thai language course and went back to Vietnam with the 1st Division Intelligence Unit. He received the Australian and Vietnamese campaign medals.

In July 1971, Rencher left the Australian Army and after reaching Britain joined the Intelligence Corps. Colleagues soon nicknamed him 'Roo'. After training at Ashford, his first posting was to Northern Ireland, where he was employed on special duties in an undercover campaign which has become known as the 'Four Square Laundry'. This was the cover name for an intriguing, to say nothing of audacious, Army intelligence-gathering operation in Republican West Belfast. Operators posed as the members of the fictional Four Square Laundry firm, which offered a cut-price door-to-door laundry service. Once collected, dirty clothes and linen were subjected to forensic testing for explosives and weapons residues before being washed and given back to each customer. If any evidence surfaced proving that the occupants of an address had handled or been exposed to explosives, weapons or ammunition, the house would either be raided and searched; or placed under surveillance for additional intelligence gathering.

Those who took part in this ingenious scheme came from various regiments and corps of the Army, including members of the Women's Royal Army Corps. Several operators were natives of Northern Ireland. As well as allowing clothes and linen to be tested, the operation fulfilled a spying function. The laundry's Bedford Commer delivery van was fitted with surveillance equipment and there was space in a false roof compartment enabling SAS soldiers to take covert photographs of targets. The laundry's 'office' was based in College Square, in Belfast city centre, and it was Rencher's job to manage that location. As he recalled later, one of the reasons he was selected for this duty was that he could pass as an Australian and not a Briton, strengthening his cover.

In September 1972, the IRA discovered that two of its members had been recruited by British intelligence. One, Kevin McKee, broke under IRA interrogation and revealed details of the Four Square Laundry operation. It was a major security error for an informant to know such information and the IRA exploited the blunder, placing the College Square premises and the laundry van under observation. Their findings appeared to confirm McKee's story. Both McKee and his fellow double agent were later taken to rural south Armagh where they were bound, hooded and executed by a gunshot to the head. Their remains were unearthed in County Meath more than forty years later, in 2015.

On the morning of 2 October 1972, having established the truth about the Four Square Laundry, the IRA mounted simultaneous attacks against the College Square office and the laundry van while it was doing its rounds in the Twinbrook estate, just outside Belfast city centre. At College Square, Rencher was in a back room when two men entered. Although they did not immediately appear hostile, Rencher later said he knew instinctively that they were terrorists. He managed to exit by a back door and sprinted away, losing himself in the city centre crowds and making his way to safety. When the gunmen realised the building was empty, they sprayed it with machine-gun fire and drove off. Meanwhile, at the Twinbrook estate, the laundry van was parked. The driver, a Royal Engineers sapper, Ted Stuart, sat at the wheel while the undercover WRAC operator, Sarah Jane Warke, stood at the front door of a house delivering laundry. Suddenly, two IRA gunmen appeared and peppered the driver's side of the van with machine-gun and rifle fire, killing Stuart instantly. Warke survived the ambush only because the woman to whom she was delivering laundry believed that Loyalists were responsible for the attack. She allowed Warke to escape through her house. Some reports stated that Warke was wounded during the incident. Rencher was later awarded the British Empire Medal (BEM) and Warke was awarded the Military Medal for bravery in 1973.

Following his experiences in Northern Ireland, Robin Rencher went on to serve in Germany, Belize and the Falklands. He rose steadily through the ranks to Warrant Officer Class 1 and was commissioned Lieutenant in August 1987 and promoted to Captain in 1989. He retired from the Army on 1 April 1991. Captain Robin 'Roo' Rencher died on 9 August 2016, aged seventy-two. His humanist funeral in Devon was well attended by his former Intelligence Corps colleagues, several of whom delivered their own eulogies to the man many described as 'the best soldier I ever served with'.

•   •   •

The following account of a typical day in the life of an agent handler in Northern Ireland is offered by former Intelligence Corps officer Lieutenant 'N' who served with the Research Office at 39 Infantry Brigade between 1978 and 1981.

Belfast, 1981. I nudged the car forward into the mid-morning traffic to head north on one of the arterial roads feeding Belfast City. It was an ordinary-looking car: bland colour, common make and, I hoped, I was an ordinary-looking driver. My hair was just long enough, I had side-burns and a moustache and wore a ubiquitous 'snorkel jacket' with fake squirrel-fur trimmed hood. I had carried out anti-surveillance drills on leaving the secure Army base and felt clean of any hostile attention.

Twenty-five minutes to go. I remember Downtown Radio was playing from the dashboard, the news commenting on the previous day's Provisional IRA rocket attack on a British Army armoured vehicle in Andersonstown, in which two soldiers were injured.

May had been a bad month for the security forces: an RUC officer shot dead on patrol in West Belfast by an IRA sniper; IRA firing ten mortars at the Army/RUC base at Newtownhamilton, injuring two; another policeman killed in his vehicle on Belfast's Springfield Road by an IRA rocket; and five British soldiers killed when their Saracen armoured personnel carrier was blown up by an IRA culvert bomb near Newry. That sort of news was as devastating as it was salutary.

The briefing had finished forty-five minutes before – the first I had given 'solo'. For a year, I was the Operations Officer, responsible for running the Operations Room and its procedures, manning the desk each time a meeting with an informant took place, liaising with all the Army units in Belfast to ensure they had the sealed envelopes with instructions on what to do if we ever jumped on their radio net and sent the emergency codeword: 'HARTSHORN, HARTSHORN'. This included letting them know how we would indicate that we were friendly forces and how they should react. But now, having attended the agent-running course, I was deemed ready to conduct my own operation on the ground.

I touched the butt of the 9mm pistol at my hip with my elbow. Nerves were kicking in. The traffic got heavier as I drove further north. I did a radio check to test communications and got the reassuring response from 'Zero Delta' and the cover vehicles. Now there were twenty minutes to go.

The cars slowed as a joint UDR/RUC vehicle checkpoint pulled in vehicles apparently at random. The policeman nodded a greeting as I wound down my window and offered my fake blue Northern Ireland driver's licence. Noticing the paperclip holding something in the back cover, he flicked open the page, saw my identity card hidden there and handed it back. His wink was almost imperceptible.

I was a bit early. I needed to lose ten minutes while the cover team did its job. I wondered now about 'SLIDING DOOR' (a fictitious agent codename that has been invented for the purposes of this book); the last coded communication with him seemed sound. He was OK for today, knew the time and knew his way to the area I needed him in. I knew the route well. I had been over it often enough, on foot and by car, together with the cover team. Nothing about his movements or actions that week indicated danger, but one can never be 100 per cent sure.

I ran over in my mind 'actions on', knowing the cover team would be there to play its part if something went wrong. Our training had covered the three major risks. First, the agent's recruitment had been a set-up job from the beginning and he was an IRA lure designed to learn our procedures then snatch one of us. That would mean torture and death. Well, they'd had that opportunity for some time and hadn't taken it and, besides, some other useful indicators allowed us to rule that out. Or maybe he was being followed by the IRA and they would see him go somewhere he shouldn't go and meet someone he shouldn't meet. But time had been spent designing a well-supported cover story to ameliorate this, with many other precautions built in. The third and worst-case scenario was based on a mix between him being seen somewhere deemed unusual and some other factor that would lead to him being 'pulled', beaten, made to confess and his mother threatened until he agreed to 'double'. Torture was used as necessary, a favourite method being an electric drill to the knee. This would be the point where, most likely, IRA's Northern

Command would step in and plan an ambush. And it would be heavy and determined, using their best men.

Habit and nerves made me check that my pistol hadn't magically disappeared. I touched the 'bug out' bag, tested the zip, felt through the material for the other weapon and gizmos I would need to use if I was ambushed, and if I couldn't drive through it and if the cover team didn't get myself and SLIDING DOOR out of the car.

SLIDING DOOR seemed a genuinely nice guy, although I had met him only a few times as co-handler. I had not been there for the 'pitch' months before when his previous handler had put to him the proposal that would lead him to risk his life, to betray his organisation and possibly his friends. There was no 'typical' agent: each had their own reasons and motivation. For some, it was money, for others, revenge, and for some, the excitement. SLIDING DOOR had seen a friend beaten by the IRA youth wing as a prelude to being 'knee-capped' for what passed as an unacceptable misdemeanour in one of West Belfast's estates. SLIDING DOOR was a Republican but saw the path to this through politics – he had no time for the bully-boys or gunmen and was prepared to help us defeat them.

Two minutes to go. The radio squawked the right codes from the cover team and I moved off. Nerves jangling, watch the red Transit parked on the left, two guys crossing ahead, delivery truck turning out on the right, cover team vehicles 'flanking' me. On cue, SLIDING DOOR appeared.

'Hello mate, how are you?' He looked as relieved as I felt. Now it began: first some quick essential protocols while I 'drilled' to clear the area, and then I started the questions – time could be critical. Fifteen minutes later I led SLIDING DOOR quietly into a secure facility, its entrance near invisible, passed unconsciously by hundreds every day. My colleague had stocked the place with food and drink and we three sat down to conduct the debrief.

In many respects, I thought the actions on the ground were a little like military parachuting: volunteers coming forward for selection, testing and incredibly exacting training, all to deliver them to a start point on the battlefield. For the agent handlers, they volunteered too, went through 'pre-select', then arduous physical training, close quarter battle and unarmed combat training, endless days on the ranges, anti-surveillance and anti-ambush drills, tradecraft lessons, meticulous plans and briefings with contingencies built in, always knowing there were some factors that can't be controlled. And the gruelling resistance to interrogation test. All to get them to the start point on their 'battlefield' where their real intelligence work started.

SLIDING DOOR was not a penetrative agent; he was not yet in a position to provide the same type of high-grade actionable intelligence as some other agents. This would come with time. These were those who could not only describe the latest IED initiating device but provide one for examination; those who could state with certainty the time, place and target of the next rocket attack, or give the location of three Armalite rifles and a half-block of Semtex; or pinpoint the judge's address that the IRA 'intelligence team' had just planned to attack and so on.

At the moment, SLIDING DOOR was still on the fringes, but he, like others, provided those essential nuggets that helped build the ever-evolving intelligence picture: two known IRA men seen entering the derelict opposite Andersonstown RUC Station; the junction where the 'Fianna' dickers (local youths used by IRA as look-outs and to monitor security forces routines) had spent the last two days; the absence of a suspected gunman from his local haunts after last Monday's shooting; the subject in Photo 317 associating with Photo 21 etc. In isolation, seemingly this was of little use but, collated, fused and analysed with other fragments, they were possibly the start of, or clincher for, other operations mounted by the Tasking Coordination Group (TCG).

There was one of these for each of the three police regions under the aegis of the Regional Head of Special Branch. They drew together potentially actionable intelligence from across the agencies for exploitation by specialist police and military units. Even if not TCG level material, the Intelligence Corps analysts in the teams at brigade or HQNI would certainly log and evaluate each fragment, add it to other intelligence, update the terrorist organisation charts, search for patterns to help assess the threat and disseminate their findings to the decision-makers. Several hours of logical and persistent questioning followed; every morsel noted and double-checked. This is where we earned our money. He earned little and wanted nothing more than expenses. He just wanted peace, and an Irish Republic, but was prepared to wait for this. All respect to him.

I made a brief call on the secure phone back to base to report a few items that were time-sensitive and received in response some specific details to add to SLIDING DOOR's tasking. These we explained carefully, then went over his personal security and communications for alerting us to particular developments around certain individuals. It was our responsibility to maintain his morale and commitment and keep him safe and alive.

It was comforting to think that, across the province, colleagues in the other two Research Offices and from the RUC's Special Branch were doing the same thing: sitting with some brave men and women who risked their lives to provide intelligence on terrorists of either side. Every fact helped build a better picture. On leaving NI, I tried to forget everything and, quite rightly, was no longer privy to any access. On a subsequent tour, years later, a colleague hinted SLIDING DOOR was responsible for the recovery of a prestige weapon, but that was in the future.

For now, we went through the next phase and infiltrated him back into his community. Later, I returned to base to produce my Contact Form (the detail of the meeting between me and the agent) and Military Intelligence Source Report – our formal intelligence reporting method – with the care and precision that SLIDING DOOR's risks warranted. I spent the evening in the Officers' Mess; he went back into the Republican heartlands to help us support the rule of law. I hope he is still alive today to enjoy all that he worked for.

• • •

Meanwhile, the operators of 14 Intelligence Company were kept just as busy. This Special Forces unit, an effective successor to the undercover military surveillance unit which carried out the previously mentioned Four Square Laundry operation, had a dedicated force of highly trained plain-clothes surveillance operatives. Members of the SAS and SBS served tours with 14 Intelligence Company, improving the unit's overall success and enhancing their own abilities as well.

Operators in 14 Intelligence Company included Corporal 'T', who was born in a South Yorkshire pit town, attended a local grammar school and then served an apprenticeship before starting a business career. Wanting something more challenging out of life, he decided to join the Army and was advised to try for the Intelligence Corps. Having passed selection and training, his first posting was to an intelligence support team in Belfast. It was here that he first became aware of 14 Company and its successes, applying to join the unit. After a rigorous selection and training programme, he was accepted and served in it for two years at the height of the Troubles.

In early 1976, a soldier manning a vehicle checkpoint reported to his Section Commander that he had been in conversation with a local man who appeared to be well connected to senior IRA members and seemed willing to talk. This lead was passed to the brigade source handlers and a qualified handler from the Intelligence Corps was tasked to assess the case with a view to possible recruitment. Corporal 'T' takes up the story in his own words.

I had just returned from several days in a Covert Observation Post and was on a day off when I was called to the operations room and tasked to participate in the provision of covert cover for the safe and secure pickup of this potential source by the brigade source handlers. I was also asked to listen in to the source meeting and provide specific questions to ask. The answers, and those received to the other questions posed by the handlers, would allow them to determine the source potential, level of access and motivation, and enable early, practical follow-up action by 14 Company to confirm the information obtained. We had to make sure he was telling the truth.

The meeting, during which the Intelligence Corps handler successfully recruited the individual, was a revelation. The source had excellent access to IRA operations, and the information he gave was current and easily confirmed. One piece of information he gave was the description of a hide within a public building which he said currently held a rifle and ammunition, and authority was obtained quickly in order to exploit this information while it was fresh. I was tasked that evening with putting together a small team of operators with the aim of gaining access to the building to confirm what was there. This was not a simple task as the building was located within a strongly Republican area and our reconnaissance showed the approach was going to be difficult.

Covert entry was made in the early hours one morning, via a window and then through an internal locked door into a central corridor. Great care was taken to ensure that the entry was clean and left no trace. Once access to the corridor was gained, two of us donned night vision helmets, which gave a good but restrictive field of view, and using a pinpoint handheld torch we moved into the pitch-black of a corridor. We made our way along the corridor and up some stairs until we came to a room, described by the source as the room containing the hide. Fortunately, the door to it was unlocked and we carefully entered. We were both very aware that we could be being lured into a trap, especially as we could see out of the room's window into Republican houses close by and streetlights cast light into the room we were in.

The location of the hide in the room was at ceiling height so, standing on a chair and unsighted, I put my hand and arm into the hide. I can still recall the exhilaration of putting my hand straight onto the barrel of a rifle. We lifted it down to the floor and then took detailed photographs of it. On returning it back to the hide I felt another object, a case, which we carefully lifted down. I gently released the clasps, and as I lifted the lid, we both instinctively looked away, worried that it may be booby-trapped – not that looking away would have helped if it had been! On opening the case we saw immediately that it was stuffed with hundreds of documents from many different sources detailing confidential and secret information about members of the RUC, Special Branch, Ulster Defence Regiment, and observation reports on movement including those of the Army. Having got a good feel for the content of the documents, we closed the lid and returned the case to the hide. We then left the building, ensuring everything was left as we had found it.

The following night we returned, anxious to record and photograph the contents of the case before it could be moved elsewhere. Having carefully checked that no lights could be seen from outside the building, quickly and quietly, we began to photograph every document in the case. With so many documents to photograph we were up against a time limit and this was especially difficult as we had to keep stopping to change the film. We completed the task just before first light and then crept away.

When the photographs had been developed and analysed, it became evident that Republican sympathisers, including employees from public and government agencies, such as the Driver and Vehicle Licensing Agency, were supplying information and documents to the IRA, obviously for use in targeting members of the security forces and establishment figures.

And what happened then? As far as I am aware, the source continued to provide first-class information for many years. And the soldier responsible for reporting the potential source was awarded a GOC's commendation. He probably never realised the value his friendly conversation with a local had on the intelligence war.

•   •   •

Despite the high number of Intelligence Corps men employed in Northern Ireland, and considering the very high element of danger for those who were employed on special duties, it is remarkable to think there was only one fatality due to direct terrorist action, and that was the result of an unlucky chance encounter rather than a planned operation. The soldier in question's story warrants inclusion in this volume.

Paul Edward Harman was born on 15 March 1950 in Ankara, Turkey, the son of a career diplomat. He was educated at Greenmore College in Birmingham and then Bromley College of Technology. Having gravitated towards science at school, he was initially employed as a laboratory assistant with the Wellcome Foundation Laboratories but moved on, eventually becoming a mortgage consultant. In September 1972, he enlisted on a three-year engagement in the 16th/5th Queen's Royal Lancers, qualified as an armoured fighting vehicle driver/signaller and was posted to his regiment at Tidworth.

On 11 July 1974, Trooper Harman applied for a transfer to the Intelligence Corps, having already spent four weeks attached to a UK-based intelligence section. That month, his squadron was posted to Cyprus for a two-month emergency tour following the Greek National Guard coup and Turkish invasion of the island, during which he was based in the Sovereign Base Area at Dhekelia. During this tour, he became friendly with several members of the Intelligence Corps, reinforcing his determination to transfer. He commenced training at the Intelligence Centre at Ashford in November 1974 and was transferred to the Corps on 15 May 1975. His first Corps posting was Germany, where he served until January 1977. He then passed selection for special duties in Northern Ireland and on completion of the course joined 14 Intelligence Company in Belfast.

For security reasons, Corporal Harman's duties with '14' cannot be disclosed, but they were to lead to his death. On the evening of 14 December 1977, he was driving his unmarked car, in plain clothes, to the 'Fort Monagh' Army base in the Turf Lodge area of Belfast. As he approached the junction of Monagh Road and Monagh Drive, he stopped so that a woman pushing a pram could cross the road. At that point, he was ambushed by at least two IRA men whose primary motive appears to have been to hijack his car, unaware of his military status. When Corporal Harman carried out the routine emergency evasion drills used in such circumstances, the IRA gunmen opened fire and he received fatal wounds. Corporal Paul Harman was twenty-seven years old when he died and is buried at St Botolph's Church at Eynsford in Kent.

●　●　●

The benefit of good, actionable intelligence, very often obtained as the result of painstaking and dangerous effort, can easily be lost as the result of premature, reckless or ill-judged action by a Commander on the ground, even against the advice of intelligence professionals. And the aftermath of such action can also result in the compromising of intelligence methodology and even the death of informants. One such example of an intelligencer's brilliant work being undone can be recounted here.

In the late 1980s, Lance Corporal 'P' was working as an analyst in the Lisburn-based signals intelligence unit when he noticed a correlation between a taxi company's radio communications and terrorist-related events on the ground. At the time, many individuals and workplaces listened to the local Downtown Radio at home and at work. This included the military, as the station often provided reports of events on the ground faster than the security forces' chain-of-command communications. Lance Corporal P was scrolling through various conversations in local short-wave radio nets when he noticed a coincidence between messages passing backwards and forwards within a particular taxi company, and IRA attacks in West Belfast. By correlating known events on the ground and other intelligence, he decoded the exchanges over a period of time. It turned out to be the command network of a West Belfast IRA Active Service Unit. The terrorists were using coded taxi management language to move weapons, extort money from 'their' pubs and even mount attacks. It was a top-class piece of analysis from Lance Corporal P, yet subsequent rash decision-making by a senior Army Commander would compromise all this good work.

Whenever the 'Taxi ASU' radio net came on the air, the IRA 'operational area' was immediately placed out of bounds, with the long-term aim of building up a sufficiently detailed picture to enable a police capture-and-arrest operation. However, the local Army Brigade Commander objected to these restrictions in his area of responsibility and demanded the General Officer Commanding tell him the reason. Although the General's Intelligence Corps Staff Officer advised against the reason being disclosed, even mounting a rearguard action to protect the information source, he was eventually overruled, meaning that the Brigadier was informed each time the Taxi ASU came live.

On the first two occasions, without consultation, the Brigadier had a pre-planned operation ready, randomly swamping the area with troops and hoping to catch the IRA in some act. This was all it took for them to realise that their signals had been compromised. On the third occasion, they used the transmissions to draw the Army into a carefully planned ambush in which one soldier was shot and injured. After that, the 'Taxi ASU' net disappeared off the air and the Army never again penetrated their communications.

For many former members of the Corps, this story represents a perfect example of the potentially valuable source of long-term actionable intelligence being sacrificed for the purposes of hasty action – some might say in order to flatter military egos.

• • •

Thursday 2 June 1994 remains the bleakest day in the history of the Intelligence Corps and the wider intelligence community in the UK and was of particular significance to those members of the Corps serving in Northern Ireland. During the early evening, an RAF Chinook helicopter was on its way from RAF Aldergrove in Belfast to a security conference at Fort George, near Inverness. It was carrying four Special Forces crew and twenty-five passengers, among them the top echelon of Northern Ireland-based Intelligence Officers within the Army, MI5 and the police. At about 6 p.m., it crashed into a hillside on the Mull of Kintyre. Everybody on board, including five Intelligence Corps officers, was killed instantly. The status of those in the helicopter, the lack of witnesses to the incident and the fact there was thick fog all complicated matters considerably. Initially, these factors led to theories that the aircraft had been brought down deliberately at a crucial time in the peace process.

The General Officer Commanding Northern Ireland at the time was General (later Sir) Roger Wheeler. He takes up the story of what remains not only the RAF's worst peacetime disaster but also an incident whose exact causes remain unclear.

I was presenting an award at Hillsborough Castle when one of my close protection officers came up and whispered in my ear. I did not hear him properly and did not want to be interrupted, knowing that everything was in hand and I was not expecting anything of importance, and so I brushed him off. A few minutes later, I was racing back to my HQ for the start of three weeks of trauma and grief. Years later, when asked at a talk I was giving to a course of military Staff Officers what was the worst day of my career, I had no hesitation in saying the Chinook tragedy.

I had bumped into three of those killed that afternoon and, as I was the General in charge of the armed forces in Northern Ireland, I knew all of those killed. They were the senior intelligence people and I saw them frequently. That evening I saw two who were due to be on that flight but did not make it because of last minute issues they had to deal with at work. On the day after, I flew over to the Mull of Kintyre. I felt I had to see it and be able to relay to the relatives what it looked like, if asked. There was this vast funnel-shaped blackened area. A man in a yellow jacket was evidently collecting debris and told me that he had seen the helicopter coming in at full speed and low over the water and disappearing into the cloud. He said, 'If it reassures you, none of them would have known anything about it.'

Unsurprisingly, intelligence operations on the ground did not miss a beat. It had crossed my mind that the Intelligence Corps would not have the experience or mechanisms for taking casualties, as we do in the infantry. There was no need for concern. Those who stepped into command roles and their colleagues, as well as all the soldiers, were outstanding, and I judged the Regimental Sergeant Major of the Joint Support Group to be one of the best I have ever met.

The second in command of the Army's agent-running unit was unable to accompany the others on the helicopter. His Commanding Officer had been on the flight, accompanied by his replacement, who was due to take over command in a few days' time. This meant the second in command had stayed behind to command current operations. He recalls:

At 6.15 p.m. I was at my desk with Sky News on in the background and caught a report that a helicopter had gone down in west Scotland. Three of those killed in the crash had been in my office just before departing to Aldergrove airport for the flight, one being the boss and another his designated successor, so it was appropriate that I had not been scheduled to go as we had a number of operations running. With much foreboding, I called Fort George, where the helicopter was due to land, but they had heard nothing at that stage. Then the phones started ringing non-stop and my worst fears were realised when the Headquarters was able to confirm that 'our' Chinook, serial number ZD576, had crashed on the Mull of Kintyre with no survivors. The news was devastating, but that is when military training and discipline kicks in. Of course, operations continued, that's what we do. We had a unit dinner planned for the end of the week following the return of the team from the Fort George conference, and we went ahead with it, in their honour. We needed a fair amount of alcohol to help us get through it.

The Chinook tragedy was a seismic event in the Intelligence Corps' history. At an emotional level, the process of grieving, leading up to a momentous memorial service, brought everybody together. This cohesion has lasted. The infantry and armoured officers who were generally in command of Army formations had not expected the Corps to manage the losses so competently. Despite the widespread shock among officers and soldiers, operations were unhindered. This was a step up in terms of recognition and respect.

Subsequent inquiries into the cause of the crash have reached different findings. The latest, published in 2011, concluded that an earlier review which had accused the pilots, Flt Lts Jonathan Tapper and Richard Cook, of gross negligence, was wrong and that ruling was set aside.

The five Intelligence Corps officers who died in the 1994 Mull of Kintyre Chinook crash are acknowledged here.

Lieutenant Colonel Richard Gregory-Smith was born on 15 September 1951 at Street in Somerset. He was educated at Wellington School in Somerset and commissioned into the Intelligence Corps in April 1972. He served his infantry attachment with 1st Battalion The Light Infantry before going on to the University of Aberystwyth, where he gained an honours degree. On returning to the Corps, he served in the UK as an Intelligence Section Commander and then moved to Germany as a Desk Officer in Security Wing. In 1980, he was appointed as an instructor to the Royal Military Academy, Sandhurst, and held this post with distinction for two years. He then moved to Joint Service Intelligence Section in Hong Kong before being promoted to Major. In 1984, he took command of 12 Intelligence and Security Company in Northern Ireland, being Mentioned in Despatches on 14 April 1987. He then served for three years as an instructor at the Specialist Intelligence Wing at Ashford and in 1989 moved to Intelligence and Security Group (Germany) as Operations Officer. He remained in that post for a year before being selected for promotion to Lieutenant Colonel and a posting to the Joint Intelligence Staff and Joint Planning Staff in Headquarters Land Forces. In July 1992, he moved to command the Force Intelligence Unit in Northern Ireland.

●　●　●

Major Roy Pugh MBE was born on 6 March 1957. He was commissioned into the Intelligence Corps in 1977. Following a short infantry attachment with the Royal Regiment of Wales, he studied Russian at the Army Languages School at Beaconsfield, qualifying as an interpreter. He then served as a Troop Commander with 14th Signal Regiment, and in 1983, as a Captain, took command of 53 Security Section in Germany. In 1986, following a brief tour in the Falklands, he was posted as SO3 Liaison at BRIXMIS, after which he went to the Force Research Unit in Northern Ireland. For the first two years of that tour, he served as a Detachment Commander and in 1989, on his promotion to Major, as the Intelligence Officer/ Adjutant. He was made an MBE in 1991. A one-year tour with the Joint Arms Implementation Group was followed by his successful attendance of Staff College, after which he was appointed Staff Officer (Intelligence) at HQ Northern Ireland.

●　●　●

Lieutenant Colonel John Tobias MBE was born on 18 December 1952 in Londonderry, Northern Ireland. He was commissioned into the Intelligence Corps in March 1973, serving his infantry attachment with 1st Battalion Queen's Lancashire Regiment. After taking the subaltern's course in 1974, he commanded 42 Security Section in Germany before being posted to 8 Detachment, where he remained until he took over the post of Adjutant of the Intelligence

Centre in 1978. In 1980, he returned to Germany in a staff appointment at HQ British Army of the Rhine, after which he moved to Northern Ireland as a Detachment Commander on special duties, a post he held for two and a half years and during which he was made an MBE. In 1984, he was posted to the Special Counter-Intelligence Team at the Ministry of Defence and in 1986 he was given command of a squadron in 13 Signal Regiment. This was followed by a security staff appointment in HQ British Forces Cyprus, after which he was appointed second in command of the group in Germany. In 1993, he had one short tour in Defence Intelligence at the Ministry of Defence. In June 1994, he was in the process of taking over, on promotion, as Commanding Officer of the Joint Support Group (Northern Ireland).

●　　●　　●

Lieutenant Colonel George Williams MBE QGM was born on 5 March 1945. He enlisted into the Intelligence Corps in 1963 and gained promotion through the ranks to Warrant Officer 1 in 1979. Most of his early soldier service was spent between the UK, Germany and the Middle East, where he served with the Trucial Oman Scouts for two years between 1966 and 1968. Later, and especially after his promotion to Staff Sergeant in 1975, he served several tours in Northern Ireland and on special duties, being made an MBE in 1977 and Mentioned in Despatches in 1980. He was commissioned in March 1980 and appointed as a Desk Officer in Security Wing of the group in Germany until 1983, when he moved to command a detachment on special duties in Northern Ireland. He became Operations Officer of this unit in 1986 and was awarded the Queen's Gallantry Medal (QGM). On promotion to Major, he commanded 3 Intelligence and

Security Company in Berlin. In 1989, after he had been selected for a Regular Commission, he returned to Northern Ireland, but in November 1990, on promotion to Lieutenant Colonel, he was appointed SO1 Instructor in Security Wing at the Defence Intelligence and Security School. He returned to Northern Ireland in June 1991 as Commanding Officer of the Joint Support Group.

● ● ●

Major (Retd) John Stewart Haynes MBE was born on 29 January 1936. He completed his National Service in the Cheshire Regiment from 1954 to 1956 and enlisted in the Intelligence Corps in 1958. He progressed through the ranks to Warrant Officer Class II, serving at various times in the UK, Jamaica, Guiana, Hong Kong and Berlin. He was commissioned in March 1972 and posted, as a Captain, as Adjutant in the UK Land Forces Group. In 1974, he became second in command of 4 Security Company in Germany and then served a one-year tour as a Desk Officer in Security Wing. He was promoted to Major in 1977 and took command of 90 Security Section in London. In 1980, he was appointed SO2 Research at HQ Northern Ireland, following which he served for two years as an instructor at the Specialist Intelligence Wing at Ashford. His final tour in the Corps was as OC 2 Intelligence Company in Germany from 1984 to 1987, for which he was made an MBE. He retired from the Army in 1987 with a total service of thirty-one years. He then joined the Security Service (MI5) and was serving with them at the time of his death.

● ● ●

As previously mentioned, the Davidson initiative – which saw the 'First 100' cadre of regular officers from other regiments being transferred into the Intelligence Corps – was a success in that it ensured well-earned regimental recognition of the Intelligence Corps within the Army. Yet it was the sixty years of continual operational service during the Cold War and in Northern Ireland between 1947 and 2007 that cemented the Corps' reputation for providing accurate and timely intelligence and guaranteed its place as a force multiplier, often thanks to the fact that small teams or individuals working alone frequently had a positive impact on operations well beyond their number, age and rank. Those six decades allowed the Corps to evolve and clarify doctrine and methods in both overt and covert intelligence gathering, while also displaying an ability to adapt to constantly changing threats on a worldwide scale.

PART FIVE

STABILITY OPERATIONS

The 1990s brought about great change for the British Army. The decade began with the de-escalation of the Cold War; and as it drew to a close, in 1998, the Belfast Agreement halted much of the violence associated with the Northern Ireland Troubles. This era marked the start of what might be termed 'stability operations', in which UK forces were committed to new theatres in order to assist failing states or to remove rogue leaders who threatened their neighbours, international order or Britain's own resources.

From 1990, Intelligence Corps units had been included in the order of battle for deployed forces and, having developed a wide range of intelligence skills in Northern Ireland and Germany, the Corps was able to use them in the Balkans, Iraq and Afghanistan. Yet intelligence challenges soon presented themselves. Whereas the IRA had operated within a framework that had some semblance of logic, and while Russia's forces and intelligence agencies were kept in check by the theory of 'mutual assured destruction', the new enemies Britain faced were far harder to pin down. Analysts had to try to assess the intentions and capabilities of an ever-changing mix of extremist groups who had no fixed rules, who often did not care about killing their own people or themselves and whose motives were driven by fundamentalist dogma or crime. This meant the conflicts in which the British Army became enmeshed were frequently confusing, chaotic and bloody.

It is too soon to be able to look back at this part of the Intelligence Corps' history in any depth or to understand its impact on the future. For one thing, some techniques employed by the Corps in carrying out duties in the 1990s are still in use today. For another, many of those who participated in Corps activities from that era are still alive and working. If certain details were divulged here, individuals and operations would, potentially, be placed at risk. With that said, a few camouflaged examples can be mentioned which demonstrate that everything which had been learned before was, and is, being put to good use. In spite of the many changes to the armed forces specifically and to society generally – to say nothing of the impact of technology – the essential characteristics of the Corps remain effective. Wherever British troops are deployed, Intelligence Corps units will be found working both overtly and covertly on the front line, overseen by a new generation of enlightened senior officers.

FORMER YUGOSLAVIA – BOSNIA AND KOSOVO, 1992–2000

After the death of Marshal Tito in 1980 and the collapse of the Soviet Union in 1991, the socialist Republic of Yugoslavia destabilised and by 1992 had dissolved into its constituent territories of Bosnia, Serbia, Croatia, Slovenia and Macedonia. The multi-ethnic and multi-religious nature of the Balkan states had been a cause of strife since Yugoslavia's formation in 1945, but tensions had largely been suppressed by authoritarian rule. The demise of Tito and the USSR allowed civil war to break out between the various ethnic groups.

BOSNIA

In Bosnia–Herzegovina in the 1990s, opposing Muslim, Serbian and Croatian groups battled for control and 'ethnic cleansing' became a grim new euphemism, with entire villages massacred by rival forces. In February 1992, the United Nations intervened by establishing a Protection Force which was given a mandate to create the conditions for peace talks. British troops, under UN control, were engaged from the start, but their limited power meant they were unable to take charge as they might otherwise have done. Following the three-week air and artillery offensive against the Bosnian Serb Army in the summer of 1995 known as Operation Deliberate Force, the Dayton Peace Accord was signed and NATO's multinational Implementation Force took over under the codename Operation Endeavour. Unrest continued in Bosnia throughout 1996 and 1997, however, and many breaches of the Dayton Accord were committed, including attacks on British soldiers and bases. In 1996, the Implementation Force was disbanded and replaced by the Stabilisation Force.

One of those whose experiences in Bosnia can be related here must, for reasons of confidentiality, be referred to only as 'Major N'. His quick thinking helped to expose an Islamist terrorist training camp whose students might have been capable of inflicting horrors on civilians and children.

Major N was commissioned from Sandhurst as a Regular Officer in 1977, aged twenty, and transferred to the Intelligence Corps in 1978. His previous duties included a tour in Northern Ireland, working in a covert surveillance unit in Germany, and a stint as a surveillance instructor in the UK before he attended Staff College in 1991. Following a UN tour in Bosnia–Herzegovina in 1994, he was commanding 2 Intelligence Company in Germany when

NATO's Implementation Force deployed to Bosnia on Operation Joint Endeavour.

Officially, NATO's Implementation Force was deployed on 20 December 1995. In fact, the lead elements of the Joint Field Intelligence Unit – the hastily created British specialist intelligence section operating under NATO's umbrella – stepped off a C130 aircraft at Sarajevo two weeks earlier, on 5 December. An Intelligence Corps Lieutenant Colonel with recent experience in the Balkans was appointed Commanding Officer and Major N was designated Operations Officer, taking with him half of 2 Intelligence Company's men. The Joint Field Intelligence Unit was under the command of the Allied Rapid Reaction Force, which led the land element of NATO's command in Bosnia.

Major N stationed the unit's three teams across Bosnia to support the British, American and French divisions while welcoming a new team at Kiseljak – a squadron from a French long-range reconnaissance and surveillance unit. His colloquial French meant he was appointed Liaison Officer.

The unit's initial tasks included assessing the plans of the various entities, gauging sources of tension between communities and evaluating potential threats to NATO. Much of this information was easily collected through covert contact with mayors, imams, local police and unit Commanders. At the same time, Major N sifted the joint field intelligence teams' reports for potential intelligence opportunities on key issues linked to Dayton Accord compliance, such as removal of heavy weapons, surrender of territory and the return of displaced persons. Through this, Major N was alerted to what appeared to be a breach of another stipulation of the Dayton Accord – a ban on 'foreign combatant' forces.

The Bosnian civil war had attracted many foreign fighters. By

February 1996, intelligence indicated that those who had supported the Bosnian Croats and Serbs had left, but there remained a sizeable number of 'mujahideen' who had fought alongside the Bosnian Army. Thanks to Major N's instincts, on 11 February the Joint Field Intelligence Unit began a surveillance operation against a suspected Islamist guerrilla training camp in a ski chalet in an isolated valley high in the mountains south of Fojnica. The aim was to confirm the intelligence Major N had seen and to collect as much information about the occupants as possible. By that evening, he and the French officers had developed a plan.

Major N and the team spent 12 February honing the idea with the French Liaison Officers. None of them had worked together before, making for an interesting test of language, doctrine and tempers as details relating to observation points (OPs) and various contingencies were thrashed out.

The plan's first phase took place that night. Due to the hazardous winter conditions and freezing temperatures, the French would only accept a Royal Navy helicopter to insert the OP teams. Major N duly persuaded the Rapid Reaction Corps to provide a Sea King and he decided to fly in its jump seat as the teams were dropped off at their various locations. As the men landed in deep snow carrying huge rucksacks, he did not envy them their six-kilometre 'yomp' through the mountains. Later that evening, Major N and Captain P, his French counterpart, briefed the troops selected for the airborne Quick Reaction Force and the Mortar Company, as well as the Follow-on Force. The Quick Reaction Force and the aircrew then rehearsed their helicopter drills until everybody was ready. Just after midnight, the observation points reported in hushed tones that they were in position.

Some movement was seen at the ski chalet, but it was not deemed to be significant. However, on the morning of 15 February, one observation point reported they may have been spotted by 'hunters'. An hour later, a second observation point reported the same concern. This was surprising given the remoteness of the target, the altitude and the deep snow. Briefings were conducted at the highest level. As the question of the target's occupants was unresolved, and as there had been a potential breach of the Dayton Accord, Major N received orders to mount an operation on the chalet. After a quick 'Orders Group' meeting, the Quick Reaction Force crammed into one helicopter, with Major N and Captain P in a second. A third helicopter flew as a reserve and to provide a distraction. Major N recalls:

We lifted from Kiseljak and the weather was clear and dry. The first helicopter dropped the Quick Reaction Force in dead ground at 1350. As they prepared for the assault, Captain P and I followed, landing in waist-high snow. The third helicopter started its distraction: cresting the tree-line, the pilot stood it on its tail, flying it at an angle of 70 degrees. The rotors blew a massive snow-wave towards the target. It had the desired effect. At 1355 three curious occupants exited the front door and were quickly overpowered. At 1409 the building was cleared and secured.

The three men were searched. Two claimed to be Bosnian caretakers, the third declared he was of a particular Middle Eastern nationality but his passport suggested otherwise and, based on a video found by the Quick Reaction Force, it was deduced that he must be a weapons instructor. All three were later confirmed as Iranian nationals.

A detailed search of the property took place. Clothing for thirty people was found and there were small rooms dedicated to disguises and key-copying, plus an armoury. Among the hundreds of automatic weapons and pistols located were some surprises including silenced sniper rifles; ammunition without headstamps; IED circuits; plus conventional and home-made explosives. Children's toys and household items such as shower-gel containers filled with Semtex were also found.

Notebooks recovered showed that the chalet was being used as a training school for the Bosnian state security service. These men were being taught how to booby-trap toys. A sketch in one notebook even showed a child's foot in a canvas shoe stepping on a booby trap. Instructional material in Farsi was also found together with cardboard models of buildings. And a manual on kidnapping a Bosnian Serb Liaison Officer in a French-guarded building in Sarajevo was also seized.

Tickets and other paperwork indicated recent travel between the Middle East and European cities and pictures of religious leaders indicated the occupants' loyalties. At 1545 one of the Follow-on Force patrols radioed to explain they had stopped three vehicles approaching. Major N allowed them through the cordon under escort and, once at the target, the vehicles' occupants were detained. Four were Bosnian government bodyguards who were furious when they were disarmed. Attention then turned to their two 'principals'. Major N spoke to both separately:

In a mixture of French, English and German each gave me the same story: they were there to help the Bosnian government, had been invited to assist with policy and agriculture and that the building was an agricultural school. Neither realised I had been through the place thoroughly and would have known this to be untrue. The first one smiled as he handed me a diplomatic passport from the same Middle Eastern country as the 'cook'. Trying to keep a neutral expression, I realised I had a potential international incident on my hands. He confirmed, on questioning, he had visited the building before and knew what was inside. I knew this anyway from evidence I had found. Managing to find the right words, I told him – with more confidence than I felt – that as there was activity and material in the building contrary to the Dayton Agreement, I considered his presence incompatible with his diplomatic status, and I was detaining him on behalf of NATO. He accepted this with a shrug.

The second man offered only a 'service passport' issued by the same country but claimed diplomatic status, so Major N dealt with him similarly. The new detainees joined the others and, in deference to their Muslim faith, were allowed to wash, pray, eat and keep warm by the fire.

Major N reported the results of the search and the detainees' details. Military and diplomatic wheels soon started turning, with a French regiment sent to bolster the effort and senior officers flying in. Later in the evening, the arms and equipment were loaded onto French vehicles, some destined for forensic testing. Major N left the scene with all the documents, including the programme for the terrorist course being run there.

The detainees were delivered to the Bosnian government and under international pressure expelled a day later. Admiral Leighton W. Smith Jr, the head of the Implementation Force, visited the scene and condemned as an 'abomination' the terrorist material that had been found. His staff later staged a press conference in Sarajevo to display it to the media. This was another crucial intelligence operation which would not have been possible without the effort of the joint intelligence teams uncovering details of the ski chalet and Major N's immediate realisation of its potential significance. That there were no casualties during the operation was a further testament to its success.

KOSOVO

In February 1998, unrest over the status and fate of the Kosovo Albanians that had simmered for years boiled over into armed conflict. Before the break-up of Yugoslavia, the Kosovo Albanians had been under Yugoslavian control. Subsequently, the newly independent states of Serbia and Montenegro had tried to exercise power over the Kosovans, resulting in the Kosovo Liberation Army (KLA) engaging in a bloody battle with Serbian forces. When diplomatic efforts to find a resolution failed, NATO sent a monitoring force into Kosovo. It proved ineffective and was withdrawn. When Serbian forces then removed over 1 million Albanians from Kosovo into Macedonia and Albania, NATO was compelled to act, bombing Serbian military targets. Thereafter, 'Kosovo Force' was formed under NATO jurisdiction with a mandate to stop Serbian aggression, disarm the Kosovo Liberation Army and bring peace and stability to the region.

In March 2000, following a 78-day and night air campaign, NATO ground forces deployed into Kosovo. NATO's mission was to ensure the withdrawal of Serb forces and to protect the majority Kosovar Albanian population. Intelligence Corps personnel were employed in NATO's HQ in Kosovo's capital, Pristina, and within each of the manoeuvre brigades. This account details how, in the latter half of 2000, human intelligence – HUMINT – made a significant contribution to Multinational Brigade Centre operations and to the wider NATO objectives of bringing about stability to Kosovo via free and fair elections.

Major 'S' was an Intelligence Staff Officer in the headquarters of 3 Commando Brigade, which had deployed to an operating base on the outskirts of Pristina in August 2000. The Multinational Brigade Centre consisted of four battlegroups – two British, one Swedish and one Finnish. The Intelligence Corps complement consisted of an intelligence section of eight operators, a counter-intelligence detachment and a field HUMINT team.

The Multinational Brigade Centre's priorities were to deter Serb aggression into Kosovo and to promote safety and stability so that democratic elections could take place on 28 October 2000. Intelligence priorities were to provide an indicator and warning capability on potential Serb aggression and to report on any local groups which were planning or conducting operations to disrupt the vote.

Brigade operations consisted of the 'cordon and search' model plus the confiscation of weapons, ammunition and explosives. The intelligence reporting that drove these operations came from the human sources run by the field HUMINT team. This reporting was fed into the Brigade Commander's daily meeting – known as 'Secrets' – by Major S and comprised a limited number of key Staff Officers and representatives from other agencies. The 'Secrets' meeting was critical to managing intelligence, determining how it could be exploited safely and deciding priorities.

Field HUMINT teams had achieved broad human source coverage since the NATO deployment into Kosovo, but in August 2000, the Ministry of Defence authorised an increase of HUMINT activity via high-risk source operations to enable the recruitment and handling of penetrative agents. This required Intelligence Corps operators and other cap-badge agent handlers – all with enhanced skills from previous service in Northern Ireland – to play key roles.

It was believed that gaining better intelligence would save the lives of innocent citizens and prevent disruption to the elections.

One source who became pivotal to this effort was given the code-name Bluebell. This individual – whose real name must remain secret even today – was initially identified in a routine stop at a vehicle checkpoint run by soldiers from a British battlegroup. Bluebell spoke English fluently, prompting a soldier to note their conversation. Following the method which had been established in Northern Ireland for such undercover contacts, Bluebell's details were given to the field HUMINT team as a potential source. Members of the team then met Bluebell on a number of occasions and began the process of assessing access and suitability. It was eventually established that Bluebell had certain qualities which were of interest to a local hard-line Serb group (hereafter referred to by the pseudo name the Draga Group), putting Bluebell in the position of being able to infiltrate it.

Bluebell was recruited and agreed to become an agent. Events moved rapidly from then on. Bluebell reported that the Draga Group was intending to go to Serbia to plot an operation designed to discredit NATO's ability to maintain security in the build-up to the election. The main purpose of the trip was to receive instructions from a senior military officer. This information was briefed at the next 'Secrets' meeting together with some collateral intelligence from other sources and a small team was formed to determine how best to exploit it.

Following the Serbia trip, Bluebell met the field HUMINT team and was able to reveal that the Draga Group had been tasked to conduct two major operations which would create chaos in the run-up to the elections. The first operation was to plant explosive devices in key government and civic sites within Pristina; the second was to target United Nations police officers who lived in the suburbs. Bluebell later provided more specific intelligence about both planned attacks. The Draga Group's idea was to place explosive devices under the cars of UN police at night which would detonate as they drove to work. Bluebell further reported that the group intended to visit Serbia again to collect explosives, detonators and mercury tilt switches from their military controller.

'Secrets' reviewed this intelligence and began outlining the ingredients of an operation to capture the Draga Group with the incriminating material. A major challenge in this type of operation is to ensure that as much control as possible is maintained over the attackers and explosives because intentions, attack options or timings might change. Bluebell was given strict instructions to communicate to the team all information on the timing or targets of the attack. As soon as the Draga Group returned from Serbia with the explosives, Bluebell was able to confirm its intent to launch both operations within seventy-two hours.

The brigade centre immediately launched an operation against the Draga Group's property to secure the explosives and arrest the would-be aggressors. The raid consisted of a battlegroup 'cordon and search' supported by drones to maintain surveillance of the general area. Bluebell's reporting was so intricate that the specialist Royal Engineer search team was given the exact location of where the explosive devices were hidden. The head of the team commented that they had never received such detailed reporting for a search. The operation resulted in the arrest of the members of the Draga Group and the recovery of the explosives, detonators and mercury tilt switches. Group members admitted under questioning that they had been tasked by the Serbian military to disrupt the elections. The outcome of the operation was then briefed to the UN's Special Representative, Bernard Kouchner.

Having proved so useful in preventing a major incident in the run-up to Kosovo's first elections, and given their proximity and role within the Draga Group, Bluebell was stood down and, for safety reasons, resettled outside of Kosovo. The operation to recruit, handle, exploit and then resettle Bluebell lasted four months. Intelligence Corps operators working in the intelligence section and in the counter-intelligence detachment all made a significant contribution to it, as did the agent handlers within the field HUMINT team. A number of Intelligence Corps personnel involved with this operation were formally recognised in an Honours and Awards List. The Bluebell case study has been briefed as an example in successful HUMINT operations, both in the UK and to international partners.

From the British Army's perspective, including the Intelligence Corps, the Bosnia–Kosovo conflicts provided a distinct set of challenges as they were 'peacekeeping' – rather than conventional war or counter-insurgency – operations. Although the intelligence production process had a different emphasis, the same skills were employed to provide the NATO allies with the intelligence required, albeit in a multi-jurisdictional environment. This was yet another example of the Corps' ability to adapt.

IRAQ

Following the Gulf War, Iraq's chemical and biological weapons programmes came under greater scrutiny. In April 1991, the United Nations Security Council passed Resolution 687, demanding the dismantling of all such weapons and requesting Iraqi acceptance of the presence of UN weapons inspectors. Although Iraq appeared to accept these demands, it began to inhibit the inspectors' work and, in December 1998, the inspectors withdrew in the face of continued

Iraqi non-cooperation. The Allied air operations to enforce the 'no-fly zones' continued, however. When the al-Qaeda militant Islamist extremist network launched a series of attacks on America on 11 September 2001, the administration of President George W. Bush became increasingly hostile to nations which were perceived as being supportive of terrorism. In January 2002, Bush declared that Iran, Iraq and North Korea formed what he called an 'axis of evil'. That November, the UN issued Resolution 1441, giving Iraq a last chance to dispose of its weapons of mass destruction and accept the presence of inspectors. Led by America and supported by Tony Blair's government, the UN came under increasing pressure to authorise military action and remove Saddam Hussein's regime. Then, in the absence of a new UN resolution, the US and UK decided on unilateral action with secondary support from other nations. The Iraq War began on 20 March 2003, when the US carried out missile strikes on Baghdad. A short but fierce ground offensive ensued involving 450,000 coalition troops in which Basra was taken by British units following an engagement with Iraqi Republican Guards. Baghdad Airport fell to US units on 3 April and US tanks entered the city two days later, completing its capture on 9 April. By 14 April, the last pockets of resistance around Tikrit had been eliminated and an end to major combat operations was declared on 1 May.

Although the war was thought to be over within six weeks, the violence was not. Dissident groups comprising regime loyalists, terrorists, Muslim extremists, disaffected Iraqis and foreign militia aligned to al-Qaeda maintained an unceasing campaign of shooting and bombing against coalition forces, foreign contractors and the coalition-trained Iraqi Army and Police. For the British forces in Iraq, Operation Telic – the codename under which all of Britain's military operations in Iraq were conducted – continued until the last troops were withdrawn in May 2011.

Intelligence Corps personnel were present during the prelude to war and during the fighting phase of Operation Telic, providing a composite military intelligence battalion which included a HUMINT company, an operational support group, a field security company plus signals and imagery intelligence specialists. Members of the Corps also served with the airborne and commando units. Although the number of Corps personnel was cut in line with the reduction of other British contingents during the post-war phase, Corps disciplines continued to be represented at all levels. There were no fatal casualties among the Corps during the war-fighting stage of Operation Telic. There were, however, three fatalities in the subsequent security operations. Each warrants acknowledgement.

Major Matthew Bacon was born on 1 August 1971 at Walton, Surrey, and was educated at Claremont Fan Court School in Esher. In 1988, at the age of seventeen, he enlisted in the Army Air Corps and completed his training as a ground crew signaller, seeing active service in the first Gulf War, Northern Ireland and the Balkans. He was then selected for officer training, graduated from Sandhurst in 1997 and was commissioned into the Intelligence Corps. His first tour with the Corps was as an Assistant Intelligence Officer with the Special Boat Service, Royal Marines. He qualified as a military parachutist at Brize Norton and completed the All-Arms Commando Course. After attending the Intelligence Course at Chicksands, he volunteered for special duties and spent two years as a Detachment Commander in Northern Ireland. Having attended Staff College, he was appointed second in command of 4 Military Intelligence Battalion and was deployed twice to Afghanistan to serve on the intelligence staff of HQ British Forces. In January 2003, he was posted to the Defence Intelligence Staff as an analyst and in June of that year he took over command of the Joint Security Unit in Cyprus. During that tour, he was deployed for a third tour in Afghanistan. He then volunteered for further operational duty and was posted to the HQ staff of the Multinational Division (Southeast) in Basra.

On 11 September 2005, Major Bacon had been to a meeting at Basra Palace and was due to return to his base at Basra Air Station by Merlin helicopter. Due to a hydraulic fault, the flight was cancelled and he had to travel by road instead. On the return journey, on the outskirts of Basra, the armoured Snatch Land Rover in which he was travelling was caught in the blast of a roadside improvised explosive device and he was killed instantly. He was thirty-four years old. Three other members of the patrol, including one Intelligence Corps NCO, were seriously injured.

• • •

Staff Sergeant Sharron Elliott was born at Hadleigh in Suffolk in 1972, the daughter of Edward, who had served in the Army, and Elsie. She attended Hadleigh High School. In 1989, her cousin, then a serving Lance Corporal in the Women's Royal Army Corps Provost Branch, was among forty-seven people killed in the Kegworth air disaster in which a Belfast-bound jet crashed near the M1. In June 1991, aged eighteen, Elliott enlisted in the Royal Electrical and Mechanical Engineers and became the first woman in the Army to qualify as an aircraft technician. Her service included two attachments to the Army Air Corps – 5 Regiment in Northern Ireland and 9 Regiment at Dishforth in Yorkshire. In June 2000, she transferred to the Intelligence Corps and served in Northern Ireland, Germany, Belize, Kosovo and Iraq. As a HUMINT specialist, in

October 2004 she was posted as an instructor to the Repton Training Delivery Wing, Defence Intelligence College at Chicksands. After that she was posted to the Cyprus Joint Security Unit. It was from Cyprus that she was deployed to Iraq to fill a temporary post, but she volunteered to extend for a six-month tour.

On 12 November 2006, Staff Sergeant Elliott was on board a Rigid Raiding Craft of 539 Assault Squadron, Royal Marines, travelling along the Shatt al-Arab waterway in Basra City and heading for the British base at the Shatt al-Arab Hotel. At approximately 1350hrs, the boat was passing under a bridge when an improvised explosive device hidden on it detonated. Bombs of this nature were common in roadside attacks, but this marked the first time that insurgents had used one on the waterway which divides southern Iraq, where most British service personnel were based, and Iran.

Staff Sergeant Elliott was killed, along with a Royal Corps of Signals Warrant Officer and two Royal Marines. Three other soldiers were also seriously injured. Staff Sergeant Elliott, who was thirty-four years old, was the first female member of the Intelligence Corps to be killed in action and the second servicewoman to die in Iraq since the invasion in 2003. She was single, her soldier fiancé having been killed in a motorcycle accident some ten years before, shortly before their wedding day.

● ● ●

Second Lieutenant Joanna Dyer was born in Berlin in February 1983, the daughter of Neill and Anne Dyer. Her father was a Lieutenant Colonel in the Royal Army Ordnance Corps and her mother a Captain in the Queen Alexandra's Royal Army Nursing Corps. After Loughborough High School, Joanna went up to Oxford

University to read philosophy, politics and economics. Upon graduating, she was accepted at Sandhurst, where she was in the same training platoon as Prince William. They became close friends.

Dyer was commissioned into the Intelligence Corps in December 2006. In order to gain operational experience in advance of her young officer course at Chicksands, she was attached to the 2nd Battalion The Duke of Lancaster's Regiment and deployed with them to Iraq on Operation Telic 9. Quickly recognised as an enthusiastic and charming officer, Dyer made her mark as the battalion's ISTAR officer (intelligence, surveillance, target acquisition and reconnaissance), a post normally reserved for a more experienced officer. Her colleagues described her as being keen to get the most out of her attachment and she soon developed a wide-ranging portfolio of skills which allowed her to be tasked with supporting the planning and conduct of ground operations alongside the other officers and Kingsmen of the battalion.

On 5 April 2007, Second Lieutenant Dyer, together with other soldiers and a local civilian interpreter, was travelling west of Basra City in a Warrior armoured vehicle which was the target of an improvised explosive device attack. Second Lieutenant Dyer and four of her colleagues, including a female member of the Royal Army Medical Corps and the civilian interpreter, were killed and another soldier was seriously injured. It was reported that the blast left a 3-foot-deep crater. When news of her death was released, a statement on behalf of Prince William was issued by Clarence House which read: 'Prince William was deeply saddened to hear the tragic news of Joanna Dyer's death. Jo was a close friend of his at Sandhurst and he is very much thinking of her family and friends right now and they will remain in his thoughts and prayers.' Second Lieutenant Joanna Dyer was twenty-four years old.

AFGHANISTAN

Afghanistan was under notional British control until 1919, when it won independence and became a monarchy. Two coups in the 1970s resulted in the communist People's Democratic Party of Afghanistan seizing control of the country. In 1979, the Soviets invaded to shore up the crumbling regime, fighting US-backed mujahideen fighters until the Soviets withdrew and the communist government collapsed in 1992. Thereafter, a civil war erupted between the mujahideen factions. This led to the emergence of the extreme fundamentalist Taliban movement which took charge from 1998, imposing Sharia law on the population. Following the attacks on America in September 2001, western intelligence agencies established links between the Taliban and the al-Qaeda terrorist group. In October 2001, a joint US–UK force invaded Afghanistan to remove the Taliban, with the British military operating under the codename Operation Veritas.

An Afghan interim government was installed and a NATO-led International Stabilisation Assistance Force formed to rebuild the country and train a new Afghan National Army and police force. In December 2004, Hamid Karzai was elected as the first democratic President and the National Assembly was established in December 2005. Attacks on international troops continued, however.

Intelligence Corps officers and soldiers provided the full spectrum of intelligence-collection activities during the invasion of Afghanistan in 2001 and throughout the subsequent counter-insurgency campaign against the Taliban. Intelligence Corps members of the Defence HUMINT Unit and 14 Signal Regiment were also deployed on the front line while other specialists of the Corps supplied operational intelligence, signals intelligence, counter-intelligence, imagery intelligence (at both tactical and strategic level) and weapons intelligence. Senior Intelligence Corps officers also served in staff appointments at formation headquarters.

Such was the demand for accurate and timely intelligence that junior NCOs of the Corps, many of them straight out of training, were deployed to serve at infantry company level as Company Intelligence Support Teams (COISTs), placing them on the front line of combat operations. One of these was a young female Lance Corporal – referred to here only as 'Lance Corporal Jenny' – who served on Operation Herrick 12 between May and October 2010. For security reasons, it is not possible to divulge specific details of this operation. This account does give an insight into what was required of a young new member of the Intelligence Corps while based in Afghanistan, however.

None of my family had any military experience. I came from a town in Hampshire, lived in a council estate and attended a state school. I left with five GCSEs and won a place on a college sports science course with the idea of going on to university to study physiotherapy, but for family reasons, I shelved these plans and took a full-time job as a leisure centre manager. I also reprised my childhood ambition and applied to join the Army. Then I spoke with a family friend who was serving with the Intelligence Corps. He opened my eyes to a world I had not heard of at the Army Careers Office and from that day I had only one choice on my application form: the Intelligence Corps.

There were twenty people vying for two places at the two-day selection board at Chicksands. Being selected was the biggest achievement of my life. Phase One training was at Pirbright. Phase Two training was at Chicksands with the Operator Military

Intelligence 3 Course. We started in May and in the December I passed out in the rank of Lance Corporal with a posting to a military intelligence section in Germany. Out of my training squad of twenty-four, eighteen were warned for pre-deployment training for Afghanistan. Several of them, including me, were destined for the role of Company Intelligence Support Team (COIST) on Op Herrick 12.

COISTs are junior NCOs, mostly Lance Corporals, who are deployed at company level with the troops on the ground. They provide immediate intelligence support and guidance to the Company Commander in the planning of local operations, targeting and force protection. It's a complex role, and the operator must be able to deal with the tasking of myriad intelligence assets and to liaise across a number of partner forces and agencies. Eventually, I learned I was to be deployed to support 'B' Company of the Danish contingent, who were operating out of Forward Operating Base Price in the Nahr-e Saraj district, about 20 miles from Lashkar Gah, the capital of Helmand province.

I had little knowledge about the Danish infantry but learned during a two-week exercise with them in Denmark that I would be doing more than acting as a COIST – I would also be teaching their designated intelligence analysts how to understand operational intelligence practices, something I found particularly odd as I had zero operational experience and had been out of training all of six months!

Before I knew it, I was flying to Afghanistan. After a quick spell at Camp Bastion, I was whisked over to Forward Operating Base Price. It was like a self-contained village with reasonable facilities including a coffee shop, medical centre and gym. My 'office' was a large shipping container equipped with the requisite IT terminals.

At any one time, only one 'B' Company platoon was at the base while the rest were at patrol bases at Barakzjai and Hazrat.

My priority was to advise the Danish Intelligence Warrant Officer on the correct content and format required for an effective Intelligence Summary. The next challenge was to obtain enough actionable intelligence to place into an Intelligence Summary that the command team would find of use when planning operations. The only way I could do this effectively was to go forward with the troops on the ground and work out of the patrol base at Hazrat.

At that time, the Danes at Hazrat were co-located with the Afghan National Army and their secondary mission was to mentor the development of the soldiering and patrolling skills of the Afghans while also providing security for the area. It seemed clear to me that if I was to have any chance of obtaining any real intelligence, it would be from patrolling with the Afghans, especially as they seemed to have a better relationship with the local nationals. Thereafter, it was decided I would take part in most of the local patrols and every operation planned.

My first patrol was part of an assurance patrol in Zumbelay, a known Taliban haven. The plan was to draw out some enemy activity and capture it on the Persistent Ground Surveillance System (PGSS) balloon for future operational planning. After about an hour on the ground, we came under attack. We had been patrolling in the fields with the intention of going up to the village when they started firing. We couldn't positively identify the shooters and the rounds were coming in from multiple directions. The Company OC was with us and he made the decision to withdraw away from the firefight as we had achieved the objective. But as we extracted, we came under heavier fire and the OC was shot in the left upper arm and left buttock. Despite his injuries, he led the patrol back to where our vehicles were and then called for a casualty extraction. A helicopter was tasked to us and he walked on like nothing had happened. The man was a machine.

We prepare for every scenario during pre-deployment training. You conduct a live-fire exercise and simulated attack phases and go through them repeatedly until the training staff are content with your performance. But nothing readies you for the whizz-bang you hear and feel when you are really shot at for the first time. Luckily, the training kicked in and the live rounds whizzing above my head didn't affect the skills that had been drilled into my subconscious. As sections, we just pepper-potted out of contact while providing covering fire – not as quickly as I'd hoped, but I think that was more to do with the Danish tactics, techniques and procedures compared to the British version. Although we didn't get anything from the ground that day, the PGSS team managed to see an array of activity from the air which gave us a starting point for future operations.

The village local to our patrol base was Sa'idan, and this was where we tried to get most of our intelligence. Because it was near the Taliban stronghold of Zumbelay, the locals would avoid speaking to us – possibly through fear of the repercussions but equally likely because they were sympathisers and didn't want us there. The village was littered with improvised explosive devices, mostly command-wired, stretching as long as 500 metres from the device. During one patrol, we'd obtained intelligence about a potential explosives cache in the Zumbelay area. As the patrol was preparing to extract, I sat down for five minutes to finalise my notes. Then I noticed what looked like a piece of string on the other side of the road. It turned out to be a command wire leading to an IED consisting of two 107mm rockets buried right next to where I had been sitting. We were there for hours as we had to provide a cordon around the device and then wait for the EOD team to come and neutralise it.

I did speak to the women in the village of Sa'idan on one of our many patrols. Naively, I thought they wanted to speak to me and hoped they would provide some vital intelligence on members of the Taliban who lived in or travelled to the village. I couldn't have been more wrong. They called me in to one of their homes to tell me I was an abomination and no woman should be doing what I do. I did get one piece of information out of them, though. They informed me the whole village was waiting for us to leave so they could get on with their lives.

We were in an area where the poppy was the main source of income and the locals had no issue with the Taliban, who would pay them for their harvest. They saw no future in making an honest living. The here and now for them was the important thing. So seeing the poppy eradication teams destroy their crop forced them to rely on the Taliban to attack the teams. I saw this in action when a 429A Order – which authorises personnel to engage an identified enemy – was executed. A man had been firing a PKM machine gun at Afghan police officers who had been told to chop down the poppy crop. Air assets were called in and I watched as a bomb fell directly onto his position. That was the hardest day of my tour. It didn't resonate well with me watching a bomb fall out of the sky onto a target who had no idea it was coming.

The highlight of the tour was gaining some intelligence, with the help of our embedded Afghan Army members, on an IED cache in Zumbelay. We'd been on a patrol and questioned some individuals. This revealed the location of the cache. After some deliberation and a battle damage assessment to determine whether we were walking into an ambush, the order was given for us to find the cache. The intelligence proved sound, but the whole building was littered with booby traps consisting mostly of low-metal-content pressure-plate-activated IEDs which were buried in the doorway, in the wall where people may lean, next to the window ledges and all inside where the equipment was stored. We were very aware of the risks, and when we'd established the safe areas, we conducted a search. Once we were content, we called in the Explosive Ordnance Disposal Unit and the Exploitation Team to do their work. This was a big win for us, as we had mainly spent our time antagonising the Taliban to draw out enemy fire. But in the grand scheme of things, this was just one cache in the middle of Helmand province.

If you read about what is expected of a COIST you would ask: how are there enough hours in the day to get everything done? Frankly, there aren't. The job is relentless, especially when you've been out on patrol and then have to come back, analyse the re-sults and produce a coherent report on what you had seen and done – a report that other people's lives may depend on. That's as well as reading and dealing with all the incoming reports that arrived while you were out when all you wanted to do was have a shower because you stink from wading through parts of the Hel-mand river. But it was only by doing the job that you learned how to decide what is important – what is it the Commander and the teams need to know.

I saw a lot happen on my tour as a COIST and learned so much in a short space of time. One thing I will always remember: if you feel something is out of the ordinary, then report it immediately, because if you think it is, then it more than likely is.

• • •

Another area in which the Intelligence Corps has been instrumental in recent years is weapons intelligence. The skills and expertise necessary for this discipline evolved over more than three decades in Northern Ireland and have become a vital part of the intelligence-gathering process which was successfully exported to the Afghanistan conflict.

A Corps operator who served in Afghanistan at the height of the conflict and who for security reasons can only be referred to as 'Corporal Z' recounts his experiences.

I deployed to Afghanistan on Op Herrick 10 in the summer of 2009 as a Corporal with Weapons Intelligence Specialist Company. For the first time, the company was forward-based, deploying to Sangin, Musa Qaleh and Gereshk. I deployed to Sangin supporting the 2 RIFLES Battlegroup whose area of operations covered the town itself along the Upper Sangin Valley as far up as Kajaki Dam. A Royal Military Police Corporal and I formed the weapons intelligence detachment based at Forward Operating Base Jackson, situated between the River Helmand and Sangin District Centre. Tragically, he was wounded in an improvised explosive device strike later in the tour and evacuated to the UK.

Our role was twofold. First, to deploy on the ground alongside the explosive ordnance disposal teams and 'exploit' the scene of any IED incident by identifying insurgent IED tactics and how this fitted into the bigger picture. Second – traditional intelligence work producing intelligence summaries and thematic papers to feed into the wider battlegroup intelligence picture. It was a point of pride for us that we attended every single incident attended by EOD teams in our area of operations.

Sangin was already notorious as an Afghan equivalent of South

Armagh's 'Bandit Country'. It was a hotbed of insurgent activity and narcotics trafficking and formed a fault line where the fiefdoms of several competing tribal groups converged. Not surprisingly, the presence of outsiders was not necessarily welcomed.

The most kinetic area was Wishtan, east of the district centre and comprising dozens of walled compounds criss-crossed by alleyways and dirt tracks, both providing ample cover for insurgents. The area was christened 'the Devil's playground'. We spent a lot of time there. The presence of a Forward Operating Base (FOB) and an Afghan National Army Patrol Base did not deter the insurgents. Civilians had long fled, with most of the compounds lying abandoned. A number of decaying Russian armoured vehicles served as a potent reminder that the locals were no strangers to conflict.

My first 'job' was here, alongside an EOD team whose mission that day was to clear devices identified in the preceding days. We had been on the ground for several hours, stopping for a short water break in an alleyway before resuming. We moved into an abandoned compound when there was an explosion. The earth was thrown up about 10 metres into the air. One of the search team had initiated an IED. When we moved forward to treat him, it was clear he was in a bad way. He had lost a leg from the knee down and the soldier next to him had also been injured, with the debris blinding him, fortunately only temporarily. I remember the smell of the smoke grenade, thrown to identify the landing site to the pilot, and I remember the medics on board screaming at us to 'get the f**k off' as we brought the casualties on board. They obviously needed to get back to the hospital in Bastion as soon as possible. It was dark by the time we made our way home, where the CO informed us the injured soldier had died.

IEDs weren't the only threat. A lot of our resupply was conducted by a contractor who operated a fleet of old Soviet helicopters with Ukrainian crews, some of whom had reportedly served in Afghanistan in the 1980s. Early one morning, we heard it approaching – a very distinctive sound – when there was a loud bang, then silence, followed by a 'Stand to!' across camp. The pilot had flown over the Green Zone, an area full of insurgents. It was an easy, prestigious target and they fired a rocket-propelled grenade, scoring a direct hit and causing it to plummet to the ground and explode, taking out a local compound in the process. The crew were killed. The wreckage burned furiously for three days afterwards and parts of the helicopter were on sale in the bazaar as 'souvenirs'. After that, the contractors refused to fly into Sangin, ending our supply of fresh food. For the rest of the tour, we mainly lived off Weetabix, boiled noodles and fried Spam.

Some of our Afghan 'counterparts' also posed a threat. Both Afghan Army and Police were based at Fort Jackson, and one ANP officer brought a Ford Ranger unarmoured pickup truck onto camp for maintenance. But when the REME mechanic looked underneath, they found a suicide vest. The police officer went 'AWOL' shortly afterwards and was never seen again; seemingly he was planning to 'martyr' himself in the base but, thankfully, never got the chance.

There were elections that summer, which the Taliban were determined to disrupt. On polling day, Jackson was subject to a number of rocket attacks but luckily all fell short. At Wishtan, three soldiers had been killed in an IED strike. We were tasked to exploit the scene and I remember waiting for the RAF Chinook to transport us there while Taliban rockets exploded to the north of the FOB. An Apache attack helicopter escorting the inbound

Chinook was engaging the firing positions from the sky directly above, with the empty cases landing among us. The 2 RIFLES Fire Support Group also fully engaged the insurgents with heavy machine guns, Javelin and snipers. It seemed like all hell was breaking loose and it was a relief to land safely at Wishtan. We patrolled out along Pharmacy Road to the site of the attack. Nearby was the wreckage of a Royal Engineers armoured bulldozer which had been hit in an IED strike some weeks prior, and we dropped our kit off here while we completed the task. The area was checked for IEDs but deemed clear. The ATO and myself had to recover the body of one of the soldiers, something I still think about every day, and then we collapsed back to the FOB.

Later, there was an explosion and, shortly afterwards, a badly injured Afghan 'military-aged male' was brought to the FOB in a wheelbarrow by a man of similar age. He had stepped on an IED placed next to the abandoned bulldozer where we had been working earlier. We suspected they were insurgents who had come to see why the device hadn't functioned when we were there. Nonetheless, the medics treated him and he was evacuated to Bastion by helicopter. It turned out the device was a new type of IED, with little to no metallic content and therefore difficult to identify. We had to patrol on foot to Jackson and we received some sporadic fire down the alleyways as we moved down Pharmacy Road – this was a 'come on' as the alleyways were heavily seeded with IEDs. We could see the tracer from the insurgents arcing into the sky as they attempted to engage an overhead Apache from behind a compound as we were patrolling past it, and one or two RPGs were fired in our direction with no success. It was with relief that we got back to Jackson, and aside from a few further attempts to hit the FOB with rockets, the Taliban gave up for the night.

We recorded over 400 IED incidents in Sangin during our tour, from 'successful' strikes against the battlegroup, to 'finds' where IEDs were identified and rendered safe. It was a challenging tour in many ways but undoubtedly the best thing I did in my career.

• • •

Four junior NCOs of the Intelligence Corps were killed while serving in Afghanistan between 2006 and 2014. As mentioned at the beginning of this book, Corporal Sarah Bryant of the 15 (United Kingdom) Psychological Operations Group died in 2008. It is only right that the other three are also remembered.

Lance Corporal Jabron Hashmi was born on 23 April 1982 at Peshawar in Pakistan, the son of Ishtiaq and Imtiaz Hashmi. He moved to Britain with his family in 1994 when he was twelve years old and settled in the Bordesley Green area of Birmingham. He was educated at Bourneville College in Birmingham, where he gained A levels in maths, chemistry and physics. He joined the Intelligence Corps in June 2004, at the age of twenty-two, completed his Phase One training at Winchester and then qualified as an Operator Military Intelligence (Op MI) at Chicksands in January 2006. He was posted to 14 Signal Regiment (Electronic Warfare) at Brawdy and eventually deployed to Afghanistan on Operation Herrick, attached to 3 PARA Battlegroup at Sangin, Helmand province. On 1 July 2006, Lance Corporal Hashmi was killed in action in a guard sanger at the Sangin base after it was attacked by Taliban fighters using a rocket-propelled grenade. A member of the Royal Signals was killed alongside him. He was the first British Muslim soldier to have been killed during operations in Afghanistan. He was twenty-four years old when he died and is buried at Handsworth Cemetery in Birmingham.

• • •

Lance Corporal James 'Jay' Brynin was born on 22 December 1990 at Shoreham-by-Sea in West Sussex, the son of Efrem and Sharon Brynin. He attended Steyning Grammar School and played for Horsham Football Club. He enlisted in the Intelligence Corps in 2011 and, following training at Chicksands, was posted to 14 Signals Regiment (Electronic Warfare). Having already served on a tour of Afghanistan in 2012, Lance Corporal Brynin was redeployed on his second tour in August 2013 as an intelligence analyst with a light electronic warfare team attached to the Brigade Reconnaissance Force (BRF), 7th Armoured Brigade. On 15 October 2013, the BRF deployed from their base at Camp Bastion to the area of Nahr-e Saraj, Helmand province, to counter an imminent threat. At the end of the operation, in the area of Karakan, they came under insurgent fire which they returned. Tragically, Lance Corporal Brynin received a serious gunshot wound during the exchange of fire and, despite immediate medical intervention, died at the scene. A subsequent inquiry determined that he had been shot accidentally by a fellow soldier of the patrol. At the time of his death, aged twenty-two, he had been selected for promotion to Corporal. His funeral was held at St Mary's Church in Pulborough.

• • •

Lance Corporal Oliver Thomas was born in Brecon, Powys, on 5 September 1987, the son of Clive and Joanna Thomas, and grew up in Kington in Herefordshire. He attended Lady Hawkins' School where he was head boy. He went on to study war, peace and international relations at Reading University, graduating with a BA in

2009. While at university, he had been a member of the University Officer Training Corps. He later completed a master's degree in conflict resolution at Manchester University. His dissertation was on the drugs trade in Afghanistan. In 2012, he moved to London to work as a researcher for the then Brecon and Radnorshire Liberal Democrat MP, Roger Williams, and enlisted in the Intelligence Corps Volunteers with the London-based 3 Military Intelligence Battalion (Volunteers). The following year, he took a sabbatical from his job and volunteered for overseas operations. On 11 December 2013, he deployed to Kandahar province in Afghanistan. On 26 April 2014, Lance Corporal Thomas was a passenger in a Lynx helicopter which crashed during a live-fire exercise in the Takhta Pul area, about 30 miles from the Pakistan border. He was killed in the accident, together with the three-man Army Air Corps crew and an RAF Intelligence Officer. A funeral for Lance Corporal Thomas, who was twenty-six, took place in Hereford in May 2014 and was followed by memorial service at St Mary's Church in Kington.

●　　●　　●

By the turn of the millennium and into the first decades of the twenty-first century, the Corps continued to provide outstanding service in support of British military operations around the world. Much of that service – specifically in the Balkans, in Iraq and in Afghanistan – was carried out in partnership with American, Australian and European allies, leading to even greater recognition of the Corps' operational professionalism. It also cemented in the minds of senior Army personnel how vital intelligence is in every military operation. Indeed, while other elements of the Army were reduced in size or scale at this time, the Corps remained unscathed.

It even increased in terms of manpower and resources, surely the ultimate vote of confidence. Furthermore, Corps officers were no longer restricted to attaining the rank of Brigadier. The new millennium saw the Corps' first promotion to Major General, with the officer being appointed to senior positions in NATO and the EU. Another officer became the first in the Corps to be appointed as Deputy Commander of a Multinational Corps, in Iraq, and later became a Divisional Commander in the UK. The third Corps officer to achieve the two-star rank of Major General was also the first to be appointed to a senior Intelligence Staff post in the Ministry of Defence. And, ultimately, a fourth officer became the Corps' first 'home-grown' three-star Lieutenant General in the post of Chief of Defence Intelligence. At the time of this book's publication, that same officer had become a full General and Commander of UK Strategic Command. With this in mind, it is no exaggeration to say that the Corps has truly come of age.

EPILOGUE

Few people, if any, who have read the accounts in this book could deny that the Intelligence Corps has a rich and distinguished history thanks to the spirited men and women who have served in it over the past century or so. These stories do great justice to this relatively overlooked element of the British Army and they will, I trust, inspire today's Corps operators to tackle the challenges they face just as vigorously as their predecessors were able to do.

As we have seen, the Corps has been involved in every theatre of operations in which the British Army has taken part since 1914. It has also been active in some places where other parts of the British Army were not present. Its officers and soldiers have always been expected to perform their duties anywhere globally, at short notice, either as a member of a team or alone and unsupported. Such tremendous responsibility speaks for itself.

It is strange to remember that the Corps was viewed with distrust and even disdain by many traditionalist military Commanders in the early part of the last century. One reason for this could be that it was, in some respects, ahead of its time. It is, however, less surprising that the value of accurate and timely intelligence was eventually acknowledged. After 1945, the Corps was able to play a major role in counter-intelligence and espionage during the Cold War, in Northern Ireland and in more than a dozen conflicts elsewhere.

With that in mind, it is clear that the Corps can be as confident in its future as it should be proud of its past. In our ever-changing world, increasing importance is attached to intelligence in general and to the Intelligence Corps in particular. Indeed, no Commander will now deploy troops and resources without the Corps also being involved. Its post-war experiences have allowed it to develop into an 'Arm' which is able to be agile and responsive in all types of situations.

The former Chief of Defence Intelligence, Air Chief Marshal Sir Stuart Peach, was kind enough to share with me his thoughts on the Intelligence Corps. He is in no doubt as to the decisive role it will play in the twenty-first century. 'History is full of examples where crucial information presented as intelligence has turned the tide of battles, campaigns and even wars,' Sir Stuart says.

The lessons are clear. As international relations remain turbulent, as the climate emergency reveals itself to be a security issue, as dealing with terrorism remains a perennial priority and as health emergencies remind us of human frailty and mortality, so we need to keep our intelligence guard up. In my own decade as an intelligencer, I came to the realisation that the Intelligence Corps – and its RAF and Royal Navy equivalents – is vital for our future. As the Chief of Defence Intelligence and the acting chair of the Joint Intelligence Committee, I understood that it was the fusion of different elements of intelligence into a single authoritative view that made the difference. It is always tempting to believe technology will save us from our problems. Cyber, AI, unmanned aerial systems and facial recognition software are all marketed with gusto by the military industrial complex. But it is people who exploit the information, turn it into intelligence and – the tricky part of the process – persuade the deciders to act that really matter, now more than ever.

The Intelligence Corps' reputation for excellence is very well deserved. I am delighted to have been able to pay tribute to it and hope that, by doing so, more people might understand and appreciate the significance of its work. The British Army is changing the way it operates. The Intelligence Corps will continue to be integral to the modern force that emerges from that reorganisation.

SELECTED BIBLIOGRAPHY

PUBLISHED WORKS

Atkin, Malcolm, *Section D for Destruction: Forerunner of SOE* (Pen & Sword, 2017)

van der Bijl, Nick, *Sharing the Secret: The History of the Intelligence Corps 1940–2010* (Pen & Sword, 2013)

van der Bijl, Nick, *To Complete the Jigsaw: British Military Intelligence in the First World War* (The History Press, 2015)

Carragher, Michael, *The Man Who Saved Paris: Roger West's Ride 1914* (Uniform, 2017)

Clark, Freddie, *Agents by Moonlight: The Secret History of RAF Tempsford During World War II* (Tempus Publishing, 1999)

Clayton, Anthony, *Forearmed: A History of the Intelligence Corps* (Brassey's (UK) Ltd, 1993)

Cole, Roger and Belfield, Richard, *SAS Operation Storm: Nine Men Against Four Hundred* (Hodder & Stoughton, 2011)

Foot, M. R. D. and Langley J. M., *MI9: Escape and Evasion 1939–1945* (Biteback Publishing, 2020) (first pub. 1979)

Foster, Steve and Clark, Alan, *The Soldier Who Came Back* (Mirror Books, 2018)

Geraghty, Tony, *BRIXMIS: The Untold Exploits of Britain's Most Daring Cold War Spy Mission* (HarperCollins, 1996)

Jeffery, Keith, *MI6: The History of the Secret Intelligence Service 1909–1949* (Bloomsbury Publishing, 2010)

Leighton-Langer, Peter, *The King's Own Loyal Enemy Aliens: German and Austrian Refugees in Britain's Armed Forces, 1939–45* (Vallentine Mitchell, 2006)

Morgan, Janet, *The Secrets of Rue St Roch: Intelligence Operations Behind Enemy Lines in the First World War* (Penguin Books, 2004)

Mortimer, Gavin, *The Long Range Desert Group in World War II* (Osprey Publishing, 2017)

Parritt, Brigadier Brian, *The Intelligencers: British Military Intelligence from the Middle Ages to 1929* (Pen & Sword, 2011)

Philo-Gill, Samantha, *The Women's Army Auxiliary Corps in France, 1917–1921: Women Urgently Wanted* (Pen & Sword, 2017)

Rée, Jonathan ed., *A Schoolmaster's War: Harry Rée, British Agent in the French Resistance* (Yale University Press, 2020)

Sadler, John, *Operation Agreement: Jewish Commandos and the Raid on Tobruk* (Osprey Publishing, 2016)

Steers, Bob, *FSS: Field Security Section* (Robin Steers, 1996)

Stripp, Alan, *Codebreaker in the Far East* (F. Cass, 1989)

UNPUBLISHED WORKS

Condon, John, 'In the Name of the Rose: In Memory of those members of the Intelligence Corps who died on active service' (2005)

Judge, Alan F. (Fred), 'The Field Security Sections of the Intelligence Corps 1939–1960' (2004)

Judge, Alan F. (Fred), 'Special Duties and the Intelligence Corps 1940–1946' (2010)

Williams, A. Lt Col (Retd), 'Intelligence Corps and SOE' (2001)

INDEX